Founding Choices

D1617582

A National Bureau of
Economic Research
Conference Report

Founding Choices
American Economic Policy in the 1790s

Edited by **Douglas A. Irwin and Richard Sylla**

The University of Chicago Press

Chicago and London

DOUGLAS A. IRWIN is the Robert E. Maxwell Professor of Arts and Sciences in the Department of Economics at Dartmouth College, and a research associate of the National Bureau of Economic Research. RICHARD SYLLA is the Henry Kaufman Professor of the History of Financial Institutions and Markets and professor of economics at New York University, and a research associate of the National Bureau of Economic Research.

The University of Chicago Press, Chicago 60637
The University of Chicago Press, Ltd., London
© 2011 by the National Bureau of Economic Research
All rights reserved. Published 2011
Printed in the United States of America

20 19 18 17 16 15 14 13 12 11   1 2 3 4 5
ISBN-13: 978-0-226-38474-0 (cloth)
ISBN-13: 978-0-226-38475-7 (paper)
ISBN-10: 0-226-38474-8 (cloth)
ISBN-10: 0-226-38475-6 (paper)

Library of Congress Cataloging-in-Publication Data

Founding choices : American economic policy in the 1790s / edited by Douglas A. Irwin and Richard Sylla.
    p. cm.
    Papers of the National Bureau of Economic Research conference held at Dartmouth College on May 8–9, 2009.
    Includes bibliographical references and index.
    ISBN-13: 978-0-226-38474-0 (alk. paper)
    ISBN-10: 0-226-38474-8 (alk. paper)
    ISBN-13: 978-0-226-38475-7 (pbk. : alk. paper)
    ISBN-10: 0-226-38475-6 (pbk. : alk. paper)   1. United States—Economic policy—18th century—Congresses. I. Irwin, Douglas A., 1962– II. Sylla, Richard Eugene. III. National Bureau of Economic Research.
HC105.F68 2011
330.973—dc22
                                                      2010015033

Relation of the Directors to the
Work and Publications of the
National Bureau of Economic Research

1. The object of the NBER is to ascertain and present to the economics profession, and to the public more generally, important economic facts and their interpretation in a scientific manner without policy recommendations. The Board of Directors is charged with the responsibility of ensuring that the work of the NBER is carried on in strict conformity with this object.

2. The President shall establish an internal review process to ensure that book manuscripts proposed for publication DO NOT contain policy recommendations. This shall apply both to the proceedings of conferences and to manuscripts by a single author or by one or more co-authors but shall not apply to authors of comments at NBER conferences who are not NBER affiliates.

3. No book manuscript reporting research shall be published by the NBER until the President has sent to each member of the Board a notice that a manuscript is recommended for publication and that in the President's opinion it is suitable for publication in accordance with the above principles of the NBER. Such notification will include a table of contents and an abstract or summary of the manuscript's content, a list of contributors if applicable, and a response form for use by Directors who desire a copy of the manuscript for review. Each manuscript shall contain a summary drawing attention to the nature and treatment of the problem studied and the main conclusions reached.

4. No volume shall be published until forty-five days have elapsed from the above notification of intention to publish it. During this period a copy shall be sent to any Director requesting it, and if any Director objects to publication on the grounds that the manuscript contains policy recommendations, the objection will be presented to the author(s) or editor(s). In case of dispute, all members of the Board shall be notified, and the President shall appoint an ad hoc committee of the Board to decide the matter; thirty days additional shall be granted for this purpose.

5. The President shall present annually to the Board a report describing the internal manuscript review process, any objections made by Directors before publication or by anyone after publication, any disputes about such matters, and how they were handled.

6. Publications of the NBER issued for informational purposes concerning the work of the Bureau, or issued to inform the public of the activities at the Bureau, including but not limited to the NBER Digest and Reporter, shall be consistent with the object stated in paragraph 1. They shall contain a specific disclaimer noting that they have not passed through the review procedures required in this resolution. The Executive Committee of the Board is charged with the review of all such publications from time to time.

7. NBER working papers and manuscripts distributed on the Bureau's web site are not deemed to be publications for the purpose of this resolution, but they shall be consistent with the object stated in paragraph 1. Working papers shall contain a specific disclaimer noting that they have not passed through the review procedures required in this resolution. The NBER's web site shall contain a similar disclaimer. The President shall establish an internal review process to ensure that the working papers and the web site do not contain policy recommendations, and shall report annually to the Board on this process and any concerns raised in connection with it.

8. Unless otherwise determined by the Board or exempted by the terms of paragraphs 6 and 7, a copy of this resolution shall be printed in each NBER publication as described in paragraph 2 above.

Contents

Acknowledgments

The chapters of this book were originally presented at a National Bureau of Economic Research (NBER) conference held at Dartmouth College on May 8 and 9, 2009. We would like to thank Karen Pelletier of Dartmouth's Economics Department and Carl Beck of the NBER for logistical support in organizing the conference. We also thank Helena Fitz-Patrick of the NBER for guiding this book through production.

The conference and this book would not have been possible without funding provided by the Dean of the Faculty Office at Dartmouth College from an endowment from Fannie and Alan Leslie ('30). For this funding we thank Dean Carol Folt, Associate Dean Michael Mastanduno, and Megan Stephen. In addition, this project was generously supported by funds from the NBER, and we thank Martin Feldstein, James Poterba, and Claudia Goldin for their encouragement and support.

The Significance of the Founding Choices
Editors' Introduction

Douglas A. Irwin and Richard Sylla

Bookstores today are awash with titles that celebrate America's Founding Fathers as courageous and far-sighted leaders who not only guided the nation through the difficult period of achieving independence from Britain, but also established a system of government that has survived relatively unchanged for more than two centuries. Almost completely ignored in this outpouring of works, however, is a sense for the economic policy achievements of the founders. The neglect of economic policy is surprising. The United States in 1790 was a relatively small economy compared to the leading nations of Europe and Asia. Within a century it would become the world's largest economy. In two centuries it would become an economic and political colossus with a larger population than any other country except China and India. The post-1790 developments were rooted to a greater extent than is generally appreciated in the economic policy decisions made in the 1790s.

This book redresses the neglect of the founders' economic choices by bringing together leading scholars to examine the early economic policies adopted by the new government under the Constitution. Ratification of the Constitution broke the gridlock that afflicted decision making about economic policy under the Articles of Confederation prior to 1789. The chapters that follow study the economic policy options that were opened up by the new framework of government, and which choices were implemented. They focus on the *choices* made by U.S. economic policymakers in the years

Douglas A. Irwin is the Robert E. Maxwell Professor of Arts and Sciences in the Department of Economics at Dartmouth College, and research associate of the National Bureau of Economic Research.
Richard Sylla is the Henry Kaufman Professor of the History of Financial Institutions and Markets and Professor of Economics at New York University, and research associate of the National Bureau of Economic Research.

immediately after 1789: what the policy alternatives were, what the political debates were about, how the new Constitution made a difference to the policy choices, how the policy decisions were made, which paths were ruled out, and how the policies were either continued, modified, or abandoned in later years. In doing so, we hope that the volume contributes to our understanding of the foundations of U.S. economic success.

A Brief Sketch of the Founding Era

By the late colonial period, the economic position of Britain's thirteen North American colonies seemed promising. Up to that time the colonies had been secure under the protection of the British army and navy, and could trade within the markets of the British Empire. Representative government generated domestic political stability and legal institutions that protected property rights and facilitated investment and exchange. The colonies experienced steady economic expansion, growing wealth, and flourishing trade that made them attractive enough to draw a steady stream of immigrants from abroad. But the colonial expansion reflected mostly high rates of population growth, as there is no evidence of modern economic growth in the sense of sustained increases of per capita product and incomes at rates approaching or exceeding 1 percent per year over extended periods.

When Britain's government, in the wake of the Seven Years' War (1756 to 1763), began to threaten the rights, institutions, and freedoms the colonists had come to expect, they began to contemplate political independence. In July 1776, after more than a year of armed conflict with Britain, the Continental Congress proclaimed American independence. Warfare in America continued for five more years, ending with the combined American-French victory at Yorktown in October 1781, although some British forces remained in the country and others continued to menace American ships. The Treaty of Paris, in which Britain formally recognized American independence, was signed two years later, in 1783.

The United States of America had gained independence, but the 1780s was a very difficult decade for the American people and the U.S. economy.[1] The War of Independence had been costly in terms of human lives and resources expended. Trade had been severely disrupted, and domestic currencies had depreciated as a consequence of excessive issuances. The transition to peace proved difficult as well. The United States found its goods and ships excluded from the markets of the British Empire. The national government was broke, unable to raise money or pay off loans it had obtained during the war from patriotic Americans and sympathetic foreign nations. Under the Articles of Confederation, the national government proved unable to take actions that would rectify this dire situation.

1. See Bjork (1964) for a discussion of the U.S. economy during this period.

The economic difficulties that the United States faced after independence were a critical factor in the decision to replace the Articles of Confederation with a new Constitution. The Constitution of 1787 marked a new political beginning for the United States. It also opened up new possibilities for economic policy. Under the Constitution, the federal government had a vast set of new powers, including the ability "To lay and collect taxes, duties, imposts and excises, to pay the debts and provide for the common defense and general welfare of the United States . . . ; To borrow money on the credit of the United States; To regulate commerce with foreign nations, and among the several states,..; To establish a uniform rule of naturalization, and uniform laws on the subject of bankruptcies throughout the United States; To coin money, regulate the value thereof . . . ; To establish post offices and post roads; [and] To promote the progress of science and useful arts, by securing for limited times to authors and inventors the exclusive right to their respective writings and discoveries." And, perhaps most controversially, the Constitution also empowered Congress "To make all laws which shall be necessary and proper for carrying into execution the foregoing powers." These powers—all in Article I, Section 8, of the Constitution—constituted much of the economic policy agenda for the new government.

President George Washington, widely admired and respected for his command of American forces during the War of Independence, provided a smooth and stable transition to the new political system. Equally important, the Washington administration undertook a series of steps to address the daunting economic challenges of the day. In the first years of the new U.S. government, America's political leaders at both the federal and state levels had a unique opportunity to lay a fresh groundwork for the nation's economic policy. They confronted a series of choices about the direction of economic policy with respect to public finance and debt management, currency and monetary policy, trade and revenue policy, land and western settlement policy, inventions and innovations, policies toward labor and business, and so forth. Many of the choices that they made would be precedent-setting and have lasting consequences.

Under the direction and guidance of Treasury Secretary Alexander Hamilton, the first Congresses enacted legislation that consolidated and funded the national debt, created a national bank, established a sound national currency, imposed import duties to collect government revenue, and protected intellectual property rights. Both the federal and state governments encouraged the formation of corporations. Some of these policy measures were uncontroversial, while others were subjects of contentious debates. In almost every case, there were many options and alternative paths that could have been taken. Some of the steps taken were altered or undone later, while others have persisted in one form or another to this day. The economic policy choices of the 1790s not only established conditions for (and removed constraints on) modern economic growth, but also provided a long-term policy framework that continued to encourage growth, the territorial expansion of the United States, and the country's influence on world affairs for decades and centuries.

Some Key Ingredients of Economic Growth

Economists usually consider growth to be increases in total economic output per person that are sustained for long periods of time. They measure it by "real"—that is, inflation-adjusted—Gross Domestic Product (GDP) per capita. They consider growth to be "modern" if real GDP per capita increases at rates of 1 percent or more per year for extended periods. For the United States and other nations, the data to measure real GDP per capita with any precision are not available for periods before the middle of the nineteenth century. In the American case, from that time to the present, all measures of economic growth are decidedly modern; they indicate annual average rates of growth of 1.5 percent per year or more.

For periods before the mid-nineteenth century, economic historians have used economic theory and models in conjunction with the more limited historical data available to make rough estimates of economic growth. Historians of the colonial era think that at best growth was modest—per capita gains of 0.3 to 0.5 percent per year (McCusker and Menard 1985)—and at worst about zero (Mancall and Weiss 1999). Around 1790, however, a different story emerges. As Richard Sylla notes in chapter 2 in this volume, the lowest estimates of U.S. economic growth for the 1790s are in the vicinity of 1 percent a year, although there remains uncertainty about how much growth there was in the first two decades of the nineteenth century.

It thus seems possible that economic growth became "modern" virtually at the start of the United States as a political entity. A recently compiled index of the output of one modern economic sector, industrial production, points to a reason why economic growth may have jumped to a higher level in the 1790s. It indicates that total U.S. industrial production grew at rates of about 5 percent per year from the 1790s to 1915, without much variation over extended subperiods of the long nineteenth century (Davis 2004). Adjusting the industrial production estimates for population growth, which was high but declining over the long century, industrial production per capita grew at approximately 1.5 to 2 percent per year in the early decades of U.S. history, and at more than 2 percent per year in later decades. The industrial or manufacturing sector, of course, was a small component of the U.S. economy in the 1790s, but its apparently high rate of growth from that time onward must have been among the reasons why real GDP per capita grew at rates substantially above those of the colonial era. As rapidly growing manufacturing and other modern economic sectors became larger and larger components of the U.S. economy, we would expect to observe a gradual acceleration in the overall rate of economic growth. Imperfect as estimates of real GDP remain for the 1790 to 1840 period, they are not inconsistent with such a gradual acceleration of economic growth. Why might U.S. growth have become "modern" in the 1790s? Could the economic policy decisions studied in this volume have made a difference? The authors of the chapters here address these questions with specificity and detail. Before summarizing their contributions, however, we ought to address the issues in somewhat more general terms.

As the world moves into the twenty-first century, it exhibits huge differences in incomes, wealth, and welfare among nations. Some, mostly in Western Europe, North America, and Japan, are rich and have been rich relative to others for a century or more. Others, termed "emerging markets," were relatively poor not so long ago, but have made giant strides in their economic growth in recent decades. These include the world's two most populous nations, China and India, as well as others in East Asia, Latin America, Eastern Europe, and elsewhere. Still others, including many in Africa, have long been and continue to be relatively poor. Why at the end of the twentieth century did the richest nations have real GDPs per capita three to five times the world average (the United States, the richest large country, was close to the top at nearly five times the world average), while Latin America as a whole was at the world average, China and India were below average but rising rapidly, and Africa as a whole languished at about a quarter of the world average?[2] Why is the world economy so unequal in our time? And, since estimates for earlier eras show less inequality across nations—the richest countries two centuries ago had real GDPs per capita less than three times the world average then, while the poorer ones were closer to the world average than they are now—why has the world economy become more unequal in the modern era?

Economic historians tend to answer these questions by focusing on why some countries in the modern era became rich. The great inequalities across nations today are mostly the result of a relatively small number of countries (such as the United States) growing quite rapidly in GDP per person for a century or two while most of the others more or less marked time, growing slowly, if at all, in terms of per capita product and incomes, rather like the American colonies during the eighteenth century.

So just why, or how, did the rich countries grow rich? Economists and economic historians provide a wide range of answers to this question, and they often disagree about the relative importance of the various factors they identify as important. Four general factors, however, seem to be a part of many explanations.

First, before most other nations, the countries that grew rich put in place *governments* that allowed economic growth and development to occur, and in many cases even fostered it through institutions and organizations they

---

2. These conclusions are derived from the comprehensive data contained in Maddison (2001).

created and by the policies they implemented. Typically, these were constitutional governments with limits on the authority of rulers and political
representation for citizens.[3]

Second, modern, developed, and prosperous nations have long had highly
articulated *financial systems* featuring strong public finances and debt management; stable currencies; good banking systems and central banks to
provide effective payment systems and stable flows of money and credit;
financial markets (money, bond, and stock markets) to fund the needs of
governments, business enterprises, and households; and business corporations, since economies of large-scale production appear to require the
corporate form of organization for their realization. The earliest economic
leaders—the city-states of Renaissance Italy, the Dutch Republic of the seventeenth century, and Great Britain after the Glorious Revolution of 1688—
developed most of these elements of a modern financial system *before* they
became leading economies. This appears to indicate a causal connection
leading from financial modernization to economic development. As other
nations emulated the Italian, Dutch, and British pioneers of financial development, they too became richer.[4]

Third, the most successful economies were ones that fostered a high degree
of *entrepreneurship*. Italian, Dutch, and British merchants and trading companies moved around the world to arbitrage their opportunities, buying low
and selling high, and thereby making themselves and their countries richer.
British tinkerers, inventors, and entrepreneurs developed new industrial
technologies on a revolutionary, mass-market scale in the eighteenth century,
providing Britain's merchants with new goods that could be bought low and
sold high. Wealth created by modern industry thus added to the mercantile
wealth already present in Britain. New and improved transportation technologies—roads, canals, railroads, and steamships—also contributed to the
expansion of markets. The new technologies raised the productivity of labor,
creating economic incentives for workers to leave farms in the countryside
for better paying jobs in factories concentrated in urban areas. Then, as the
industrial revolution spread from Britain, other nations also able to create
a healthy climate for entrepreneurial innovation grew progressively richer.[5]

Finally, since modern, rich economies have most of their goods and services produced by business enterprises ranging from quite small to very large
ones, they had to develop *managerial capabilities* to make these organizations work effectively. Successful entrepreneurs may have started out small,
but as their enterprises grew they had to learn how to manage them and their

---

3. Studies examining the historical roots of governments that enable or hinder economic
growth include Olson (1982, 1993), and North, Wallis, and Weingast (2009).
4. See Ferguson (2001, 2008) and Demirgüç-Kunt and Levine (2001).
5. For a comprehensive history of entrepreneurship throughout history, see Landes, Mokyr,
and Baumol (2010). For better and worse ways to elicit vibrant entrepreneurship, see Baumol,
Litan, and Schramm (2007).

growth, or employ others who were able to do that. All business enterprises need to be managed, but the need for effective management is especially important for large and complex enterprises, the ones whose economies of scale and scope have been largely responsible for the productivity advances that made rich countries rich. Economists measure improvements in productive efficiency by changes in total factor productivity (TFP), the increment in output over time that cannot be explained by increases in the conventional economic inputs of labor, capital, and land or natural resources. The sources of TFP growth remain something of a mystery. Improved managerial capability in productive enterprises is probably one source of TFP growth over time, although it so far has defied measurement. Without effective management, large-scale enterprises could not exist for very long.[6] In many of the world's nations, for much of modern history, few such enterprises got started or lasted for long. Growing economies, in contrast, long have invested considerable resources in educating and training those who manage large-scale enterprises.

In short, on most lists of the key ingredients of economic success for any nation, one likely would find good government, effective financial systems, healthy entrepreneurship, and improved managerial capabilities, especially for the large and complex enterprises that generated so much of the productivity advances that made rich countries rich. How did the rich countries manage to create these ingredients? How did the United States do it? The chapters that follow indicate that in the American case, decisions made early in the country's history, including the economic policy choices of the 1790s, may have had a lot to do with the outcome.

This Book in Summary

In chapter 1, "The Constitutional Choices of 1787 and Their Consequences," Sonia Mittal, Jack Rakove, and Barry Weingast explain how the founders in the 1780s sought by means of the Constitution to replace an ineffective national government with one that they hoped, but could not really know, would be much more effective. Later generations have known that the founders' hopes were realized, but success was far from certain in 1787, or even in 1800. The authors explain how the new Constitution provided ways of solving many problems that remained unsolved under its predecessor, the Articles of Confederation, as well as accommodating adaptations of policies and institutions. As far as economic growth and development are concerned, the Constitution contributed to market-preserving federalism, a concept explained in the chapter, by giving the new federal government the authority to solve a variety of national problems, while

6. Studies of the historical role of management include Chandler (1977, 1990) and Lamoreaux and Raff (1995).

allowing the states of the union to address in an experimental, even competitive way, other problems that were not of a national nature. In terms of our discussion here, as a result of the Constitution and the manner in which its provisions were implemented by the founding and later generations, the United States put in place a governmental system that proved to be highly compatible with, and in many ways supportive of, modern economic growth.

Chapter 2, "Financial Foundations: Public Credit, the National Bank, and Securities Markets," by Richard Sylla, explains how a second key ingredient of economic success—a modern, articulated financial system—quickly emerged in the Washington administration. As has long been understood by historians, Alexander Hamilton was the founder most responsible for the financial revolution of the early 1790s. But how could so much financial change happen so fast? Sylla shows that Hamilton, who became a student of financial history while an officer on General Washington's staff during the War of Independence, realized that financial modernization was needed both for effective government and economic growth. When President Washington named him to be the nation's first secretary of the treasury, Hamilton used his authority to implement a plan that had been developing and maturing in his mind for years. With the cooperation of Congress, Hamilton implemented the federal revenue system the Constitution authorized, restructured the national debt and placed it on a sound financial footing, argued for and obtained a national banking corporation, and defined the new U.S. dollar and provided for its coinage by calling for a federal mint. Hamilton's policies prompted the states to charter many more banks and other corporations. And all the new federal bonds and national bank stock that resulted from his plan induced investors, brokers, and dealers to create active markets for the new securities. As Hamilton had predicted, the new and modern financial system almost immediately increased the power of the federal government and helped to raise the rate of economic growth toward modern levels. Effective government and modernized finances, two key ingredients of economic success, were realized in very short order in the 1790s. That was quite an achievement.

In chapter 3, "Revenue or Reciprocity? Founding Feuds over Early U.S. Trade Policy," Douglas Irwin looks at import duties as the key method by which the new federal government raised revenue to fund its operations and pay the national debt. As noted earlier, the national government was essentially broke under the Articles of Confederation. In addition, the national government had no authority over trade policy so it could not retaliate against other countries for discriminating against U.S. exports. Marking a huge break from the Articles, the Constitution gave Congress the power to levy import tariffs, giving the government an independent source of revenue and the potential to strike back at Britain's restrictions on U.S. commerce. In the debate over which objective deserved emphasis, Hamilton insisted upon revenue. In Irwin's view, Hamilton was aware that the American public would resist many domestic excise taxes, so he had to rely on import taxes as the principal revenue-raising device of the government. Import duties were a critical part of his funding scheme. By funding the debt, Hamilton improved the country's creditworthiness (which might be needed in times of war); by nationalizing the debt, Hamilton allowed states to reduce the burden of their local taxes, thus increasing support for the Constitution. But imports could be easily disrupted, making it a fragile base on which to depend for supporting the nation's finances. Keenly aware of the country's financial fragility, Hamilton desperately wanted the United States to remain neutral in any European conflict. For this reason, he strongly opposed efforts by Thomas Jefferson and James Madison, who wanted to use tariffs to retaliate against Britain in the hope of forcing open the markets of the British Empire to U.S. commerce. Hamilton feared that British reprisals would severely diminish the steady flow of revenue from import duties, on which his financial plans hinged.

Peter Rousseau in chapter 4, "Monetary Policy and the Dollar," argues that the United States gained considerably in the early 1790s after the Constitution ended the colonial and 1780s monetary system that allowed provincial and then state governments to issue their own fiat paper currencies, and replaced that system with the new specie dollar and currency union of all the states. Under this new system, banks, not governments, would provide most of the nation's money stock by issuing deposits and bank notes convertible into the specie-dollar base. The founders' motivation for the change was the sad experience during the War of Independence, when both the Continental Congress and the states financed their military forces by overissuing fiat paper currencies to the point where they lost much of their value and risked a hyperinflation. The "Continental Currency" issued by Congress essentially collapsed by 1779 or 1780 because Congress lacked the authority to levy taxes to be paid in Continentals. Holders of depreciating Continentals were instead taxed by inflation as their dollars depreciated in value. States did have powers of taxation, and their currencies during and after the war fared better than Continentals, but not well, because states were reluctant to levy unpopular taxes. The Constitutional solution to these problems, implemented as a part of Hamilton's financial revolution, was to ban the states from issuing fiat moneys, and to place the United States on the specie-based dollar defined in terms of gold and silver. Under the new system, money was created not by government officials printing it to finance public spending, but by banks issuing it to finance trade, investment, and entrepreneurial innovation. The new system, unlike the old, gave Americans more confidence in the long-term value of their currency holdings, anchored as they were in silver and gold dollars, and it allowed the money stock to expand in accordance with requirements of a growing economy.

Howard Bodenhorn's chapter 5, "Splendid Associations of Favored Individuals: Federal and State Commercial Banking Policy in the Federalist Era and Beyond," deals with the founding choices about the banking system in the United States. There were two main options: one in which banks were to be loosely regulated in their operations, accountability, and governance, or one in which regulations embodied in bank charters were more restrictive in these areas. Bodenhorn shows that Robert Morris's Bank of North America, the nation's first bank when chartered in 1781 to 1782 (by Congress and also several states) exemplified the first approach. The loose regulation of Morris's bank, and its behavior in attempting to stifle competition, produced a backlash by the mid-1780s; the bank lost its Pennsylvania charter temporarily and only regained a new one by extensive politicking and accepting more restrictions on its operations.

Hamilton was a keen observer of these events. Therefore, when as treasury secretary he crafted the charter of the Bank of the United States in 1791, its operational latitude was more carefully delimited. It was made accountable to the federal government which, in a Hamiltonian innovation, owned 20 percent of the Bank's stock, and its governance provisions balanced the interests of large and small stockholders. At the same time, Hamilton's charter allowed the Bank to open branches throughout the United States. Both the first and second Banks did that, providing the country with nationwide branch banking in its early decades. After the second Bank lost its federal charter in the 1836, nationwide branch banking would not return until the 1990s. Despite that setback, Bodenhorn demonstrates that Hamilton's charter, with its many restrictions on bank operations, became the model for most American banks and, he notes, most Canadian banks. Canada's banks operated branch systems throughout the country, but U.S. state laws and federal regulatory deference to those laws until late in the twentieth century restricted banks to operate from one office (unit banking), one city, or at most one state.

Founding choices about the sort of banking Americans should have seem eerily relevant in the aftermath of the banking and financial crises of the early twenty-first century. Once again, regulatory laxities are thought to have led to bad outcomes. Reforms embodying stricter regulation of U.S. banking and financial services are therefore at the top of legislative agendas.

In chapter 6, "The Other Foundings: Federalism and the Constitutional Structure of American Government," John Wallis notes that after the Constitution provided a stable and accommodative government at the national level during the 1790s (as established by Mittal, Rakove, and Weingast in chapter 1 of this volume), most of the interactions between political and economic development took place at the level of the states. Wallis explains that it was difficult politically for the federal government to maintain a presence in banking (the two Banks of the United States were discontinued) or to play much of a role in the development of the nation's economic infrastructure; for example, improvements in internal transportation. That left the states to become the laboratories in which the important experiments in banking, corporations, and infrastructure development were made.

Initially, states strove to keep taxes low by investing in banks and other corporations, and by borrowing extensively for transportation improvements in the expectation that they would, in one way or another, pay for themselves. But such policy choices also provided incentives for state governments to restrict these developments. Dividends and other revenues states obtained from investment in banks and corporations as well as toll revenues on state-owned canals would be greater if there were not so many banks, corporations, and canals. Less competition meant greater earnings on state investments. At the same time, extensions of the political franchise and the rise of mass political parties created pressures to provide more access to banking and the corporate form, as well as more infrastructure investment. The economic and financial crises of the late 1830s and early 1840s brought these conflicts between economic and political development to a head. Banks, other corporations, and state transportation projects failed. State revenues declined precipitously everywhere, and eight states and one territory defaulted on their debts.

Citizens were outraged by these embarrassing outcomes, and reacted by calling for constitutional changes at the state level to ensure that they would not happen again. And so, within a stable framework of national government, many states rewrote their own constitutions to disentangle their governments from banks and corporations, and to provide more open access to both by enacting free banking and general incorporation laws. These laws allowed citizens to start banks and corporations without the specific sanction of state legislatures. They also placed restrictions on state borrowing for public purposes—henceforth, such borrowings, if proposed by public officials, could be made only after a public vote approved tax increases to service the debts to be incurred. Wallis explains how these developments represented a major shift in American political economy. The founders had worried about the democratic excesses, particularly in state legislatures, and wrote the Constitution to curb them by diminishing state authority, and even national authority, through an intricate system of political checks and balances. In the ensuing decades, American politics nonetheless became more democratic. By rewriting their constitutions, Wallis argues, states reconciled greater democracy with more responsible political decision making and more open access to financial and other corporate institutions that fostered economic growth.

Robert Wright's chapter 7, "Rise of the Corporation Nation," continuing Wallis's discussion of corporations, draws attention to a dramatic rise in the chartering of business corporations during the 1790s. Only eight such corporations had been chartered in the long colonial era, and another twenty-one during the 1780s. During the 1790s, 290 more corporations, ten times as many as in all previous colonial and U.S. history, appeared. Wright attributes this to the implementation of the new Constitution, which gave entrepreneurs the encouragement they needed to invest their efforts and funds in new, large-scale enterprises. But the appearance of a "corporation nation" in the 1790s was just a beginning; Wright notes that by 1860 the country would have some 20,000 corporations, far more than any other nation. Still, Americans had to overcome a great deal of suspicion about corporations, which many believed were privileged institutions with too much market and political power. An obvious solution to this problem, or at least part of it, was to make the corporate form available to almost anyone or any group of Americans who desired it—to turn the corporation from a privileged monopoly for the few into a competitive form of enterprise for the many.

Why were corporations important? In Wright's view, the increased availability of the corporate form of business organization stimulated entrepreneurship by broadening the menu of organizational-form choices available to entrepreneurs. Most corporations had limited liability, which encouraged shareholders to pool their capital to achieve economies of scale and scope. That led to innovative primary markets for the new issuance of shares, and to active secondary or trading markets that provided shares with liquidity. Finally, the appearance of so many corporations so early in U.S. history meant that Americans more or less had to learn how to govern and manage complex corporate entities. The training and experience in management that Americans gained in the early corporations no doubt came in handy later, when even more and larger corporations appeared to take advantage of technologies of mass production and distribution. Via its impact on corporate development, the Constitution thus contributed to vibrant entrepreneurship and managerial capabilities.

In chapter 8, "Land Policy: Founding Choices and Outcomes, 1781–1802," Farley Grubb argues that the U.S. government became "land rich" even before the Constitution when the original states with claims to land between them and the then-western border of the country, the Mississippi River, began to cede those claims to the national government. The problem, as Grubb notes, was that the land would not have been worth very much had the national government tried to sell it quickly to pay its debts, although that idea, as well as the thought of exchanging land for public debt, was considered. Instead, under the Constitution, Congress opted to survey the lands and sell them gradually as the nation expanded and population grew, and to pledge the revenue from future land sales to debt retirement via the sinking fund that Hamilton had created as a part of his financial reforms. Grubb estimates that at prevailing land prices, the federal government's holdings of land in the 1790s had a value well in excess of the national debt. Even if that value could not have been realized had the land been sold quickly, it served to give domestic and foreign creditors of the government confidence in its ability to honor its obligations in later years and decades. Thus, the land policy choices of the 1790s supported public credit. That credit, as Grubb notes at the end of his chapter, had an early payoff when the United States in 1803 doubled its size by obtaining the Louisiana Territory from France "on relatively cheap and easy terms."

In chapter 9, "Free and Slave Labor," Stanley Engerman and Robert Margo review how the abundance of land in America implied, as the other side of the coin, a shortage of labor. This shortage was mitigated not only by rapid natural increase (births greater than deaths), but also by immigration of free labor, indentured labor, convict labor, and slave labor. The Constitution itself said little about the immigration of labor. The implicit default was free immigration since the land/labor ratio remained high, and that was made more explicit in Hamilton's prescient 1791 Report on Manufactures. Still, in the Constitutional era, in-migration of indentured labor began to decline and an independent United States rejected convict labor from Europe. But the Constitution did deal with slavery by stipulating that the slave trade—immigration of slave labor—could not be ended for at least twenty years (the slave trade was ended by law in 1808), and that slavery itself was left to the states as an issue to be resolved. Northern states had few slaves, and they enacted laws ending slavery, gradually in most cases. Southern states had most of the slaves, and they wanted slavery taken off the table as a matter of national debate. These compromises over slavery most likely were the price of having a unified country in the early decades, something very much in doubt at the time. Six decades later the slavery issue did divide the country, leading to a costly civil war.

The Constitution also said little about factors affecting the stock of human capital, such as education, training, health, and internal labor mobility. These were considered matters with which the states would properly deal, and the authors conclude that was likely a good thing because it promoted experimentation and competition between states.

Engerman and Margo discuss the effects of slave policy choices in comparison with options not adopted. The ban on slave imports, in comparison with no ban, raised the price of slaves, and especially of female slaves, the only remaining source for expansion of the slave labor stock. If slavery itself had been ended by the Constitution, the authors conclude that the U.S. economy would have had less output and a different structure than it did with slavery, and they point to the post-Civil War era after slavery ended as tending to confirm their analysis.

Finally, Zorina Khan's chapter 10, "Looking Backward: Founding Choices and Intellectual Property Protection," documents that the American system of patent and copyright protections authorized by the Constitution, as implemented by legislation in the 1790s and after, was a departure from European precedents in directions that were conducive to economic growth. American patents were for "first and true" inventors and for new and original inventions, not merely ones imported from another country or copied from another inventor. As of 1790, patents were subject to an examination system to enforce these strictures. Application fees for patents were lower than in Europe, and were intended to cover administrative expenses rather than enhance government revenues. Property rights were strong; those granted patents were not restricted in how they could exploit them. That encouraged an active market in licensing and assigning patents. The system was open and transparent; with an inventor's rights protected, knowledge of new inventions was made widely available, as was knowledge that patent protection had expired. Patents did not grant monopoly rights; that was not their purpose. The purpose, as stipulated in the Constitution, was "to promote the progress of science and useful arts" by means of granting temporary exclusive rights for novel and original inventions.

In contrast to inventors, the copyrights of American and foreign authors were less protected than in Europe. American copyright piracy may have been to the advantage of the public, and encouraged the widespread dissemination of learning and literature. But it was met by retaliation from foreign countries, which was not to the advantage of the most successful American authors. Over time, as the market for American cultural products expanded, the founding regime of strong patents and weak copyrights changed to one that was more balanced. Khan suggests, however, that further change may have gone too far, giving the United States a system of weak patents as well as strong copyrights. Today, the enforcement of copyrights seems to be more in the interests of their owners, which often are firms that can afford extensive lobbying of lawmakers, than in the public interest.

The chapters of this book, summarized here, indicate that the founding choices made in the Constitution and then implemented during the 1790s did indeed give the United States a governmental and financial system conducive to economic growth. They also gave rise to institutions such as the competitive business corporation and the patent system that encouraged innovation, vibrant entrepreneurship, and the development of managerial capabilities. Given that so many ingredients of long-term economic success were put in place by the founding choices, perhaps we should not be surprised that the higher rates of economic growth characteristic of modern economies began in the 1790s and continued for more than two centuries. The United States got many things right at the start of its national history. It went on to become perhaps history's most successful "emerging market" economy.

Alternative Approaches and Explanations

Was America's economic success really a matter of the policy choices of the 1790s? Or might it have been preordained regardless of those choices? Some influential recent research appears to diminish the importance of policy choices in favor of more fundamental causes. This research on the underlying foundations of economic growth indicates that a country's underlying institutions matter more than policy choices, and are largely responsible for whether it becomes prosperous or not. These institutions include the protection of property, security against expropriation of private wealth, and the sanctity and enforcement of contracts. Such institutions are viewed as being essential to promote the entrepreneurship and investments that lead to economic growth and development.[7]

Where do these institutions come from? Searchers for the "deep roots" of America's and other countries' institutions contend that differences among them were endogenously based on factors such as geography, climate, and disease environments. Engerman and Sokoloff (2008, 124), for example, suggest that "the institutions that emerged across the colonies established by Europeans do seem to have varied systematically with aspects of the environment, such as climate, land types, and natural resources." According to this line of thinking, the mild climate and natural resources of North America favored certain types of economic activity and promoted European settlement, dispersed and smaller land holdings, and thus greater economic equality. These characteristics in turn fostered demands for political participation and the adoption of measures favorable to economic development such as a greater provision of educational opportunities. In contrast, the hotter climates and natural resources of the Caribbean and large parts of Central and South America were conducive to plantation agriculture and extractive mining activities. This led to fewer European settlers, larger land holdings, extensive use of slave labor, and greater economic inequality, all of which detracted from long-run economic development (Engerman and Sokoloff 1997).

A related but different view is that of Acemoglu, Johnson, and Robinson (2001, 2002, 2005), who study European colonialism and see institutional differences among colonies less as developing from climate and resource differences and more as choices made, or imposed, by the European colonizers. Exploitative, extractive institutions were imposed in initially (circa 1500) more densely populated regions with higher mortality rates for Europeans, such as parts of Latin America, as compared with initially less densely populated and lower mortality regions such as North America, where private property institutions were adopted. The former were more prosperous at the time the European colonizers appeared, but in the long run the latter, including prominently the United States, in a reversal of fortunes became more prosperous than the former. Institutions matter for economic performance, but were chosen by colonizers rather than being dictated by geographical conditions.

Still another view of institutional origins suggests that different legal traditions transplanted by various European colonizers were important in shaping the economic futures of colonies.[8] This work begins with the observation that legal rules protecting investors and limiting the extent of expropriation

---

7. For a recent overview of work on good institutions, see Haggard, MacIntyre, and Tiede (2008).

8. This body of work is summarized in La Porta, Lopez-de-Silanes, and Shleifer (2008).

vary systematically across countries. In particular, common law countries of British origin appear to provide greater investor protections than civil law countries with legal codes originating from Roman and French traditions. Differences in legal origins, which were exogenously placed around the world as a result of colonization or other means, had implications not just for financial development, but also for government ownership and regulation. Common law countries tend to have less government intervention, greater contract enforcement, and greater protection of property rights. Simply put, in this view a country such as the United States simply had the good fortune to be a British colony and to inherit British institutions.

Such research has led to reconsiderations of the underlying roots of different economic outcomes. It might seem to suggest that the importance of government economic policy is overrated, and that there are deeper roots to a country's economic success (or failure) than simply implementing the right (or wrong) policies. In this view, initial conditions, not the policy choices made by a particular generation of leaders, were most responsible for a country's economic success or lack of it.

Yet to attribute all or most of U.S. economic success to its initial geographic and climatic conditions and its colonial inheritance perhaps goes too far in discounting the role of different institutional arrangements and different economic policy choices in affecting long-term outcomes. The United States may well have had the climatic and geographic endowments that were conducive to the importation of good institutions, and it may have inherited good institutions from its original colonizer, but that does not mean that success was predetermined. As Acemoglu, Johnson, and Robinson (2001, 1395) observe, there are "substantial economic gains from improving institutions, for example as in the case of Japan during the Meiji Restoration or South Korea during the 1960s." Japan's Meiji leaders, in a setting of limited natural resources, adopted modern institutions and policies that quickly catapulted it ahead of other Asian countries. South Korea and North Korea in the 1950s had virtually the same ethnic and cultural heritages and levels of income; half a century later South Korea's per capita income was ten times North Korea's. Barbados and Jamaica, two Caribbean island economies inhabited mainly by descendants of African slaves, as former British colonies inherited nearly identical political, legal, and economic institutions; yet in the latter half of the twentieth century Barbados, by making better economic policy choices, grew nearly three times faster than Jamaica in real per capita income.[9] Clearly, there are substantial variations in policies and outcomes within countries having the same or similar geographies, climates, and legal origins. There are also reasons for doubting that

---

9. See Henry and Miller (2009). Barbados and Jamaica are not entirely similar. Barbados, smaller and more densely populated, experienced out-migration, whereas Jamaica had more land so that people could leave the plantation sector for small farms. But in that sense Jamaica was more like the United States than was Barbados, which might reinforce the view that policy choices indeed matter as much or even more than inherited institutions.

protection of property is constant over time in countries of a given legal origin.[10]

Even within a given colonial inheritance, there can be a variety of political institutions. A pertinent example is, of course, the United States. The Articles of Confederation provided for one system of political rules, but those rules did not seem promising in ensuring the nation's economic success. Yet the American political system was flexible and adaptable enough to make adjustments by scrapping the Articles of Confederation in favor of the Constitution. If powerful vested interests had a stake in preserving the status quo under the Articles, as some historians suggest, they might have been able to prevent the political change, leaving the United States with a very different institutional mix. Instead, a consensus among the Founding Fathers flexibly adapted the political rules to creating market- and growth-promoting institutions. The alternative arrangements under the Articles could not survive without the political support of important, commercially engaged segments of society that favored a stronger national government. Fearful of excessive government power, however, the founders also ensured that the Constitution included the separation of powers and many checks on executive discretion, which helped to make more credible the promises of the government to respect property rights.[11]

Among the greatest contributions of the Constitution to the well-being of the nation was to preserve, even extend, a large and open market area. The economic benefits of an expanding free-trade area reduced the incentives of individual states or groups of states to break away and form independent countries. Not only would independent states potentially jeopardize the large and open national market of the American union, but as the history of Europe amply demonstrates, they could have been a source of political friction and even military conflict. The Constitution's failure to resolve the slavery issue, a failure that likely was the price of having a union of the original thirteen states, would lead to a costly Civil War eight decades later. But it is likely that other interstate conflicts were avoided because of the federal union and its commitment to free trade among states. Research by economists and political scientists amply documents the devastating and

10. See Haber, North, and Weingast (2008). As Haggard, MacIntyre, and Tiede (2008, 219) note: "Chile and Iraq are both civil law countries; Ireland and Sierra Leone common law countries. Yet does anyone believe that the performance of Sierra Leone or Iraq is likely to be explained to any significant degree by its legal system, however defined?"

11. See Weingast (1995, 1997). One potential contributor to America's economic success is the abundance of natural resources. Yet it has also been argued that natural resources can be a curse to economic development because they create rents that can breed domestic conflicts over control of those resources. Several factors allowed the United States to avoid the problems associated with resource abundance. America's resource base was widespread and accessible to most individuals (for example, the Homesteading Act). Thus, free entry and widespread land holding prevented the creation of scarce and valuable rents that would generate domestic conflict. In addition, America's democratic political institutions were sufficiently entrenched and had legitimacy to push conflict over resource rights to political and legal institutions rather than to other forms of power grabbing. See Lederman and Maloney (2007).

destructive economic effects of civil conflict, which can even threaten a wider breakdown of law and order.[12]

What Have We Missed?

Just as there were founding choices, there are choices to be made in making a collaborative study and putting together a book on founding choices. After the coeditors organized the project and secured the participation of the authors represented here, discussions with them and with others indicated topics that we might have included but did not.

One is national security, an area in which the founders had many concerns and choices to make. Important recent books have shed new light on national security concerns at the founding. Historian Max Edling (2003) argues that founders, traditionally thought to have written the Constitution to check the excessive democracy of state legislatures because they deemed it to be inconsistent with both the common good and minority rights, were as much if not more concerned about building a strong national state that could stand up to the predatory inclinations of larger, stronger European states. And well they might, since Britain, France, and Spain posed real threats to the fledgling American republic during the 1790s and early 1800s. Political scientist David Hendrickson (2003) amplifies the argument by contending that the Constitution was in effect a peace pact between sovereign but divided states and communities. These entities chose to make peace amongst themselves in 1787 and 1788 so that they could better put up a united front against the European predations they feared. We might remember that the United States founded a coast guard and a navy in the 1790s to complement its army, and that after his influential role as the first secretary of the treasury from 1789 to 1795, Alexander Hamilton was commissioned a major general and served in effect as chief of staff of the U.S. army from 1798 to 1800. The military policies of the United States were quite controversial during the 1790s. After that they became less controversial, and the military played no small role in the territorial and economic expansion of the country, as well as its increasing role in the world of empires and nations.

Another topic we have slighted, although not totally ignored, is the judiciary. The federal judiciary was to play an important role in the system of governmental checks and balances designed by the founders. The Supreme Court would pronounce the laws of Congress and state legislatures as well as the actions of the federal executive branch to be unconstitutional. The federal courts would settle disputes between states and between citizens of different states. The judiciary role in the 1790s was, however, less important than it became in subsequent decades as the country expanded. A number of landmark Supreme Court decisions under Chief Justice John Marshall who headed the Court from 1801 to 1835 proved instrumental in delineating fed-

12. See Collier (1999).

eral and state powers, in protecting private property rights, and in preserving the U.S. common market as a free trade area. In the case *Dartmouth College v. Woodward* (1819), the Marshall Court ruled that the contract clause of the Constitution limited the power of a state to overturn a corporate charter, thereby extending the protection of contracts between individuals to corporations. In *McCulloch v. Maryland* (also 1819), the Court affirmed the constitutionality of the Bank of the United States and more broadly the power of the federal government to pursue explicit or implicit constitutional ends by appropriate means to those ends. *Gibbons v. Ogden* (1824) upheld the constitutional authority of Congress, and not a state, to regulate interstate commerce. On the other hand, the decision of Chief Justice Roger Taney in *Dred Scott v. Sandford* (1857), which enhanced the rights of slaveholders, contributed to dividing the nation.

Finally, education receives little attention in this volume. As Engerman and Margo note in their chapter, the founders chose, perhaps wisely, to leave most decisions about education to the states and localities. The first state-sponsored universities were established in the 1790s, in North Carolina and Georgia. We might also have given more attention to the effects of founding choices on the distributions of political power and incomes. No doubt there are other omissions, but we hope that we have treated the most important founding choices.

What is evident in the pages that follow is that the economic policy choices of the founding era released a burst of energy that would persist for more than two centuries. In half a century the land area of the United States would triple in size, spreading from sea to sea. In a century, the American economy would be the largest of any of the world's nations, drawing to it large numbers of immigrants from around the world. In two centuries, a nation that in 1790 had less than half a percent of the world's population would become the world's third most populous nation, one in which 5 percent of the world's people would produce some 20 to 25 percent of world economic output, and enjoy a standard of living unimaginable a century or two ago. Such economic size and strength made the country politically what some would describe as the world's sole superpower and even a hyperpower. In 2010, Americans as usual, maybe even more than usual, worry about their own and their country's economic problems. The founders, we surmise, would have a different view. They would take a measure of pride in the long-term results of their economic policy choices.

References

Acemoglu, D., S. Johnson, and J. A. Robinson. 2001. The colonial origins of comparative development: An empirical investigation. *American Economic Review* 91:1369–401.

————. 2002. Reversal of fortune: Geography and institutions in the making of the modern world income distribution. *Quarterly Journal of Economics* 117:1231–94.

————. 2005. Institutions as a fundamental cause of long-run growth. In *Handbook of economic growth*, ed. P. Aghion and S. Durlauf, 384–472. Amsterdam: Elsevier.

Baumol, W. J., R. E. Litan, and C. J. Schramm. 2007. *Good capitalism, bad capitalism, and the economics of growth and prosperity.* New Haven: Yale University Press.

Bjork, G. 1964. The weaning of the American economy: Independence, market changes, and economic development. *Journal of Economic History* 24:541–60.

Chandler, A. D. 1977. *The visible hand: The managerial revolution in America.* Cambridge, MA: Harvard University Press.

————. 1990. *Scale and scope: The dynamics of industrial capitalism.* Cambridge, MA: Harvard University Press.

Collier, P. 1999. On the economic consequences of civil war. *Oxford Economic Papers* 51:168–83.

Davis, J. H. 2004. An annual index of U.S. industrial production, 1790–1915. *Quarterly Journal of Economics* 119:177–215.

Demirgüç-Kunt, A., and R. Levine. 2001. *Financial structure and economic growth: A cross-country comparison of banks, markets, and development.* Cambridge, MA: MIT Press.

Edling, M. M. 2003. *A revolution in favor of government: Origins of the U.S. Constitution and the making of the American state.* Oxford: Oxford University Press.

Engerman, S. L., and K. L. Sokoloff. 1997. Factor endowments, institutions, and differential paths of growth among New World economies: A view from economic historians of the United States. In *How Latin America fell behind*, ed. S. Haber, 260–98. Stanford: Stanford University Press.

————. 2008. Debating the role of institutions in political and economic development: Theory, history, and findings. *Annual Review of Political Science* 11:119–35.

Ferguson, N. 2001. *The cash nexus: Money and power in the world, 1700–2000.* New York: Basic Books.

————. 2008. *The ascent of money: A financial history of the world.* New York: Penguin.

Haber, S., D.C. North, and B. Weingast, eds. 2008. *Political institutions and financial development.* Stanford: Stanford University Press.

Haggard, S., A. MacIntyre, and L. Tiede. 2008. The rule of law and economic development. *Annual Review of Political Science* 11:205–34.

Hendrickson, D.C. 2003. *Peace pact: The lost world of the American founding.* Lawrence: University Press of Kansas.

Henry, P. B., and C. Miller. 2009. Institutions versus policies: A tale of two islands. *American Economic Review Papers and Proceedings* 99 (2): 261–67.

Lamoreaux, N. R., and D. M. G. Raff, eds. 1995. *Coordination and information: Historical perspectives on the organization of enterprise.* Chicago: University of Chicago Press.

Landes, D. S., J. Mokyr, and W. J. Baumol. 2010. *The invention of enterprise: Entrepreneurship from ancient Mesopotamia to modern times.* Princeton, NJ: Princeton University Press.

La Porta, R., F. Lopez-de-Silanes, and A. Shleifer. 2008. The economic consequences of legal origins. *Journal of Economic Literature* 46:285–332.

Lederman, D., and W. F. Maloney. 2007. *Natural resources: Neither curse nor destiny.* Washington, DC: World Bank.

Maddison, A. 2001. *The world economy: A millennial perspective.* Paris: Organization for Economic Cooperation and Development (OECD).

Mancall, P. C., and T. Weiss. 1999. Was economic growth likely in colonial British North America? *Journal of Economic History* 59:17–40.

McCusker, J. J., and R. R. Menard. 1985. *The economy of British America, 1607–1789.* Chapel Hill: University of North Carolina Press.

North, D.C., J. J. Wallis, and B. R. Weingast. 2009. *Violence and social orders: A conceptual framework for interpreting recorded human history.* New York: Cambridge University Press.

Olson, M. 1982. *The rise and decline of nations: Economic growth, stagflation, and social rigidities.* New Haven: Yale University Press.

———. 1993. Dictatorship, democracy, and development. *American Political Science Review* 87:567–76.

Weingast, B. 1995. The economic role of political institutions. *Journal of Law, Economics, and Organization* 7:1–31.

———. 1997. The political foundations of democracy and the rule of law. *American Political Science Review* 91:245–63.

I

Politics

1

The Constitutional Choices of 1787 and Their Consequences

Sonia Mittal, Jack N. Rakove, and Barry R. Weingast

1.1 Introduction

The choices made in the creation of a constitution have immediate political results and, often enough, lasting economic consequences. That, at least, is the overall thesis of this book, which examines the economic significance of the Federal Constitution drafted in Philadelphia in the late spring and summer of 1787. The Constitution occupies so large a place in our collective understanding of American history and politics, and is so vital a symbol of national identity that it is difficult to recall that the American federal republic might easily have evolved along alternative paths. Of course, it is well known that some matters *were* hotly contested in 1787, such as the disputes over representation that dominated the first seven weeks of debate at Philadelphia, and that others, notably the absence of a declaration of fundamental rights, became objects of public controversy as soon as the Constitution was submitted to a sovereign people for ratification. But to emphasize the big dramatic issues—the purported "great compromise" over representation, the assuaging of Anti-Federalist doubts with the proposal of a "bill of rights"—is still only to confirm what a heroic episode it all was. Other contingent choices that set the Convention on its course, or that gave the Constitution its essential ability to endure, remain obscure.

In this chapter, we treat three interrelated issues involving the constitu-

Sonia Mittal is a PhD candidate in political science at Stanford University. Jack N. Rakove is the William Robertson Coe Professor of History and American Studies and professor of political science at Stanford University. Barry R. Weingast is the Ward C. Krebs Family Professor in the department of political science at Stanford University, and a senior fellow at the Hoover Institution.

The authors gratefully acknowledge John Carey, Farley Grubb, Douglas Irwin, Pauline Maier, and John Wallis for helpful conversations.

tional choices of 1787. First, we examine various defects of the Articles of Confederation, including basic institutional failures and their consequences for public policy. Several features of the Articles made enforcement of federal measures virtually impossible, and thus hindered the capacity of the national government to adapt to unforeseen circumstances. An array of crises emerged under this political system, many associated with states that had incentives to shirk their federal obligations and pursue their self-interest at the expense of the common good. The lack of reliable and independent sources of revenue left the national government financially dependent on the states. Similar problems emerged in other policy domains: foreign relations, internal trade barriers, and paper money. Congress under the Articles also failed to solve other problems, such as enforcing the Treaty of Paris, the British closure of its Caribbean ports to American ships, and asserting control over the western frontier. Retiring the public debt and establishing public credit remained major difficulties. Even as these problems became clear, the Article's institutional constraints prevented their resolution. The unanimity rule necessary to revise the Articles rendered amendment and adaptation of its institutions impossible. Try as they might, advocates of greater powers for the national government could not convince every state to go along.

Second, we emphasize that the dramatic paradigm shift inherent in the adoption of the Constitution—from a federal union premised on the voluntary compliance of the states with federal measures to one in which two governments would each act *legally* on their common citizenry—was not inevitable. Instead, it was one choice among many. The Founders could easily have followed a less risky strategy by proposing more limited though still significant adjustments within the framework of the Articles. That they did not ultimately pursue this path reflects their understanding of the Articles' failures and the drastic change needed in any future constitutional solution. Equally important, the framers' success was not inevitable. Institutional innovations incorporated into the Federal Constitution of 1787 were new and untested. Although it is easy for us to believe that more than two centuries of relative political stability means that success was inevitable, the history of previous confederations and republics suggests otherwise.[1] A stable republican constitution capable of governing a society as large as the United States, for example, had never existed.

Finally, we examine how the Constitution's features allowed Americans both to solve the wide range of policy problems and to adapt policy and institutions as circumstances required. The new Constitution had effects on policies on two levels: directly, reflecting the national government's addressing various problems under its new authority; and indirectly, reflecting the

1. In making this claim, we do not, of course, overlook the dark and bloody ground of the Civil War or the major shift in federal relations to which it led. However, we see that conflict not as a *constitutional* failure per se, but rather as a crisis rooted in two fundamentally incompatible visions of the nature and value of the federal Union itself.

states acting to address other problems within the context of the newly created market-preserving federalism.[2] For our purposes, two of the most important institutional innovations include the replacement of the unicameral consultative Continental Congress by a true bicameral legislature, and the shift toward a centralized federalism to replace the decentralized system of the Confederation.[3] In contrast to the Articles, the new constitutional system proved remarkably adaptable, allowing the nation to confront new challenges. As an illustration of both the successes and limitations of this system, we discuss the persistent problem of slavery in the antebellum years.

This chapter proceeds as follows. In section 1.2 we reconstruct the larger realm of constitutional choice that shaped the deliberations of 1787, and then reflect on the lasting significance for American economic development of key decisions that were taken. In section 1.3, we turn to the consequences of the Constitution, both direct and indirect. This discussion begins with the new policies chosen to address the various policy dilemmas under the Articles, turns to the consequences of the new centralized federalism, and then ends with the long-term consequences of the ability to adapt, including a special look at the ongoing difficult problem of slavery within the republic. Section 1.4 concludes.

1.2   The Road to Philadelphia

Once past the opening words of the preamble, the Constitution is a prosaic text. Most of its clauses are devoted to allocating different powers and duties among the great departments of government, sketching the relationship and boundaries between national and state governments, describing the modes of appointment of particular officers, and detailing their terms of service. Yet the larger enterprise of constitution-*making* cannot be wholly reduced to the sum of these provisions. Or rather, these provisions, properly construed, illuminate the multiple dimensions of the American constitutional project of the late 1780s. Four dimensions deserve particular notice.

First, the immediate occasion for the calling of the Convention was the perceived need to establish a new framework within which key public policy and public goods problems of the 1780s could be adequately addressed and satisfactorily resolved. Those problems were primarily consequences of the war for independence and the immediate aftermath of the treaty of peace (Edling 2003; Marks 1986; Rakove 1979).

A short list of these specific policy concerns include at least the following:

2. Market-preserving federalism is a type of federalism that places states in competition with one another in the context of policy and tax authority over local public goods while requiring them to face the financial consequences of their decisions (i.e., the hard budget constraint); see Weingast (1995).

3. Riker (1987) describes the American invention of centralized federalism in 1787.

- Providing the national government with independent and reliable sources of revenue to meet its basic expenses.
- Funding or retiring the public debt accrued during the war, thereby enabling the United States to have future access to credit markets at home, but especially abroad.
- Developing effective strategies for responding to the twin economic threats to postwar prosperity: the flooding of American markets with European goods, and the closure of British harbors, particularly in the West Indies, to American merchantmen.
- Enforcing key provisions of the Treaty of Paris relating to the rights of British creditors seeking payment of prewar debts and loyalists seeking recovery of confiscated estates.
- Securing effective control of the new national domain above the Ohio River and maintaining the political loyalty of trans-Appalachian settlers more generally, especially after Spain closed the Mississippi River to American navigation in 1784.

Many of these problems stemmed from the incentives of states to shirk their duties rather than cooperate. Insufficient coercive power under the Articles led to shirking by the states. States, for example, faced free-rider incentives to limit their tax collection for the national government. The national government had no means to ensure cooperation or to punish states that shirked. Similar problems arose in other areas, such as honoring treating obligations, internal trade barriers, and paper money.

Together, these five clusters of issues defined the issue space within which questions of public goods and public policy began to converge with issues of constitutional authority and institutional design. Absent these specific concerns, there would have been no occasion for anything like the Federal Convention to be held. But even with them, the putative reformers favoring a stronger federal union had to ask whether their optimal strategy was one of piecemeal amendment or wholesale revision of the Articles of Confederation. Until early 1786, political prudence favored the idea of gradual change; by the close of the year, political desperation tipped the calculation toward comprehensive change. Yet, had the delegates who straggled into Philadelphia in May 1787 acted more cautiously, many contemporaries would have applauded their good judgment in not making the best the enemy of the good.

A second major dimension of the constitution-making project of the late 1780s is that it involved a substantial rethinking of the republican assumptions that informed the drafting, a decade earlier, of both the initial state constitutions that replaced the *ancien régime* of colonial government and the Articles of Confederation. This rethinking is what gives the constitutional debates of 1787 to 1788—both the deliberations at Philadelphia and the broader public discussion that followed—their dramatic character and intellectual significance. To draft the Constitution and to secure its ratification, the framers and their Federalist supporters had to challenge basic premises under which the revolutionaries had acted a decade earlier (Wood 1969). Part of that challenge was directed, of course, to such classic questions as the optimal size of republics or the degree of virtue necessary to their preservation. But a substantial part focused on basic matters of institutional competence and constitutional design—that is, to the real stuff of the practical constitution-making enterprise.

Third, that enterprise was also a negotiated compact among a preexisting set of established polities. Whether the original states are better described as fully sovereign entities or, more narrowly, as autonomous jurisdictions for purposes of internal governance, their delegates at Philadelphia and the subsequent ratification conventions did not operate behind any veil of political ignorance when it came to assessing how adoption of the Constitution might affect vital interests. The Convention's compromises over the composition and election of the political branches were only the most obvious examples of the bargaining process that went into constitution-making. The Constitution also operated as a mutual security pact among the existing states, sharply limiting their capacity to threaten each other militarily. Equally important, the Constitution also collectively assured the territorial integrity of the states against separatist movements within their claimed boundaries (Onuf 1983; Hendrickson 2006).

But, in the fourth place, those states—or rather, their governments—were no longer the sole or even primary parties to the federal compact being renegotiated. Nor was the Constitution simply an agreement to be promulgated by a group of dignitaries once they had resolved all the questions their deliberations had raised. For the Constitution to become fully constitutional, it also had to be ratified by the people themselves, acting through popularly elected conventions in each of the states. The relative ease with which this new rule of ratification was adopted and applied, and the Federalist success in restricting the true decisions of these conventions to up-or-down votes on the Constitution in its entirety, guaranteed that the new system of government would begin its operation with a remarkable measure of legitimacy (Rakove 1996; Siemers 2002). As passionately as Americans would soon begin debating the meaning of particular clauses, their disputes never denied the legitimacy of the constitutional revolution of 1787 to 1788. That was not an outcome that could have been taken completely for granted when the movement for constitutional reform risked the calling of a general convention, or even after the luminaries at Philadelphia finished their work.

To survey these multiple facets of constitution-making is to identify one final aspect of the great enterprise of 1787. No obvious, transparent agenda was destined or predetermined for the Convention to pursue; but, instead, a range of possible outcomes existed among which choices had to be made. The otherwise rich documentary record of the debates of 1787 to 1789 is

strikingly thin when it comes to knowing what either the delegates themselves or the American public initially expected the Convention to accomplish. The one great exception to this is the evidence we have for James
Madison's preparations for Philadelphia, and given his key role in setting
its agenda, that evidence goes far toward explaining why the Convention
took the course it did.[4]

Even so, it is important to stress that multiple paths of constitutional
reform were available in 1787. The Convention could have easily pursued a
more prudent path. Nor should one forget that the logic of radical reform in
1787 also rested on the perceived "imbecility" of the Articles of Confederation, especially as manifested in the absurd rule requiring the unanimous
approval of the state legislatures for its amendment. Had any of the amendments to the Confederation previously proposed surmounted that obstacle,
the case for an extraordinary plenary convention might never have been
made, much less prevailed at that time. The American Union could then have
evolved along any number of counterfactual paths. But the fact remains,
the contingencies of historical action did break one way, not another, and
fundamental choices were made. Not least among them was the decision
to abandon the framework of the Confederation and to proceed with radically different notions of the institutional structure and legal authority of
the Union.

1.2.1   The Initial Agenda of Constitutional Reform

Drafted in 1776 to 1777, the Articles of Confederation reflected the
dominant republican assumptions that also shaped the first state constitutions. Overall coordination of the struggle for independence belonged to
Congress; the states would implement its decisions, acting not as sovereign
judges of the propriety of its resolutions, but as administrative auxiliaries
with superior knowledge of local conditions and the representative political
authority to rule by law. This understanding accorded well with American
experience. Governance in colonial America had always been highly decentralized; the authority of the empire never penetrated into the countryside,
and there was no national administrative apparatus to speak of. Congress
itself was a badly undermanned institution. Its members typically served
some months during a yearly term or two before insisting that others bear
the burden of long absences from home and family. It made completely good
sense to expect the states to do the real work of mobilizing the country's
resources for war.[5]

---

4. See Rakove (1996, chapter 3); but for a characteristically provocative and perverse dissent
on just this point, *counterfactual*, see McDonald (1985, 205).

5. Which is not to say that all states were equally competent in mobilizing those resources.
See the provocative comparison of the capacities of northern and southern states in Einhorn
(2006). The best single study of how an individual state went about complying with federal
measures is Buel (1980).

This expectation that the states would strive to do their duty also rested, Madison rightly recalled, "on a mistaken confidence that the justice, the good faith, the honor, the sound policy, of the several legislative assemblies would render superfluous any appeal to the ordinary motives by which the laws secure the obedience of individuals" (Madison 1787). The first American federalism was thus grounded on the public-spirited values of republicanism, and those values were sorely tested by the duration of a bitterly fought war and the enormous strain it placed on both the capacity of the states and the virtue of their citizens.

By 1780 the discouraging results of this test were apparent. Such efforts as the states made to levy taxes were clearly inadequate to meet the open-ended demands of the war. One response to this continuing shortfall was to rely on the customary methods of currency finance, printing money and trying to withdraw it from circulation before it depreciated too badly. But depreciation occurred regardless, and in 1779 the specie value of the continental dollar fell to 20:1. In that year, Congress made the painful decision, first to stop printing money, and then to adopt a new requisitioning system of "specific supplies" to be demanded from particular states (Rakove 1979). The fits and starts of that conversion, compounded by the worst snowfalls in decades, made the winter of 1780 the absolute nadir of the war effort.

It was also the moment from which we can date the emergence of the reformist impulses that ultimately led to the Federal Convention of 1787. Perhaps it is only a symbolic coincidence that Madison entered Congress in March 1780, or that a few months later Alexander Hamilton drafted the mini-treatise on political economy (as a letter to New York delegate James Duane) that first exhibited his keen financial intelligence. More noteworthy is the fact that members of the national political elite already recognized that the still-unratified Articles of Confederation were inadequate to the real problems of governance the war had exposed. Thus, even as Congress worked to bring Maryland, the last holdout, to end its dissent, delegates like Madison were already contemplating the amendments needed to give Congress adequate authority.

After Maryland ratified the Confederation early in 1781, Congress quickly sent its first amendment to the states, requesting permission to levy a 5 percent impost on foreign imports, meant not as a source of operating revenue, but as security against which Congress might attract foreign loans. Congress also appointed Robert Morris as its first (and only) superintendent of finance. Amid his heroic labors in keeping the Continental Army in the field in advance of the decisive victory at Yorktown, Morris found time to begin drafting a comprehensive program to secure adequate revenues and establish public credit. When Rhode Island effectively killed the impost in 1781, the Morris program to vest Congress with authority to levy land, poll, and excise taxes became the basis for months of sharp debate and political maneuvers. To pressure Congress to adopt his program, Morris attempted to mobilize public creditors throughout the states while exploiting unrest in the army. Morris overplayed his hand, however, and eventually lost the support of a key bloc of delegates who joined Madison in promoting a compromise measure. The states would be asked to assign permanent revenues of their own choosing to Congress, a new impost would be proposed, and the unwieldy formula of the Confederation for apportioning the common expenses of the Union on the basis of the assessed value of improved land would be replaced by a simple population rule (with slaves counting as three-fifths of free persons). This was the basis for the package of resolutions that Congress sent to the states on April 18, 1783, and it marked the first major component of the agenda of federal constitutional reform.

Over the course of the next year, two other sets of issues emerged to enlarge the potential agenda for constitutional reform. One was concerned with the dual crises that afflicted American commerce in the first year of peace, when scores of British ships entered American harbors, bringing imported goods war-deprived consumers were all too happy to purchase, to the detriment of local artisans, while London simultaneously barred American merchantmen from imperial harbors, most importantly in the West Indies, the traditional market for American agricultural surpluses. A second set of issues had to do with the effective governance and political control of the trans-Appalachian interior. Above the Ohio River, Congress gained title to a national domain established through the voluntary cessions of states claiming interior lands. Its ability to develop this land, however, was threatened by several factors: the free flow of squatter-settlers into southern Ohio, opposition from indigenous peoples who were surprised to learn that they had just been defeated in the Revolutionary war, and the retention by the British of frontier forts from which they could encourage resident tribes to resist American expansion. Below the Ohio, the future states of Kentucky and Tennessee were still part of Virginia and North Carolina, respectively, but settlers there were deeply troubled by the Spanish decision to prohibit the transshipment of American produce through New Orleans into the Gulf of Mexico. If Congress could not find a way to relax the Spanish choke hold, the loyalty of these settlers would be up for grabs, and the United States might forfeit the generous territorial settlement it had gained in the peace negotiations of 1782 and 1783.

In April 1784, Congress responded to the first set of issues by asking the states to approve two additional amendments to the Confederation. Stopping well short of recommending a plenary power to regulate foreign trade, these proposals would have empowered Congress to retaliate against nations that discriminated against American merchants. In dealing with the new national domain, Congress adopted a land ordinance (forerunner to the Northwest Ordinance of 1787) that anticipated the eventual admission to the Union of a number of new states, on essential conditions of equality with its original members. That was a visionary statement of a core constitutional principle of state equality, and one which promised that the interior of the continent would not be developed as internal colonies of the older societies on the seaboard. But the greater challenge Congress faced in the west stemmed from its inability to project national power beyond the Appalachians. Without the resources to maintain armed forces in the Ohio Valley, there was little chance that Congress could overawe either squatter-settlers or the Indians they were antagonizing, much less induce Spain to open the Mississippi to American navigation.

In the end, then, it all (or mostly) came down to revenue, and from 1783 to 1786, that prospect in turn depended on unanimous state acceptance of the package of amendments Congress had proposed in April 1783. The basic obstacle to reform remained the unanimity rule of the Confederation, a rule predicated in part on the belief that the states were quasi-sovereign jurisdictions, but also fortified by the perception that republican convictions of the public good should make consensus attainable. Whether decisions about essential public goods should require that high a degree of agreement was the great question that the mid-decade constitutional stalemate left unresolved. Insofar as the failure to attain unanimity challenged core republican assumptions, the stringent rule of amendment worked to make calculations of interest rather than appeals to virtue the denominator of American politics. The unanimity rule of the Articles greatly limited the ability of Americans to adapt to new circumstances and to adjust their institutions as practice diverged from expectations.

1.2.2   Madison's Agenda

Taken individually or collectively, none of these measures portended a radical shift in the character or structure of the Confederation. Well into 1785, the agenda of constitutional reform remained gradualist, not radical. All of the powers being considered could be vested in the same unicameral body that had governed national affairs since 1774. Nationally minded politicians hoped that the specter of an "imbecile" Congress (as it was often disparaged) and the bite of commercial depression would somehow enable Americans to recognize that an assembly appointed by their own state legislatures did not pose the same dangers as a distant Parliament once had.

For this strategy to succeed, however, success had to begin somewhere, and in practice the unanimity rule of the Confederation made its amendment impossible. As the nation seemed to sink into commercial depression by 1785, a committee of Congress, led by James Monroe, drafted yet another amendment giving Congress the sole power "of regulating the trade of the States, as well with foreign Nations, as with each other," including authority to levy "such imposts and duties upon imports and exports, as may be necessary for the purpose," with the resulting revenues accruing to the states in which they were collected (Ford 1904–37, 494). But with the previous amendments still in limbo, it seemed pointless to add a fresh one to the queue.

These issues of revenue and public credit, foreign commerce, and control of the interior remained the great national questions. But within the states, other developments were taking place that would ultimately lead to a significant expansion in the agenda of constitutional reform. The most important of these concerned efforts by individual states to retire their own public debts and to remove the financial detritus of the war. That involved imposing higher levels of taxation than an exhausted population was inclined to favor, and amid the depressed economic conditions of the mid-1780s, calls for tax and debtor relief and the issuance of paper money were hardly surprising. As these demands mounted, and as the politics of individual states—notably Rhode Island—came under the sway of pro-paper money factions, stalwart defenders of basic property rights persuaded themselves that the republic was endangered by what we might call economic populism *avant le fait*. If the advocates of paper money prevailed now, they worried, who could guarantee that the American people might not come to favor a confiscatory redistribution of other forms of wealth as well, even an Agrarian law modeled on the precedent of Roman antiquity and a radical strain in modern republican thinking that ran from More and Machiavelli to Harrington and Locke and even, perhaps, to Jefferson (Holton 2007; Nelson 2004).

No one was more alarmed over these developments than Madison, and in our view, his key role in shaping the ultimate agenda of constitutional reform makes close attention to his developing views a key element in any account of what happened in 1787. There is no question that a brooding concern over the security of the rights of creditors and landowners helped inspire Madison's efforts to rethink the basic premises of republican government (Rakove 1996). Scholars who equate his originality as a constitutional thinker solely with the "extended republic" and "ambition counteracting ambition" hypotheses of Federalist 10 and 51 overlook the extent to which the real source of his creative insights lay in his acute analysis of the institutional workings and defective outputs of state legislatures. Two years of service in the Virginia assembly, after he had been term-limited out of Congress in 1783, turned Madison into a keen student of the science of legislation, especially as that applied science was practiced, not by the all-wise "lawgiver" of Enlightenment philosophy, but by rustic provincials who were prone to error and all too responsive to the parochial concerns of their constituents. By August 1785, he was convinced that the crying need of republican government within the states was to find ways to "give *wisdom* and steadiness to legislation" (Rakove 1999). This need was closely tied to his emerging recognition, as he would state it in Federalist 10, that "The regulation of these various and interfering [economic] interests forms the principal task of modern legislation, and involves the spirit of party and faction in the necessary and ordinary operations of the government" (Cooke 1961a, 59). From this concern evolved the critical conviction that no solution to the problems of federalism would be complete that did not reach the matter of legislative misrule within the states.

Whether that concern would ever become the basis for action, however, depended on the uncertain fate of the amendments of 1783 and 1784. In late January 1786, the Virginia legislature invited other states to join it in sending delegates to a special convention to consider the nation's commercial woes. Though Madison was initially a reluctant supporter of this scheme, he soon concluded that this meeting offered a more promising path to constitutional reform than adherence to the rules of the Confederation. From his correspondent James Monroe, he knew that Congress was considering yet another set of amendments to the Articles. But believing that Congress itself was too politically discredited to be an agent of its own transformation, Madison agreed that other steps were necessary.

Had the eventual Annapolis convention of September 1786 been better attended, it might have framed a new and more expansive amendment vesting broad commercial powers in Congress; akin, perhaps, to the recommendation Monroe's committee had prepared in 1785, or to similar proposals that were presented to Congress in the summer of 1786. But the dozen commissioners from five states who quaffed a few tankards at Mann's Tavern in mid-September 1786 were too small a gathering to propose anything of their own authority. Rather than adjourn empty-handed, however, they seized upon a clause in the credentials for the New Jersey deputies, and proposed instead that a new meeting be held at Philadelphia the following May. That call was eventually heeded by every state except Rhode Island and endorsed by Congress as well.

In the winter and early spring of 1787, Madison set about preparing a working agenda for the Philadelphia meeting. Much has been written about the extent to which this course of reading and reflection led him to hypothesize that a large diverse republic might better resist the "mischiefs of faction" than the small, homogeneous nurseries of disinterested civic virtue beloved of traditional republican theorists. But for purposes of framing an agenda for action, other aspects of Madison's reflections and preparations appear more consequential.

First, and arguably most important, Madison concluded that any system of federalism grounded on the voluntary compliance of the state governments with national measures was doomed to failure.[6] As independent jurisdictions, the interests of the states were too disparate, and their politics too prone to manipulation by "courtiers of popularity," to be expected to

---

6. As mentioned earlier, Madison clearly perceived the commitment problem at the heart of state shirking. "A distrust of the voluntary compliance of each other may prevent the compliance of any, although it should be the latent disposition of all" (Madison 1787, 73).

comply regularly and enthusiastically with the recommendations of a tooth-less Congress. Even when their interests should coincide, doubts about their mutual good faith in fulfilling federal obligations would discourage active compliance. It followed that the national government had to be empow-ered to operate as all true governments do, with constitutional authority to enact, administer, and adjudicate its own laws, which would apply directly to citizens and involve the state governments as little as possible. That, in turn, meant replacing the unicameral Continental Congress with a bicam-eral legislature while also creating a constitutionally independent executive and judiciary. (Here is where the lessons to be drawn from the experience of republican government in the states would prove most salient.)

Second, Madison's rich critique of the "Vices of the Political System of the U. States" (1787) indicted the shortcomings of state-based politics on additional grounds. States were defaulting on their federal duties in other ways: by arrogating congressional authority; violating international treaty obligations (especially by obstructing British creditors seeking recovery of prewar debts); trespassing on each other's rights (his leading example being the designation of paper money as legal tender); and by showing a "want of concert in matters where common interest requires it," a "defect [that] is strongly illustrated in the state of our commercial affairs" (Madison 1787, 69–71). Implicit in this list of criticisms was the idea that constitutional reform had to extend beyond the principal purpose of making the Union independent of the states. It required as well an effort to curtail the authority of the states themselves, especially as their residual sovereignty constrained the pursuit of national objects or the harmony of interstate relations.

Third, Madison's analysis extended to the internal vicissitudes of state policy, or what he called the "multiplicity," "mutability," "injustice," and "impotence" of state lawmaking. It would not be enough, he concluded, to restrict the states from jeopardizing the pursuit and attainment of common interests. It was also essential to check their legislative excesses—to provide a federal remedy, through a congressional negative on state laws, that could check the factious forces swirling through state politics. That negative could be deployed defensively, to block the states from adopting measures that threatened federal policies and national interests. But it could also be used for interventionist purposes, to protect individuals and minorities against the unjust or ill-considered laws that dominant majorities were likely to adopt. And there is no question that the class of legislation that most wor-ried, indeed obsessed Madison was the quasi-populist, anticreditor, prore-lief measures that various states had either adopted or were still discussing (Rakove 1996; Holton 2007).

Fourth, all of Madison's concerns at this critical moment rested on a perception that the future politics of the republic would pivot around efforts by interests—whether defined in terms of communities, classes, or occupa-tions—to exploit the positive lawmaking authority of both state and national governments for their own purposes. Today this seems like a truism, and wholly unsurprising. But in the eighteenth century, the reigning political ideology viewed representative assemblies first and foremost as checking institutions, not as the adaptive and preference-aggregating forums they were in the process of becoming. Madison, by contrast, had developed an acutely modern notion of legislation. Drawing in part on the experience of wartime governance, but accurately foreseeing the more active use of legislative power in an age of economic development and improvement, he was deeply concerned with promoting the proper use of legislative power. In the states, where the bulk of economic regulation would still take place, it was important to guard against the dominance of factious, self-interested majorities. At the national level, however, it might be possible, through the refining mechanisms of election and deliberation, to promote a more considered, less impulsive understanding of the "public good." His notion of what the particular public goods comprising the broader public good of res publica might consist of was probably less expansive or complex than that of his northern counterparts, particularly his current ally and future rival, Alexander Hamilton. But the idea of improving the quality of legislative deliberation through the election of a superior class of representatives was premised on the belief that republican governments would be active governments capable of responding effectively to a wide variety of challenges through informed processes of collective deliberation.

1.2.3   At Philadelphia

In the eight months between the Annapolis and Philadelphia conventions, there must have been many private conversations about the potential agenda for constitutional reform. It was "not uncommon," treasury commissioner Samuel Osgood wrote John Adams, "to hear the principles of Government stated in common Conversation. Emperors, Kings, Stadtholders, Governors General, with a Senate, or House of lords, & House of Commons, are frequently the Topics of Conversation." Some favor "abolishing all the state Governments" and "establishing some Kind of general Government," Osgood added, "but I believe very few agree in the general Principles; much less in the Details of such a Government" (Rakove 1979, 387). Absent a pre-Convention planning conference in which proto-Federalist notables could have mapped strategy, and given the lack of published speculation as to what the Convention might do, the extent to which Madison's own preparations ultimately mattered in shaping the agenda of discussion becomes more evident. Short of abolishing the states outright, or impracticably trying to equalize their net influence by a creative redrawing of state boundaries, it is difficult to conceive how anyone could have fashioned a more expansive agenda than Madison worked out in the roughly two months preceding the appointed meeting day of May 14.

Having issued the original invitation to Philadelphia, the Virginians were

punctual about attending. The same could not be said for the other delega-
tions. While waiting for their arrival, the Virginians crafted the fifteen articles that Governor Edmund Randolph introduced as the Virginia Plan on
May 29. In contrast to all prior discussions of constitutional reform, which
had focused on the specific additional powers the Union was deemed to
need, the Virginia Plan was far more concerned with structure than authority. Article 6 would empower the new bicameral legislature "to legislate in all
cases to which the separate States are incompetent, or in which the harmony
of the United States may be interrupted by the exercise of individual Legislation" (Farrand 1966, I, 21). Although it is possible that the Virginians really
did intend to vest a future congress with this kind of plenary power, it seems
more likely that this formula was meant to serve as a placeholder whose contents would be specified later, once the great disputes over representation that
consumed the first seven weeks of debate were resolved. Madison's political
strategy was to insist that the Convention must first agree that representation in *both* houses of the legislature had to be proportioned to population,
and that the quantum of power the large states would be willing to vest in
the new government depended on the satisfactory resolution of this issue.

That strategy held even after William Paterson proposed the New Jersey
Plan in mid-June. Although this plan's provisions were more reminiscent of
the kinds of reforms that had been discussed over the past few years, this
alternative scheme proved a brief distraction from the debates over representation. Once the New Jersey Plan was dispatched, the convention spent
another four weeks trying to solve the representation conundrum. The basic
story is familiar to every schoolchild: a good compromise was finally struck
allowing the fearful small states to preserve an equal vote in the Senate,
while an evil but perhaps necessary bargain enabled the slaveholding states
of the South to count their human chattel for purposes of representation.
Often overlooked in this moral calculus is the reality that slavery was the
real, material, palpable interest that had to be accommodated if a lasting,
intersectional Union was to be created, and with it the benefits of economic
integration the Constitution was intended to promote. The ostensible conflict between small and large states, by contrast, was ephemeral and false,
since the size of the state in which one works and votes has never identified
an actual interest deserving or requiring promotion (Rakove 1996, 57–93).

Once the twin issues of representation were resolved in mid-July, the delegates were finally free to turn their attention to what they actually wanted
the government to *do.* That task was entrusted to the committee of detail
that met during the ten-day adjournment from July 26 to August 6. Its report
marked the point at which the open-ended grant of legislative power in the
Virginia Plan began to be transformed into the enumerated Article I, Section
8 powers of the final draft.

Once the Convention took up the committee's proposals, the ensuing dis-
agreements on matters of substance were few. Vesting Congress with the

power to levy and collect taxes and regulate foreign and interstate commerce were foregone conclusions. On economic matters, the two main sticking points were the prohibition of taxes on exports and the proposal that navigation acts—laws regulating foreign commerce—require two-thirds majorities in both houses. There were some sharp exchanges on both points, but the convention found little difficulty in treating the retention of the prohibition as a concession to the commodity-exporting states of the South, and eliminating the two-thirds requirement as a fair bargain with the commercial North.

One other matter would prove a source of significant controversy after the Constitution was ratified. On August 18, Madison included among a list of further legislative powers to be considered the power "To grant charters of incorporation in cases where the Public good may require them, and the authority of a single State may be incompetent." That same day, Charles Pinckney proposed a simpler version of the same power, dropping Madison's qualifying phrases (Farrand 1966, II, 325). When the committee of detail and the committee on postponed parts failed to report a suitable clause, Madison renewed his motion on September 14, three days before the Convention adjourned. After brief debate, the motion failed, eight states to three. Madison could reasonably infer that the Convention had thereby denied Congress the power in question. A few years later he learned he was wrong, and that the Necessary and Proper Clause was capacious enough to fill the textual gap—or so Secretary of the Treasury Hamilton said, and President Washington finally agreed.

Compared to the lengthy debates over representation in June and July, many a scholar has wished that the delegates could have spent more time in August and September hashing out their ideas of what they expected the new national government, if ratified, to do. There are notable differences between the extended speeches of the first weeks of deliberation, and the more concise and clipped exchanges of August and early September. Perhaps Madison's exhaustion as the consensus note taker explains part of the discrepancy, but it is just as plausible to think that the later debates took the form they did because the delegates were already deeply united in their notions of the expanded powers the Union should exercise.

1.3   The Constitution's Effects

As section 1.2 suggested, perhaps the most striking contribution of the Constitution—and one too often taken for granted—was the creation of a successful, stable, republican government: a national government at once responsive to the interests of citizens, yet limited in scope and capable of respecting a wide range of rights. Without this accomplishment, the United States is unlikely to have achieved its long-term history of economic growth over the next two centuries. Moreover, this form of government was a major new invention: a stable republican government over an extended territory as large as the United States had never before existed, and many thought it impossible.

The Constitution, however, did not create a competitive polity and a competitive market economy. Long-term economic growth did not automatically follow. Only in the most general sense did the Constitution create "a machine that would go of itself" (Kammen 1986). To survive and thrive in an uncertain and ever-changing world, Americans had to solve a host of important economic and political problems. This required that they devise a variety of new institutions, frameworks, and policies, including national defense; financial markets; policies with respect to trade, intellectual property rights, land, labor, money, and bankruptcy; the promotion of economic growth through public goods and infrastructure; education; political, economic, and geographic expansion; and the one problem that would prove the most difficult to manage, sectional conflict.

In a real sense, therefore, the Constitution's most important accomplishment was to create a framework within which Americans could cooperate to devise the institutions and policies necessary to support economic and political development, resolving various threats to cooperative activity as they arose (Mittal [2010, 2008]; also see Landau [1973, 1969]).

The Constitution's most general direct economic effect was to create a common market and the basis for specialization and exchange that emerged over the next two generations. As North (1961) argued, over the first generation under the Constitution, economic producers in different regions came to specialize in different economic activities. The South produced export crops (originally tobacco, rice, and indigo; later sugar, and especially cotton). The Northeast concentrated on transportation and financial services for southern exports (financing of exports, insurance, marketing, and the transportation of exports). The Northwest, largely independent at first, increasingly specialized in the production of food, shipped south along the waterways and, once the transportation infrastructure grew, shipped east along the canals and, later, the railroads (Callender 1902; Goodrich 1960).

This system of specialization and exchange and the national prosperity it helped to produce did not occur on its own. Because economic and political actors are reluctant to undertake specialized investments that are vulnerable to political change, a stable republican governmental structure underpinned these investments. A host of national and especially state policies also supported this accomplishment. As discussed in the next section, the investments resulting in regional specialization also required complementary action by state governments. The purpose of this chapter is to explain the institutions that promoted this outcome.

We divide the Constitution's effects into three categories. First, the direct effects: making new national policies. Second, the indirect effects: the creation of market-preserving federalism, fostering competition among the states, and allowing them to solve a wide range of important political and economic and political problems. And third, the forward-looking effects of problem solving and bargaining. We discuss these in turn.

1.3.1 Direct Effects: Promotion of New National Policies

Our discussion of the Constitution's direct effects on national policy-making will be brief, in large part because the other contributions to this volume represent extended investigations into these effects.

We now take American national defense and security for granted, but this is in part because the Founders successfully promoted security (Edling 2003; Hendrickson 2006). As emphasized in section 1.2, providing security proved difficult under the Articles. The national government lacked independent and reliable sources of revenue. It could not retire existing debt or fund new debt if the need arose, it could force the British to honor some provisions of the Treaty of Paris, secure the trans-Appalachian domain, and it had no means to devise strategies for dealing with various problems with foreign governments, such as the closure of British harbors to American merchantmen.

The Constitution helped the new national government solve these problems by granting the national government adequate revenue sources, and by creating a new legislature with sufficient powers to devise new policies and adapt these as circumstances changed.

Working under the new government, political officials solved a range of other important problems that plagued the United States under the Articles. For example, under the Articles, internal trade barriers hindered commerce among the states. Several clauses of the Constitution, notably the commerce clause and privileges and immunities clause, prohibited various types of internal trade barriers by states against the goods and services of other states, fostering a common market central to the growth of specialization and exchange over the next generation. The national government also became the locus of authority of monetary affairs, eliminating another source of conflict (e.g., Rhode Island's inflationary policies whose costs spilled over into other states).

The national government also made new policies in a series of areas dealing with national public goods. Beginning with his landmark *Report on Public Credit* (1790), Alexander Hamilton helped provide several national public policies necessary to underpin financial markets, including the establishment of public credit (including the assumption of state revolutionary war debts), the national Mint, and the Bank of the United States (Sylla, chapter 2, this volume). The government also established a national post office to improve communications among the states (John 1995). Congress also passed a bankruptcy law, an important institution that lowered both the transactions cost of removing failed enterprises and the incentives for failed enterprises to seek political bailouts.

1.3.2 Indirect Effects: A Stable, Centralized Federal System and its Implications

As Wallis (2007) reminds us, the Constitution did not create the states, and all states had ongoing constitutions in 1787. Adoption of the Constitution did not make the states impotent or secondary players with respect to policy. Indeed, states remained the nexus of economic regulation and the promotion of economic growth. Nor did the Constitution provide a road map for economic and political development.

The Constitution did, however, change the environment in which states operated, inventing a new form of "centralized federalism" that had never existed (Riker 1987). Two important new features of the post-Constitutional environment are relevant for our discussion. First, the most important change was creating a stronger national government capable of policing the common market. The national government had no such powers to prevent states from acting opportunistically under the Articles. The Constitution's commerce clause prevented states from regulating interstate commerce and restricted the federal government to truly national public goods, endowing the United States under the new Constitution with one of the largest common markets in the world.

The second feature was that the Constitution created the conditions of market-preserving federalism (Weingast 1995), matching the economists' prescriptions for fiscal federalism, including competition among subnational jurisdictions (Oates 1972; Tiebout 1956). The importance of market-preserving federalism is that it unleashed the creative engines of state government through competition, all within a common market protected by the federal government.

Federal systems differ across many dimensions, and only some promote fiscal federalism, competition among subnational jurisdictions, and economic development. In addition to a hierarchy of governments, market-preserving federalism requires four conditions:

- States have power over policies within their jurisdictions, including taxation and the ability to regulate their local economies.
- States participate in a common market.
- States face a hard budget constraint.
- National institutions provide incentives for national officials to honor the rules so that federalism is self-enforcing.

Satisfying these conditions seems natural in the American context, but few modern federal systems meet them (Weingast 1995).[7] Each of these

7. For example, modern Germany, Mexico, and Russia fail the policy independence condition. Argentina and Brazil fail the hard budget constraint. From 1950 through the early 1990s, India failed the policy independence and self-enforcing conditions (with respect to the latter, the national government used its authority to take over successful opposition state governments).

conditions is necessary to create effective interjurisdictional competition among the states. States without policy-making authority lack the power to tailor policies to their local environments, so that they cannot design new policies and programs to compete with their rivals. The absence of a common market policed by the national government diminishes the competitive pressures of interjurisdictional competition and allows states to insulate their economy from competitive pressures through internal trade barriers. A soft, as opposed to hard, budget constraint allows states to live beyond their financial means, often ignoring the effects of interjurisdictional competition through the ability to support or bail out noncompetitive local enterprises. Finally, federal systems that are at the discretion of the national government or that fail to prevent that government from manipulating the policies and innovations of subnational governments inhibit competition; for example, when the national government removes governors or governments for policies at variance with those of the national government (as has occurred at times over the last twenty-five years in India, Mexico, and Russia).

For the early United States, the institutions of market-preserving federalism launched the "laboratory of the states." Federalism fostered state experimentation that became critical not only as the competition among the states, but central to the economic growth of the early United States.

We tend to take the new political stability of the national government for granted. But this stability, including the stability of the federal system itself, is necessary for the interregional specialization and exchange necessary to promote prosperity. When states and economic actors feel threatened or believe the system at risk, they are less likely to promote and undertake specialized investments that are vulnerable to political opportunism from other states or the national government.

The main consequence of the Constitution's system of market-preserving federalism is that states developed many of the important policies promoting economic and political development. American states were the frontier of new rights and public goods, including franchise (Sokoloff and Engerman 2000), education (Mariscal and Sokoloff 2000), and party organization (Hofstadter 1969; Holt 1999; North, Wallis, and Weingast 2009, ch. 6). Consider education. In the United States, the leading liberalizers in the nineteenth century were not the original thirteen and wealthier colonies, but new ones (Mariscal and Sokoloff 2000). This pattern arose in part because newer states competed both with each other and with the established states for scarce labor. In order to attract labor to the frontier, states liberalized rights and provided public goods, including education. By midcentury, "more than 40 percent of school-age population in the United States overall was enrolled and nearly 90 percent of white adults were literate" (Mariscal and Sokoloff 2000, 161).

States were also the dominant providers of market-enhancing public goods, especially infrastructure investment and banks to help finance the flow of goods and crops to markets, a topic we discuss later (Callender 1902; Goodrich 1960; Wallis and Weingast 2005). They were also the primary locus of economic and social regulation (as Callender [1902]; Handlin and Handlin [1947]; Hartz [1948]; and Hughes [1977] emphasize in different ways). States also controlled the definition and enforcement of most economic property rights, including those pertaining to land and slavery. They were also the principal creators of open access for corporations, with general incorporation acts emerging in the 1840s. Until the Voting Rights Act of 1965, states were also the primary locus of the regulation and administration of elections (subject to the qualification of the federal experiments during reconstruction). Finally, states collected most direct taxes imposed on citizens (such as the property tax), with the dominant form of national revenue being raised through tariffs.

With respect to the economy, the national government eclipsed the importance of the states only in the mid-twentieth century. Until then, state governments remained the dominant force in taxation, economic regulation, the provision of public goods, and the management of the economy more broadly.

1.3.3   Some Illustrations of State Promotion of Economic Development

States in the early republic were remarkably active in the design of markets and the promotion of economic activity. Competition within the framework of market-preserving federalism fostered both state innovation and imitation of successful innovations by others. We illustrate this point with two examples, the evolution of state rules regulating banking and with government promotion of economic development through infrastructure provision.

Banking in the Early United States

Developing countries often create privileges and rents in the design of new markets (North, Wallis, and Weingast 2009). This is easily seen in banking, where most developing countries restrict the number of banks to limit entry, and sell bank charters as a means of creating economic rents that can be shared among the banks, the government, and specific citizens and firms who receive scarce loans (Haber 2008). Because the government has significant interests in banking, the exchange of privileged rights often explicitly or implicitly grants the government privileged access to loans. Moreover, as Haber (2008) argues, organizing the banking sector in this way limits its ability to provide the basic banking functions of an economy, notably, mobilizing capital to highest valued users who create new enterprises or seek to expand profitable ones. Instead, most loans go to the government, insiders, high government officials, and their relatives. An inevitable consequence of this structure, therefore, is limited competitiveness of the financial sector and, hence, limits on the degree to which banks help foster long-term economic growth.

The United States was no exception to the rule about restricting entry to create rents shared among bankers and the government.[8] In 1800, most states used this system, including Pennsylvania, whose commercial center of Philadelphia was the country's banking center.

States competed in an environment of strong market-preserving federal structure throughout the late eighteenth and nineteenth centuries. Consistent with the previous conditions of market-preserving federalism, states had nearly exclusive regulatory control over markets within their borders, they participated in a common market with product and factor mobility, and they faced a hard budget constraint. Moreover, states raised virtually all of their own revenue. This structure allowed states to design and redesign the rules governing various markets.

In the decade following 1800, Massachusetts slowly switched systems. Beginning with the monopoly approach, it created one large bank, in which it invested heavily, and several smaller banks. The state also imposed a tax on bank capital, which worked against the smaller banks. As the majority owner of the large bank, the state effectively paid part of its own tax. Over time, the state found it raised more taxes from the smaller banks than it did in dividends from the large bank.

The state's fiscal incentives led it to make two changes. It sold its interest in the larger bank, and it stopped limiting entry and selling charters. Under the new system, Massachusetts combined relatively low taxes on bank capital with more open entry into banking. This type of market gave Massachusetts banks a competitive advantage over all other U.S. banks. Merchants, enterprises, and transactions funded in Boston—such as financing, insuring, marketing, and transporting export crops to Europe—had an economic edge over their competitors from other states.

Under the new system, Massachusetts's fiscal incentives differed from those in other states, including Pennsylvania. Because a competitive banking sector maximizes the size of its tax base, Massachusetts now promoted the growth of a competitive banking sector. This system was so successful, that by the early 1830s, Massachusetts had more banks and bank capital than any state in the country. It also received over 50 percent of its revenues from the tax on bank capital, allowing it to reduce the principal tax falling on its citizens, the property tax. This was a win-win policy for that state.

Based on its competitive banking sector, Massachusetts eclipsed Philadelphia as the nation's banking center. A number of years later, New York also switched fiscal systems, emulating Massachusetts, and New York City eclipsed both Boston and Philadelphia as the nation's banking center. Many other states subsequently switched to the system that worked. Had the United States been a centralized federalism, as modern Mexico, the na-

---

8. Our discussion of banking in the early United States draws on Wallis, Sylla, and Legler (1994).

tional government would have had little incentive to alter the original system of limited entry once it was in place.

Market-Enhancing Public Goods in the Early Republic

Early American governments devoted substantial resources to promoting economic development.[9] Remarkably, state governments, not the national government, played the central role as promoters of development. State financial efforts were nearly an order of magnitude larger than the federal government's. Between 1790 and 1860, state and local governments spent over $450 million on transportation improvements; in contrast, the federal government spent $60 million (Goodrich 1960).

With millions of acres of fertile land, much of it virgin soil, the early United States was an agrarian economy. Economic growth necessitated investment in both transportation infrastructure (roads, canals, and railroads) to open the frontier to markets, and in banks to finance shipment of goods to markets. State governments financed both large-scale internal improvements and financial institutions (Callender 1903; Goodrich 1960; and Larson 2001). Many of the early projects, such as the Erie Canal, proved immensely profitable for the states.

Importantly, the state and national governments financed development projects in different ways. Congressional politics allowed the national government to finance large collections of small projects (such as lighthouses), but not large projects concentrated in one state or a small number of states (Wallis and Weingast 2005). Congressional majorities would not finance large projects benefiting one or a few states while drawing taxes from the rest. In principle, the national government could have used benefit taxation to solve this problem—raising taxes for the project from the states in proportion to their benefits from the projects—but the constitutional provisions for national taxation prohibited this. To the extent that the national government financed transportation investment, it did so through something-for-everyone programs. In contrast, states financed large projects using benefit taxes, assessing property owners in proportion to their expected economic gains from the new project. This fiscal mechanism allowed them to solve the political problems that plagued the national government.

This pattern of infrastructure finance reveals the incentives underlying the limits on the power of the national government operating in early America. The Constitution created a series of political constraints that made it politically impossible for the federal government to finance large infrastructure projects. Federal efforts came either in the form of financing large collections of small projects, or formal allocation formulas to distribute funds to every state. In short, the national government was politically impotent with respect to the provision of the highest valued infrastructure projects. States filled this gap.

---

9. This discussion draws on Wallis and Weingast (2005).

Other Illustrations

In the same way, states carried out a host of policies, from the form and security of property rights to economic regulation. Moreover, states did not limit creation of rights and promotional policies to commerce. As Sokoloff and Engerman (2000) demonstrate, suffrage represents an interesting case. Virtually all states at the time of independence had property restrictions on the vote. Universal (white) male suffrage tended to emerge on the frontier, as new territories and states sought to be attractive to scarce labor. The innovations of these states, in turn, forced established states to liberalize and remove their suffrage restrictions. Mariscal and Sokoloff (2000) make a similar argument for public education.

1.3.4   Adaptive Efficiency

Political stability requires that countries preserve cooperation even as they must adapt to changing circumstances, including various crises. Adaptation, in turn, requires that the different interests in society have a means of finding and implementing bargains that at once solve new problems as they emerge while maintaining cooperation. In particular, all parties with the ability to disrupt the constitutional system—for example, through secession or a coup—must judge themselves better off under the new bargain than disrupting the system. If the constitutional system lacks the ability to make the necessary agreements credible, then the bargaining parties will fail to solve their problems, not because a solution fails to exist, but because they lack the means to find and implement this bargain credibly.

Following Hayek (1960), North (2005) uses the term "adaptive efficiency" to describe a society's ability to solve problems and react to crises within an existing constitutional framework. Mittal (2010) argues that adaptive efficiency reflects the epistemic features of a political system that allow or hinder it to learn and adapt as circumstances require (see also Ober [2008]). Some countries are more likely to weather crises, even if severe. Other countries, such as those in Latin America and Africa, are prone to lapse into disorder and failure in the face of crises.[10]

Adaptive efficiency is one of the central features of the American constitutional system, which has proved relatively adept at allowing Americans to address problems and crises (Mittal 2010).[11] This adaptability was not inevitable, however. The unanimity requirement under the Articles prevented virtually all adaptation, even in the face of a wide range of debilitating cooperation failures and free-rider problems. Had the Founders merely proposed revisions of the Articles rather than devising a bold, new plan to take its place, it is unlikely that much of the adaptation under the Constitution

---

10. Using North, Wallis, and Weingast's terminology, these differences in performance reflect differences in limited access versus open access societies.

11. The essays in this volume show how, in a wide range of areas, the American Constitutional structure allowed Americans to devise solutions to a range of policy problems.

would have occurred. Sequential, piecemeal strengthening of the Articles would have undermined the creation of a truly national government capable of addressing a wide variety of crises and problems.

One of the principal concerns of *The Federalist* is addressing problems inherent in preserving constitutional stability in periods of unforeseen change. The essays argue that the commitment problem of maintaining an effective federal union is a perpetual one in the sense that it recurs in many guises as circumstances change. Problems of state shirking and disunion are dynamic. To preserve the union given the problems of new circumstances and unforeseen change, the government must possess sufficient power to address a wide variety of threats to cooperative activity over time.

Federalist 23 to 36 argues for the need to create exactly such a capacity to address unforeseen circumstances. Political stability requires an energetic constitution with the power to provide for defense and the people's welfare in unanticipated circumstances.

> Constitutions of civil government are not to be framed upon a calculation of existing exigencies, but upon a combination of these with the probable exigencies of ages, according to the natural and tried course of human affairs. Nothing, therefore, can be more fallacious than to infer the extent of any power, proper to be lodged in the national government, from an estimate of its immediate necessities. There ought to be a CAPACITY to provide for future contingencies as they may happen; and as these are illimitable in their nature, it is impossible safely to limit that capacity. (Cooke 1961b, Federalist 34, 210–11)

In designing the Federal Constitution of 1787, America's constitution-makers recognized that improving the quality of legislative deliberation was central to maintaining political stability. When it came to designing a constitution that would last, they understood that they could not foresee what the future would bring. Rather than leave the future to future generations, they radically reconsidered the role of legislation in society and drew on the latest scientific principles to design a legislative system capable of addressing threats that could not be foreseen.

From the perspective of *The Federalist,* the legislative process consists of much more than a representative forum—it is the nation's primary means of adaptation, especially in the face of crises. Previous republics tended to conceive of representative bodies more narrowly; for example, granting them veto power to check the power of others who had the power to devise new proposals (such as a nobility in the Italian city-state republics).[12] Congress was granted powers sufficient to create new legislation on an ongoing basis.

---

12. Montesquieu and Machiavelli consider legislatures primarily as rights-protecting institutions, not the adaptive and preference-aggregating forums they were later to become. The *Federalist* represents a critical transition from a negative, rights-protecting approach to lawmaking to a positive understanding of the role of law of in a changing world.

This modern legislative form is typical of legislative powers in the developed world today, but it was novel in 1787.

In designing a legislative system to respond to a wide variety of threats, Federalists relied heavily on the leading political science of the day. Liberal incorporation of scientific principles such as competition, redundancy, and diversity in the design of the Federal Constitution suggests that Federalists subscribed to a Humeian view of political science that argued that people, no matter where they are, respond to similar incentives similarly. Implicit in their political science was a response to the challenges of *fortuna* and uncertainty as they conceived of it.

In order for a single legislative process to adapt to problems of increasing complexity, government officials needed to have constant incentives to search for and create solutions to new and pressing problems that threatened to undermine cooperation. To respond to this challenge, America's constitution-makers designed a political system that puts self-interested elected officials in competition with each other.

Legislative competition is created by concurrent jurisdiction inherent in the separation of powers and federal systems (Federalist 32). Instead of trusting the creation of law to a body of enlightened statesmen, the legislative process involves inputs from many actors embedded in competition (Federalist 10). Within competitive systems, officials in the different institutions invest in expertise to avoid exploitation at the hands of their competitors.

Competition ensures that "ambition counteracts ambition" and inhibits encroachments on the constitutional rules, whether by departmental, federal, or state officials. But competition in the federal and separation of powers systems was not simply created to preserve a set of constitutional limits over time. A complementary goal of intragovernmental competition is to create adaptive efficiency by improving the quality of legislative deliberation, and the ability of legislatures to solve problems as they arise (Mittal 2008). Overlap (or redundancy) in the jurisdiction of these branches creates competitive pressures among them. Competition, in turn, forces each branch not only to check the others, but to invest in skills and knowledge. Competition is also an impetus behind institutional change. By increasing the stock and quality of institutional knowledge (Mokyr 2002), competition in the legislative process improves adaptive efficiency.

In order to respond effectively to unanticipated circumstances, legislative actors need more than political incentives to create legislation that will prove effective in restoring cooperation. They also need the *ability* to create such legislation. The Federalist framework for adaptive efficiency created a legislative process that restores and reinforces cooperative activity in the face of problems and crises by *aggregating, aligning, and codifying* knowledge.[13]

---

13. Focusing on ancient Athens, Ober (2008) articulates the importance of institutions for aggregating, aligning, and codifying knowledge in the success of democratic regimes.

With regard to aggregation, American constitution-makers sought to ensure that the system as whole would locate effective solutions to new problems. The Federalists sought to widen the epistemic base of government by creating *many* players with competitive interests in finding legislative solutions. Under the Articles, the unicameral Congress was the sole legislative body. Under the Federal Constitution, two branches of the legislative, the executive, and the judiciary each have a role in creating federal legislation.

In addition to creating many problem-solvers in government, the Constitution created *different* problem-solvers. Page (2007) uses mathematical modeling to show how groups that display a range of perspectives outperform groups of like-minded experts. He argues that diverse groups of people bring to organizations more and different ways of seeing a problem and, thus, faster and better ways of solving it.[14] Each branch of the federal government and every state has a distinct culture, experiences and knowledge, and approach to deliberation. The electoral system also contributes to diversity of approach by introducing new representatives with different perspectives into the lawmaking process (Federalist 62).

In addition to aggregating knowledge and producing legislative solutions, it is also critical that the central government *coordinate* on a legislative solution suited to the problem. In this context, the legislative process is the principal means of aligning a diverse population and set of political institutions on a particular solution to a problem. The required consent of several legislative bodies promoted alignment on moderate proposals. Extreme legislation would pass only in periods with unusual levels of consensus.

Finally, adaptive efficiency requires that solutions to new problems be codified and disseminated quickly. Preserving political stability in a crisis requires that knowledge of the legislative solution be quickly and efficiently dispersed throughout society. Without access to new information, each American state will operate on outdated information—leading to the familiar story of miscalculation, crisis, and disorder. American approaches to codification stem from thoughtful analysis of the Articles of Confederation. Uniformity and clarity in state legislation on issues was a direct response to Madison's concern with the "multiplicity, mutability, and injustice" of state law. Issues of naturalization, trade, and bankruptcy required greater uniformity of treatment and procedure than could be obtained from independent state action.

Our earliest political leaders understood that their work in 1787 would not be perfect (Federalist 85). While a wide variety of threats to cooperative activity could be addressed through legislation, they recognized some situations would require changes to the constitutional framework. With the bitter memory of the Articles' unanimity requirement for amendment fresh

14. Ober (2008) argues that bringing together people with different knowledge and perspectives was part of ancient Athens's success.

in their minds, the Federalists ensured that amendment of the Federal Constitution could be achieved with greater ease.

Turning to the specifics of adaptation, we have already discussed several ways in which the American system proved adaptive. With respect to western expansion, the American Constitutional framework proved adaptive. The mechanisms for settling western lands and the rules for supervising these units ensured that they would be self-constituting units and that they would be brought into the union on the same terms as existing states (see Grubb, chapter 8, this volume). This framework limited the potential rent-extraction from existing states and ensured that the new states would enjoy the same incentives possessed by existing states created by the market-preserving federalism environment. As new opportunities arose for expansion, the new nation took advantage of them, such as in the Louisiana Purchase and its settlement.

With respect to financial institutions, the national government promoted aspects of national capital markets, particularly sound public credit and a national bank. Federalism, especially competition among jurisdictions, prompted states to address a range of problems as a means of promoting a healthy economy and outcompeting rivals for scarce capital and labor and for the means of economic prosperity. Notable examples include the banking system and infrastructure to promote economic development. This system was not automatic, however, and often Americans faced seemingly intractable problems.

The most enduring and difficult problem that would episodically trouble Americans over their first century concerned sectional conflict, particularly over slavery. In the nineteenth century, the United States faced five sectional crises; conflicts between Northerners and Southerners over the nature of the Constitution and the future of the republic. In each crisis, the future of the country was at risk, and one—the fourth—resulted in a devastating Civil War when each of the proposed compromises of 1861 failed. With considerable difficulty, Americans solved the other four crises. Those in 1820, 1833, 1850, and 1877 resulted in adaptation of the constitutional bargain through an official Compromise, congressional acts that typically resolved the immediate issue of the crisis but also set rules governing future policies.

None of these compromises officially amended the Constitution. Yet each of the four compromises changed the rules of the political game, resulting in what Eskridge and Ferejohn (2001) call "super-statutes." These statutes represent more than ordinary legislation and can therefore be thought of as small "c" constitutional changes, changes in the structure of the bargain underlying the political system.

From the beginning of the republic, Americans had to confront the issue of whether one section, North or South, would gain the ability to dominate the national government. This issue underlay each of the five nineteenth-century crises. Americans constructed the Constitution to balance the interests of the sections so that neither would dominate (Ellis 2000; Finkelman

1996; Rakove 1996). In particular, it provided a range of credible commitments to protect slavery, including federalism's decentralization of property rights to states, and the three-fifths clause granting Southerners additional representation in Congress based on their slaves.

Perhaps the most important credible commitment to protect slavery was the *balance rule,* the idea that the country would maintain an equal number of free and slave states (Weingast 1998, 2002). Sectional balance provided each section with a veto over national policy-making through equal representation in the Senate; in particular, it granted Southerners the ability to veto any national legislation over slavery. Sectional balance first emerged with the admission of Kentucky (1792) and Tennessee (1796), bringing each section's delegation up to eight states. Americans maintained this balance through 1850 with the lone admission of California. Attempts to restore balance over the next decade (for example, the Kansas-Nebraska Act in 1854, and the 1858 attempt to admit Kansas as a slave state under the Lecompton constitution that was mired in allegations of voter fraud) added to the crisis.

A critical feature of sectional balance as a major institutional protection for slavery is that it required the two sections to grow in parallel, in turn requiring that each section have sufficient territory within which to expand. Three of the four antebellum crises emerged in moments when one section potentially had an edge, as in 1819 to 1820, 1846 to 1850, and 1854 to 1861.

As an example, consider the Compromise of 1820. The immediate concern in the 1819 controversy over Missouri was whether to admit Missouri as a slave state. With no obvious free territory looming in the wings, this admission would have tipped the balance in favor of the South, and Northerners reacted in the House of Representatives (where they had a majority) by admitting Missouri subject to conditions of gradual emancipation of all slaves. Southerners used their equal representation in the Senate to prevent this provision from becoming law, and a crisis ensued.

The Compromise of 1820 resolved the crisis on three different levels. First, it admitted Maine (broken off from Massachusetts) as a free state to balance the admission of Missouri, maintaining sectional balance. Second, it divided the remaining territories between free and slave, removing ambiguity as to their status and the uncertainty over the future disposition of those territories and the resulting states. Third, the Compromise made explicit the balance rule for the future admission in states. For the next three decades, states were admitted in pairs (Arkansas and Michigan in the mid-1830s; Florida, Texas, Iowa, and Wisconsin in the mid-1840s). In similar ways, Congress passed compromises in 1833 and 1850 to resolve crises over sectional issues.

In all four antebellum crises, secession and the potential failure of the American Constitution and democracy were live issues, as demonstrated by the secession winter of 1860 to 1861 and the following Civil War. American constitutional stability, therefore, rested on the ability of Americans to resolve their differences and to provide solutions to new problems as they arose.

Thinking broadly to include federalism and the engine of competition among the states, the Constitution created a framework within which Americans could resolve most of their problems, including the most vexing one of slavery and the balance between the two sections within the Union. Although this framework failed to create a solution in 1861, the constitutional system did allow Americans to resolve their conflicts for three generations prior to the Civil War. This framework provided the basis for ongoing cooperation between the sections, and to foster specialization and exchange of a growing economy. In addition, twenty-five years after the start of the Civil War, Southern states had been readmitted on roughly the same terms as they had left, with the major change being the abolition of slavery.

1.4   Conclusions

The most striking contribution of the Constitution—and one too often taken for granted—was the creation of a successful, stable, republican government capable of adapting to the wide variety of changes future generations would face. Without this accomplishment, the United States is unlikely to have achieved its long-term history of sustained economic growth. In contrast to the Articles, which provided incentives for states to shirk their responsibilities, the Constitution created a system in which Americans cooperated to solve a range of problems.

In the Constitution's first decade, new policies addressed a range of problems, most notably the policy failures under the Articles: providing security for the new nation; addressing a wide range of problems of public finance, including raising sufficient revenue, retiring existing debt, and creating the basis for new debt when needed; asserting control over the frontier; trade policies aimed at the flooding of foreign goods on the American markets and the closing of foreign ports to American shipping; enforcing provisions of the Treaty of Paris; and limiting a range of problems among the states, such as internal trade barriers.

The Constitution also provided the means and incentives for Americans to solve new problems as they arose. Many solutions occurred directly through congressional policy-making. We illustrated this point with the various compromises aimed at solving the episodic problems that arose around slavery, the territories, and westward expansion. The Constitution also created indirect incentives for Americans to solve their problems through the market-preserving federalism. States not only had incentives to create strong systems of property and other rights as a means of competing against neighboring states, but to adapt their policies and institutions as circumstances changed. With respect to banks, for example, states originally created a system of

local monopolies; but gradually, following the innovations in Massachusetts, states moved to a system of competitive banking. By the Civil War, the
United States had more banks than any other economy. Competition among
the frontier territories and states for scarce capital and especially labor led
them to expand political rights and education, resulting in universal enfran-
chisement, at least for white males.

The result was one of the biggest common markets in the world, largely
free of government regulation. In combination, the national and state
governments provided a secure environment for investment with a relative
absence of political opportunism or threat of expropriation. Significant specialization and exchange resulted, producing long-term economic growth.

References

Buel, R. 1980. *Dear liberty: Connecticut's mobilization for the revolutionary war.*
    Middletown, CT: Wesleyan University Press.
Callender, G. S. 1902. The early transportation and banking enterprises of the states
    in relation to the growth of corporations. *Quarterly Journal of Economics* 17 (1):
    111–62.
Cooke, J. E., ed. 1961a. Federalist 10. In *The Federalist*, Alexander Hamilton, James
    Madison, and John Jay, 59. Middletown, CT: Wesleyan Press.
———. 1961b. Federalist 34. In *The Federalist*, Alexander Hamilton, James Madi-
    son, and John Jay, 210–11. Middletown, CT: Wesleyan Press.
Edling, M. 2003. *A revolution in favor of government: Origins of the U.S. Constitution
    and the making of the American state.* New York: Oxford University Press.
Einhorn, R. 2006. *American taxation, American slavery.* Chicago: University of Chi-
    cago Press.
Ellis, J. J. 2000. *Founding brothers: The revolutionary generation.* New York: Alfred A.
    Knopf.
Eskridge, W. N., and J. Ferejohn. 2001. Super-statutes. *Duke Law Journal* 50 (5):
    1215–76.
Farrand, M. 1966. *The records of the Federal Convention of 1787.* New Haven: Yale
    University Press.
Finkelman, P. 1996. *Slavery and the founders: Race and liberty in the age of Jefferson.*
    Armonk, NY: M. E. Sharpe.
Ford, W. C., ed. 1904–37. Proposed Amendments to the Articles of Confederation,
    August 7, 1786. Report of Continental Congress. In *Journals of the Continental
    Congress, 1774–1789*, journal 31: 494. Washington, DC: Government Printing
    Office.
Goodrich, C. 1960. *Government promotion of canals and railroads, 1800–1890.* New
    York: Columbia University Press.
Haber, Stephen. 2008. Political institutions and financial development: Evidence
    from the political economy of bank regulation in the United States and Mexico.
    In *The political economy of financial development.* Edited by Stephen Haber, Doug-
    lass C. North, and Barry R. Weingast. Stanford: Stanford University Press.
Handlin, O., and M. Handlin. 1947. *Commonwealth: A study of the role of govern-*

ment in the American economy, Massachusetts, 1774–1861. New York: New York University Press.

Hartz, L. 1948. *Economic policy and democratic thought: Pennsylvania, 1776–1860*. Cambridge, MA: Harvard University Press.

Hayek, F. A. 1960. *The Constitution of liberty*. Chicago: University of Chicago Press.

Hendrickson, D.C. 2006. *Peace pact: The lost world of the American founding*. Lawrence, KS: University Press of Kansas.

Hofstadter, R. 1969. *The idea of a party system*. Berkeley: University of California Press.

Holt, M. F. 1999. *The rise and fall of the American Whig Party: Jacksonian politics and the onset of the Civil War*. New York: Oxford University Press.

Holton, W. 2007. *Unruly Americans and the origins of the Constitution*. New York: Hill and Wang.

Hughes, J. 1977. *The governmental habit*. New York: Basic.

John, R. R. 1995. *Spreading the news: The American postal system from Franklin to Morse*. Cambridge, MA: Harvard University Press.

Kammen, M. G. 1986. *A machine that would go of itself: The Constitution in American culture*. New York: Knopf.

Landau, M. 1969. Redundancy, rationality, and the problem of duplication and overlap. *Public Administration Review* 29 (4): 346–58.

———. 1973. Federalism, redundancy, and system reliability. *Publius* 3 (2): 173–96.

Larson, J. L. 2001. *Internal improvement: National public works and the promise of popular government in the early United States*. Chapel Hill: University of North Carolina Press.

Madison, J. 1787. Vices of the political system of the U. States. In *James Madison: Writings*, ed. Rakove, 69–79. New York: Library of America.

Mariscal, E., and K. L. Sokoloff. 2000. Schooling, suffrage, and the persistence of inequality in the Americas, 1800–1945. In *Political institutions and economic growth in Latin America: Essays in policy, history, and political economy*, ed. S. Haber, 159–218. Stanford: Hoover Institution Press.

Marks, F. W., III. 1986. *Independence on trial: Foreign affairs and the making of the Constitution*. Wilmington, DE: Scholarly Resources.

McDonald, F. 1985. *Novus ordo seclorum: The intellectual origins of the Constitution*. Lawrence, KS: University Press of Kansas.

Mittal, S. 2008. A necessary precaution: The separation of powers and political stability. Paper presented at the annual meeting of the MPSA Annual National Conference, Chicago, April.

———. 2010. Constitutional stability in a changing world: Institutions, learning, and adaptive efficiency. Stanford University, Department of Political Science. Working Paper.

Mokyr, J. 2002. *The gifts of Athena: Historical origins of the knowledge economy*. Princeton, NJ: Princeton University Press.

Nelson, E. 2004. *The Greek tradition in republican thought*. Cambridge: Cambridge University Press.

North, D.C. 1961. *The economic growth of the United States: 1790–1860*. New York: W.W. Norton.

———. 2005. *Understanding the process of economic change*. Princeton, NJ: Princeton University Press.

North, D.C., J. J. Wallis, and B. R. Weingast. 2009. *Violence and social orders: A conceptual framework to interpret recorded human history*. Cambridge: Cambridge University Press.

Oates, W. 1972. *Fiscal federalism*. New York: Harcourt Brace Jovanovich.

Ober, J. 2008. *Democracy and knowledge: Innovation and learning in classical Athens.* Princeton, NJ: Princeton University Press.

Onuf, P. S. 1983. *The origins of the federal republic: Jurisdictional controversies in the United States, 1775–1787.* Philadelphia: University of Pennsylvania Press.

Page, S. E. 2007. *The difference: How the power of diversity creates better groups, firms, schools, and societies.* Princeton, NJ: Princeton University Press.

Rakove, J. N. 1979. *The beginnings of national politics: An interpretive history of the Continental Congress.* New York: Knopf.

———. 1996. *Original meanings: Politics and ideas in the making of the Constitution.* New York: Knopf.

———, ed. 1999. James Madison to Caleb Wallace, August 23, 1785. *James Madison: Writings.* New York: Library of America.

Riker, W. H. 1987. The invention of centralized federalism. In *The development of American Federalism,* ed. W. H. Riker, 17–42. Boston: Kluwer Academic Publishers.

Siemers, D. J. 2002. *Ratifying the republic: Antifederalists and Federalists in constitutional time.* Stanford: Stanford University Press.

Sokoloff, K. L., and S. L. Engerman. 2000. Institutions, factor endowments, and paths of development in the New World. *Journal of Economic Perspectives.* 14 (3): 217–32.

Tiebout, C. 1956. A pure theory of local expenditures *Journal of Political Economy* 64:416–24.

Wallis, J. J. 2007. American government and the promotion of economic development in the national era, 1790 to 1860. In *Government and the American economy.* ed. P. Fishback and D.C. North, 148–86. Chicago: University of Chicago Press.

Wallis, J. J., R. E. Sylla, and J. B. Legler. 1994. The interaction of taxation and regulation in nineteenth century U.S. banking. In *The regulated economy: A historical approach to political economy,* ed. C. Goldin and G. D. Libecap, 121–44. Chicago: University of Chicago Press.

Wallis, J. J., and B. Weingast. 2005. Equilibrium federal impotence: Why the states and not the American national government financed infrastructure investment in the antebellum era. NBER Working Paper no. 11397. Cambridge, MA: National Bureau of Economic Research, June.

Weingast, B. R. 1995. The economic role of political institutions: Market-preserving federalism and economic development. *Journal of Law, Economics, and Organization* 11 (1): 1–31.

———. 1998. Political stability and civil war: Institutions, commitment, and American democracy. In *Analytic narratives,* ed. R. Bates, A. Greif, M. Levi, J.-L. Rosenthal, and B. R. Weingast, 148–93. Princeton, NJ: Princeton University Press.

———. 2002. *Institutions and political commitment: A new political economy of the American Civil War era.* Hoover Institution, Stanford University. Unpublished Manuscript.

Wood, G. S. 1969. *The creation of the American republic, 1776–1787.* Chapel Hill: University of North Carolina Press.

II

Policy

2

Financial Foundations
Public Credit, the National Bank, and Securities Markets

Richard Sylla

The financial foundations of the United States and its federal government were created in three years, 1790 to 1792. Before 1790, the government was effectively bankrupt. Without tax revenues until late in 1789—after the newly created Treasury Department opened in September of that year, it managed to collect by year end a grand total of $162,200 in custom duties—the U.S. government was in default on almost all of its large domestic debts left over from the Revolution, as well as on most of its foreign debts incurred in the struggle. The new nation lacked a national currency, a national bank, a banking system, and regularly functioning securities markets. It had only a couple of dozen business corporations the states had chartered during the 1780s.

The financial revolution of 1790 to 1792 changed all that. In 1793, the government collected almost $4.7 million in tax revenue, more than enough to fund government operations and meet interest payments on the national debt. By 1793, a federally chartered Bank of the United States had opened in Philadelphia with branches in several cities, as had the U.S. Mint, to produce silver and gold coins in the newly defined dollar unit of account. Several states had chartered ten more banks to join the first three bank start-ups of the 1780s, one of which operated without a corporate charter until 1791.

Richard Sylla is the Henry Kaufman Professor of the History of Financial Institutions and Markets and Professor of Economics at New York University, and a research associate of the National Bureau of Economic Research.

The author thanks Eric Hilt, Farley Grubb, Douglas Irwin, Naomi Lamoreaux, Hugh Rockoff, Jon Wallis, Thomas Weiss, Robert Wright, other participants in the Founding Choices conference, and two anonymous reviewers for comments and suggestions that he hopes have improved this essay. Some material in the chapter is based upon work supported by the National Science Foundation under Grant no. 0751577, "U.S. Corporate Development, 1801–1860." Any opinions, findings, and conclusions expressed in this chapter are those of the author and do not necessarily reflect the views of the National Science Foundation.

Along with the national bank and its branches, these banks were interacting with one another as a banking system.

Forty-four new business corporations, including the banks, received charters in 1790 to 1792: more in three years than the total of seven in the entire colonial era and the total of twenty-four in the 1780s. Securities markets in Philadelphia, New York, and Boston priced every business day the $63 million of restructured domestic U.S. debt that began to appear in late 1790, as well as the $10 million in stock of the Bank of the United States and the stock of state banks and nonbanking corporations.[1] These markets had even survived their first bubbles, panics, and crashes in 1791 and 1792 (Sylla, Wright, and Cowen 2009). Financially, by 1793 the United States looked surprisingly modern. In 1789 it was decidedly premodern.

Because of the events of 1790 to 1792, from that time forward Americans and most of their historians could assume, correctly, that a modern financial system always existed in their country. But, too often incorrectly, they also assumed there was nothing special, unique, or even good about it. Since modern economies by definition have modern financial systems, much of U.S. financial historiography has focused on the unseemly, negative features of these systems. Taxes and public spending are too high. The national debt is too big and ought to be reduced. Large banks are a threat to economic stability and perhaps even the people's liberties. Banks take too many risks and too often fail. Stock markets are the dens of speculators and thieves, and too often they crash. Business corporations have too many privileges and too much influence in American life.

These widely trumpeted opinions of our time are nothing new. They have been voiced throughout U.S. history since 1790. But they were not voiced in America before 1790, or in most other countries until long after 1790.

The United States was one of the first nations to modernize its finances. Only two nations did so earlier—the Dutch Republic (the modern Netherlands) about two centuries before the United States, and Great Britain starting perhaps a century earlier. Neither modernized as completely as the United States did by 1800, and neither did it within three years, or even three decades (Rousseau and Sylla 2003, 2005; Sylla 2009).

This chapter attempts to answer several questions. How did so much modernizing economic and financial change happen so quickly at the start of U.S. history? What were the specific choices made and actions taken during 1790 to 1792 that made it happen? How were they challenged? How were they defended? Did the financial revolution happen as easily as is sometimes assumed from its sheer rapidity? And finally, what difference did the financial revolution make for what happened after it occurred? In particular, what was its impact on the growth of the U.S. economy?

---

1. An additional $12 million of foreign debt raised the total national debt to approximately $75 million as of 1790. Most of the foreign debt was owed to France, for French loans during the War of Independence and arrears of interest on those loans.

2.1   Hatching and Shaping the Plan

The origins of the financial revolution of the early 1790s can be traced to the seemingly insurmountable financial difficulties of the last years of the War of Independence. Then, the Confederation Congress saw its paper money become worthless and, having no tax powers, it struggled to find ways to pay its army and its debts (Ferguson 1961). Congress appointed Robert Morris, a wealthy merchant and financier, to be superintendent of finance in 1781. Morris managed to fund the decisive Yorktown campaign and victory in October of that year, and to persuade Congress to charter the first American bank, the Bank of North America, shortly thereafter. But Congress failed to enact most other financial reforms Morris recommended, and he resigned in frustration in 1784.

Financial difficulties in countries are common, particularly during times of war, and there were lots of such times during the eighteenth century. Financial revolutions, however, are rare. How, then, did the financial difficulties experienced by Americans during the War of Independence lead to a financial revolution a decade later?

Subsequent events would reveal that the initial plans for a U.S. financial revolution were hatched in several letters—more accurately essays—on political economy that Alexander Hamilton wrote between late 1779 and early 1781. Hamilton at the time was a lieutenant colonel in the Continental Army and the principal aide de camp to General Washington, the American commander. In his long letters to U.S. leaders, Hamilton demonstrated an unusual understanding of financial history, gained from his recent study of the works of Malachy Postlethwaite, David Hume, Richard Price, Adam Smith, and others (McDonald 1979, 35). The letters indicate that Hamilton knew quite a lot about the successful financial revolutions of the Dutch and the British, and the aborted efforts of John Law in France. From those histories he drew the conclusion that finance was the key both to state power and economic growth. Applying his historical understanding to the situation of the United States, he began to formulate plans for what would become the U.S. financial revolution a decade later. In 1789, as the first secretary of the treasury of the new federal government, Hamilton would execute a more refined version of a plan he had hatched a decade earlier and then developed during the 1780s.

The setting for Hamilton's letter-essays was the dire situation of the American revolutionaries in 1779 to 1781. The war had dragged on for five years. Paper "Continental Currency," first authorized and issued by Congress in 1775, and then issued to excess by 1778 to 1779, was well on its way to becoming worthless by 1780. Taxation, then, was in the hands of the states. To meet the requisitions of Congress, states were supposed to levy wartime taxes payable in Continentals as well as in their own state paper currencies. That would support the values of the paper currencies by making them acceptable as a means of paying taxes and by reducing the amounts outstanding. But taxes levied and collected by the states were woefully inadequate to the task, so Continental paper dollars depreciated to the point where it took about forty paper dollars to purchase a dollar in hard-money coins by the start of 1780, and about one hundred paper dollars to buy a dollar in specie by the beginning of 1781 (Perkins 1994, 97). Borrowing, an alternative to taxation and money printing as a method of public finance, also proved difficult both at home and abroad, in part because ineffective taxation and excessive money printing undermined whatever confidence lenders might otherwise have had in the revolutionary cause.

In his first letter on the dire U.S. financial situation (undated, but thought to have been written between December 1779 and March 1780), Hamilton argued that the main solution to the wartime financial problems of the Americans had to be a foreign loan, most likely from France, which already supported the American cause financially and militarily. "The most opulent states of Europe in a war of any duration are commonly obliged to have recourse to foreign loans and subsidies. How then could we expect to do without them. . . ." Part of the loan might be used to buy up superfluous paper currency, but Hamilton thought it would be better to turn it into merchandise (military supplies) overseas and import the supplies to aid the undersupplied Continental Army. If that were done, the Americans might be able to carry on the war for two or three more years. By itself, however, a foreign loan would do little to restore the currency to a sound basis (Syrett 1961–1987, II, 234–51, quote at 237–38).

A better plan, Hamilton reasoned, was to have Congress charter for ten years what he already in 1780 called a "Bank of the United States," and use the foreign loan to provide some of the bank's capital, with the rest to come from subscriptions to the bank's stock by private investors. The way to restore private confidence in paper money was to have the Bank's notes replace fiat paper money such as Continentals. The Bank would hold specie reserves (gold and silver coins) and its notes would be convertible into hard money. Bank paper money convertible into specie would achieve the goal of currency stability. The U.S. government would own part of the Bank and share in its profits. And, it would receive a large loan from the Bank, at 4 percent interest, to finance the ongoing war.

As precedents for his plan, Hamilton referred to John Law's failed plans for financial reforms in France, which nonetheless had some good features. "It will be our wisdom to select what is good in [Law's] plan and in any others that have gone before us, avoiding their defects and excesses." He also drew on the experience of the Bank of England, a "striking example" of how far paper credit could be increased "when supported by public authority and private influence." He admired how British public debt was absorbed and managed by the Bank of England, which strengthened the Bank and enhanced the ability of the British government to borrow. Unlike the Bank of England, however, Hamilton's proposed Bank of the United States was not to have exclusive privileges. While Hamilton supported increased state power, he was opposed to monopoly as inimical to economic growth. "Large trading companies must be beneficial to the commerce of a nation, when they are not invested with [exclusive privileges]; because they furnish a capital with which the most extensive enterprises may be undertaken (Syrett 1961–1987, II, 245, 249, 250).

Hamilton's first letter on financial reform foreshadowed several of the key elements of modern financial systems, most notably a *central bank* issuing paper money (bank notes) convertible into specie, which the bank would hold as reserves. It was a plan to *stabilize the currency* of a country whose paper currency had lost most of its value. The bank would also lend to the government, thus strengthening *public finances* and supporting *a public debt market*. It would be a *corporation* without exclusive privileges, and such enterprises would foster economic growth.

Hamilton addressed a second letter-essay in September, 1780, to James Duane, a New York delegate to the Continental Congress. In it Hamilton's political economy advanced to a higher plane. The fundamental problem of the United States was that the national government did not have sufficient vigor, and especially sufficient means, to meet public exigencies. The national government needed to be altered. It needed to have the power of the purse. "All imposts [import taxes] upon commerce ought to be laid by Congress and appropriated for their use, for without *certain revenues* a government can have no power; that power, which holds the purse strings absolutely, must rule."

There were two sets of remedies. First, the national government had to have the power to govern and wage war. Hamilton asserted that Congress, having declared the independence of the United States, already had such powers, but—fearful of state objections—Congress was too timid to use them. Recognizing that few would agree with his bold call for Congress to assert sovereign powers, Hamilton recommended that Congress immediately convene a convention of the states to provide the national government with competent powers. This, in 1780, appears to be the first call by any American for a constitutional restructuring of U.S. government, and issues of public finance were at the heart of it. Passages in the letter, in fact, sound a lot like Article I, Section 8, of the U.S. Constitution written seven years later (Syrett 1961–1987, II, 400–18, quote at 404).[2]

2. Compare Article I, Section 8, with this from Hamilton's 1780 letter to Duane: "Congress should have complete sovereignty in all that relates to war, peace, trade, finance, and to the management of foreign affairs, the right of declaring war and raising armies, officering, paying them, directing their motions in every respect, of equipping fleets and doing the same with them, of building fortifications arsenals magazines &c., &c., of making peace on such conditions as they think proper, of regulating trade, determining with what countries it shall be carried on, granting indulgences laying prohibitions on all articles of export or import, imposing duties granting bounties & premiums for raising exporting importing and applying to their own use the product of these duties, only giving credit to the states on whom they are raised in the general account of revenues and expences, instituting Admiralty courts &c., of coining money, establishing banks on such terms, and with such privileges as they think proper, appropriat-

Second, to supply the army, Hamilton proposed to Duane a four-step approach: a foreign loan (most likely from France), pecuniary taxes, a tax in kind, and a bank founded on public and private credit. In connection with the bank proposal, Hamilton discussed the origins of modern banking in Venice, the Banks of Amsterdam and England, and the flaws in John Law's system in France. The bank he outlined was similar to the Bank of the United States proposed in the earlier letter, but now Hamilton says that it should have three branches in three different states. Later, Hamilton's 1790 proposal for a Bank of the United States, enacted with a Hamilton-drafted congressional charter in 1791, permitted the bank to have branches, and the Bank would open several branches ranging from Boston to Charleston in 1792.

A third Hamilton letter-essay was to Robert Morris in April, 1781, shortly after Congress had appointed Morris as its superintendent of finance to salvage revolutionary finances after the collapse of paper Continentals.[3] After stressing the crucial importance of finance—"'Tis by introducing order into our finances—by restoring public credit—not by gaining battles, that we are finally to gain our object" (Syrett 1961–1987, 606)—Hamilton said he intended to give Morris some ideas he had on financial administration, and a plan that, while "crude and defective," might be a "basis for something more perfect." First, he estimated the revenue capacity of the country and compared it with an estimate of necessary civil and military expenses. The latter greatly exceeded the former, leaving a revenue shortfall that had to be financed. Foreign loans might help, but could not do it all. So a plan had to be devised, and Hamilton's plan calls, as did the plans outlined in his two previous letters, for establishing a national bank. He goes on to discuss the pros and cons of national banks in theory and in history, including a statement of how banking development and the expansion of credit promote both state power and economic growth:

> The tendency of a national bank is to increase public and private credit. The former gives power to the state for the protection of its rights and interests, and the latter facilitates and extends the operations of commerce among individuals. Industry is increased, commodities are multiplied, agriculture and manufactures flourish, and herein consist the true wealth and prosperity of a state.
>
> Most commercial nations have found it necessary to institute banks and they have proved to be the happiest engines that ever were invented for advancing trade. Venice Genoa Hamburgh [sic] Holland and England are examples of their utility. They owe their riches, commerce, and the figure

ing funds and doing whatever else relates to the operations of finance, transacting every thing with foreign nations, making alliances offensive and defensive, treaties of commerce, &c., &c" (Syrett 1961–1987, II, 408).

3. In the September 1780 letter to Duane, after recommending that Congress appoint "great officers of State" to execute its decisions—the idea of an executive branch—Hamilton endorsed Robert Morris to head the department of finance (Syrett 1961–1987, 408–09).

they have made at different periods in a great degree to this source. Great Britain is indebted for the immense efforts she has been able to make in so many illustrious and successful wars essentially to that vast fabric of credit raised on this foundation. 'Tis by this alone she now menaces our independence. (Syrett 1961–1987, II, 618)

Much of the remainder of Hamilton's letter to Morris is given over to proposing and discussing twenty articles, "only intended as outlines," that would comprise the national bank's charter. The bank would be, for example, by law a *corporation,* which seemed so obvious to Hamilton and to a businessman such as Morris that it "needs no illustration," although in America as elsewhere there were few business corporations then. The letter ends with a brief discussion of the national debt after the war is over. The debt would not present a problem, Hamilton said, because the country's growth and a good financial administration will easily enable the United States to pay it off in a matter of decades. In fact, properly managed, it will be "a national blessing . . . a powerful cement of our union" (Syrett 1961–1987, II, 635).

Morris replied to Hamilton that he had been thinking along similar lines, although the Bank of North America (BNA) that he soon proposed to Congress was more realistic and less ambitious in scale and scope than the national bank Hamilton recommended (Syrett 1961–1987, II, 645–46). Interestingly, the proceeds of a foreign loan, as in Hamilton's plans, did become the source of most of BNA's capital.

Hamilton's letter-essays of 1779 to 1781 dealing with finance, state power, and economic growth touched on all the main components of modern financial systems—government revenues and public debts, money, banking and central banking, corporations, and, at least implicitly, the securities markets that would arise to give liquidity to government debt and corporate securities; that is, bonds and stocks. They demonstrate an unusually modern grasp of the role of finance in political and economic history. They also foreshadow the financial revolution Hamilton would execute a decade later as treasury secretary.

The remarkable aspect of Hamilton's early letter-essays on political economy and finance is their demonstration of his historical learning, the lessons for the United States he saw in financial history, and his grasp of the components of a modern, articulated financial system, and the support each component gives to the others. On the basis of the limited historical evidence and other information available to him, Hamilton drew the right conclusions. He also realized that in America public opinion, not just the views of leaders, mattered for policy change. With that in mind, Hamilton in 1781 to 1782 published six essays entitled *The Continentalist* in a New York newspaper. These essays were simpler versions of the ideas embodied in his three letter-essays to leaders.

By the time Hamilton became secretary of the treasury a decade later, the plans that he started to shape in 1779 to 1781 were more refined. In the interim, Robert Morris appointed Hamilton receiver of Continental revenues for New York State, an experience that provided lessons in the difficulties of financing a national government by means of requisitions from states. As Congress' superintendent of finance from 1781 to 1784, Morris tried without success to implement many of the financial reforms that Hamilton would successfully implement a decade later. It is one thing to have a plan, and quite another to be able to execute it. Likely the different outcomes resulted from the constitutional changes of 1787 to 1788. (Hamilton, as we have seen, called for such changes in 1780.)[4]

In September 1789, shortly after approving Congress' bill establishing the Treasury Department, President Washington nominated Hamilton to head it, with Congress approving the nomination the same day. Hamilton immediately arranged loans from the Banks of North America and New York that financially launched the new federal government. Revenues from recently enacted duties on imports and tonnage were still absent, and one of Hamilton's early tasks as treasury secretary was to organize the system for collecting federal revenues.

Having developed his financial plan for the country over the course of the previous decade, Hamilton now was in a position to execute it, with the help of his allies in and out of Congress. That was not to prove so easy. Each step of the implementation featured political controversy; partisan attacks became increasingly bitter. As leaders took positions in favor of or against Hamilton's program, the U.S. financial revolution soon engendered the two-party system of politics that ever since has been a staple of American life.

Despite the political divisions, the financial revolution happened, and with great rapidity. By the time Hamilton retired as treasury secretary in 1795, the finances and debt management of the new federal government would be firmly established, and the U.S. economy would have a modern, articulated financial system jump-starting and sustaining its growth.

2.2   Executing and Implementing the Plan

Ten days after becoming secretary of the treasury in 1789, Hamilton was directed by the House of Representatives to prepare a plan "for the support of the public credit, as a matter of high importance to the national honor and prosperity." He delivered his report in January 1790. On the basis of fairly solid information, Hamilton estimated the debts of the United States, including arrears of interest, at $54.1 million, of which $11.7 million was owed to foreign governments and investors, and $42.1 was owed to domestic

---

4. Ver Steeg (1954) provides a full account of Morris's financial program and its relationship to Hamilton's.

creditors. In addition, he estimated from less solid information that state debts incurred mostly during the War of Independence, including arrears of interest, were $25 million. Because they had been incurred in the common cause, Hamilton argued that the state debts ought to be assumed by the federal government. The grand total of the national debt estimated by Hamilton amounted to $79.1 million (Syrett 1961–1987 VI, 87–88), about 40 percent of the estimated gross domestic product (GDP) in 1790 (Johnston and Williamson 2009).

If the United States were to pay interest on this mass of debt on the terms under which it had been borrowed, Hamilton calculated that the annual expenses would come to $4.587 million—$4.045 million on the domestic debt and $0.543 on the foreign debt. Could the government, with tax revenues just beginning to trickle in, have paid this huge annual interest expense along with its annual operating expenses, which he estimated at $0.6 million?[5] Hamilton thought that to do so "would require the extension of taxation to a degree, and to objects, which the true interest of public creditors forbids" (Syrett 1961–1987, VI, 88). Therefore, he recommended that interest on the foreign debt be paid in full, but that domestic debt holders voluntarily agree to have the full value of their debts funded by a new loan at a reduced rate of interest amounting essentially to 4 percent instead of the original 6 percent.[6] That would reduce the annual interest on the domestic debt to a little over $2.7 million, potentially manageable, instead of $4 million.

To induce domestic creditors to make the voluntary conversion, Hamilton offered call protection—only a small amount of the debt could be retired annually even if market interest rates declined, as he confidently predicted they would. To give the creditors further assurances, he proposed a federally administered sinking fund to apply surplus revenues and money borrowed at home or abroad to open-market purchases of public debt "until the whole of the debt shall be discharged" (Syrett 1961–1987, VI, 107; Sylla and Wilson 1999). Investors thus could count on the government not merely to pay interest on its debt, but ultimately to redeem it. And, the government gained the ability to conduct open-market purchases to support debt prices.

After half a year of protracted debates in Congress and some side deals to attract the needed votes, Congress essentially adopted Hamilton's proposal. The most crucial of the side deals involved federal assumption of state debts.

5. Hamilton was too optimistic with his $0.6 million estimate of federal operating expenses. In the governments first full year of operation, 1790, domestic operating expenditures came to $0.829 million.

6. Hamilton, in his January 1790 Report on Public Credit, laid out a menu of debt management options for Congress to consider. Congress adopted one of them with a minor modification that was more generous to public creditors than Hamilton's proposal. But it was also less generous because Congress reduced the rate of interest the government would pay on the new debt representing arrears of interest to 3 percent, whereas Hamilton had proposed that arrears receive the same interest rate as the original principal sums borrowed. See Swanson and Trout (1992).

As Thomas Jefferson, the secretary of state, reported on a 1790 conversation with Hamilton, "He [Hamilton] opened the subject of the assumption of state debts, the necessity of it in the general fiscal arrangements and it's [*sic*] indispensible necessity toward a preservation of the union: and particularly of the New England states, who had made great expenditures during the war . . . [and who] would make it a sine qua non of a continuance of the Union" (cited by Elkins and McKitrick [1993, 155]). But most southern members of the House of Representatives were opposed to assumption, and in early votes they had prevented it from passing. At Hamilton's behest, Jefferson hosted a dinner for Hamilton and Madison in June, 1790, at which Madison, a member of the House from Virginia, agreed to twist the arms of some southern Congressmen to switch their votes to favor assumption in return for Hamilton arranging a move of the national capital from New York to a new capital city on the Potomac River (after a ten-year stay in Philadelphia to secure Pennsylvania's support for the deal). This is how Washington, DC, came to be, and how Hamilton obtained federal assumption of state debts (McDonald 1979, chap. VIII; Elkins and McKitrick 1993, chap. III; see also the further discussion of assumption in section 2.3 following).

The U.S. foreign debt, owed mostly to France, would be discharged by new foreign loans, arranged primarily through Dutch bankers. This roll-over of the foreign debt was completed by 1795. Interest on the domestic federal debt—the new loan took the form of three new securities: a 6 percent bond (6s), a 3 percent bond (3s), and a 6 percent bond with interest deferred (deferreds) for ten years, with public creditors receiving a package of the three yielding 4 percent interest in exchange for the old debt—began to be paid quarterly in 1791. Assumed state debts were funded by a similar exchange, but interest payments were delayed until 1792, with interest accrued to 1792 being added to the principal.

Exchanges of old debt for new debt went smoothly. By September 1791, $31.8 of an eventual total of $64.5 million had been converted. From then to the end of 1793, an additional $26.2 million was exchanged. By the end of 1794, a month before Hamilton stepped down as treasury secretary, $63.1, or 98 percent of the total domestic debt, had voluntarily been exchanged for the new 6s, 3s, and deferreds (Bayley 1884, 403). Substantial increases in the market values of the three federal debt securities in the early 1790s aided the conversion process by confirming predictions Hamilton had made when he unveiled his plan for supporting public credit.

Even with interest charges on domestic debt reduced from $4 to $2.7 million, adding in the interest on the foreign debt ($0.5 to 0.6 million in 1790) raised projected total annual interest to $3.2 million. Adding further to that amount a conservative estimate of ordinary federal operating expenses of at least $0.8 million (see footnote 4), the annual cost of Hamilton's program adopted by Congress in 1790 would come to more than $4 million by 1792, when it became fully operational.

Where was the money to come from to cover $4 million or more of government expenditures? In the early 1790s, Hamilton recommended some increases and extensions of the import duties levied in the original tariff of 1789. He also persuaded Congress to enact some excise taxes. But rates of taxation were kept low. The purpose of the tariff was revenue, not protection, and Hamilton knew that Americans detested taxes of any kind. The key to the success of Hamilton's bold gamble to establish public credit solidly and quickly would not be tax increases. Instead, it would be a higher rate of economic growth—rising American incomes would draw in more imports and swell customs collections—plus an ability of the Treasury to borrow what was needed to cover shortfalls of tax revenue that might arise before growth generated enough tax revenue to pay the expenses of the federal government.

That is why two other financial foundations—the Bank of the United States and the securities markets—were so important to Hamilton's plan. As he had outlined to Robert Morris nearly a decade before, a national bank would "increase public and private credit," with public credit giving "power to the state for the protection of its rights and interests," while private credit "facilitates and extends the operations of commerce among individuals." The Bank would be a source of loans to the government to cover revenue shortfalls, and it would lend also to the private sector to extend commerce and facilitate growth. Securities markets operated in a similar way: their existence increased the power of the state to borrow by selling debt securities. At the same time, securities markets offered private investors liquidity and income, and provided corporate entrepreneurs with a means of raising equity and debt capital. In Hamilton's plan, visionary for its time, state power and economic growth indeed went hand in hand. Each was needed for the other to succeed.

In his January 1790 report, Hamilton asked Congress to ask him to prepare a proposal for a national bank. Congress obliged in August. The Bank Report came in December. Hamilton listed three principal advantages of the Bank, the first of which emphasized its contributions to economic growth. Bank lending to business would create bank or credit money in the form of bank notes and deposits, augmenting the money supply, and "thus by contributing to enlarge the mass of industrious and commercial enterprise, banks become the nurseries of national wealth. . . ." The second and third advantages were governmental: the Bank would be a source of loans to the government, "especially in sudden emergencies," and it would facilitate the payment of taxes, both by lending to those who owed taxes and by increasing "the quantity of circulating medium and the quickening of the circulation" (Syrett 1961–1987, VII, 309).

The Bank of the United States, as proposed by Hamilton, was to be a private corporation chartered by Congress, to avoid "a calamitous abuse of it" when "temptations of momentary exigencies" might lead to inflationary excesses "should the credit of the Bank be at the disposal of the Government" (Syrett 1961–1987, VII, 331). Here Hamilton espoused what later would be called central bank independence. But he called for the U.S. government to own 20 percent of the Bank's $10 million of capital stock, to be purchased initially by a loan from the Bank and repaid over ten years, and for the government to have some oversight of it. So, it was really a mixed private-public corporation, but one whose levers Hamilton could employ in central banking operations.

Private investors owning the majority of the Bank's stock could pay for one-fourth in specie and three-fourths in the recently issued U.S. 6s. The latter provision increased the demand for 6s, market prices of which rose to par. So the Bank supported the public debt, just as the debt supported the Bank.

The Bank would also be allowed to open branches, although Hamilton thought it advisable to wait until the institution was firmly established in one place, and the managerial issues posed by a branch bank were well understood, before it opened branches. He saw the advantages of a large, well-managed branch bank as being greater lending capacity and less danger of bank runs. In the Bank Report, Hamilton formalized the aforementioned provisions and others into twenty-four articles of a proposed constitution, which became the basis for the Bank's charter enacted by both houses of Congress in January and February 1791.

That was not quite the end of the story. The president had to approve the Bank bill, and Washington hesitated when three of his trusted advisors, Madison in Congress, and Jefferson and Randolph in the cabinet, argued that the Bank was not authorized by the Constitution. Hamilton effectively countered their argument in a defense of the Bank that set forth the doctrine of implied constitutional powers. Washington signed the bill. But Hamilton's victory may have been part of a complex deal to approve the Bank while assuring the southerners who had tactically opposed it that the national capital, as earlier agreed, would move to the Potomac by 1800 (McDonald 1979, 199–210).

The Bank had its public offering of stock, heavily oversubscribed, in July 1791, and it opened in Philadelphia in December. Several branches—New York, Boston, Baltimore, and Charleston—opened in 1792. By its model and its expanding presence, the Bank prompted states to charter more banks of their own, ensuring a rapid expansion of the U.S. banking system. Some states such as New York did this for defensive reasons; they feared that if they did not charter state banks, the federal bank's branches would dominate banking in those states. Other states such as Rhode Island chartered a bank for just the opposite reason; they thought it would help attract a branch of the federal bank (Sylla 1998, 2008). The three state banks existing in 1790 thus became twenty by 1795, and twenty-eight by 1800. These state banks interacted with one another and with the five branches of the Bank of the United States in a rapidly developing nationwide banking network.

The U.S. securities markets also expanded rapidly as a result of Hamilton's program. How could they not? The debt restructuring created more than $60 million (par value) of new U.S. 6s, 3s, and deferreds, while the Bank added $10 million of equity shares (par $400 per share) between 1790 and 1794. Markets, even nascent stock exchanges, for all these new securities began actively to trade the new federal securities and Bank stock in several cities—Philadelphia, New York, and Boston in 1790, followed closely by Charleston and Baltimore—almost as soon as they appeared (Sylla 1998; Wright 2002, 2008). These markets also facilitated the finances of state governments, which owned securities paying interest and dividends. Banks and other business corporations, which the states increasingly chartered, raised capital by issuing securities, and like state governments some of the corporations earned income by investing in securities.

Financial development unleashed by Hamilton's financial revolution apparently raised the rate of growth of the U.S. economy to modern levels in the early 1790s, as was intended (see section 2.4). And it is a good thing that it did because increased growth was the key to solving rather pressing financial problems that Hamilton's program created for the government. Recall that the federal government needed to finance at least $4 million of spending by 1792; that is, $3.2 million of interest payments on its debt and at least $0.8 million in operating expenses. It was able to do this, which led later scholars of the era to assume it was not much of a problem at all. For example, Elkins and McKitrick (1993, 226) contend that after Congress enacted the excises Hamilton proposed in early 1791,

[T]he first phase of Hamilton's financial program was complete. The federal government now had an income sufficient to cover current expenses and to pay full interest on the entire debt. This meant that the tax potential which had long impressed European financiers was no longer a projection but a fact, and as Hamilton's predictions about the Treasury's ability to meet its obligations without undue strain were borne out, the price of federal securities would continue to move toward par. They would thus be less and less viewed as an item for speculation.

While Hamilton certainly wanted people at the time to think that federal finances were fundamentally sound—that was part of his strategy—he should not be allowed to keep scholars two centuries later under that illusion.[7] He did give a number of hints as to the direness of the fiscal outlook around the time he came into office. Writing in October 1789 to Lafayette

---

7. About the only one who did not succumb to the illusion of fiscal soundness in the early 1790s was Riley, who noted that in 1792, "interest payments on the American debt amounted to $3.2 million, a figure equivalent to 87 percent of tax revenues totaling $3.67 million. Debt charges including redemptions equaled no less than $7.26 million, or 198 percent of tax revenues. . . . [S]uch ratios . . . exceeded current levels among even fiscally straitened European governments." Further, "When one strikes a balance on the liquid and potential assets and liabilities of the federal government in the years to 1796, one must acknowledge the calculation points to insolvency" (Riley 1980, 188–91).

in France, Hamilton asked if France could delay payments of the debt the United States owed to it, and make it look as though it was a French idea. "I venture to say to you, as my friend, that if the installments of the Principal of the debt could be suspended for a few years, it would be a valuable accommodation to the United States. . . . Could an arrangement of this sort meet the approbation of your Government, it would be best on every account that the offer should come unsolicited as a fresh mark of good will" (Syrett 1961–1987, V, 426). A day later he communicated the same ideas to William Short, an American representative in Europe, implying that Short should hint to France that "a voluntary and unsolicited offer" to delay debt payments would be most welcome (Syrett 1961–1987, V, 429–30).

The closest Hamilton came to revealing the unpromising fiscal outlook in a public document is in the January 1790 Report on Public Credit. After noting that the annual interest on the public debt, domestic and foreign, according to the original terms of borrowing would be $4.6 million, Hamilton goes on:

The interesting problem now occurs. Is it in the power of the United States, consistently with those prudential considerations, which ought not to be overlooked, to make a provision equal to the purpose of funding the whole debt, at the rates of interest which it now bears, in addition to the sum which will be necessary for the current service of the government.

The Secretary will not say that such provision would exceed the abilities of the country; but he is clearly of the opinion, that to make it, would require the extension of taxation to a degree, and to objects, which the true interest of the public creditors forbids. It is therefore to be hoped, and even to be expected, that they will cheerfully concur in such modifications of their claims, on fair and equitable principles, as will facilitate to the government an arrangement substantial, durable and satisfactory to the community (Syrett 1961–1987, VI, 87).

Hamilton here is saying, in other words, that public creditors, in their own long-term interest and in that of the country, should be willing to accept what later would be called a "haircut," a reduction of what they were contractually owed, because the government did not have sufficient funds to pay all of what it owed, and if it tried to obtain the funds by raising taxation the result could easily be a taxpayers' revolt that ended up in their getting even less than Hamilton was prepared to offer. The haircut did not reflect a write-down of debt principal, which was fully funded. Rather, by reducing the interest paid on the new debt in effect from 6 to 4 percent, Hamilton's restructuring of the national debt gave investors a package of securities that had a lower market value than it would have had if 6 percent had been paid on all of it (Garber 1991).

Less than three months later, on March 29, 1790, Hamilton formally wrote to President Washington that the Treasury did not have enough

Table 2.1   Federal tax revenues by year, 1789–1800

Year	Revenue (in thousands)	Year	Revenue (in thousands)
1789	162	1795	6,115
1790	1,640	1796	8,378
1791	2,648	1797	8,689
1792	3,675	1798	7,900
1793	4,653	1799	7,547
1794	5,432	1800	10,849

Sources: 1789–1793: Van Eeghen Papers, Archives of the University of Amsterdam; 1794–1800: Historical Statistics of the United States (2006, 5–80).

money to pay the members of Congress and their staffs, the salaries of other government officials, the requirements of the War Department, and an interest payment in arrears on Dutch loans. It therefore needed to obtain a loan of $100,000. Two days later, the president authorized the loan (Syrett 1961–1987, VI, 328, 333). The new government of the United States was living from hand to mouth.

Just how tenuous was the fiscal situation of the federal government in the early 1790s, and just how much Hamilton counted on economic growth to change that situation is evident in the table 2.1, which shows federal revenues from sources other than loans growing year by year from 1789 to 1800.[8]

Revenues (excluding loans) grew 3.3-fold from 1790 (the first full year of revenue collection) to 1795, or 26 percent per year. Most of this revenue (100 percent in 1790, 91 percent in 1795) was from duties on imports and tonnage. Although some duties were added (as were excises, which raised $209 thousand in 1792, their first year, and $338 thousand in 1795), and other duties were increased, these innovations cannot account for the entire revenue upsurge. Nor can the outbreak of the French Revolutionary Wars in 1793, often cited as an unexpected source of prosperity for the United States, since the most rapid gains in revenue were from 1789 to 1793.

8. Scholars may have been fooled by a quirk in virtually all reports of federal fiscal data, which lump the years 1789 to 1791 together seemingly as one year. The table here is based on quarterly and half yearly financial reports from 1789 through 1793 that I discovered in the Van Eeghen documentary collection of early Americana, located in the archives of the University of Amsterdam. Dutch investors in America such as the Van Eeghens, as a part of their due diligence, gathered whatever intelligence they could obtain in the United States and sent it back to the Netherlands to be pasted in scrapbooks for future reference. Van Eeghen & Co., in the later nineteenth century, donated their scrapbooks to the university. The quarterly and half yearly statements of federal revenues and expenses are printed sheets that I surmise were created by the Treasury for the information of Congress at the time. In the United States they do not appear to exist, probably because they were regarded as ephemera that could be discarded after more up-to-date statements appeared. The Dutch did Americans a favor by preserving a part of early U.S. financial history that apparently was not preserved in America.

It is therefore difficult to avoid a conclusion that the upsurge in revenue was due in good part to a higher real rate of economic growth along with a rising price level that resulted from monetary expansion rooted in both domestic (bank expansion) and foreign (capital inflows as foreign investors purchased American securities) sources (Rousseau and Sylla 2005; Rousseau, chapter four, this volume). A part of the growth resulted from expanding exports (Goldin and Lewis 1980). More rapid growth also led to more taxable imports, which is why expanding trade was an essential ingredient of Hamilton's fiscal planning (Irwin, chapter three, this volume).

As happened often in later U.S. history, economic growth ratified the risky bets on the future of entrepreneurs. In the early 1790s, the main entrepreneur was the secretary of the treasury, who bet that his comprehensive program of financial innovation and reform would jump-start economic growth and make it possible for the federal government to pay much more interest on its debt than seemed possible when the decisions were made to make those payments in 1790. Hamilton won his bet, but it was by no means the easy win historians often assume it was. Hindsight is 20-20, but a look at the government's finances during 1790 to 1792, when the future was unknown, indicates that some good things had to happen for Hamilton's bold debt-funding gamble to succeed.

2.3   The Financial Policy Debate of the 1790s

There was a high-level financial policy debate of sorts in the mid-1790s. On one side was Albert Gallatin, a Republican congressman from western Pennsylvania and future treasury secretary in the Jefferson and Madison administrations. Gallatin was the Republican opposition's financial expert, a role that corresponded to Hamilton's role in the Federalist Party. The two parties had formed either to support Hamilton's financial policies or to oppose them, although both had precursors in the Federalist versus Anti-Federalist debates over the Constitution. Gallatin in 1796 presented his reasoned critique of Federalist financial policies along with extensive data drawn from government documents in *A Sketch of the Finances of the United States* (Adams 1960, III, 69–206).

Although Gallatin most likely was unaware of it, Hamilton essentially responded to Gallatin's critique before Gallatin wrote and published it. In a lengthy but never completed essay, "The Defence of the Funding System," dated July 1795, six months after stepping down as treasury secretary, Hamilton reviewed the decisions he had made while in office and the reasons he had made them (Syrett 1961–1987, XIX, 1–73). The two essays deal with the same issues—taxes and spending, public debt management, the Bank, securities markets, and the economic and political effects of the measures adopted. We, therefore, can read them as a policy debate, even though the two debaters were not on a platform confronting one another. Gallatin's is the more polished of the two, but Hamilton's rough draft is the more penetrating because he had made the key policy decisions, and he used "The Defence" to explain them in considerable detail.

Like other Republican leaders, Gallatin thought most public debts were bad, and his principal charge against Hamilton's policies was that the assumption of state debts in 1790 had made the national debt larger than it needed to be by at least $10.9 million. Most state debts, $18.3 million, were assumed in 1790, and each state's debt assumed by the federal government was charged to it in a settlement of state accounts to equalize across states the per capita costs of financing the War of Independence. The settlement of state accounts was not completed until a few years after 1790. When it was completed, creditor states—ones that had contributed more than their fair shares of the war costs—were found to be owed $3.5 million. The debtor states that had contributed less than their fair shares had an equivalent negative balance. Creditor states were issued some $4 million in new federal bonds to cover the $3.5 million in their favor plus arrears of interest. That swelled the amount of state debt assumed to $22.5 million. The debtor states for political reasons were forgiven the corresponding balances they owed.[9]

With elaborate arithmetical calculations, Gallatin demonstrated that if assumption had been postponed until the settlement of accounts had occurred, the states could have been put in exactly the same position as they were with a federal assumption of only $11.6 million. Hence, the national debt was $10.9 million larger than it needed to be. So why was the federal assumption of state debts done in 1790 instead of waiting until the settlement of state accounts had been completed? Gallatin listed the ostensible reasons as, first, some states were heavily burdened by their debts in 1790 and could not realistically wait for a final settlement to occur, if indeed they could be sure it would ever occur; second, the new federal government would be strengthened if more state creditors depended on it for debt payments; and third, it might be easier for the federal government to pay the debts. Gallatin's own view was darker. The additional debt had weakened, not strengthened, the union and had rendered additional taxes necessary. He also suspected that "some influential characters [most likely including Hamilton] whose wish was to increase and perpetuate the debt," had pushed for a quick assumption, possibly to foster "private interest and speculation" (Adams 1960, III, 131).

In "The Defence," Hamilton essentially agreed with the ostensible reasons for assumption as set forth by Gallatin. Some states were heavily burdened with debts in 1790, and were not in a position to wait for a final settlement of accounts that possibly might never occur. If those states had to resort to higher taxes to service their debts, the result might be more taxpayer

9. Perkins (1994, chapter 9) provides a good treatment of how the settlement of state accounts took place in the early 1790s.

revolts such as Shays' rebellion in Massachusetts in 1786. If that did not happen, Hamilton thought that higher taxes in the heavily indebted states would promote emigration from them to lightly taxed states, making the debt burden yet more difficult to bear. Hamilton also agreed with Gallatin that assumption tended "to strengthen our infant Government by increasing the number of ligaments between the Government and the interests of Individuals," but that "this was the consideration upon which I relied least of all" (Syrett 1961–1987, XIX, 39–41). Why? The tendency of having more domestic creditors to give support to the federal government was offset by the necessity of resorting to unpalatable modes of taxation that "jeopardized [the government's] popularity and gave a handle to its enemies to attack." And in any event, the increased ligaments between the federal government and domestic creditors would be temporary as foreign investors purchased more of the debt and as the debt was gradually paid down, both of which Hamilton expected to happen.

Hamilton also agreed with Gallatin's point that the federal government, having sole access to customs and tonnage duties, could more easily pay debts. But his strongest reason for favoring assumption in 1790 was that he feared conflicts over tax bases between state and federal governments if both had large debts to service. The Constitution had given the states and the federal government concurrent powers over all tax bases except imports, a plan that involved "inherent and great difficulties" even though it was a better plan than the alternatives. Hamilton saw these difficulties as "the Gordian knot of our political situation."

> To me there appeared but one way of untying or severing it, which was in practice to leave the states under as little necessity as possible of exercising the power of taxation. The narrowness of the limits of its exercise on one side left the field more free and unembarrassed to the other and avoided essentially the interference and collisions to be apprehended *inherent* in the plan of concurrent jurisdiction (Syrett 1961–1987, XIX, 23).

If the state debts had not been assumed, Hamilton wrote, the United States as a nation and all public creditors would have been subject to "the weakness and embarrassment incident to fifteen or perhaps to fifty different systems of finance" (Syrett 1961–1987, XIX, 25). His assumption plan, in contrast, had three advantages: it lightened the burdens of all citizens; it equalized the burdens of the citizens of one state with those of another; and it brought immediate relief to the states with the heaviest debt burdens while facilitating the eventual settlement of state accounts. "It is curious fact which has not made its due impression," Hamilton wrote in 1795, "that in every state the people have found relief from assumption while an incomparably better provision than before existed has been made for the state debts" (Syrett 1961–1987, XIX, 35).

Recent research on state taxation during the 1780s and 1790s confirms Hamilton's point. "[S]tate governments were relieved of both payments on Congress's requisitions and on their own state debts. Freed from these expenses, the state governments could reduce direct taxation by as much as seventy-five to ninety percent" (Edling and Kaplanoff 2004, 736). The federal government was able to relieve the states from the necessity of raising taxes, indeed to allow them substantially to lower taxes, without resorting to direct taxes such as the property and poll taxes that were the mainstays of state revenues. The fear that the federal government would resort to direct taxes—Hamilton's Gordian Knot of concurrent federal and state tax bases—led to the Constitution's stricture that federal direct taxation had to be apportioned to the states on the basis of population. Still, the fear that the federal government might tax citizens in a direct way persisted into the ratification debates and beyond.

Since Hamilton believed that there was one national debt that had been incurred in the common cause of independence, he scoffed at the notion Gallatin came close to promoting, namely, that the debt had been increased by assumption. "Assumption did nothing more than transfer the particular debts to the Union. . . . The MASS OF PUBLIC DEBT remained the same, on the infallible evidence of a mathematical axiom that WHOLE cannot be greater that ITS PARTS" (Syrett 1961–1987, XIX, 44).

A minor aspect of Gallatin's critique of Treasury Department management is interesting in the light of recent research findings. Gallatin, in his close perusal of the Treasury's accounts, had noticed that expenditures on debt reduction were made by the sinking fund in 1791 and 1792, and later repaid from the proceeds of foreign loans arranged by Dutch bankers *before* the foreign loans had been received in the Treasury. He charged that "the transaction was illegal, but no otherwise criminal than as it was illegal." But he then went on to say, ". . . the result of the purchases made at that period was useful by accelerating the raising of the price of stock to its nominal value" (Adams 1960, III, 110–12).

What Gallatin apparently did not know, in part because Hamilton had not wanted it to be widely known, was that the Dutch funds were used to repay domestic bank loans incurred to finance Hamilton's open market purchases of government securities during two financial crises—the collapse of the Bank scrip bubble in August and September 1791, and the collapse of securities prices in the financial panic of March and April of 1792, when panicked selling caused market prices of U.S. debt securities to fall 25 percent in two weeks. Well aware of the collapses of French Mississippi and the British South Sea bubbles in 1720, Hamilton knew that financial modernization carried with it an increased probability of financial crises. He had given some thought to how a finance minister or central banker ought to react to such crises. When the 1791 and 1792 crises broke out, Hamilton fought them in modern ways by making open market purchases of securities, fostering banker-dealer cooperative agreements to increase market liquidity, and encouraging banks to keep lending (Sylla, Wright, and Cowen 2009).

Gallatin certainly knew about and mentioned the 1792 crisis, but he did not make the connection it had with the financial operations of the Treasury (Adams 1960, III, 134–35). The 1791 and 1792 financial crises ended quickly as a result of Hamilton's actions, with seeming little or no disruption of the economic expansion taking place at the time. But the Republican opposition had a field day, claiming that Hamilton's policies were turning the country into a nation of stock-jobbers and speculators, and that Hamilton abetted speculative activity by illegally committing the proceeds of foreign loans before they had been received. When his enemies in Congress, including Gallatin, questioned the financial transactions, Hamilton coyly responded that the expenditures were for reducing the public debt, which everyone would agree was a good thing. He did not mention that the Treasury's purchases of U.S. debt helped to bail out the banks, brokers, and dealers of Wall Street and Chestnut Street during two financial meltdowns. After the crisis wound down, in May 1792, a number of the securities dealers Hamilton had bailed out joined with others in the Buttonwood Agreement that marked the founding of the New York Stock Exchange and a better trading system for securities (Sylla 2005; Sylla, Wright, and Cowen 2009).

Gallatin, contrary to the views of many in his Republican party, agreed with Hamilton that the Bank of the United States, as well as banks in general, were useful for making loans to the government as well as to the private sector. As treasury secretary, he would later argue unsuccessfully for the Bank to be rechartered in 1811. But he felt that the Federalist administration had abused the Bank by borrowing too much from it instead of reducing expenditures and raising taxes. The heavy borrowing from the Bank, Gallatin contended, had created an apprehension that it "might become a political engine in the hands of the government," and also reinforced the conviction among many (mostly in his Republican party) that Congress did not by the Constitution have a right to incorporate such an institution (Adams 1960, III, 135–36).

Hamilton earlier had addressed both of these issues, in the Bank report and in his lawyerly opinion that the Banks did not violate the Constitution. But once he had decided to fund all federal and state debts at par, revenue shortfalls gave him no choice other than to borrow a lot from the Bank, which is why he fought so hard for its establishment. By 1796, as Gallatin noted, the government had borrowed $6 million, 60 percent of the institution's capital, and the Bank asked for much of it to be repaid. Wolcott, Hamilton's successor, against his own and Hamilton's wishes, was forced to sell nearly half of the government's shares in the Bank to pay down the loans (Cowen 2000, 215). This weakened the ties between the government and the national bank, probably making it easier for anti-Bank forces to prevail when the Bank's charter came up for renewal in 1811.

Gallatin closed his *Sketch* with a challenge to the view that the debt funding plan "had created a large productive capital which did not exist before." His view was that "every nation is enfeebled by a public debt," and that the best policy was to extinguish public debt as quickly as it was feasible to do so by cutting spending and increasing taxes. He lamented the fact that foreign investors had purchased so much of the U.S. debt and other American securities, which only led the American sellers "to consume, to spend more, and they have consumed and spent extravagantly."

> Taking in the great number of elegant houses which have been built within a few years in all the large cities, and which, however convenient to the inhabitants, afford no additional revenue to the nation, it may be asserted that the greater part of the capital thus drawn from Europe for purchases of stock has been actually consumed, without leaving in its stead any other productive capital, and thus as the nation still owes the whole, it has been impoverished even by the only consequence of the funding system that has made any temporary addition to the apparent wealth of the country. That wealth is, in a great degree, consumed and destroyed, and the whole debt remains to be paid. (Adams 1960, III, 149)

Substitute China for Europe in this passage, and Gallatin's message would seem rather similar to arguments one often hears today, more than two centuries later. Other passages in his essay indicate that he would subscribe to "crowding out"—the idea that public borrowing and spending reduces private investment—as well as Ricardian equivalence—the notion that people react to increases in public debt by increasing their savings in order to be able to pay the increased taxes necessary to service a larger public debt.

The solution to the problem, Gallatin argued in a way that foreshadowed Jefferson's and his policies as Treasury Secretary after 1800, was to get rid of the debt as quickly as possible. One way of doing that would be to sell land to pay down the debt. Another would be to exchange public land for debt. But even if that were done, there would still be a need for more revenue, as the Treasury had converted the 6 percent debt to 8 percent annuities in the mid-1790s in a plan drawn up by Hamilton and implemented by Wolcott, which raised the annual cost of servicing the debt. And the deferred 6 percent component of the debt would commence paying interest in 1801. Tax increases were therefore necessary. But, Gallatin wrote, customs duties were already as high as they should be, and excises were disliked and had a low revenue potential. Therefore, "the other general species of American capital, the other great branch of national revenue, lands, must be resorted to; must be made to contribute by direct taxation" (Adams 1960, III, 168). Gallatin, in short, called for a national property tax. Whereas Hamilton had severed the Gordian Knot of concurrent federal and state tax bases, Gallatin recommended that it be retied.[10]

Hamilton disagreed with most of Gallatin's analysis. Sales of American securities to foreign investors, far from encouraging lavish consumption, brought in capital that made the U.S. economy grow faster:

Whoever will impartially look around will see that the great body of the new Capital created by the Stock has been employed in extending commerce, agriculture, manufactures, and other improvements. Our own *real* navigation has been much increased. Our external commerce is carried on much more upon our own capitals than it was. . . . Settlements of our waste land are progressing with more vigour than at any former period. Our Cities and Towns are increasing rapidly by the addition of new and better houses. Canals are opening, bridges are building with more spirit & effect than was ever known at a former period. The value of lands has risen everywhere.

These circumstances (though other causes may have cooperated) . . . are imputable in a great degree to the increase of Capital in public Debt and they prove that the predictions of its dissipation in luxurious extravagance have not been verified. . . . The universal vivification of the energies of industry has laid the foundations of benefits far greater than the interest to be paid to foreigners can counterbalance as a disadvantage. (Syrett 1961–1987, 65–66)

For Hamilton, public debt was indeed a blessing. Since it was traded in the markets of Europe, it was relatively easy for Europeans threatened by wars to emigrate to America and bring their capital with them. All they had to do was to purchase the U.S. stock in European markets, and easily convert it to cash on arrival in America by utilizing U.S. securities markets. Americans enjoyed a similar advantage from liquid securities markets. "All property is capital," wrote Hamilton, and "that which can quickly and at all times be converted to money is active capital. It is nearly the same thing as if the possessor had an equal sum of money on hand" (Syrett 1961–1987, 67).[11] In fact, owners of government debt used it as collateral for bank loans; by 1792, the 6 percent debt was accepted at par value as collateral for such loans (Sylla 1998).

It was a great policy debate between the top financial and economic experts of the two contending political parties of the 1790s. Gallatin and

10. In 1798, the federal government, suffering from reduced customs collections as a result of French predations on U.S. international commerce, and a lack of access to European capital because the Amsterdam market had been cut off after the French revolutionaries overran the Dutch Republic, imposed a direct tax during the Quasi War with France. It did so again during the War of 1812 with Great Britain. The two direct taxes were highly unpopular and politically divisive, as Hamilton had surmised they would be.

11. On the early integration of U.S. and European securities markets, see Sylla, Wilson, and Wright (2006).

Hamilton were not directly addressing one another, but one would hardly know that.

2.4 Growth

So who won the debate? Gallatin, with his view that Federalist financial policies had saddled the country with excessive debt that was enfeebling it, with the only solutions being to cut spending, impose a national property tax, and extinguish the debt? Or Hamilton, who viewed his planned financial revolution as having the salutary effects on public credit, state power, and economic growth that he long had predicted they would have?

It is the nature of such policy debates that the winners and losers cannot be known at the time they take place. The debate is about the future, not known at the time and only revealed by the passage of time and the march of events. There were neither GDP and industrial production data nor stock market indices in the 1790s, so Gallatin and Hamilton could not use such data to score debating points. Gallatin in 1796, however, did not counter the optimistic view that Hamilton and others took of the U.S. economy's progress. Rather, in general terms, he endorsed it. "[I]n proportion to our population, we [are] one of the first commercial nations . . . we are by far the first agricultural nation . . . [but] we are not yet a manufacturing nation" (Adams 1960, III, 168). The country had too much debt, however, and the blame for that, Gallatin implied without naming names, could be laid at Hamilton's doorstep.

Various analyses, data sets, and estimations of the GDP and its components developed much later to describe early U.S. economic growth, tenuous as they are and not always agreeing with one another, tend to support Hamilton's optimistic view of the economic changes taking place. North (1961, 53), relying heavily on balance of payments data, called the period 1793 to 1808 "years of unparalleled prosperity." He traced the prosperity to Hamilton's policies and the trade boom in neutral America created by European wars. The latter was a temporary factor that went away after Jefferson's embargo in 1808. Goldin and Lewis (1980), also relying on international trade data, estimated U.S. real per capita income growth in the range of 1.03 to 1.51 percent per year from 1793 to 1800, and in the range of 0.84 to 1.32 percent per year from 1793 to 1807.

Several attempts have been made to estimate the U.S. GDP (total and per capita, nominal and inflation-adjusted) annually, back to 1790. These estimates rely on modern-type GDP series that begin for years around 1840, benchmark GDP estimates between 1790 and 1840, interpolations between benchmark years using annual series that relate to components of the GDP, and assumptions about the relationship of nonagricultural productivity (about which little is known, especially before 1820) to agricultural productivity (about which more is taken to be known).[12] The three real GDP per capita series in Carter et al. (2006, table Ca9-19, 3–23ff.) all indicate rapid growth at modern rates ranging from about 1 to 3 percent per year from 1790 into the first years of the nineteenth century, and considerably slower growth from then until around 1820. Indeed, two of the series (Ca11 and Ca16) show almost no growth of per capita GDP in these two decades, but the text discussing these series indicates that this is based on the assumption that nonagricultural productivity experienced no growth because that is what agricultural productivity did. Still a third series (Ca17, the Berry series) indicates per capita growth of about 1 percent per year from a peak in 1801 to a peak in 1822. An accompanying series (Ca19) on industrial production, one of the components of nonagricultural production, grows at 5.4 percent per year from 1790 to 1802, and at 3.7 percent per year for the next two decades; these rates are well above the rate of population growth, which was just under 3 percent per year (Davis 2004). This raises doubts about the assumption that nonagricultural productivity did not grow.

An updated version of series Ca16 in Carter et al. (2006) is that of Johnston and Williamson (2009) that indicates rapid growth in real GDP per capita of 2.72 percent per year from 1790 to an 1802 peak, slower but still modern growth of 0.85 percent per year from 1802 to 1814 (peak to peak), and then essentially no growth in the decade after 1814.[13] Overall, this series, which can be said to make use of the latest information relevant to GDP estimation, shows per capita real GDP growing at a rate of 1.27 percent per year during the three decades 1790 to 1820. The rapid economic growth of 1790 to 1802 might be confirmed, or at least supported, by a recently compiled stock market index extending back to 1791, which claims to have discovered America's first bull market, 1791 to 1803, when U.S. equity prices rose 47 percent (Taylor 2009).[14]

Although the various estimates of historical GDP do not entirely agree on the precise rates of early U.S. growth, they do agree that the rates from the 1790s onward were "modern," that is, in the vicinity of 1 percent or more per capita in real terms. They also agree that there was a tendency of U.S. growth to accelerate gradually over time, as one might expect if

12. See Carter et al. (2006, vol. 3, 3–16 to 3–19) for a good discussion of the problems of estimating annual GDP series in the "Statistical Dark Age: 1790–1840." The various series follow in table Ca-19 starting on 3-23.

13. The U.S. GDP and other macroeconomic data from 1790 to 2007, updated annually, are from Johnston and Williamson (2009), at http://www.measuringworth.com/growth, a site that also features graphing capabilities and a calculator allowing computation of growth rates between any two years.

14. The 12-stock index is not adjusted for inflation, which was some 3 percent per year in the 1790s, and it shows price appreciation, not dividends. No doubt it will be extended and refined to show real appreciation and real returns. The index, series SPXD, is available from http://www.globalfinancialdata.com.

an initially small but rapidly growing modern sector—the commercial and industrial activities that most utilized bank credit and capital markets—gradually became a larger and larger component of the entire economy. By extension, they also agree that the United States was growing considerably faster than the economy of Great Britain, which from all the discussions of the first industrial revolution, one might have thought would have been the fastest growing economy. In fact, what some regard as the best estimates of British growth (output per person) also show a gradual acceleration, but it was from a rate of 0.35 percent a year during 1781 to 1801 to 0.52 percent a year during 1801 to 1831 (Crafts 1987; Sylla 2009). If these estimates are accurate, the celebrated first industrial revolution in its early decades had a fairly muted impact on average British incomes. And it appears that British growth during the first industrial revolution was at roughly half the rate of growth of the U.S. economy during the same era.

Gallatin and Hamilton agreed that there was considerable prosperity in the United States at the time of the Gallatin-Hamilton debate. But would it last? Did it mark the beginning of modern economic growth, the sustained growth that lasted for decades and centuries? We now know that it did. GDP per capita grew at long-term rates of about 1 percent or more per year from 1790 to 1860, with little variation among subperiods of any length. By 1860, thanks to its rapid growth, the United States had a larger GDP than the United Kingdom, the mother country and the workshop of the world, and (although this is more controversial) essentially the same GDP per capita according to Officer and Williamson (2009).

Did U.S. policies, including those that produced the financial revolution of the 1790s, make the country grow faster than its neighbors and other "new" countries? The evidence to answer this question is limited. But what there is suggests an answer of "yes." Angus Maddison's estimates for benchmark dates of 1700 and 1820 indicate that in 1700 Mexico's GDP per capita was 107 percent of the U.S. (colonial) level; in 1820, it was 60 percent of the U.S. level. Maddison also reports similar data for "other Western offshoots" besides the United States, with that category including Canada, Australia, and New Zealand. In 1700, these other offshoots (dominated by Canada, as Westerners had yet to settle Australia and New Zealand) had a GDP per capita that was 76 percent of the level Maddison estimated for the colonial United States; by 1820, the other offshoots were only 60 percent of the U.S. level (Maddison 2001, table B–21, 264).[15] The faster growth of the early United States in comparison to the growth of its northern and southern neighbors and other "new" countries suggests that U.S. policies launched in the 1790s did make a difference in relative economic performance.

15. For Canada, Maddison does not have a separate number for 1700, but for 1820, he reports one. It indicates that Canada then had a GDP per capita that was 71 percent of the U.S. level. See Maddison (2001, table TA1-c, 185).

2.5   Conclusion

What were the alternatives to Hamilton's public credit, banking, and capital market policies? As regards public credit, the two alternatives discussed at the time were to give debt holders a worse deal than Hamilton did by repudiating some of the debt on grounds of financial exigency, or to retire the debt rapidly by raising taxes—at both the state and federal levels with no federal assumption of state debts, or at the federal level with assumption. The former, repudiation, was never a serious option as it violated most leaders' sense of honor and would have made future borrowing capability problematic. Rapid debt retirement by means of raising taxes was tried by Massachusetts in the 1780s, and led to Shays' Rebellion. That enhanced the appeal of Hamilton's approach, which involved funding the entire debt at a reduced rate of interest with a blend of new and liquid federal securities (6 percents, 6 percent deferreds, and 3 percents), along with a gradualist approach to debt retirement based on economic growth increasing federal tax revenues as the U.S. population and economy expanded (Perkins 1994, chaps. 7–10).

Federal assumption of state debts was a closer call, and succeeded only by means of linking it to other issues such as the location of the country's temporary and permanent capital cities. Without assumption, as Hamilton argued in his 1796 "Defence of the Funding System" (Syrett 1961–1987, XIX, 1–73), the United States would have had (a) multiple systems of state and federal public finance, (b) weaker governments and capital markets, and (c) greater conflicts between heavily and lightly debt-burdened states that might have threatened to break up the Union. With assumption, those problems went away and the burdens on state public finance were greatly reduced. Eventually, the ability of the states to borrow on their own for internal improvements and other purposes was greatly enhanced as the pristine public credit of the federal government and the well-functioning securities markets engendered by Hamilton's policies rubbed off on them.

The alternative to the Bank of the United States was, of course, no central bank. One need not speculate on the alternative because subsequent U.S. history gives examples. Congress allowed the first Bank to lapse in 1811 when its twenty-year charter expired and was not renewed. That added to the financial embarrassments of the federal government during the War of 1812, as well as economic instability. Both paved the way for Congress in 1816 to reestablish a central bank in the form of a new and larger second Bank of the United States, again with a twenty-year charter. Under the leadership of Nicholas Biddle after 1823, the second Bank and the U.S. economy thrived. When Congress voted to renew the Bank's charter in 1832, President Andrew Jackson vetoed the renewal and prevailed. That left the United States without a central bank from 1836 to 1914.

The absence of a central bank did not prevent the U.S. economy from growing to become the world's largest in the long interim. But banking panics and economic recessions were more frequent than they had been in the early decades when a central bank was present. Also during the long interim, other leading countries established central banks and experienced greater economic stability than did the United States. The U.S. financial panic of 1907 set in motion a sequence of events that led to the establishment of a third Bank of the United States, better known as the Federal Reserve System, in 1914. Once again banking panics and financial crises became less frequent. The advent of the Fed was a vindication of Hamilton's original U.S. financial architecture.

Hamilton's public debt restructuring and Bank injected tens of millions of dollars of high-grade debt and equity securities into securities markets from 1790 to 1795 while he was treasury secretary. Federal bonds and Bank stock became the national market securities traded in all markets that were established quickly in the country's leading cities. In each city, the national market securities were joined by a growing list of local securities—those of banking, insurance, transportation, and other corporations chartered by the states, and also in time a host of state and local governmental debt securities. The presence of capital markets from the start encouraged the formation of corporations (Wright chapter 7, this volume). It also encouraged foreign investors to purchase American securities, thereby transferring capital to the United States, by assuring them that liquid markets for their investments existed in the new country (Sylla, Wilson, and Wright 2006). Absent Hamilton's policies, capital markets most likely would have emerged and developed much more gradually in U.S. history, as they did in other countries. It was a great advantage, both economic and political, for the United States to have modern capital markets virtually from the nation's founding.

Hamilton's strategic planning and execution paid off for the U.S. government and the American economy. On any fair assessment he deserves the place he occupies in the pantheons of the American founders and world statesmen. It was he who first realized the strategic dependence of state power *and economic growth* on financial development. It was he who first saw that financial modernization, and hence state power and economic growth, would be difficult to achieve without changing the form of American government. It was he who worked as hard as anyone to bring about U.S. constitutional change. It was he who then deftly executed his well-conceived plan for a financial revolution in the first term of Washington's administration, and defended it when political opposition and events threatened to, and sometimes did, erode the institutions he created. Part of his genius as a political entrepreneur was to base his plan on precedents with which many Americans were familiar. The federal revenue system based on import and excise taxes was a postcolonial version of what the colonies, and then the states, had long used. The Bank of the United States was modeled to an extent on the Bank of England, an institution with which many Americans were familiar. It made sense, as both Jefferson and Hamilton realized, to model the silver U.S. dollar on the Spanish peso that had long been the most commonly encountered coin in the thirteen colonies and states. Hamilton's system, while innovative in both some of its particulars and its sweeping comprehensiveness, was not wholly new. That served to enhance its appeal and make it a practical success.

A century ago, the noted American historian Charles Beard (1913, 100; 1915, 131) was not far off the mark when he described Hamilton as "the colossal genius of the new system," the one who "displayed that penetrating wisdom which placed him among the great statesmen of all time." Compared to when Beard wrote, economists and historians now have a better understanding of the importance of financial development for economic growth, together with a vastly larger store of historical data on the long-term performance of the U.S. economy. They also have more knowledge of what Hamilton did at the beginning of U.S. history, how he came to do it, and what the effects of his policies were. Their findings serve to reinforce Beard's assessment of Hamilton's key role in developing the institutions that raised the trajectory of U.S. economic growth. He established the financial foundations that would make the United States the most successful emerging market in the nineteenth century, and the economic colossus of the next that some would call "the America century."

References

Adams, H., ed. 1960. *The writings of Albert Gallatin.* New York: Antiquarian Press.
Bayley, R. A. 1884. History of the national loans of the United States from July 4, 1776, to June 30, 1880. In *Tenth census, report on valuation, taxation, and public indebtedness in the United States,* 7, 295–486. Washington, DC: Government Printing Office.
Beard, C. A. 1913. *An economic interpretation of the Constitution of the United States.* New York: Macmillan.
———. 1915. *Economic origins of Jeffersonian democracy.* New York: Macmillan.
Carter, S. Gartner, M. Haines, A. Olmstead, R. Sutch, and G. Wright. 2006. *Historical statistics of the United States: Earliest times to the present.* Millennial Edition. Cambridge: Cambridge University Press.
Cowen, D. J. 2000. *The origins and economic impact of the first bank of the United States, 1791–1797.* New York: Garland.
Crafts, N. F. R. 1987. British economic growth, 1700–1850: Some difficulties of interpretation. *Explorations in Economic History* 24 (3): 245–68.
Davis, J. H. 2004. An annual index of U.S. industrial production, 1790–1915. *Quarterly Journal of Economics* 119 (4): 1177–215.
Edling, M. M., and M. D. Kaplanoff. 2004. Alexander Hamilton's fiscal reform: Transforming the structure of taxation in the early republic. *William and Mary Quarterly* (third series), 61:713–44.

Elkins, S., and E. McKitrick. 1993. *The age of federalism: The early American republic, 1788–1800.* New York: Oxford University Press.

Ferguson, E. J. 1961. *The power of the purse: A history of American public finance, 1776–1790.* Chapel Hill: University of North Carolina Press.

Garber, P. M. 1991. Alexander Hamilton's market based debt reduction plan. *Carnegie-Rochester Conference Series on Public Policy,* 35 (1): 79–104.

Goldin, C., and F. D. Lewis. 1980. The role of exports in American economic growth during the Napoleonic Wars, 1793–1807. *Explorations in Economic History* 17 (1): 6–25.

Johnston, L. D., and S. H. Williamson. 2009. What was the U.S. GDP then? MeasuringWorth. Available at: http://www.measuringworth.org/usgdp/.

McDonald, F. 1979. *Alexander Hamilton: A biography.* New York: Norton.

Maddison, A. 2001. *The world economy: A millennial perspective.* Paris: Organization for Cooperation and Development.

North, D.C. 1961. *The economic growth of the United States, 1790–1860.* New York: Prentice Hall.

Officer, L. H., and S. H. Williamson. 2009. Annualized growth rate and graphs of various historical economic series. MeasuringWorth. Available at: http://measuringworth.com/growth/.

Perkins, E. J. 1994. *American public finance and financial services, 1700–1815.* Columbus: Ohio State University Press.

Riley, J. C. 1980. *International government finance and the Amsterdam capital market, 1740–1815.* Cambridge: Cambridge University Press.

Rousseau, P. L., and R. Sylla. 2003. Financial systems, economic growth, and globalization. In *Globalization in historical perspective,* ed. M. D. Bordo, A. M. Taylor, and J. G. Williamson, 373–415. Chicago: University of Chicago Press.

———. 2005. Emerging financial markets and early U.S. growth. *Explorations in Economic History* 42 (1): 1–26.

Swanson, D. F., and A. P. Trout. 1992. Alexander Hamilton, conversion, and debt reduction. *Explorations in Economic History* 29 (4): 417–29.

Sylla, R. 1998. U.S. securities markets and the banking system, 1790–1840. *The Federal Reserve Bank of St. Louis Review* 1998 (May/June): 83–98.

———. 2005. Origins of the New York Stock Exchange. In *The origins of value: The financial innovations that created modern capital markets,* ed. W. N. Goetzmann and K. G. Rouwenhorst, 299–312. Oxford: Oxford University Press.

———. 2008. The political economy of early U.S. financial development. In *Political institutions and financial development,* ed. S. Haber, D.C. North, and B. R. Weingast, 60–91. Stanford: Stanford University Press.

———. 2009. Comparing the UK and U.S. financial systems, 1790–1830. In *The origins and development of financial markets and institutions, from the seventeenth century to the present,* ed. J. Atack and L. Neal, 209–39. Cambridge: Cambridge University Press.

Sylla, R., and J. W. Wilson. 1999. Sinking funds as credible commitments: Two centuries of U.S. national-debt experience. *Japan and the World Economy* 11 (2): 199–232.

Sylla, R., J. W. Wilson, and R. E. Wright. 2006. Integration of trans-atlantic capital markets, 1790–1845. *Review of Finance* 10 (4): 613–44.

Sylla, R., R. E. Wright, and D. J. Cowen. 2009. Alexander Hamilton, central banker: Crisis management during the U.S. financial panic of 1792. *Business History Review* 83:61–86.

Syrett, H. C. 1961–1987. *The papers of Alexander Hamilton,* 26 volumes. New York: Columbia University Press.

Taylor, B. 2009. *America's first bull market.* Los Angeles: Global Financial Data.
Van Eeghen & Co. Papers. 1789–1793. Archives of the University of Amsterdam.
Ver Steeg, C. 1954. *Robert Morris, revolutionary financier.* Philadelphia: University of Pennsylvania Press.
Wright, R. E. 2002. *The wealth of nations rediscovered: Integration and expansion in American financial markets, 1780–1850.* New York: Cambridge University Press.
———. 2008. *One nation under debt: Hamilton, Jefferson, and the history of what we owe.* New York: McGraw Hill.

3

Revenue or Reciprocity?
Founding Feuds over
Early U.S. Trade Policy

Douglas A. Irwin

"Our treasury still thinks that these new encroachments of Gt.
Brit. on our carrying trade must be met with passive obedience
and non-resistance, lest any misunderstanding with them
should *affect our credit, or the prices of our public paper.*"
—Thomas Jefferson, 1791

"Every gust that arises in the political sky is the signal for measures tending to destroy [our] ability to pay or to obstruct the
course of payment."
—Alexander Hamilton, 1794

3.1 Introduction

An important motivation for the Constitutional Convention of 1787 was
to permit the national government to impose import tariffs and regulate
foreign commerce, something that it was not empowered to do under the
Articles of Confederation. Once Congress was granted this authority, the
use of these powers became the subject of immediate controversy. Should
import duties be imposed simply to collect revenue, or should they be used to
strike back against countries that imposed barriers against U.S. commerce?
Debate over precisely this issue—using import tariffs for revenue purposes alone or to achieve reciprocity as well—divided President George
Washington's administration in the early 1790s. The debate pitted Treasury

Douglas A. Irwin is the Robert E. Maxwell Professor of Arts and Sciences in the Department of Economics at Dartmouth College, and a research associate of the National Bureau
of Economic Research.

Secretary Alexander Hamilton against Secretary of State Thomas Jefferson and his congressional ally James Madison. Seeing imports as the critical tax base on which he planned to finance government expenditures and fund the public debt, Hamilton advocated modest, nondiscriminatory import duties to ensure a steady stream of revenue into the treasury coffers. He also wanted a stable commercial relationship with Britain to avoid any conflict that might disrupt imports and diminish customs revenue. By contrast, Jefferson and Madison saw trade policy as an instrument for achieving reciprocity, a weapon to be wielded against what they perceived to be Britain's grossly unfair discrimination against U.S. commerce. They sought to impose countervailing restrictions in an effort to force Britain to improve its treatment of U.S. goods and shipping in its home and colonial markets.

To some degree, these objectives were conflicting and mutually exclusive. Revenue considerations meant that nothing should be done to jeopardize the receipts coming from taxes on imports, suggesting that Britain's discriminatory trade practices should be tolerated so that the public debt could be funded. Reciprocity considerations suggested that retaliatory barriers should be imposed against British goods even at the risk of jeopardizing the government's most important source of revenue because it held out the promise of freer trade in the longer term.

Thus, early U.S. policymakers faced a dilemma: were import tariffs more important as a means of raising revenue, or as a tool for achieving reciprocal market access? Put this way, the choices hardly seem fundamental. But, in fact, the stakes were considerable and the decision had ramifications for the funding of the public debt and the role that overseas commerce would play in America's economy. This chapter examines how the nation's founding policymakers confronted this dilemma and evaluates the merits of different trade policy options. The main conclusion is that the Federalist policy of moderate tariffs, nondiscrimination, and conflict avoidance provided much needed stability during the first decade of the new government. Some of the potential pitfalls that were avoided during this crucial period can be illustrated by examining, briefly, how policy changed when the Jeffersonian Republicans took over in 1801 and initiated a more aggressive approach to trade relations with Britain.

3.2   From the Articles of Confederation to the Constitution

As a philosophical matter, America's political leaders were largely favorable to the idea of free trade after the nation achieved its independence. As students of the Enlightenment and rebels against British mercantilism, the Founding Fathers wanted to have free and open commerce among nations. This did not mean the absence of import tariffs, because such duties were recognized as essential for revenue purposes. Instead, "free trade" meant something along the lines of unconditional most-favored nation (MFN) status in which discriminatory restraints and exclusive preferences that inhibited trade would be abolished.[1]

But the newly independent United States found itself in a decidedly mercantilist world. No longer part of the British Empire, Americans faced a host of restrictions on their goods in Britain and its West Indies colonies. Other European powers similarly protected their home market and sought to keep trade with their colonies for themselves.[2] This harsh reality tempered the initially high hopes that the United States could enjoy the fruits of unrestricted international commerce. In 1785, for example, Thomas Jefferson wrote that the United States should embrace free trade "by throwing open all the doors of commerce and knocking off all its shackles." Yet, he immediately qualified this hope: "But as this cannot be done for others, unless they do it for us, and there is no probability that Europe will do this, I suppose we may be obliged to adopt a system which may shackle them in our ports, as they do us in theirs." James Madison expressed a similar view: "Much indeed is it to be wished, as I conceive, that no regulations of trade—that is to say, no restriction or imposts whatever—were necessary. A perfect freedom is the System which would be my choice." But, he added, "before such a system will be eligible perhaps for the U.S. they must be out of debt; before it will be attainable, all other nations must concur in it."[3]

Madison's observation, that before the United States could adopt free trade it had to be free of debt and have access to other markets, underscored two key weaknesses of the Articles of Confederation. Under the Articles, the national government lacked the ability to impose taxes or regulate foreign commerce. These two weaknesses created two enormous problems: the government could not fund its operations, finance its debt, or pay for national defense, and it could not credibly negotiate treaties of commerce with foreign powers. These closely intertwined problems had long been recognized. In 1782, Alexander Hamilton wrote that "the vesting of Congress with the power of regulating trade ought to have been a principal object of the Confederation for a variety of reasons. It is as necessary for the purposes of commerce as of revenue."[4] Yet the states, jealous of their sovereignty and

1. As McCoy (1980, 86–87) explains, "Many republicans eagerly embraced an eighteenth century ideology of free trade, whose leading spokesmen included Montesquieu, Hume, Adam Smith, and the French physiocrats. According to these writers, foreign as well as domestic commerce should be freed from all restraints so that it might flourish and, in the process, humanize men by refining their manners and morals. . . . Given their hostility to Britain and the mercantilist model, it is not surprising that many Americans in the early years of independence embraced this outlook and tied it directly to the spirit of their revolution."
2. Shepherd and Walton (1976) examine the reorientation of U.S. trade and shipping as a result of achieving independence.
3. PTJ 8: 633; PJM 8:333–34. This chapter will use PTJ to refer to the Papers of Thomas Jefferson (University of Virginia Press), PJM for the Papers of James Madison (Princeton University Press), and PAH for the Papers of Alexander Hamilton (Columbia University Press).
4. PAH 3: 75–76.

fearful of creating a dominant national government, designed the Articles with such weakness in mind.

With respect to revenue, Congress's inability to impose any taxes left it entirely dependent on requesting funds from the states, without any ability to compel them to pay. And through the 1780s, the states proved increasingly reluctant to respond to Congress's repeated requests for funds. In October 1781, just after the victory at Yorktown, Congress requisitioned $8 million from the states in 1782. By January 1783, Congress had only received $420,000 of that amount (Baack 2001). Later requisitions fared no better. By March 1787, states had paid two-thirds of the October 1781 and April 1784 requisitions, one-fifth of the September 1785 requisition, and two percent of the August 1786 requisition. "By the end of 1786," Brown (1993, 25) notes, "Congress literally was receiving no money from the states for current federal needs and expenses." An attempt by Congress to float a loan in October 1786 failed completely, without having attracted a single subscriber. This forced Madison to conclude: "Experience has sufficiently demonstrated that a punctual and unfailing compliance by thirteen separate and independent Governments with periodical demands of money from Congress, can never be reckoned upon with the certainty requisite to satisfy our present creditors, or to tempt others to become our creditors in future."[5]

Attempts to remedy this shortcoming by modifying the Articles of Confederation failed repeatedly during the decade. The Articles could be amended only by the unanimous consent of the states. In February 1781, Congress requested that the states amend the Articles and empower the Congress to levy an import duty of 5 percent. To allay the fears of the states that this would create an overly powerful central government and threaten their sovereignty, the proceeds of this tariff would be devoted exclusively to paying the interest and principal on the national debt and the duties would be abolished when the debt had been retired. Enactment of the measure looked promising: the proposal was approved by eleven states within a year, but then it stalled in the Rhode Island legislature. In November 1782, the Rhode Island legislature unanimously rejected the proposal, choosing to finance its state government with import duties rather than direct taxes and desiring to keep all the revenue from any import taxes for itself.

Undeterred, in early 1783 James Madison proposed a similar revenue plan that called for limited twenty-five-year authorization for Congress to impose specific duties on enumerated items and a 5 percent duty on all other imports; the duties would be administered in part by state authorities. Congress approved the measure in April 1783, but the unanimous approval of the states again proved to be out of reach. By July 1786, every state had approved the proposal except for New York. The legislature had rejected the

5. PJM 6:144–45.

revenue plan in 1785, after upstate agricultural interests realized that their taxes would go up if the state gave up its claim on the collection of import duties in the port of New York City. Then New York passed it in 1786 with the requirement that the state oversee the collection of the import duties, determine how much would be given to the national government, and make payments to Congress in New York currency. These conditions were unacceptable to Congress, which required gold and silver coin to repay foreign creditors, leaving the matter at an impasse.[6]

Writing in 1787, James Madison concluded:

> the present System neither has nor deserves advocates; and if some very strong props are not applied will quickly tumble to the ground. No money is paid into the public Treasury; no respect is paid to the federal authority. Not a single State complies with the requisitions, several pass over them in silence, and some positively reject them. The payments ever since the peace have been decreasing, and of late fall short even of the pittance necessary for the Civil list of the Confederacy. It is not possible that a Government can last long under these circumstances. (Brown 1993, 27)

The situation was no better when it came to regulating foreign commerce in an attempt to negotiate better terms for U.S. goods in foreign markets. After it achieved independence, the critical foreign-trade problem facing the United States was the loss of its preferential access to the markets of the British Empire. The nation's economy depended upon exports, which amounted to 12 percent of the gross domestic product (GDP) around 1790, and the loss of British-controlled markets was keenly felt. Not only did American producers now face higher duties on their goods in Britain, but, in July 1783, the British government banned American ships from ports in the British West Indies and outlawed the importation of selected American goods as well. This action sharply curtailed demand for America's shipping services and severely harmed New England shipowners and fishermen, fish being one of the products excluded from the West Indies. Some American products, such as lumber, flour, and livestock, could be brought to the British West Indies, but only in British vessels. Prior to independence, more than a quarter of U.S. merchandise exports were destined for the West Indies and the trade employed a sizeable share of America's merchant marine. Britain's actions also created difficulties for the U.S. balance of payments because, in the prerevolutionary period, the nation's trade surplus on the West Indies trade helped finance trade deficits with Britain itself.

Under the Articles of Confederation, the thirteen states could not for-

---

6. "The failure of constitutional revision in 1786 reflected less a division of opinion—all the states had endorsed a federal impost in principle—than the inherent difficulty of securing unanimous agreement to any proposal," notes Ferguson (1961, 337). "It appeared that the Articles of Confederation could not by constitutional procedure be amended to give Congress the limited accretion of power which majority opinion already sanctioned."

mulate a unified national response to Britain's discriminatory trade policies. Article IX of the Articles expressly stated that "no treaty of commerce
shall be made whereby the legislative power of the respective States shall be
restrained from imposing such imposts and duties on foreigners, as their own
people are subjected to, or from prohibiting the exportation or importation
of any species of goods or commodities whatsoever." As a result, there was
no national trade policy at all, but rather thirteen state trade policies.[7]

The national government tried to negotiate commercial agreements with
Britain and other European trading partners, but the negotiations failed
because the American diplomats had nothing to offer. They could not commit the states to any particular policy. By making demands on others without the ability to give something in return, the U.S. diplomatic overtures were
doomed from the start. "The commerce of America will have no relief at
present, nor, in my opinion, ever, until the United States shall have generally
passed navigation acts," Adams wrote to John Jay. "If this measure is not
adopted we shall be derided; the more we suffer, the more will our calamities
be laughed at."[8]

Some states tried to retaliate against Britain's exclusionary policies, but
the lack of coordination undermined those efforts. In response to the West
Indies prohibition, for example, Massachusetts prohibited British ships
from loading American goods in its ports. But when Connecticut refused
to follow this example, British ships simply shifted their destination from
Boston to New Haven, and Massachusetts was forced to suspend its action
a year later (Marks 1973, 82). Indeed, the neighboring states of New York
and New Jersey, Pennsylvania and Delaware, could not enact strict shipping
legislation unilaterally without simply diverting trade to the adjacent state.
Some states were persistent: in 1787, New York attempted to lay duties on
goods coming from Connecticut, and New Jersey as well, to punish them for
not levying additional duties on British goods or tonnage. Still, that effort
failed and the duties were soon abolished because no other states cared
to join New York; smaller states tended to free ride off of the retaliatory
actions of larger states, and thus undermine the effort. The British easily

7. Eleven of the thirteen colonies passed their own tariff laws during the 1780s. New Jersey
and Delaware, the only two states that did not pass tariff legislation, lacked the large seaports
of Massachusetts, New York, and Pennsylvania, and wanted to provide every encouragement
to trade they could. Most of the import duties in the state tariffs were relatively low, at about
five percent, and the structure of duties was quite similar across the states (Shepherd 1993). This
decentralized tariff system produced many problems, but trade wars between the states were not
among them. By the end of the 1780s, the tariffs of the states were converging with one another.

8. John Adams was impatient for action: "Patience, under all the unequal burthens they
impose upon our commerce, will do us no good; it will contribute in no degree to preserve the
peace with this country. On the contrary, nothing but retaliations, reciprocal prohibitions, and
imposts, and putting ourselves in a posture of defense, will have any effect. . . . Confining our
exports to our own ships, and laying on heavy duties upon all foreign luxuries, and encouraging
our own manufactures, appear to me to be our only resource, although I am very sensible to
the many difficulties on the way" (Davis 1977, 99).

evaded the differing state-by-state policies on navigation and simply went to the most welcoming ports.[9]

As was the case with taxation, efforts to amend the Articles of Confederation to remedy this shortcoming came to naught. In December 1784, Congress appointed a committee to change Article IX of the Articles and give Congress "the powers to regulate the commercial intercourse of the States with other powers." The committee recommended that Congress be given the "sole and exclusive" authority of "regulating the trade of the States, as well with foreign nations, as with each other, and of laying such imposts and duties upon imports and exports as might be necessary for the purpose." New England states, with their mercantile base, were desperate to give Congress the power to deal with the foreign trade situation, and the Mid-Atlantic states were supportive as well. But the proposal floundered due to the sectional jealousies. Southern states were much less adversely affected by British shipping regulations in the West Indies and elsewhere and objected out of concern that the power would be used to exclude British competition for the shipment of U.S. exports, putting the South at the mercy of New England merchants. In essence, the South feared that it would face a northern monopoly on the shipping of its staple exports, raising transport costs and diminishing its export sales.

New England merchants and politicians were incensed at the South's reluctance to act. In their view, the South was refusing to act out of its own interest without considering the economic distress felt in other parts of the country. "They may get their goods to market cheaper if our ships have nothing to do," one correspondent complained to John Adams (Davis 1977, 85). New England wanted some preferences for American shipping, such as a tax on goods arriving or departing on British vessels, to strengthen the American shipbuilding and shipping industry.

The commercial distress was so acute in New England that there was even talk of seceding from the union if the South continued to block commercial reform.[10] Madison worried that the issue might dissolve the fragile nation. Mad-

9. The national government had no power to formulate a collective solution to this problem. A British magazine recognized this: "By the latest letters from the American States, the restraint laid upon their trade with the British West Indies has thrown them into the utmost perplexity; and by way of retaliation they are passing laws inimical to their own interest; and what is still worse, inconsistent with each other. . . . Hence the dissensions that universally prevail throughout what may be called the thirteen Dis-United States" (Marks 1973, 83).

10. In August 1785, Madison reported to Jefferson: "The machinations of G.B. with regard to Commerce have produced much distress and noise in the Northern States, particularly in Boston, from whence the alarm has spread to New York and Philada. . . . the sufferers are every where calling for such augmentation of the power of Congress as may effect relief. . . . If any thing should reconcile Virga. to the idea of giving Congress a power over her trade, it will be that this power is likely to annoy G.B. against whom the animosities of our Citizens are still strong. They seem to have less sensibility to their commercial interests; which they very little understand, and which the mercantile class here have not the same motives if they had the same capacity to lay open to the public, as that class have in the States North of us. The [high] price of our Staple since the peace is another cause of inattention in the planters to the

ison, who thought that the advantages of giving Congress the power to regulate trade "appears to me not to admit of a doubt," repeated these fears to others:

> I conceive it to be of great importance that the defects of the federal system should be amended, not only because such amendments will make it better answer the purpose for which it was instituted, but because I apprehend danger to its very existence from a continuance of defects which expose a part if not the whole of the empire to severe distress. The suffering part, even when the minor part, can not long respect a Government which is too feeble to protect their interest; but when the suffering part come to be the majority part, and the despair of seeing a protecting energy given to the General Government, from what motives is their allegiance to be any longer expected. Should G. B. persist in the machinations which distress us; and seven or eight of the States be hindered by the others from obtaining relief by federal means, I own, I tremble at the anti-federal expedience into which the former may be tempted.[11]

By the mid-1780s, there was a growing consensus among national political leaders that the current system of government was unworkable and should be reformed to strengthen the national government. The nation's unsatisfactory experience with the Articles of Confederation in the 1780s gave a compelling economic and foreign policy rationale for creating a stronger national government. Although many other factors were involved, the belief that the federal government should have an independent source of revenue and credible authority to negotiate with foreign powers over navigation rights and market access were both important motivations for the Constitutional Convention of 1787.[12]

At the convention, delegates had no difficulty in agreeing to give Congress the power to impose import duties. Article I, section 8, clause 1 of the new Constitution contained the key provision relating to trade policy, which stated:

> The Congress shall have power to lay and collect taxes, duties, imposts and excises, to pay the debts and provide for the common defense and general welfare of the United States; but all duties, imposts and excises shall be uniform throughout the United States.

This uncontroversial provision was adopted without significant debate or apparent dissent. Few disagreed with John Rutledge's observation that "taxes on imports [were] the only sure source of revenue" for the government (Farrand 1911, 3: 126, 327).

The proposal to grant Congress the general power to regulate foreign

---

dark side of our commercial affairs. Should these or any other causes prevail in frustrating the scheme of the Eastern and Middle States of a general retaliation on G.B., I tremble for the event. A majority of the States deprived of a regular remedy for the distresses by the want of a federal spirit in the minority must feel the strongest motives to some irregular experiments. The danger of such a crisis makes me surmise that the policy of Great Britain results as much from the hope of effecting a breach in our confederacy as of monopolising our trade" (PJM 8:344).

11. PJM 8: 334–35.

12. Brown (1993) stresses the finance motive while Marks (1973) and Edling (2003) stress the foreign policy motives, although they were all intertwined.

commerce, such as shipping regulations, was more contentious. The shipping states of New England desperately wanted to give the federal government the authority to regulate commerce so that American navigation laws could be enacted. In their view, enacting preferential duties for American ships in U.S. ports through differential tonnage duties would not only promote the domestic shipping industry, but would put the government in a better position to negotiate an elimination of foreign regulations that blocked U.S. access to foreign markets.[13]

As before, Southern states feared giving Congress the power to regulate commerce. With their prosperity dependent upon large exports of agricultural staples, they wanted maximal competition to ensure inexpensive shipping services. If competition from British ships was seriously handicapped by American navigation laws, the South believed that it would be exploited by New England shipping interests and charged exorbitant freight rates that would reduce the price and volume of its exports. The South wanted to deny Congress the power to regulate commerce, or at least require a two-thirds vote in Congress to enact such regulations, to prevent hostile legislation that would leave it completely dependent upon New England shipping interests.

How were the sharply opposing views of the North and South reconciled? The ability to regulate commerce became bound up with the slave trade and formed part of the "dirty compromise" that played out over a few days in late August.[14] The essence of the "dirty compromise" was that "the South Carolina delegation would support the commerce clause if New England would support protection for the slave trade and a prohibition on export taxes" (Finkelman 1987, 214). This interregional agreement allowed the convention to get around these contentious issues, but each part of the compromise was controversial.

Thus, the desire to vest Congress with the power to tax and regulate foreign commerce was one of the major forces behind the chain of events that led to the new Constitution. As Madison later recalled,

It was well known that the incapacity [of the States to regulate foreign commerce separately] gave a primary and powerful impulse to the transfer of the power to a common authority capable of exercising it with effect. . . . In expounding the Constitution and deducing the intention of its framers, it should never be forgotten, that the great object of the Convention was to provide, by a new Constitution, a remedy for the defects of the existing one; that among these defects was that of a power to regulate foreign commerce.[15]

Like many others, Alexander Hamilton was struck by the nation's structural problems in the 1780s and supported these constitutional changes. In

---

13. From the standpoint of his region, Nathaniel Gorham of Massachusetts argued that there was little other reason for drafting a new constitution because "the eastern states had no motive to union but a commercial one" (Farrand 1911, 2: 374).

14. See Finkelman (1987) and Goldstone (2005).

15. Letters of James Madison 4:251.

the Federalist papers, Hamilton made two arguments for granting Congress powers over trade. First, if there was to be a national government, it was imperative that it be able to raise revenue and not depend upon contributions from the states. "A nation cannot long exist without revenue," Hamilton argued in Federalist 12. "Destitute of this essential support, it must resign its independence and sink into the degraded condition of a province. . . . Revenue therefore must be had at all events." Hamilton observed that the United States would at first depend largely upon import duties as the means of raising revenue, but suggested that "unless all the sources of revenue are open to its demands, the finances of the community under such embarrassments, cannot be put into a situation consistent with its respectability, or its security."

Second, Hamilton made the case for a national trade policy to achieve reciprocity, so that "we may oblige foreign countries to bid against each other, for the privileges of our markets." In Federalist 11, Hamilton argued that imposing trade restrictions against Britain "would provide a relaxation in her present system" that hindered U.S. commerce, and such a relaxation would be beneficial "from which our trade would derive the most substantial benefits." Hamilton emphasized the bargaining advantages of federal powers over commerce:

> By prohibitory regulations, extending, at the same time, throughout the States, we may oblige foreign countries to bid against each other, for the privileges of our markets. . . . Suppose, for instance, we had a government in America, capable of excluding Great Britain (with whom we have at present no treaty of commerce) from all our ports; what would be the probable operation of this step upon her politics? Would it not enable us to negotiate, with the fairest prospect of success, for commercial privileges of the most valuable and extensive kind, in the dominions of that kingdom?

Thus, Hamilton held out the hope that American navigation laws would "produce a relaxation in her system" and enable the United States to enjoy the commerce of the West Indies once again. Furthermore, such an agreement "would be likely to have a correspondent effect on the conduct of other nations."

As the first treasury secretary, Hamilton vigorously sought revenue, but—as we shall see—shied away from reciprocity.

3.3   Trade Policy in Practice: Revenue

The first order of business for the new Congress under the new Constitution was raising revenue to fund the government's operations and service the public debt. On April 8, 1789, two days after the Congress first achieved a quorum, Madison introduced a bill in the House of Representatives to levy duties on imports. Citing the urgent revenue requirements of the new government, Madison argued that a tariff should be imposed without delay so that the spring importations from Europe could be taxed. As a temporary expedient, Madison proposed a tariff structure based on that approved by the Continental Congress in 1783. The 1783 proposal called for a general 5 percent ad valorem tax on all imports and higher specific duties on such commodities as wine and spirits, tea, and coffee. Madison suggested that a more permanent tariff structure be crafted at a later date, but that Congress should act quickly to avoid missing the spring imports and to allow revenue to start flowing into the treasury coffers.[16]

Madison's proposal sparked a debate as to whether revenue should be the sole objective of the tariffs on imports. Several members argued that import duties should be levied to promote domestic manufactures as well as raise revenue. As Thomas Hartley of Pennsylvania put it, "No argument . . . can operate to discourage the committee from taking such measures as will tend to protect and promote our domestic manufactures . . . I think it both politic and just that the fostering hand of the General Government should extend to all those manufactures which will tend to national utility."[17]

Knowing that this highly controversial issue would produce an extended and contentious debate, thereby delaying the imposition of import duties and exacerbating the government's financial problems, Madison sought, and succeeded, in postponing a debate over protective duties. Indeed, at this early stage, the United States did not seriously consider "protectionist" policies, in the sense of high tariffs designed exclusively to protect domestic producers from foreign competition without any revenue motive. The simple political economy explanation for the lack of interest in protectionist trade policies is that the nation, from the merchant shipping interests in New England and New York to the staple exporters in the South, was completely dominated by pro-trade interests. There were very few import-competing manufacturers, mainly around Philadelphia, and they lacked the political strength to press for a high tariff policy. Partly for this reason, Alexander Hamilton's controversial proposals for federal aid to fledgling industries in the *Report on Manufactures* (1791) were not seriously considered by Congress.[18] Hence, there was no great debate over protectionism in the first decade under the 1787 Constitution; such policies did not emerge until after the War of 1812 when the country had begun to establish a manufacturing industrial base that demanded protection from foreign competition. At least initially, the greater concern was that the nation so disliked taxes that

16. Madison argued that "the deficiency in our Treasury has been too notorious to make it necessary for me to animadvert upon that subject." "Let us content ourselves with endeavoring to remedy the evil. To do this a national revenue must be obtained; but the system must be such a one that, while it secures the object of revenue, it shall not be oppressive to our constituents."

17. *Annals of Congress*, vol. 1, April 9, 1789, 114.

18. On Hamilton's report, see Cooke (1975), Nelson (1979), Peskin (2003), and Irwin (2004).

Congress had to be careful about raising import tariffs to such an extent as to promote smuggling or provoke a popular backlash.

Madison's tariff proposal became the second piece of legislation passed by Congress and was signed by President Washington on July 4, 1789. The preamble of the law stated that import duties were necessary "for the support of government, for the discharge of the debts of the United States, and the encouragement and protection of manufactures." By the standards of later tariff legislation, the first tariff bill was not fiercely contested.[19] The first tariff schedule consisted of three parts: specific duties on select commodities, ad valorem duties on most other goods, and duty free treatment for a small number of items.[20] The specific duties were largely levied on alcoholic beverages, although some of these duties provided incidental protection to some producers. For example, although domestic spirits were subject to an excise tax, it was much less than the import tariff. Other specific duties were imposed explicitly for the benefit of domestic producers, such as those on boots and shoes, nails and spikes, and fish and hemp. Almost all other imports were subject to ad valorem duties. Four levels of ad valorem duties were established: 15 percent (on carriages and parts), 10 percent (on china, stone, and glassware, among others), 7.5 percent (on cotton and woollen clothing, hats, hammered or rolled iron and other metal manufactures, and leather manufactures, among others), and 5 percent on all other articles not specified.

In September 1789, Alexander Hamilton became secretary of the treasury and emerged as the chief architect of economic policy in the Washington administration. Hamilton almost singlehandedly reorganized the nation's finances, managing debts and establishing the public credit, as Richard Sylla's chapter discusses. He also performed the vital task of setting up the customs service that was charged with collecting import duties at the principal U.S. sea ports. By all accounts, he managed the customs service with efficiency and great attention to detail, ensuring that it operated smoothly and functioned free of corruption.[21]

19. Peskin (2003, 91) notes that the tariff rates were generally lower than those in Pennsylvania and Massachusetts.

20. The list of goods subject to specific duties were initially imposed on thirty-six goods, including beer, wine, spirits, molasses, salt, sugar, tobacco, tea, and coffee. The specific duties were viewed as a tax on luxuries consumed mainly by the wealthy; their main purpose was to raise revenue.

21. Dalzell (1993, 142) writes that "putting customs collection on a sound footing represented a crucial first step in Hamilton's program, and the Secretary of the Treasury kept as close a watch on the customs houses as he could manage from the capitol. Through a steady stream of circulars, instructions and advice to the collectors, Hamilton vigorously exerted his authority over the customs collectors. He assumed control over major customhouse expenditures; asked to be apprised of all seizures and attempts to defraud the revenue; and most importantly dispense general interpretations of the revenue laws to govern their implementation in the ports. Energetic and determined to implement an efficient, uniform system of operation, Hamilton more than any other single figure left an enduring stamp on the experiment of federal customs collection, marking it with his distinctive ideas of federal style, financial policy, and political economy."

The revenue collected from customs duties increased sharply after the federal government took over the customs service. The returns from the ports of New York, Philadelphia, Baltimore, and Charleston jumped from $1.975 million over the period 1785 to 1788 to $11.845 million during the period 1792 to 1795, an increase of 600 percent (Edling and Kaplanoff 2004). The revenue growth was partly due to a revival of foreign trade after the adoption of the Constitution, but also an increase in the rates of duty (which were roughly double those of New York in the 1780s) and the efficiency of the customs service in collecting them.

This administrative achievement was critical because the federal government was almost completely dependent upon customs revenues for its revenue. In 1792, for example, customs duties (on imported merchandise and shipping tonnage) accounted for $3.4 million of the $3.7 million of total government receipts. In that year, government expenditures amounted to about $5.1 million, resulting in a substantial revenue shortfall. Hamilton recognized the precarious fiscal situation of the federal government and sought to raise these early tariffs to generate additional revenue. Indeed, given that virtually all government revenue was derived from customs receipts, and that the revenue generated by the initial tariffs was uncertain, the specific duties were fine-tuned almost immediately in order to provide additional revenue.

In January 1790, in his first report on public credit, Hamilton proposed that Congress increase the duty on Madeira wine, Hyson tea, coffee, and chinaware, as well as other adjustments to the tariff code. The highest revenue-raising duties were imposed on wine, spirits, tea, and coffee because they were goods for which demand was relatively inelastic. "Experience has shown, that luxuries of every kind lay the strongest hold on the attachments of mankind, which, especially when confirmed by habit, are not easily alienated from them." Hence, Hamilton concluded: "it will be sound policy to carry the duties, upon articles of this kind, as high as will be consistent with the practicability of a safe collection. This will lessen the necessity, both of having recourse to direct taxation, and of accumulating duties, where they would be more inconvenient to trade, and upon objects which are more to be regarded as necessaries of life" (PAH 6:100). Congress enacted most of these recommendations in August 1790.

Still more increases followed. Acting again on Hamilton's advice, Congress increased the duties on spirits in March 1791. At this point, Hamilton believed that "the duties on the great mass of imported articles have reached a point, which it would not be expedient to exceed" for fear of offending the merchant class and diminishing the revenue.[22] Therefore, he advocated an excise tax on domestically produced spirits to diversify the government's sources of revenue: "it is clear that less dependence can be placed on one species of funds [import duties], and that too, liable to the vicissitude of the

22. Second Report on Credit, December 1790 (PAH 7: 232).

continuance, or interruption of foreign intercourse, than upon a variety of different funds, formed by the union of internal with external objects. . . . to attempt to extract wholly from duties on imported articles, the sum necessary to a complete provision of the public debt would probably be both deceptive and pernicious, incompatible with the interests, not less of revenue than of commerce."

Yet, the revenue requirements of the government continued to grow. In 1792, in order to finance expenditures related to the protection of the western frontier, Congress advanced the ad valorem tariff schedule by 2.5 percentage points, pushing the base rate from 5 percent to 7.5 percent. In 1794, the basic schedule was raised another 2.5 percentage points, bringing the base rate to 10 percent, and duties on sugar and wine were increased to begin retiring the public debt. In 1797, Congress imposed higher specific duties on sugar, molasses, tea, cocoa, and other products, along with an increase in the base rate to 12.5 percent. In each of these cases, the primary purpose of the adjustment was to raise revenue to finance government operations and the payment of the debt.

Figure 3.1 shows the evolution of the average tariff during this period. Although import tariffs were relatively low in 1790 and 1791, at around 12 percent, on average, subsequent revisions to the initial duties quickly brought the average tariff up to about 20 percent by the mid-1790s. Each of the early tariff spikes—in 1794, 1797, and 1804—is proximately related to

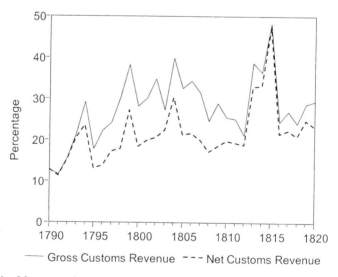

Gross Customs Revenue   − − − Net Customs Revenue

Fig. 3.1   Measures of average tariff, 1790–1820
Note: calculated as customs duties divided by value of imports for consumption.
Source: Irwin (2003, table 1).

legislation that raised import duties. These revisions were motivated almost exclusively by revenue considerations, and were relatively free from political controversy.

These estimates indicate the relative height of import duties over time, but reveal nothing about the structure of those duties. As a rough approximation, the specific duties were levied on consumption items for revenue purposes while the ad valorem duties were levied for the protection of some domestic producers. The higher average tariff was largely due to increases in specific duties, which ranged between 40 percent and 60 percent, on average (Irwin 2003). The ad valorem duties on manufactured and other goods remained relatively low through the 1790s, rising from 5 percent to just over 13 percent by 1800, by which time the base rate was 12.5 percent.

Levying taxes on imports proved to be an economically and politically efficient method of raising revenue. Imports arrived at just a few large seaports on the coast and required relatively few officials to collect the taxes upon landing. The administrative cost of enforcing import duties was just 4 percent of the gross revenue collected, while the cost of collecting domestic excise taxes was 20 percent of the gross revenue (Balinky 1958, 57).

An equally important consideration was the fact that import duties were a politically efficient way of raising revenue. The tax on imports was automatically built into the domestic price of imported goods and avoided the "political minefield" of excise taxes (Brown 1993, 238–39). In the aftermath of the fight over the Constitution and the fragile nature of support for the federal government, Hamilton and others were reluctant to impose domestic taxes that might trigger a domestic political resistance, as indeed they did with the Whiskey Rebellion in 1794. Hamilton's fiscal and revenue program brought about a large and welcome shift in the nation's tax system. Edling and Kaplanoff (2004) note that leading states had to rely on direct taxes (poll and land taxes) to a much greater extent than on customs duties. These intrusive and burdensome taxes sparked a political backlash. By reducing the burden of debt on the states—which allowed states to reduce those direct taxes by a significant margin, as much as 75 percent in many states—and substituting trade taxes for direct taxes, the perceived tax burden on the public fell sharply. The frequent protests over state taxes in the 1780s had largely disappeared by the 1790s.

Still, Hamilton sought to supplement and diversify revenue sources away from customs duties, which were subject to vicissitudes of trade, to more dependable forms of internal revenue, such as excise taxes. Confronting the argument that the government should rely solely on import duties without any internal taxes, Hamilton warned that it would "deprive the government of resources which are indispensible to a due provision for the public safety and welfare . . . if the government cannot then resort to internal means for the additional supplies, which the exigencies of every nation call for, it will be

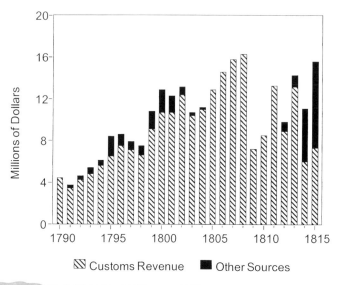

Fig. 3.2   Sources of federal government revenue
Source: U.S. Bureau of the Census (1975, series Y-352-353).

unable to perform its duty or even to preserve its existence. The community must be unprotected, and the social compact be dissolved."[23] Yet domestic taxes were highly unpopular and Congress was reluctant to enact them.[24] As a result, as figure 3.2 shows, Hamilton only managed to diversify the source of government revenue to a modest extent.

Despite the growth in customs revenues that came with expanding trade in the early 1790s, the fiscal position of the federal government remained precarious. In 1792, interest alone on U.S. debt soaked up 87 percent of total tax revenue. The United States covered the revenue shortfalls only through a large loan from the Netherlands, which helped pay off previous foreign loans and allowed for the redemption of significant amounts of domestic debt (Riley 1978). Still, this refinancing meant that the nominal value of the national debt did not fall during the 1790s. (It was not until 1796 that the government's tax revenue would cover federal debt and nondebt expenditures.) This left Hamilton open to charges from the Jeffersonian Republicans that he was not serious about retiring the debt. But as noted, there were political and economic constraints on further increasing either import duties or excise taxes. As Edling (2007, 306) puts it, "Faced with a choice between raising taxes to pay off the debt rapidly or accepting indebtedness for at least the foreseeable future, Hamilton opted for the latter alternative."

23. PAH 11: 85–86.
24. The stability of excises as a source of revenue was at least partly balanced by the unrest they caused. The Whiskey Rebellion in western Pennsylvania was triggered when Congress, acting on Hamilton's advice, boosted the excise tax on spirits in 1791.

These revenue constraints made Hamilton extremely careful to husband the government's meager financial resources and maintain the country's creditworthiness. For this reason, he desperately wanted the United States to remain neutral in any European military conflict, fearing that U.S. involvement would destroy the nation's finances. Becoming entangled in a war for which it was unprepared would ruin the nation's finances; government expenditures would soar and its revenues would collapse. This fear deeply colored Hamilton's approach to the issue of trade reciprocity.

3.4   Trade Policy in Practice: Reciprocity

In Federalist 11, Hamilton argued that threats to close the U.S. market to British goods, or to impose discriminatory restrictions against British shipping, could force that country to improve its treatment of American goods in its home and colonial markets. Yet, as secretary of treasury, Hamilton aggressively fought every effort to implement such a policy. Instead, he put overwhelming emphasis on the economic goal of maintaining and increasing customs revenue. Given the fragility of the nation's finances, Hamilton believed that the overriding priority of the Washington administration should be to ensure that the government could finance the interest on the public debt: "Nothing can more interest the National Credit and prosperity, than a constant and systematic attention to husband all means previously possessed for extinguishing the present debt, and to avoid, as much as possible, the incurring of any new debt."[25] Given the revenue constraints facing the government, the United States, in his view, had to avoid any significant drop in imports or the customs revenues that they generated, and also had to avoid any sudden, unexpected rise in spending. Both events would occur should the country become embroiled in a war and nothing, in his view, could destroy the nation's finances and credit rating faster.

Thus, economic policy dictated foreign policy: the nation had to maintain political neutrality between Britain and France in order to avoid conflict. Neutrality, in turn, required that import duties be imposed on a nondiscriminatory basis so as not to offend British officials. Yet the public continued to harbor bitter feelings against Britain, whose postwar policies with respect to American commerce helped sour relations even further. Many Americans resented the country's continuing commercial dependence on Great Britain; the overwhelming majority of U.S. imports came from Britain, many exports were sent to Britain or her colonies, and trade finance was still largely British. Britain did not treat the commerce of the United States as favorably as it had when it was a colony, and had begun to interfere with U.S. shipping with the outbreak of the war with France in 1793.

Despite the public sentiment, Hamilton wanted to stifle the temptation to

---

25. PAH 11:141.

strike back at Britain. Hamilton vigorously opposed commercial discrimination aimed at Britain because he feared it could start a trade war. (Indeed, a representative from Britain warned him that any discriminatory measure would bring about not a relaxation of British mercantile regulations, but retaliation instead.) A trade war would dry up the flow of customs revenues arising from British imports and jeopardize Hamilton's entire fiscal program. America was in a much weaker position than Britain, in Hamilton's judgment, and therefore had much more to lose as a result of a commercial or military conflict.

By contrast, James Madison (in the House) and Thomas Jefferson (as secretary of state) desperately sought commercial discrimination against Britain. Although the United States had won its political independence, they believed that it had not achieved economic independence and was much too reliant on commercial and financial ties with Britain. At the same time, they attacked mercantilist regulations that kept American goods and ships out of Britain's home and colonial markets. They advocated adopting the retaliatory policies endorsed by Hamilton in Federalist 11.[26] In their view, discriminatory measures against Britain would force it to open up the West Indies market to American shipping and improve its treatment of U.S. goods in its market. (Ironically, if these measures succeeded in changing Britain's policies, America would only become further dependent on commerce with Britain and its colonies.)

The basis for Jefferson and Madison's confidence that trade measures could force Britain to change its policy came from the colonial period. After the passage of the Stamp Act in 1765 and the Townshend Duties in 1770, some American colonists organized a boycott of British goods. In the case of the Stamp Act, British merchants who saw their exports to the colonies fall flooded Parliament with petitions demanding accommodation to end the nonimportation. The British government complied and repealed the act. In the case of the Townshend Duties, British merchants did not protest the lost exports because there was a domestic economic boom, but a change in the British government resulted in a repeal of the duties. From this pattern of American resistance through nonimportation followed by British retreat, the colonists drew the conclusion—correctly in the case of the Stamp Act, but incorrectly in the case of the Townshend Duties—that British policy could be manipulated with American trade embargos.

Between 1789 and 1794, Madison and Jefferson tried repeatedly to implement discriminatory trade measures against Britain.[27] Each time they failed as the politically adroit Hamilton maneuvered to defeat them.

26. But Hamilton saw the Madison-Jefferson approach as threatening his conception of U.S. trade and revenue policy. Although Hamilton had been closely allied with James Madison in securing the creation and implementation of the Constitution, they diverged sharply in their view of trade policy, as well as many other matters of economic policy (Schwartz 2007).
27. See Peterson (1965), McCoy (1974), and Ben-Atar (1993).

The first attempt came in the summer of 1789 as the new Congress was debating the first tariff bill. Along with the tariff on imported merchandise, Congress imposed duties on the tonnage of ships entering U.S. ports. These duties favored U.S.-owned ships: the duty was six cents per ton on American vessels versus fifty cents per ton on foreign vessels. But Madison wanted further discrimination among foreign ships, distinguishing between those from countries that had a commercial agreement with the United States (such as France) and those that did not (such as Britain). Madison and Jefferson believed that the United States possessed enough economic leverage to harm Britain's trade and force the country to relax its restrictions on American commerce. In their view, Britain depended more on commerce with America than the other way around because the United States sent essential food and raw materials—necessities, in their view—to Britain in exchange for manufactures and luxuries, which could be safely done without. In a trade war, Britain's commercial interests would be "wounded almost mortally, while ours are invulnerable," Madison explained. "I have, therefore, no fears of entering into a commercial warfare with that nation; if fears are to be entertained, they lie on the other side."[28]

Although Madison's proposal easily passed the House, it failed in the Senate, due to what proponents attributed to the British influence coming from the city of New York. President Washington lamented the Senate's action, calling it "adverse to my ideas of justice & policy." But apparently he did not recognize that, behind the scenes, his soon-to-be treasury secretary, Alexander Hamilton, helped energize Senate opposition to the measure.[29]

In early 1790, Madison used a petition from merchants demanding higher tonnage duties on foreign vessels to reopen the debate over tonnage discrimination. A House committee recommended doubling the tonnage duties on foreign ships from fifty cents per ton to one dollar per ton. Madison proposed that the doubling only applied to countries without a commercial treaty with the United States, so that it would apply to Britain, but not France. The House passed the measure and Jefferson praised the "salutary effect" it would have on Britain's behavior. However, once again, the bill languished and died in the Senate, where Hamilton apparently worked hard to ensure its demise.

A third opportunity to introduce discrimination came in January 1791, when France argued that it was exempt from the tonnage laws under the 1778 Treaty of Commerce. Jefferson disagreed with the French construction of

---

28. PJM, May 4, 1789, 248.

29. In Washington's view, "The opposition of the Senate to the discrimination in the Tonnage Bill, was so adverse to my ideas of justice & policy, that, I should have suffered it to have passed into Law without my signature, had I not been assured by some members of that body, that they were preparing another Bill which would answer the purpose more effectually without being liable to the objections, & to the consequences which they *feared* would have attended the discrimination which was proposed in the Tonnage Law" (PGW 3: 323–24).

the treaty, but wanted to grant France an exemption as a gesture of good will.[30] Hamilton agreed with Jefferson's interpretation of the treaty, that the United States was not obligated to grant an exemption, but set forth a series of polite but firmly stated objections to Jefferson's proposal. In Hamilton's view, one problem was the "want of reciprocity in the thing itself"—that is, French ships would be given the same treatment as American ships in U.S. ports, but American ships would only get most-favored nation treatment in French ports. Hamilton believed that such a policy would have little practical effect, but the concession would set a dangerous precedent. "The introduction of such a principle without *immediate* reciprocity, would be a high price for the advantage which it is intended to compensate."[31]

Hamilton also pointed out that the tonnage duties were earmarked for paying down the public debt. "I do not mention this as an insuperable objection but it would be essential that the same act which should destroy this source of revenue should provide an equivalent," he argued. "This I consider as a rule which ought to be sacred, as it affects public Credit." He summed up his position in this way:

> My commercial system turns very much on giving a free course to Trade and cultivating good humour with all the world. And I feel a particular reluctance to hazard anything in the present state of our affairs which may lead to commercial warfare with any power; which as far as my knowledge of examples extends is commonly productive of the worse kind of warfare. Exemptions & preferences which are not the effect of Treaty are apt to be regarded by those who do not partake in them as proofs of an unfriendly temper towards them.[32]

Although President Washington forwarded Jefferson's brief on the issue to Congress, the Senate defeated any concessions for France for a third time. Jefferson was outraged: "Our treasury still thinks that these new encroachments of Gt. Brit. on our carrying trade must be met with passive obedience and nonresistance, lest any misunderstanding with them should *affect our credit, or the prices of our public paper.*"[33] As Jefferson complained bitterly to Washington:

> My system was to give some satisfactory distinctions to the French, of little cost to us, in return for the solid advantages yielded us by them; and to have met the English with some restrictions, which might induce them to abate their severities against our commerce. I have always supposed this coincided with your sentiments; yet the Secretary of the Treasury, by his

30. PAH 7: 408.
31. Hamilton suggested that a new treaty of commerce with France could formalize reciprocity as a permanent principle. This "would perhaps be less likely than apparently gratuitous and voluntary exemptions to beget discontents elsewhere"—referring to the dim view that Britain would take of such a grant.
32. PAH 7: 426.
33. PTJ 20: 236.

cabals with members of the legislature and by high-toned declamations on other occasions, has forced on his own system, which was exactly the reverse.[34]

Hamilton had his own complaints, writing that Jefferson was "an avowed enemy to a funded debt." In his view, Jefferson was consistently proposing policies that could undermine his financial plans: "Jefferson with very little reserve manifests his dislike of the funding system generally, calling in question the expediency of funding a debt at all. . . . I do not mean that he advocates directly the undoing of what has been done, but he censures the whole on principles which, if they should become general, could not but end in the subversion of the system." Foremost among these risks were Jefferson's overtures to France, which he thought could create a hostile wedge with Britain and undermine his ability to fund the national debt. Hamilton believed that the foreign policy views of Madison and Jefferson were "unsound and dangerous." "Attempts were made by these Gentlemen in different ways to produce a Commercial Warfare with Great Britain. . . . Various circumstances prove to me that if these Gentlemen were left to pursue their own course there would be in less than six months *an open War between the U States & Great Britain*." Such a war would destroy Hamilton's financial policies and therefore "the Neutral & the Pacific Policy appear to me to mark the true path" that the country should follow.[35]

To Washington, Jefferson complained that the charge of his having a "desire of not paying the public debt" was completely untrue:

every word, and act on the subject . . . prove that no man is more ardently intent to see the public debt soon and sacredly paid off than I am. This marks the difference between Colo. Hamilton's views and mine, that I would wish the debt paid tomorrow; he wishes it never to be paid, but always to be a thing wherewith to corrupt and manage the legislature.[36]

Jefferson accused Hamilton of taking on so much debt such that the country was "obliged to strain the *impost* till it produces a clamour, and will produce evasion, and a war on our own citizens to collect it: and even to resort to an *Excise* law, of odious character with the people, partial in its operation, unproductive unless enforced by arbitrary and vexatious means, and committing the authority of the government, in parts where resistance is most probable, and coercion least practicable."[37]

This policy dispute came to a head in early 1794, when the threat to Hamilton's fiscal system was perhaps the greatest. The outbreak of war between Britain and France in February 1793 triggered a debate about whether the United States should back France, its ally during the revolutionary war, and

34. PTJ 24: 353–354.
35. PAH 11: 429–430.
36. PTJ 24: 355.
37. PTJ 23: 536.

thereby risk war with Britain, or remain neutral. With the European powers attempting to destroy the trade of the other, they—but primarily Britain—began intercepting American shipping and confiscating the cargoes, actions that fueled anti-British sentiment. Washington took Hamilton's advice and issued the neutrality proclamation in April 1793, but Jefferson and Madison, who strongly supported a tilt toward France, made one last bid for economic nonneutrality.

In December 1793, the outgoing secretary of state sent Congress a report on commercial discrimination. Jefferson's report documented the manifold foreign barriers placed on U.S. goods and shipping in foreign markets, particularly those controlled by Britain. Jefferson's preferred course of action was "friendly arrangements"—trade agreements—with foreign countries to remove the impediments to trade. However, Jefferson argued at length that

> should any nation, contrary to our wishes, suppose it may better find its advantage by continuing its system of prohibitions, duties, and regulations, it behooves us to protect our citizens, their commerce, and navigation, by counter prohibitions, duties, and regulations, also. Free commerce and navigation are not to be given in exchange for restrictions and vexations, nor are they likely to produce a relaxation of them.

He then outlined a policy of strict reciprocity, in which high duties would be met with high duties and prohibitions with prohibitions, all in an effort to free trade from such impediments.[38] The thinly veiled message was that the United States should strike back at British restrictions on U.S. commerce.

Jefferson's report prompted Madison to raise the issue of discrimination once again. Madison proposed to implement Jefferson's reciprocity policy by imposing higher duties on goods and shipping from countries without a commercial treaty with the United States. Clearly aimed at Britain, without mentioning the country's name, Madison argued that "what we receive from other nations are but luxuries to us, which, if we choose to throw aside. . . . if we are force, in a contest of self-denial." Therefore, the United States could "make her enemies feel the extent of her power." Discrimination would also diversify trade away from Britain: "They would produce, respecting many articles imported, a competition which would enable countries who do not now supply us with those articles, to do it, and would increase the encouragements on such as we can produce within ourselves."[39]

---

38. Jefferson discounted the risk of foreign retaliation: "It is true, we must expect some inconvenience and practice from the establishment of discriminating duties. But in this, as in so many other cases, we are left to choose between two evils. These inconveniences are nothing, when weighed against the loss of wealth and loss of force, which will follow our perseverance in the plan of indiscrimination. When once it shall be perceived that we are either in the system or in the habit of giving equal advantages to those who extinguish our commerce and navigation by duties or prohibitions, as to those who treat both with liberality and justice, liberality and justice will be converted by all, into duties and prohibitions" (*American State Papers, Foreign Relations*, 1: 300ff). See also Peterson (1965).
39. PJM 15: 182ff.

Hamilton worked feverishly in Congress and within the Administration to defeat these proposals and avoid a potential conflict with Britain.[40] Hamilton argued that "The folly is too great to be seriously entertained by the discerning part of those who affect to believe the position—that Great Britain . . . will submit to our demands urged with the face of coercion and preceded by acts of reprisal. . . . it is morally certain that she will not do it." Hamilton mobilized his Congressional allies to speak out strongly against any reciprocity measure that involved discrimination against Britain. Indeed, Hamilton wrote the main speech against Madison's proposals, delivered by William Loughton Smith of South Carolina.[41]

Sensing that he did not have sufficient political support for his proposals, Madison sought to delay any vote by the House. Still, anti-British sentiment was running high in Congress because of attacks on American neutral shipping. In March, Congress imposed a one-month embargo on trade with Britain. In April, Congress considered a proposal to sequester payments to British creditors and to prohibit trade indefinitely. Hamilton wrote to Washington that these actions—stopping debt repayment or enacting an embargo—"cannot but have a malignant influence upon our public and mercantile credit. . . . Every gust that arises in the political sky is the signal for measures tending to destroy [our] ability to pay or to obstruct the course of payment." In particular, an embargo would lead to the "derangement of our revenue and credit." Such a precipitous act would

give a sudden and violent blow to our revenue which cannot easily if at all be repaired from other sources. It will give so great an interruption to commerce as may very possibly interfere with the payment of the duties which have heretofore accrued and bring the Treasury to an absolute stoppage of payment—an event which would cut up credit by the roots.

40. In 1792, Hamilton drafted a reply to Jefferson's impending report, which began by noting: "The commercial system of Great Britain makes no discriminations to the *prejudice* of the UStates as *compared* with other foreign powers" and "There is therefore no ground for a complaint on the part of the UStates that the system of G Britain is particularly *injurious* or *unfriendly* to them" (PAH 13:412).

41. The speech argued that setting up such trade barriers would hurt the United States more than Britain, and that it was completely unrealistic to expect British policy to change as a result of such actions. Hamilton through Smith ridiculed "a Government attempting to aid commerce by throwing it into confusion; by obstructing the most precious channels in which it flows, under the pretense of making it flow more freely." He warned of "the impracticability and Quixotism of an attempt by violence, on the part of this young country, to break through the fetters which the universal policy of nations imposes on their intercourse with each other." "The main argument for the chance of success, is, that our supplies to Great Britain are more important to her than hers to us. But this is a position which our self-love gives more credit to than facts will altogether authorize . . . while a commercial warfare with Great Britain would disturb the course of about one-sixth of her trade, it would disturb the course of more than one-half ours." *Annals of Congress*, January 13, 1794, 196, 203, 202. As Jefferson wrote to Madison, "I am at no loss to ascribe Smith's speech to its true father. Every tittle of it is Hamilton's except the introduction. There is scarcely any thing there which I have not heard from him in our various private tho' official discussions. The very turn of arguments is the same, and others will see as well as myself that the style is Hamilton's" (PTJ 28:49).

Table 3.1   Trade dependence, circa 1792

	United States (%)	Great Britain (%)
Share of exports to other	24	19
Share of imports from other	88	6

Sources: American State Papers, Commerce and Navigation, vol. 1, 194. Mitchell (1988, 494).

Hamilton also responded to Madison's claim that the United States possessed great commercial strength:

> Tis as great an error for a nation to overrate as to underrate itself. . . . Tis our error to overrate ourselves and to underrate Great Britain. We forget how little we can annoy how much we may be annoyed. . . . To precipitate a great conflict of any sort is utterly unsuited to our condition to our strength or to our resources.

Which view was a more accurate appraisal of the situation? In terms of economic leverage, the figures on bilateral trade shown on table 3.1 seem to confirm Hamilton's view. While Britain sent nearly a fifth of its exports to the United States, only six percent of its imports came from the United States. On the other hand, the United States was much more dependent on Britain for its exports and imports. Of course, Madison argued that these percentages were misleading: the United States exported essential food and materials to Britain, whereas it imported trifles from that country. Therefore, he concluded, the United States had much more economic leverage than these shares might indicate. Yet subsequent attempts to coerce British policy through economic means demonstrated that other countries could, in fact, supply Britain with similar goods. When they had the opportunity to give their policies a test from 1807 to 1812, Jefferson and Madison were repeatedly surprised and frustrated by the ineffectiveness of trade sanctions to bring about the desired change in Britain's policy.

In terms of the dependence of U.S. commerce on British shipping, the European war rendered the debate over tonnage discrimination completely moot. The war diverted the British merchant marine into the navy, allowed American ships to take over the carrying trade left in the British wake. As figure 3.3 shows, the British share of the tonnage entering U.S. ports fell sharply after 1792. American ships began to dominate the Atlantic carrying trade, and U.S. commerce experienced a boom in reexport trade (Goldin and Lewis 1980).

Finally, Hamilton's fears about the financial market reaction to these events are borne out by the price of U.S. government debt in New York. Figure 3.4 illustrates Hamilton's remark that "Every gust that arises in the political sky is the signal for measures tending to destroy our ability to pay or to obstruct the course of payment" by showing that the price of U.S.

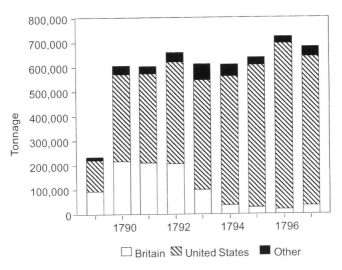

Fig. 3.3   Tonnage of shipping entering U.S. ports, by ship owner, 1789–1797
Source: Senate Document No. 16, 19th Congress, 1st Session, Serial Set Volume 125, January 9, 1826, p. 6.

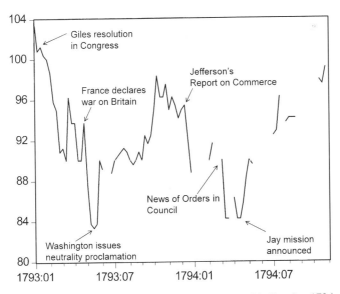

Fig. 3.4   Price of U.S. securities in New York, January 1793–October 1794
Source: Sylla, Wilson, and Wright. US 350, U.S. 6s. National Bond. Available at: http://eh
.net/databases/early-us-securities-prices.

Table 3.2   House of Representatives vote on doubling tonnage duties on British vessels, May 10, 1794

	Yea	Nay
New England	2	19
Mid-Atlantic	3	24
South	19	24
Total	24	55

Source: Annals of Congress, 1794.

government debt in New York appears to have been highly sensitive to political events during 1793 to 1794. The market reacted negatively to Congressional attacks on Hamilton (Giles resolutions), the European war, Jefferson's report on commerce, and reacted positively to Washington's neutrality proclamation and the Jay peace mission.

In the end, Hamilton again won the debate in Congress and within the Washington administration. Hamilton convinced Washington to defuse the immediate crisis by sending John Jay to negotiate a treaty with Britain concerning neutral shipping rights.[42] With the Jay mission underway, Congress easily defeated the proposal to impose discriminatory tonnage duties on Britain. (See table 3.2; Madison's proposal for discrimination was a minority position even among representatives from the South.) The controversial Jay treaty led to one of the most divisive foreign policy debates in American history. Under the terms of the treaty, the United States agreed not to discriminate against Britain in its commercial policy in exchange for a British opening of the West Indies market. After a heated national debate, the Senate endorsed the treaty by the slimmest possible margin.

By putting the issue of discrimination to rest, the Jay treaty completed Hamilton's system. With commercial peace with Britain secure and the reexport trade booming, the government was finally able to begin paying down the debt. While the nominal value of the national debt was little changed over the 1790s, Hamilton did make an effort to pay down the debt after 1794, although this was partly masked by borrowing during the quasi-war with France.[43] However, Hamilton's policy of commercial peace did allow a sharp reduction in the debt to GDP ratio, even if the nominal value of the debt did not decline, as figure 3.5 shows. In his Farewell Address (drafted by Hamil-

42. PAH 18: 451–52. As he left office, Hamilton wrote an analysis of the Jay Treaty for President Washington in which he argued that "the greatest interest of the Country in its external relations is that of peace." Any commercial advantages from particular treaties was much less important. Peace would allow the country to buy time to strengthen. "War at this time would give a serious wound to our growth and prosperity. Can we escape it for ten or twelve years more, we may then meet it without much inquietue and may advance and support with energy and effect any just pretensions to greater commercial advantages than we may enjoy."
43. On Hamilton's financial program, see Garber (1991), Swanson and Trout (1992a, 1992b), and Edling (2007).

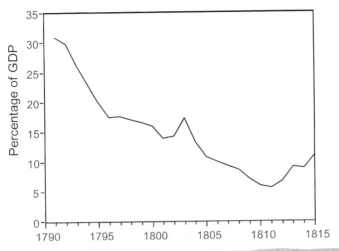

Fig. 3.5   U.S. federal government public debt to nominal GDP ratio, 1791–1815
Sources: Public Debt: U.S. Department of Commerce (1975, Series Y 493). Nominal GDP: Johnston and Williamson (2003).

ton), Washington stated that the public credit was "a very important source of strength and security," which should be used "as sparingly as possible, avoiding occasions of expense by cultivating peace." The Adams administration continued the Federalist policies of neutrality, nondiscrimination, and moderate tariffs until the end of the decade.

3.5   The Jefferson Administration

A detailed discussion of the Jefferson administration's economic policies is beyond the scope of this chapter, but the period gives us a glimpse at the possible consequences of the Republican alternative to Federalist policies.

Thomas Jefferson's election as president in 1800 portended significant changes to Federalist economic policy. Jefferson appointed Albert Gallatin as treasury secretary. Gallatin had written a sharp attack on Hamilton's policies in 1796, arguing that Hamilton's complex financial management lacked transparency and that little effort had been made to retire the debt. Yet once in office, Gallatin and the Republicans made relatively few changes to Hamilton's fiscal system: a functional revenue system was in place, and the Jay Treaty prevented any major changes to trade policy. Over Gallatin's objections, internal taxes were abolished, which left the government completely dependent upon customs duties for fiscal revenues, as figure 3.3 shows. They matched increases in spending with increases in import duties, levying higher rates in 1804 to pay for military action against the Barbary pirates, and began paying down the national debt at an accelerated pace.

After the Jay treaty expired in 1805, however, the Jefferson administration took a much less accommodating stance with respect to Britain. The renegotiation of a successor agreement failed because of the British impressment of American sailors. Without a formal agreement establishing an understanding about neutral shipping rights, the risk of a conflict between the two countries increased. Such an event occurred in June 1807, when the British navy attacked the *U.S.S. Chesapeake.*

Rather than declare war, Jefferson proposed an embargo on all overseas shipping starting in December 1807 to safeguard American merchants and punish Britain for its cavalier treatment of U.S. ships and sailors. This experiment in "peaceable coercion" failed to change Britain's policy, but, in bringing the nation's foreign commerce to a halt, severely disrupted the U.S. economy. The embargo was enormously costly: one estimate suggests that the loss of trade cost the United States about 5 percent of its GDP in that year (Irwin 2005). As the economic pain and political unrest caused by the embargo increased through 1808, pressures mounted for its abolition. Federalists vociferously opposed the embargo as harming the nation's prosperity and debilitating the government's finances, arguing that the measure was futile and would ultimately fail to coerce Britain into changing its policies. Even Jefferson's treasury secretary, Albert Gallatin, thought that it was "entirely groundless" to hope that the embargo would win concessions from Britain. The embargo was lifted in early 1809 and was replaced with selective nonimportation measures.[44]

Although the embargo was a failure, it created surprisingly few fiscal problems for the United States. This is because the disruption to exports was much greater than the disruption to imports. The Jefferson administration allowed American ships that had spent the winter in a European port to return home in the spring of 1808 and unload their cargoes, so imports fell significantly less than exports that year. Still, customs revenues fell off as a result of the embargo and nonimportation, forcing Gallatin to confront a significant budget deficit. Fortunately, as table 3.3 shows, the Treasury could absorb the shortfall by dipping into its cash reserves. Unlike the experience of 1794, the market price of U.S. government debt was virtually unaffected during this period and the government did not need to borrow to finance its expenditures. Yet, the embargo could not have been sustained for much longer without forcing the U.S. government to borrow. In the event, however, the federal government continued paying down the debt, and U.S. credit remained strong until the War of 1812.

---

44. "Despite overwhelming evidence to the contrary," Ben-Atar (1993, 171) argues, Jefferson "continued until the end of his public life, to hold on to an inflated assessment of the strength of the United States and its commerce." In 1794, Hamilton predicted that any embargo would be short-lived because it would fail to affect Britain and the domestic consequences "may occasion the most dangerous dissatisfaction & disorders in the community and may drive the government to a disgraceful retreat—independent of foreign causes" (PAH 16: 275).

Table 3.3   Federal government finances, 1807–1811 (millions of U.S. dollars)

	Receipts	Disbursements	Operating balance	Specie in treasury
				$8.5 (October 1, 1807)
October 1807–September 1808	$17.9	$12.6	+$5.3	$13.8 (October 1, 1808)
October 1808–September 1809	$9.3	$17.3	–$8.0	$5.8 (October 1, 1809)
October 1809–September 1810	$8.7	$11.1	–$2.4	$3.4 (October 1, 1810)

Source: Treasury Reports, American State Papers, Finance.

3.6   Alternative Paths and Roads Not Taken

This chapter has described the economic policy debate concerning trade and revenue policy in the 1790s. This debate was relatively narrow in the sense that there existed a broad consensus that import duties should be the principal source of revenue. There was no debate about whether there should be import duties or whether the public debt should be funded. Given this consensus, there were relatively few policy options that could have taken the country in a different direction. The disputes about the role of excise taxes, and the gains from discriminating against British shipping, were relatively minor in comparison to a decision to repudiate the public debt or rely on inflationary finance.[45]

The most obvious counterfactual to consider is: what if Washington had taken the advice of Jefferson and Madison instead of Hamilton with regard to commercial discrimination? In some sense, the issue was of greater symbolic importance than the underlying economic stakes might suggest. For example, the direct financial price of discriminatory tonnage duties would have been small. In 1791, the Treasury collected $3,171,474 in duties on imported merchandise and only $145,347 on tonnage.[46] Thus, the effect of discrimination on the government's fiscal balance would have been relatively small—in the absence of any British retaliation. Of course, the presumed absence of British retaliation is a key qualification. It is very difficult today to judge the likelihood of Britain's reaction if such a policy had been attempted.

A Republican program of "aggressive reciprocity" might have generated commercial benefits if it succeeded in expanding U.S. access to foreign markets, but it also could have led to counterreprisals. It was clearly a riskier strategy, with the potential to disrupt trade much more than the Federalists' passive approach. Although the fiscal impact of the Jeffersonian embargo was relatively mild because imports continued to arrive in early 1808 and

45. Of course, the country had already experienced the debilitating effects of inflation during the Revolutionary War and did not want to repeat the experience. Bordo and Vegh (2002) contrast the early U.S. experience with that of Argentina.
46. American State Papers, Commerce and Navigation, 140–141.

the Treasury's specie balance could be run down, the government did not have this financial cushion in the early 1790s. Therefore, the financial consequences from disrupted trade would likely have been much greater earlier in the nation's history.

Two other alternative paths also would have changed the course of history. If the Articles of Confederation had been amended to allow Congress to lay duties on imports, the Articles could have been perpetuated as a governing framework because the revenue issue would have been at least partly solved. While solving the government's financial problem, the United States still would have been saddled with a weak governmental framework that would probably have caused greater political problems down the road.

Another path would have been trade protectionism through excessively high duties. The economic costs of such a policy would likely have been smaller than the political threat such a policy would have posed to the union. The United States was not the "united" states yet; the union was still fragile, and many sections would have strongly opposed trade restrictions for infant industries. In later years, such extreme trade policies threatened the nation's unity. During the War of 1812, sentiment in New England ran in favor of breaking away from the Union because the antishipping, antitrade policies of the Jeffersonian Republican dominated the federal government's approach. If the United States could not err too much in terms of antishipping policy without alienating New England, it also risked erring on the side of too much anti-import, pro-protection for manufacturers policy that would have offended the South. One of the most serious antebellum threats to the union was the Nullification Crisis of 1832 to 1833. After the passage of the Tariff of Abominations in 1828, South Carolina vowed not to enforce the federal tariff and even threatened to secede from the union.

Thus, approached without the spirit of compromise, the issue of trade policy had the to potential to tear the country apart. That such extreme measures were avoided in the 1790s helped cement the union of states.

3.7 Conclusion

The Washington administration, blending George Washington's sound judgement and Alexander Hamilton's fiscal acumen, successfully navigated the tricky economic transition from the difficult days under the Articles of Confederation in the 1780s to the new government under the Constitution of 1787. The financial foundation of the new federal government depended on its conduct of trade policy, which at the time was largely revenue policy. By avoiding many pitfalls, at a time when the political union and its finances were exceedingly fragile, the Washington administration helped put the nation on a sound economic basis.

References

Baack, B. 2001. Forging a nation state: The Continental Congress and the financing of the War of American Independence. *Economic History Review* 54 (4): 639–56.

Balinky, A. 1958. *Albert Gallatin: Fiscal theories and policies.* New Brunswick: Rutgers University Press.

Ben-Atar, D. S. 1993. *The origins of Jeffersonian commercial policy and diplomacy.* New York: St. Martin's Press.

Bordo, M. D., and C. A. Vegh. 2002. What if Alexander Hamilton had been Argentinean? A comparison of the early monetary experience of Argentina and the United States. *Journal of Monetary Economics* 49: 459–94.

Boyd, J., ed. 1950. *The papers of Thomas Jefferson.* Princeton, NJ: Princeton University Press.

Brown, R. H. 1993. *Redeeming the republic: Federalists, taxation, and the origins of the Constitution.* Baltimore: Johns Hopkins University Press.

Cooke, J. E. 1975. Tench Coxe, Alexander Hamilton, and the encouragement of American manufactures. *William and Mary Quarterly* 32:369–92.

Dalzell, F. A. B. 1993. *Taxation with representation: Federal revenue in the early republic.* PhD diss. Harvard University, Cambridge, Massachusetts.

Davis, J. L. 1977. *Sectionalism in American politics, 1774–1787.* Madison: University of Wisconsin Press.

Edling, M. M. 2003. *A revolution in favor of government: Origins of the U.S. Constitution and the making of the American state.* New York: Oxford University Press.

———. 2007. "So immense a power in the affairs of war": Alexander Hamilton and the restoration of public credit. *William and Mary Quarterly* 54:287–326.

Edling, M. M. and M. D. Kaplanoff. 2004. Alexander Hamilton's fiscal reform: Transforming the structure of taxation in the early republic. *William and Mary Quarterly* 61:713–44.

Farrand, M. 1911. *Records of the Federal convention of 1787.* New Haven: Yale University Press.

Ferguson, E. J. 1961. *The power of the purse: A history of American public finance, 1776–1790.* Chapel Hill: University of North Carolina Press.

Finkelman, P. 1987. Slavery and the Constitutional Convention: Making a covenant with death. In *Beyond confederation: Origins of the Constitution and American national identity,* ed. R. Beeman, S. Botein, and E. C. Carter II, 188–225. Chapel Hill: University of North Carolina Press.

Garber, P. M. 1991. Alexander Hamilton's market-based debt reduction plan. *Carnegie-Rochester Conference Series on Public Policy* 35:79–104.

Goldin, C., and F. D. Lewis. 1980. The role of exports in American economic growth during the Napoleonic Wars, 1793–1807. *Explorations in Economic History* 17: 6–25.

Goldstone, L. 2005. *Dark bargain: Slavery, profits, and the struggle for the Constitution.* New York: Walker & Co.

Hutchinson, W. T., and W. M. E. Rachal, eds. 1962. *The papers of James Madison.* Chicago: University of Chicago Press.

Irwin, D. A. 2003. New estimates of the average tariff of the United States, 1790–1820. *Journal of Economic History* 63:506–13.

———. 2004. The aftermath of Hamilton's report on manufactures. *Journal of Economic History* 64:800–21.

———. 2005. The welfare costs of Autarky: Evidence from the Jeffersonian embargo, 1807–1809. *Review of International Economics* 13:631–45.

120   Douglas A. Irwin

Johnston, L., and S. H. Williamson. 2003. The annual real and nominal GDP for the United States, 1789–Present. Economic History Services. Available at: http://www.eh.net/hmit/gdp/.

Marks, F. W. 1973. *Independence on trial: Foreign affairs and the making of the Constitution.* Baton Rouge: Louisiana State University Press.

McCoy, D. R. 1974. Republicanism and American foreign policy: James Madison and the political economy of commercial discrimination, 1789–1794. *William and Mary Quarterly* 31:633–46.

———. 1980. *The elusive republic: Political economy in Jeffersonian America.* Chapel Hill: University of North Carolina Press.

Mitchell, B. R. 1988. *British historical statistics.* New York: Cambridge University Press.

Nelson, J. R., Jr. 1979. Alexander Hamilton and American manufacturing: A reexamination. *Journal of American History* 65:971–95.

Peskin, L. A. 2003. *Manufacturing revolution: The intellectual origins of early American industry.* Baltimore: Johns Hopkins University Press.

Peterson, M. D. 1965. Thomas Jefferson and commercial policy, 1783–1793. *William and Mary Quarterly* 22:584–610.

Riley, J. C. 1978. Foreign credit and fiscal stability: Dutch investment in the United States, 1781–1794. *Journal of American History* 65:654–78.

Schwartz, M. 2007. The great divergence reconsidered: Hamilton, Madison, and U.S.-British relations, 1783–89. *Journal of the Early Republic* 27:403–36.

Shepherd, J. F. 1993. State tariff policies in the era of confederation. Presented at Western Economic Association, Lake Tahoe, Nevada. Unpublished Manuscript.

Shepherd, J. F., and G. M. Walton. 1976. Economic change after the American Revolution: Pre- and post-war comparisons of maritime shipping and trade. *Explorations in Economic History* 12:397–422.

Swanson, D. F., and A. P. Trout. 1992a. Alexander Hamilton's hidden sinking fund. *William and Mary Quarterly* 49:108–16.

———. 1992b. Alexander Hamilton, conversion, and debt reduction. *Explorations in Economic History* 29:417–29.

Sylla, R., J. Wilson, and R. E. Wright. Early U.S. securities prices, 1790–1860. Available at: http://eh.net/databases/early-us-securities-prices.

Syrett, H. C., ed. 1961. *The papers of Alexander Hamilton.* New York: Columbia University Press.

U.S. Department of Commerce, Bureau of Economic Analysis. 1975. *Historical statistics of the United States, bicentennial edition.* Washington, DC: Government Printing Office.

4

Monetary Policy and the Dollar

Peter L. Rousseau

Twenty-first century Americans take for granted that a dollar is worth a dollar, meaning that a given Federal Reserve note at a point in time carries a fixed purchasing power regardless of who tenders it or where it is tendered. And though one may rightfully say that prices of goods with identical physical characteristics can and do differ across localities, and that a dollar may therefore not purchase the same quantities of goods everywhere, an apple in New York is a distinct economic good from an apple in Cleveland. This again just means that a dollar is worth a dollar with no questions asked of its holder.

When the United States adopted the dollar as a common currency shortly after the ratification of the Federal Constitution in 1788, it represented the birth of the monetary system that for the most part continues to the present day—a system that eventually led to the dollar's universal acceptance and rise to its position as the world's leading currency. With it came a central bank, a mint, the start of modern banking operations and securities markets, and a newly found confidence among investors in the ability of the young nation to service its financial obligations. The new system and its specie standard represented a marked improvement over the fiat paper money systems that had operated in the British North American colonies prior to their independence in 1776, and an enormous improvement over the rapidly deteriorating monetary conditions that existed during the during the Revolutionary War (1776–1781) and under the Articles of Confederation (1781–1788).

Peter L. Rousseau is professor of economics at Vanderbilt University and a research associate of the National Bureau of Economic Research.

The author thanks Michael Bordo, Doug Irwin, Richard Sylla, two anonymous reviewers, and conference participants for helpful comments and suggestions.

During the war, unbacked paper money issued by the Continental Congress gave way to an inflationary spiral, debt depreciation, and a scarcity of real money balances. Later issues of paper money by individual states in the 1780s fared somewhat better, but in most cases were also unable to retain their value. The need to unify the currency and to restore public confidence in it through adoption of a specie standard must have weighed heavily in the minds of the Founding Fathers as they drafted a constitution that forbade emissions of paper money by individual states.

These men probably based the decision on their more recent experiences with the Continental (Hammond 1957, 95) and with state currencies in the 1780s, yet the experiments with fiat paper monies conducted in the colonies in the eight decades prior to Independence can hardly be considered a woeful failure. At the same time, the colonial monetary systems were vastly different from the one now used in the United States. While the colonists did indeed exchange "pounds" for goods in many of their transactions, they were not the British pound sterling. Rather, individual colonies issued their own "pounds," each with markedly different and frequently varying relative valuations from one another and against the British pound. These variations generated uncertainty as to what the local currency might be worth at any point in time, present or future. And though these local "pounds" were usually employed as the unit of account in each colony, meaning that prices of all goods were generally set in terms of them, a wide range of exchange media might be accepted in actual payment for goods including, but not limited to, a colony's own paper pounds, those of other colonies, and various foreign coins that traded at varying rates against the local "pound."

Often money did not change hands at all. Rather, those desiring goods received credit from a shopkeeper, who would then record a debt for the local currency value of the goods extended. Repayment might then occur in goods acceptable to the merchant and in a quantity that would erase the debt, or in any of the monetary forms described above. Sometimes transactions occurred by simple barter between two individuals, such as a two bushels of wheat for eight hours of work on the farm.

Given these conditions, it would seem that the colonists could have benefited from standardizing at least their paper currencies, if not their coins as well. Article 1, Section 8 of the Constitution speaks to this issue by granting Congress the exclusive right to "coin money [and] regulate the value thereof." This, in combination with the clause in Article 1, Section 10 that "No state shall emit bills of credit," in effect turned the United States into a common currency area. But the fact remains that the colonial arrangements worked reasonably well most of the time, especially in light of restrictive policies imposed by the mother country. It was only when the supply of paper money increased to great excess that bouts of hyperinflation and depreciation would destroy wealth and lead to public consternation. Because these events were relatively rare, it is not immediately obvious that the Founding

Fathers should have preferred the ban on state currencies that eventually made its way into the federal Constitution.

In this chapter I develop the argument that, though perhaps not an obvious decision at the time, the ban on state-issued currencies was in retrospect a very good idea. This is because the transition to the dollar and all that came with it succeeded in *monetizing* the modern sector of the U.S. economy, a feat that was not possible in an era when colonial legislatures were unable to commit credibly to controlling currency emissions. And though the rapid spread of banks and banking that followed may not have been anticipated by all who debated Article 1, Section 8, its later interpretation led to a beneficial privatization of the money creation process that linked money more closely to the provision of credit. In making the case, I will describe how the monetary systems of the colonial and confederation periods operated, and compare these systems with those put in place early in the nation's Federal period and under today's more familiar Federal Reserve. Some aspects of these systems, including how colonial paper monies managed to retain their value, are ones of current academic discussion. In these instances, I review the alternative viewpoints in the course of synthesizing an overall view of how the monetary systems in America worked before and after the transition to the dollar.

4.1   The Economics of a Currency Union

The property that a U.S. dollar is worth a dollar regardless of its holder, or in other words, that the states today operate as a single currency area within a monetary union, has its advantages. Consider the alternative of a loosely connected group of territories, as were the colonies, with each operating under its own monetary standard. In such a world, an agent buying goods outside of his or her area would first need to exchange that area's money with a currency that was valid in the area where the purchase would occur. Either that, or the purchaser's currency would likely be accepted at a lower value than it could command in its own area. The discount would be taken because transporting the "foreign" currency back to the location where it could ultimately be redeemed involved costs, and because of uncertainty regarding how much the currency would be worth upon its return. These "deadweight" losses, as economists call them, have to fall somewhere, and often upon the consumer. Today, such a system of separate currency areas within a single nation would likely be rejected as inefficient and trade inhibiting, and replaced with a system based on a common currency. Even in the case of connected yet distinct nations seeking greater adhesion, such as the European Union, separate currencies and exchange rates across them often give way to a common currency, as has occurred with the euro.

One consequence of operating under a common currency is some loss in the ability of individual areas within the union to control the amount of money available to their citizens, and therefore to control the general level of prices in any particular area. For example, prior to the establishment of the euro zone, if, say, the Bank of France believed that putting more francs (i.e., the former French currency) into circulation would keep prices stable in the midst of heightened economic activity, the central bank could buy a bond from the government, printing francs to do so, and the government could then use these francs to pay for some form of consumption or investment. If there were enough of the government's bonds already outstanding, the Bank could, of course, also accomplish this by buying some of these bonds back from the public.

If, on the other hand, the monetary authority believed that stabilizing the franc's external value with respect to other currencies was a higher priority than stabilizing prices within France, it might instead create money only if it found the franc appreciating excessively against other currencies. Though achieving both internal price stability and a fixed exchange rate with another currency is generally not possible in economic theory and in practice, the fact remains that under a national currency individual governments and their central banks have some degree of autonomy in deciding which of their policy goals are the most important to pursue.

Now consider a common currency, say the euro. Continuing the example, if economic activity were to increase in France, there would be downward pressure on French prices as the same euros would now have to suffice for purchasing a larger quantity of goods. The downward price pressure would draw euros from other members of the European Union into France as they sought to purchase cheaper goods, but it might take some time for prices to return to their original level. In the meantime, if economic activity were to remain stable outside of France, the draw of euros into France would decrease the money supply elsewhere, lowering prices in other parts of the union. In this case, the European Central Bank (the monetary authority of the euro zone) might attempt to stabilize prices by anticipating how much money the zone would need to absorb the heightened activity in France and inject a commensurate amount of reserves. But the injection might impact prices in some member countries more than others, meaning that the monetary policy action could disadvantage some. The inability to execute independent monetary policies may be somewhat offset by independent fiscal policies, but members of most currency areas usually agree to limit their scope.

At the same time, a common currency allows a monetary authority to keep the money supply of the currency zone on some predetermined long-run path, thereby controlling inflation and maintaining the strength of the common monetary unit. A common currency also often goes hand in hand with an integrated banking system and financial markets that reduce redundancies and improve the efficiency with which financial transactions take place. All of this can lead to better synchronization of business cycles across member countries, counteracting their loss of monetary independence. Uncertainties about exchange rate fluctuations within the zone between times of contracting for goods and paying for them are also eliminated, and could well increase trade among the member countries. For example, Rose (2000) estimates that the volume of trade within currency unions is three times greater than the members would conduct in the absence of a union. Though this effect seems too large, most economists would agree that the increases in trade are considerable. Finally, a common currency may render its members better insulated from speculative attacks and the financial crises that can often follow in small countries with inadequate reserves. Of course, if the currency of a large region such as the euro zone were to come under a successful attack the damages would be catastrophic.

As timely as the issues surrounding the establishment of a monetary union may seem in today's financial climate, it may come as a surprise to some readers that the United States came to grips with many of the same issues more than two centuries ago in the years that followed the 1788 adoption of the federal Constitution. At that time the nation officially made the transition from a loose confederation operating under a system of multiple state-issued fiat currencies to a nation in which transactions were unified under a single unit of account.[1]

The coordination problems associated with the lack of a monetary union were quite serious in the colonies. Currencies of distant colonies did not pass in hand-to-hand transactions at their stated values, but rather for considerably less. Currencies of nearby colonies, such as those within New England, however, were often accepted at their stated values. Though the latter arrangement may have some features of a monetary union, it was nonetheless problematic in that there was no central authority to control the total supply of paper currency in the region.

Figure 4.1 shows the course of the per capita supply of paper money in the New England colonies from 1720 through 1751, with all local pounds converted into sterling equivalents to facilitate direct comparisons. This was done by dividing the amount of outstanding paper money by the total population of each colony, and multiplying the result by average annual sterling exchange rates for Massachusetts.[2] In this case, with specie (i.e., gold and silver coins) effectively driven from the New England area by 1723, paper money represented the entire money stock for most of the period in the figure (Brock 1975).

1. Rolnick, Smith, and Weber (1993) contend that the colonies operated under flexible exchange rates and that the desire to eliminate them was the main reason why the U.S. Constitution forbade state currency emissions.

2. The quantities of outstanding bills of credit for the New England colonies are from Brock (1992, table 1). Colonial populations are from U.S. Bureau of the Census (1975, 1168, series Z-3, Z-6, Z-7, Z-11) and use constant growth rates to interpolate between decadal benchmarks. Sterling exchange rates are annual averages of local pounds per one hundred pounds sterling from McCusker (1978, table 3.1, 138–45).

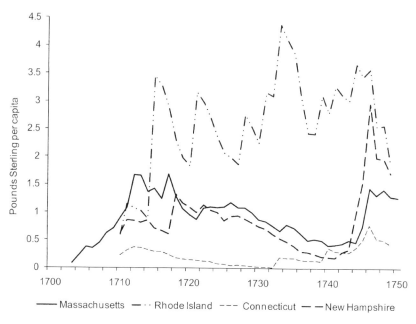

Fig. 4.1   Bills of credit per capita, New England colonies 1703–1749

A few observations can be made at this point. First, the per capita stock of paper money declined in Massachusetts, New Hampshire, and Connecticut through the 1720s and 1730s. By 1740 it had fallen to less than £0.5 sterling in all three. Second, the behavior of Rhode Island's money stock was much different, following an upward trend from 1710 through 1747. Apparently the legislature of this small state, with a population of 25,000, one-sixth that of Massachusetts, had discovered that it could issue paper money that would depreciate only to the extent that it undermined confidence in the money stock of the entire *region*. This in effect allowed Rhode Island to levy taxes indirectly on its neighbors. The issues can be considered taxes because they could be used to purchase goods outside of Rhode Island, thereby increasing the usable money supply of the neighboring colonies and leading to inflation. (After all, inflation is just a way of taxing those who hold money by eroding its value.) Finally, when the New England colonies all began to emit larger quantities after 1745 to pay for King George's War, the ensuing expansion of the region's money supply led to a rapid inflation.

Recognizing its difficulties in managing paper money, Massachusetts reformed its currency between 1749 and 1754, at first using most of a parliamentary grant of £183,650 that was belated compensation for expenditures made by the colony during King George's War to purchase silver (and some copper) to retire its paper money. After that, Massachusetts issued only "treasurer's certificates," which bore interest and were redeemable on demand in silver. This effectively placed Massachusetts on a specie standard for the remainder of the colonial period (Brock 1975, 244–56).

Rhode Island's ability to exploit the system of currency finance underscores an important disadvantage of monetary independence in a tightly wound regional economy—the domestic value of one currency becomes dependent on actions taken by other members of the "union." The forbidding of state bills of credit, formation of a central bank, and growth of the banking system after 1790 can be viewed as actions to reduce the possibility of these problems arising.

This is not to say that the young United States decisively tackled the problems of monetary control within a currency union either, but by settling upon the dollar as the monetary standard it certainly made progress in that direction. Indeed, most of the discussion at the Constitutional Convention of 1787 indicates that the inherent instability of multiple issues of paper money was the main justification for establishing the currency union even though many colonies, unlike Rhode Island, managed their currency issues responsibly. It was not until the ratification process was under way in 1788 that the father of the Constitution, James Madison, proposed a more modern argument in Federalist Paper no. 44, stating that "Had every State a right to regulate the value of its coin, there might be as many different currencies as States, and thus the intercourse among them would be impeded" (Madison 2009, 228). It is not clear why the advantage of expanded trade within the union was not explicitly stated earlier.

Much of the credit for crafting the U.S. financial system is appropriate to bestow upon the nation's first secretary of the treasury, Alexander Hamilton. By establishing a federal mint in 1792, Hamilton brought order under a bimetallic standard to the collection of foreign coins and various local currencies that had previously comprised the nation's money stock, and formally introduced the dollar as the common unit of account. Hamilton also succeeded in building legislative support for the charter of a national bank, the First Bank of the United States. And though its charter was not renewed in 1811 for political reasons, the functions performed by the First Bank as the federal government's fiscal agent helped to demonstrate the advantages of a common currency with centralized control over the government's deposits and disbursements. For one, the Bank made it easier for the government to deposit revenues in certain regions and disburse them in entirely different ones. The Second Bank of the United States, formed in 1816 and surviving until 1836, continued along the path set by the First Bank, and with a much expanded capitalization, was able to further the monetary and financial integration of the nation.

Interestingly, there is little evidence that banks or banking were discussed at the Constitutional Convention. The delegates were certainly aware of banks, bank notes, and their monetary uses, however, given that the Bank of North America in Philadelphia had been chartered by Congress in 1781.

Hammond (1957, 105) suggests that banks were not included in the Constitution or openly discussed at the Convention because the "subject was too touchy," with many delegates favoring their creation while the populace generally did not. Bank notes did not seem to be of great concern either, as they were considered to be surrogates for money rather than money itself due to their ready convertibility to specie. Thus, bank notes, unlike state-issued fiat paper money, could be interpreted as consistent with Article 1, Section 10, which prohibited the states from making "anything but gold and silver coin a tender in payment of debts." At the same time, even though the Constitution did not explicitly authorize Congress to charter corporations, the omission was interpreted by Hamilton shortly thereafter as implicitly permitting it, which led to the active chartering of commercial banks.

Whether initially a "touchy" issue or not, the banking system would grow rapidly over the early Federal period. While only three banks were chartered in the 1780s, twenty-eight new banks obtained state charters in the 1790s and another seventy-three were chartered in the decade that followed (Van Fenstermaker 1965a, 13). The profitability of these early banks, for which annual dividends of more than 8 percent were common, sparked a rapid expansion in their number that reached a high-water mark of 834 state banks by 1840. Then, after a brief decline during the depression of the early 1840s, by 1860 the number of state banks nearly doubled again. Figure 4.2 shows

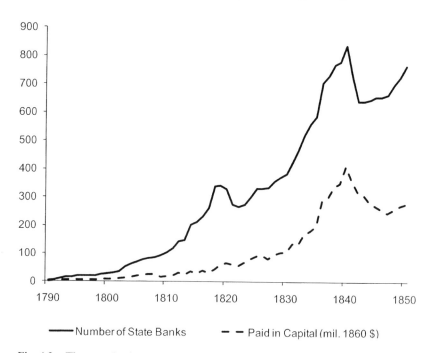

Fig. 4.2   The growth of state banks, 1790–1850

this evolution along with estimates of paid-in banking capital.[3] Like the rise in number, the increase in capital (in 1860$) from $3 million in 1790 to $426 million by 1840 reflects the growing role of banks in mobilizing resources and in providing credit and other financial services.

The most substantive change, however, was the transfer of much of the control over the money supply from the public to the private sector. Rather than a system in which government officials and politicians controlled the issuance and redemption of paper—functions that placed them at the center of a credit allocation process aimed largely at the agricultural sector—banks were able to amass private capital and issue notes that could promote invest-ment and foreign trade by seeking the highest returns.

By issuing notes, I mean that individual banks could now print their own paper money, redeemable into specie on demand at the bank's counter, and allow these notes to circulate among the public over the time between issu-ance and redemption. At first this may seem to represent little improvement over the colonial system, where at least there were legislators and the crown to keep track of the quantities issued, but over-issuance of demand notes by banks turned out to be the exception rather than the rule. One reason for this was that most banks feared large and unpredictable presentations of paper at their counters for immediate redemption in specie, and practiced some restraint in issuing notes for this reason. Another reason was that a loss in a bank's reputation could lead to difficulties in raising capital. At the same time, many banks were known to have over-issued notes, and especially in the 1830s. Yet the central bank, at the times when one existed, could and did impose some discipline on over-issuing banks by accumulating notes of such banks and then presenting them all at once to the issuer for redemption. In other words, excessive note issues by a large number of soon-to-be-insolvent banks in one region could disrupt the economy generally if they undermined confidence in other banks, but the excesses of a single issuer (i.e., in this case a single bank), unlike that of an entire colony, were unlikely to disrupt the entire financial system.

At the same time, it can be fairly said that bank money in the early United States was not homogeneous in that its value did depend on the ability of the issuing bank to make good on the promise to redeem its own notes on demand and in specie. Uncertainty about the strength of these prom-ises and the costs of verifying them did cause bank notes to pass at dis-counts away from their points of issue (Gorton 1996), and the use of notes

3. Total paid-in capital for state banks was constructed by extending backward the series for 1837 to 1850 that appears in U.S. Bureau of the Census (1975, series X587). This was done by multiplying the paid-in capital of reporting state banks in each year from 1803 to 1837 by the ratio of the total number of state banks to the number of reporting ones (Van Fenstermaker 1965a, 66–8; 1965b, 406), and joining the result to the Census series. I then used percentage changes in the authorized capital of all state banks from 1790 to 1802 (Van Fenstermaker 1965a, 13) to approximate the series through 1790, and converted to 1860 dollars using the consumer price index from David and Solar (1977, 16).

of closed banks and counterfeiting did occur (Mihm 2007). But in the end a note was always tethered to its place of issue by the redemption option and would eventually return there, limiting the extent to which excessive issues could disrupt prices in nearby states. So, even if lacking some features of a full currency union in the modern sense, the early United States had many of such a union's advantages.

4.2   The Challenges of Monetary Control

The currencies of the colonies were essentially fiat monies, meaning that they were deemed an acceptable means of payment by government decree. Given this, one question that often arises is how the colonial bills of credit managed to retain their value as well as they did amidst a wide range of monetary and real economic shocks. Indeed, why would anyone value them at all? One could well ask the same question with regard to today's U.S. currency, which is also a fiat money, yet the "full faith and credit of the U.S. government" means a lot more today than it meant 250 years ago. This is because the Federal Reserve has for some time maintained a commitment to control the quantity of money that is available in the economy, and is equipped with the means for doing so through interactions between the banking sector and the purchases and sales of the government's debt securities.

For example, if the Federal Reserve Bank chooses today to increase the supply of money, perhaps with the objective of achieving some targeted rate of interest, it purchases outstanding government debt securities (i.e., Treasury bills, notes, bonds, or other acceptable paper) from the public and many of the payments go into the sellers' checking accounts where they immediately become reserves for the banking system. Individual banks then create money by lending on the new reserves. Since banks need only maintain a fraction of their deposits as reserves, an additional dollar in reserves in ordinary times supports the creation of many new dollars through the making of loans. For example, with a reserve requirement of 10 percent on deposits, one additional dollar in reserves can be multiplied into ten dollars of new money. This occurs because loans are initiated by creating checking account deposits for the borrowers, and checking deposits are part of the narrowly defined money supply (i.e., M1). An economist would say that the expansion had occurred through a "money multiplier" effect, with the multiplier in this case taking a value of ten.

To contract the money supply, possibly with the objective of making money more scarce and thereby raising interest rates, the Federal Reserve does the opposite, selling treasury securities to the public, reducing the checking balances of those who buy them and draining reserves from the banking system. A so-called "reverse money multiplier" then takes over through which each dollar of lost reserves forces an affected bank to reduce its assets by the multiplier. If, as in the previous example, the reserve requirement is

10 percent and the "multiplier" is therefore ten, each dollar of drained reserves forces the bank to contract deposits by ten dollars, a task that is sometimes accomplished by calling in loans.

When the federal government needs money to finance its expenditures that cannot be acquired through taxes, it instructs the Federal Reserve Bank of New York to conduct an auction that sells bonds to the public on its behalf. If the debt is purchased by domestic entities and the government spends the funds quickly, it generates only a temporary reduction in the money supply. It is temporary because the reserves drained in the sale make their way back into the banking system quickly as the government spends the funds and the recipients deposit them.

If the debt is purchased by foreigners using dollar-denominated balances in banks outside of the United States, the effective money supply would increase because the government would spend the fresh funds and they would end up in individual checking accounts, where they would increase domestic reserves and be subject to the multiplier effect. All else the same, this would place downward pressure on interest rates. To hold interest rates at the target, the Federal Reserve may therefore choose to sell some of its own inventory of securities to offset the expansion coming from foreign sources.

The main point here is that this system of "open market operations," as employed in the United States today, is more or less effective in controlling the main monetary aggregates.

There were no such open market operations to control the money supply in the British North American colonies. To use a modern analogy, increasing the money supply in a colony would have been much like today's federal government forcing the Federal Reserve to purchase its IOU, printing cash to do so, and the Federal Reserve choosing not to offset the resulting increase in the money supply with its own open market sales. The fiscal authority could, however, promise to exchange the cash at some future date for individual tax obligations and to ultimately return these tax payments to the Federal Reserve for shredding. This would extinguish the original IOU and remove the cash from circulation.

If executed according to design, such a system would tax the public only once—in advance through the monetary emission. If the public were to maintain confidence in the government's resolve to redeem and destroy the cash according to a well-defined schedule, this anticipation would dampen inflationary pressures associated with the emission since it would be understood to be temporary. Interestingly, the greatest challenge of monetary control faced by the colonies involved the timely "retrieval" of currency through later taxation.

Of course, the individual colonies did not have central banks, nor any real banks to speak of other than a few small, private ones operating primarily in New England, so colonial legislatures, in conjunction with the crown, had to function as their own central bankers. When a colonial legislature needed money (perhaps to finance skirmishes with its French, Spanish, or Native American neighbors, or to pay its employees or make loans to farmers for land purchases), it authorized itself, usually with the consent of the crown, to print paper money (i.e., write the public an IOU). It would then spend the newly printed "bills of credit," as they were called, increasing the money supply of the colony and imposing an indirect tax on holders of previously issued bills. Inflation would sometimes ensue, the extent of which would depend on the size of the issue, the quantity of gold and silver coins in circulation, the growth of real activity, and most importantly, the credibility of the legislature's plans to redeem the bills.

In the middle colonies such as Pennsylvania and New York, bills of credit were usually issued with specific schedules for redemption in the form of the cancellation of individual tax liabilities. The bills would be burned after collection, thereby reining the money supply back. Some scholars believe that when the public was confident that these operations were being carried out as planned, as they were most of the time in the middle colonies, the bills of credit were in effect "backed"—not necessarily by gold or silver, but by their promised acceptance in payment of future taxes (Smith 1985).[4] Indeed, in a growing economy where it is known that paper money issues will be removed from circulation in a timely manner and the emissions are not excessive, the government's balance sheet may be relatively unaffected and inflationary tendencies dampened (Sargent and Wallace 1981; Sargent and Smith 1987). This is because the paper issues represent a liability for the government that is offset by a receivable, namely future tax receipts.

In other colonies, such as those of New England in the 1740s and South Carolina before 1730, however, the commitment to collect and destroy bills of credit according to schedule was less steadfast than in the middle colonies. After all, defending against neighboring foes was seen as crucial to the survival of the British Empire, so the colonial legislatures met with little resistance from the crown when emitting paper money in amounts sufficient for funding such conflicts. But once the new money was spent, it was hard to commit to accepting it in lieu of taxes. Even if collected, there was a temptation to recycle the bills for new expenditures rather than destroying them. Even outright theft could and did sometimes occur.

Thus, when the need for the new money ceased with the end of military operations, if other sectors of the economy had not grown adequately in the meantime, there was often too much money in circulation to hold prices steady. This was a recipe for inflation, depreciation, and the destruction of wealth. Colonists would first try to exchange the bills for specie in the course of everyday transactions when confidence in them fell, but the bills would quickly depreciate. In this scenario, a speculative attack was avoided only

4. Others disagree, most prominently Michener (1987) and McCallum (1992).

because the colonial legislatures did not attempt to peg the bills to gold or silver, or in other words, did not commit to maintaining fixed exchange rates between bills and specie.

The period of the Revolutionary War and the provisional government under the Articles of Confederation, though ending in military and political triumph for the former colonies, saw further deterioration of monetary control. Calomiris (1988), Perkins (1994), and Michener and Wright (2005), among others, describe how the Continental Congress, a political body that lacked the power to ensure redemption of paper money by levying taxes, authorized their issue anyway to finance the conflict. Given the history of problems that the colonies had faced in redeeming their bills of credit even with the authority to impose taxes, it is in retrospect not surprising that the new paper money depreciated virtually to the point of worthlessness.

The saga of the "continental" currency is a classic example of what economists refer to as the "time inconsistency" problem in monetary policy. The burden of financing the Revolutionary War, which was much greater than experienced during the French and Indian War (1755–1763), called for drastic measures. The former colonists had never experimented with a common currency, and when debt proved difficult to sell domestically, fiat money became a viable option for financing the Revolution. Uncertainty about the size of the new issues and perhaps even misplaced optimism about the terms of their redemption allowed the bills to retain their value long enough to support expenditures in the first year or two. But when the paper depreciated the Continental Congress could not successfully turn to the device a second time. The Continental was officially devalued at 40:1 in 1781, and in the end Hamilton's funding plan of the 1790s provided for redemption of the remaining bills at a ratio of 100:1 (Perkins 1994, 97–8).[5]

The thirteen states also issued their own fiat currencies during and immediately after the War of Independence, and rapid depreciation commenced on many of these as well. By the mid-1780s, seven states had reissued fiat currencies that were backed by future tax collections, but these never managed to circulate at par. Pennsylvania, for example, which is often credited with having among the more stable of these later arrangements, saw the value of its currency depreciate by 20 percent against sterling between November 1780 and June 1785 (Bezanson 1951, 346). At the same time, the federal government was in default on its foreign debts, primarily to the French government and to Dutch investors. The 1780s saw attempts by financial leaders such as Robert Morris and Hamilton to hasten the privatization of the financial system by establishing the nation's first real banks in the commercial centers of Philadelphia and New York (Perkins 1994, esp. ch. 6). Political opposition to these banks was strong, however, and they were

---

5. The popular phrase "not worth a continental" has its origins in experiences with this currency.

at that time unable to serve as much more than a model for the changes that were to come (Sylla 2002; Rousseau and Sylla 2005).

In other words, the ability of the young United States to finance its military efforts in the Revolutionary War does not imply that its monetary policies in this transitional period were optimal or stable. After all, an ability to write-down (and effectively write-off) state and federal obligations at pennies on the dollar can hardly be considered a desirable policy—even among a general population that was reluctantly willing to accept the Continental issues as the taxes that they were. Further, the depreciating currency, in the absence of a banking system or organized and liquid securities markets, was the only domestic financial asset that could function of a store of value. It is clear why savings and capital accumulation were stunted under such conditions.

When the transition to the dollar occurred in the 1790s, an accompanying flurry of activity led to the establishment of a banking system and a central bank that achieved better control over the money supply. This is not to say, however, that a system similar to today's "open market operations" was achieved—this did not occur until the founding of the Federal Reserve Bank in 1914. The main problem was that the First Bank of the United States, with its large-for-the-time capitalization of $10 million, still lacked several features of a modern central bank. For one, it lacked the capital and mandate to act as a lender of last resort and, in effect, guarantee the notes of the banking system in times of crisis. Indeed, an expansion of its own note issues in late 1791 and early 1792 and then a sharp contraction as the Bank lost reserves probably contributed to the first financial panic of the Federal period in March and April of 1792. In the end it was Secretary Hamilton who arrested the panic by using Federal monies to purchase bonds and inject liquidity into the New York market (Sylla, Wright, and Cowen 2009). In addition, the First Bank lacked the span-of-control required to fine-tune the aggregate money supply in an era when banks were not bound by reserve requirements.

At the same time, the Bank was able to set an important example of how to handle note issue responsibly, and a decentralized system of individual banks soon followed the lead and issued their own demand notes backed by gold and silver coins. The backing of the paper money supply with specie increased the confidence of foreign investors in the commitment of the United States to make scheduled payments of interest on its public debts in hard money, encouraging capital flows to the young nation.

From that point until 1914, the quality of the money supply in the United States was based upon the acceptability of bank notes. Even though banks in most states operated without any form of reserve requirements until the 1860s, state banks realized that they would be out of business quickly if they allowed specie balances in their vaults to get too low. Financial panics remained an important part of the antebellum economic landscape, with notable ones occurring in 1814, 1819, 1837, 1839, and 1857, but it is worth noting that hyperinflations such as those experienced by the colonies and the provisional government became a thing of the past in the United States. At the same time, banks were able to expand note issues as the needs of commerce increased, and while contracting the supply of bank notes was still more difficult than expanding it, the money supply saw greater elasticity in the fifty years following the Constitution than it ever did beforehand (Rousseau 2006).[6] Transferring control of the money supply to a series of quasi-public and private banks was at the time the right decision, and establishing a specie standard was an important intermediate step that would set the stage for the fiat system that would evolve in the latter half of the twentieth century.

4.3   Backing of Paper Currencies and the Potential for Economic Growth

Thus far, I have proceeded under the premise that the acceptability of the paper money issued by the colonies for the cancellation of future tax liabilities was among the features that gave real economic value to these emissions. Put another way, it was the credibility of the government's promise that the bills would someday be usable at their nominal values to pay an unavoidable debt that limited the extent to which the bills could depreciate before that date. This form of "backing" was quite different from the system that existed after the adoption of the Constitution in which it was public confidence in the readiness of convertibility to specie that rendered a bank note as good as specie or better, at least in the vicinity of the issuing bank.

One of the fundamental tenets of monetary economics is that the relationship between money, output, and prices can be described, to a first approximation, by a simple identity commonly known as the "quantity theory of money." In its most basic form, the quantity theory posits the following "equation of exchange":

(1) $$MV = PY$$

where M is the quantity of money in circulation, V is the velocity of money, or the number of times that a typical single dollar is used in transactions over some fixed period of time, P is the general level of prices, and Y is the extent of transactions carried on, often measured by real output or gross domestic product. This expression shows that, assuming Y and V to be fixed in the short term, an increase in the supply of money should be quickly reflected in an increase in the level of prices, or put differently, that money should

6. It can be argued that the bank-based monetary system had a procyclical elasticity, meaning that the money stock could be expanded during booms and contracted as business activity slowed, and that the colonial systems were perhaps better equipped for implementing countercyclical policy. But the impediments that the colonial legislatures faced in contracting money suggest that the practical importance of such potential countercyclicality was small.

depreciate in value. Similarly, a decrease in the money supply should quickly lead to a proportionate decline in prices and increase in the value of money. The quantity theory is of particular interest to scholars of the colonial period because some evidence suggests that the predicted direct and proportionate relationship between money and prices did not always hold at that time. For example, West (1978) estimated the relationship between the quantity of bills of credit in circulation and prices in New York, Pennsylvania, and South Carolina using a standard linear regression model and found no significant correlation between the two, while Smith (1985) obtained similar results for Maryland and the Carolinas. These findings ignited a discussion that has persisted for decades about whether the West-type regressions capture a failure of the quantity theory or simply a failure of the extant data for the colonies to reflect the quantities of interest.

Michener (1987) develops a theoretical model of the colonies in which paper money and specie are substitutes, meaning that emissions of paper drive specie out of circulation and reductions generate offsetting specie inflows, thereby keeping the total money supply (i.e., paper plus specie) on some stable long-run path. If true, failure to find the relationship between money and prices implied by the quantity theory could just reflect the exclusion of specie from the measured money supply. This opens up the possibility that econometric tests would support the quantity theory if only the money supply could be measured accurately. It is also consistent with the view that paper money retained its value in the face of new emissions (i.e., did not have the expected effects on the price level) because offsetting specie outflows would leave the total money supply unaffected. In the latter case, money would depreciate via the quantity theory only after enough bills of credit had been issued to drive all specie out of a colony, and further emissions had begun to increase the total money supply even more. Prior to this, paper money and specie would be exchangeable at some fixed rate. Given the observed lack of correlation between paper money and prices, the theory is most plausible if there was a lot of specie in the colonies most of the time to support the fixed exchange rate.[7] It also requires an ability of colonial legislatures to contract paper money quickly to keep the total supply steady in the face of specie inflows. As stated earlier, the colonies had great difficulties in accomplishing this.

Advocates of the backing theory, such as Smith, interpret the failed correlation between paper money and prices not as one of measurement, but rather as a direct violation of the quantity theory. In this view, specie and paper money are not perfect substitutes, but rather complements much of the time, so that fluctuations in the supply of paper money would indeed

---

7. Michener (1987, 253–6) is careful to note that his model is expository, and that exchange rates were not fixed at all times, as the model requires, and that specie was not always abundant.

closely reflect movements in the total money supply. Under these conditions, the quantity theory fails because the public believes that new emissions of paper money will at some point be removed from circulation, which delivers a smaller impact on current prices than the quantity theory would predict, and possibly no impact at all.

Formally, the backing theory as proposed by Sargent and Wallace (1981) and Sargent and Smith (1987) predicts a zero inflationary response to paper money issues only under technically stringent conditions. In particular, the colonial legislature making the emission must commit to raising future taxes at the same rate as it has increased the supply of money through currency issues, thereby increasing the current demand for currency as an asset, and must maintain confidence in the promise that the bills will be collected later. Another way to think of it is that the government puts the new money into circulation by purchasing physical assets, and the future returns to these assets are passed back to citizens through the later acceptance of the bills for taxes. In this case, the present value of the returns from the assets must equal the value of the new notes in order for the price level to remain undisturbed.

Even if not operated precisely in the noninflationary manner described, the Wallace-Sargent-Smith mechanism would still dampen inflationary pressures in an economy where bills of credit are perceived as tax anticipatory notes. The theory is thus consistent with West's failure to find statistically significant correlations between paper money quantities and prices.

The backing theory does not imply offsetting inflows and outflows of specie as the supply of paper money contracts and expands. It also does not imply fixed exchange rates between paper and coins, but rather exchange rates that fluctuate with the ebbs and flows of paper, specie, and real activity. Further, the system could work in a region where specie was scarce, and would be consistent with the view, supported by much of what was reported in the contemporary press, that the colonies issued paper money because they could not maintain a supply of coins that was large and stable enough to keep prices from fluctuating excessively.

The controversy between the backing and quantity theorists, at the end of the day, hinges on how much specie was in the colonies. Unfortunately, scholars of the period will probably never know the answer to this question with certainty.

An alternative that I have proposed in Rousseau (2007) supports the quantity theory of money while retaining elements of the backing theory, and does not require fixed exchange rates or an abundance of specie in the colonies. Returning to the equation of exchange, I assume velocity (V) to be constant but allow monetized transactions (Y) to vary. In this arrangement, increases in the supply of money could encourage more individuals to use it in transactions because of its greater convenience over barter or bookkeeping entries. Indeed, economies experiencing growth in modern sector activity (i.e., manufacturing, construction, commerce), such as those of the colonies and the young United States, might have found money to be increasingly useful from a development perspective.

If such a mechanism was operating in the colonies, emissions of paper money would direct more transactions through the formal market sector of the economy, with the possible side effect of increasing the amount of activity occurring in the market sector itself, in either case raising Y in the equation of exchange. Thus, increases in M on the left-hand side would be at least partially offset by increases in Y on the right-hand side, requiring long-run prices (P) to move less, or in the case of complete absorption of the new money, not at all.

To work in the colonies, it would have been essential for legislatures to keep the money supply from expanding more rapidly than it could be absorbed in newly monetized transactions. To the extent that the public believed that the new money would be accepted as future tax payments, this would have helped money to retain its value as the public began to use the new bills in a wider range of transactions, and would have allowed for lags between the actual emissions and associated increases in modern sector activity. While fixed exchange rates are not required, exchange rates between specie and paper money could still have remained relatively stable over extended periods provided that the stock of specie was adequate. In other words, since the new paper money could be absorbed in newly monetized activities and ultimately by increases in output, it would serve as a complement to specie and therefore not drive it out of the issuing colony. On the other hand, at times when specie was scarce, the bills of credit would still be backed by future tax collections. In either case, only excessive issues would erode public confidence in the backing and lead to inflation.

It is important to note that the quantity theory holds under the mechanism that I propose, yet the extent to which money could be created in the colonies, despite an excess demand for its services, was limited by the extent to which colonists could be convinced of the colonial legislature's resolve to redeem the notes. This means that the colonial monetary systems could have been growth-promoting, and certainly more so than in a system without paper money, but that the power of this mechanism was limited by the gradual and incremental manner in which it could be utilized. It also suggests that breaking away from the constraints on money creation inherent in the colonial systems, as occurred early in the Federal period, could lead to improved macroeconomic outcomes. Rearranging (1) with V held constant immediately yields

(2) $$Y = F(M/P),$$

a relation in which real activity in the market (i.e., modern) sector is a direct function of real money balances. Rousseau (2007) offers support for finance-led growth of this type for colonial Pennsylvania and the early United States in a set of vector error correction models in which real money balances exert a positive influence on modern real sector activity, with this effect strongest in the early Federal period.[8] The mechanism is most likely to have operated at times when the amount of specie available in the colonies was small, meaning when they were undermonetized. The next section examines the prevalence of this condition.

4.4   Specie Shortages and Undermonetization in Colonial America?

Specie shortages seem to have been common in the colonies during the period preceding the Revolutionary War. Shortages arose because England prohibited exports of specie in the course of commerce from the mother country to the colonies, and prohibited the colonies from minting their own coins. Though the colonists did manage to produce some copper coins on their own in direct disobedience of the crown, the specie base in the colonies consisted mainly of the small quantities of British coins that did make it across the Atlantic to reimburse military expenses and to pay British soldiers stationed there, and other foreign coins. The most common foreign coin, the Spanish silver dollar, or "piece of eight," arrived primarily from the West Indies in the course of international trade with other countries and parts of the globe. Other coins in common circulation included the Spanish gold pistole, and the Portuguese gold Johannes (or "Joe" as it was called by the colonists), and the Portuguese gold moidore. It is very likely that this collection of coins, due to their shortage as well as their minting in denominations too large to be useful in most transactions, was inadequate to support all of the exchange activity for which some form of money would have been desirable.

The scholarly record also suggests that the supply of specie was usually inadequate. For example, Brock (1975, 532) asserts that "in ordinary times, the supply of specie was at best meager and uncertain, and was not infrequently wanting altogether." The second chapter of Bezanson (1951, 10) opens with the claim that between 1770 and 1775 only "a minor amount

---

8. Specifically, assuming velocity constant, I proxy for Y using real exports and demonstrate that long-run (i.e., cointegrating) relationships consistent with a long-run version of the quantity theory of money existed between Y and M/P for Pennsylvania between 1723 and 1774, and for the United States as a nation between 1790 and 1850. These long-run relationships also indicated that Y responded to low-frequency movements in real money balances in both periods, but that these responses occurred more rapidly in the early Federal period than in colonial Pennsylvania. Since Y in the theory represents monetized transactions rather than aggregate output, and such transactions were more prevalent in modern sectors such as shipping and international commerce than in traditional ones, trends and fluctuations in real exports provide the best available combined indicator of the demand for money and the economy's ability to absorb it (Rousseau 2007, 267).

of coin furnished the medium of exchange in domestic trade." Lester (1938, 326) states that "gold and silver coins were a luxury in the colonies." In terms of quantitative estimates, McCusker and Menard (1985) place the share of specie at about 25 percent of the money supply, and Grubb (2004) estimates that specie was used in about 20 percent of market transactions. If these scholars are anywhere close to the mark, money would certainly have been in insufficient supply if limited to specie alone.[9]

If we are to believe, then, that specie was in short supply, it would seem unlikely for the colonial bills of credit to have maintained fixed exchange rates against the British pound sterling. The extant data on exchange rates also indicate that they moved around quite a bit (McCusker 1978), so that if they were indeed fixed, they fluctuated within very wide bands. All of this suggests that the notion of the colonies operating under a version of the quantity theory in which specie need not be abundant, and in which exchange rates need not be fixed, is plausible.

Despite the inefficiencies and crises that many scholars focus upon, the colonial experience with paper money was far from a complete failure. Several colonies were able to control the rate of depreciation of their paper money and to keep it in circulation for decades. And even though the possibility of rapid depreciation made colonists less willing to hold currency as a store of value, it had little effect on their willingness to use it in hand-to-hand transactions. Thus, an actively circulating medium was able to increase wealth generally. At the same time, the negative experiences with currency depreciation that did occur led all colonists to place some positive weight on the possibility that their currency might one day become worthless. This limited the volume of bills that colonial governments could issue.

The more stable experiments with paper money in Pennsylvania, New York, and New Jersey avoided catastrophic depreciations because issues remained manageable. It does not follow from this, however, that these colonies had an optimal monetary arrangement. McKinnon (1973) shows how, in the absence of a well-articulated financial system, money and capital can be complements in a developing economy due to money's role as a conduit for savings. This did not occur in the colonies because of the failure of paper money as a store of value. Rather, these colonies had great difficulty monetizing, at least if measured by the real value of paper money in circulation.

9. This is not to say that there is universal agreement about the amount of specie in the colonies. Using the results of Jones's (1980) study of colonial probate records from 1774, Michener (1987, 528) estimates that about two-thirds of the money supply in New York and Pennsylvania was comprised of specie. Problems with using probate records to estimate the money stock, and most importantly, that such measures represent the specie holdings of wealthy individuals and are thus unrepresentative of the population at large, are described in Smith (1988, 29) and McCusker and Menard (1985, 264–5). Smith (1988) includes a summary of other estimates of the colonial money supplies and the conceptual problems associated with each. Michener (1987, 278–9) discusses inconsistencies in McCusker and Menard's calculation.

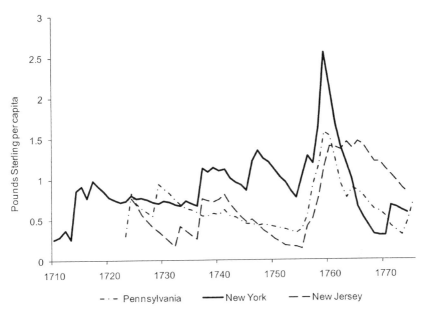

Fig. 4.3   Bills of credit per capita, Mid-Atlantic colonies 1710–1775

Figure 4.3 shows the per capita stock of paper money from 1710 to 1775 in these mid-Atlantic "successes" after converting to sterling equivalents.[10] It may be surprising that Pennsylvania (given by the dotted line in figure 4.3), often touted as the great example of currency finance at its best, saw its per capita stock of paper money fall steadily from 1724 until 1755. It rose from 1755 to 1760 in the midst of the French and Indian War, but then fell rapidly, reaching its lowest point in the pre-Independence period by 1773. In 1750, bills per capita were about £ 0.7 (14 s.) in local Pennsylvania currency or £ 0.4 in sterling equivalent. This amount could purchase, for example, using December prices from Cole (1938, 31–2), one gallon of rum (3 s.), one bushel of wheat (4.5 s.), one bushel of corn (2.5 s.), and two pounds of cot-

10. Bills of credit in circulation for Pennsylvania are from Brock (1992, table 6). For New Jersey they are from Brock (1975, table VI, 93) for 1724 to 1752, and Brock (1992, table 5) for 1753 to 1774. The amount of outstanding bills for New York is available on an annual basis after 1747 from Brock (1992, table 5). For 1709 to 1747 Brock (1975, 66–73) includes records of emissions, anticipated redemptions, and many actual redemptions, as well as a few benchmark estimates of the overall stock of bills. Using this information and linear interpolation for missing years in the time paths of individual issues and their retirements, I approximated the stock of bills for New York. Colonial populations are from U.S. Bureau of the Census (1975, 1168, series Z-9, Z-10, and Z-11) and use constant growth rates to interpolate between decadal observations. Sterling exchange rates are annual averages of local currency per 100 £ sterling from McCusker (1978, table 3.5, 162–7 for New York; table 3.6, 172–3 for New Jersey; and table 3.7, 183–8 for Pennsylvania), with interpolations filling in between occasional missing observations.

ton (2 s.). In other words, the stock of paper money could have supported purchases of staple goods if it had changed hands frequently enough. Yet any savings or other hoarding of coin would have lowered velocity, and the colonists were faced with other cash expenses such as building materials, capital goods, and farm maintenance costs.

A comparison of bills of credit per capita in Pennsylvania with England's per capita money stock further suggests that the colonies were undermonetized. Cameron (1967) estimates England's M2 in 1750 at about 52 million in 1790 sterling. Since England's population was about 6 million in 1750 and the consumer price index (1790 = 1) was 0.779, real money per capita was about £ 6.80—much more than the £ 0.4 sterling equivalent for Pennsylvania. Even allowing for the generous possibility that specie accounted for two-thirds of Pennsylvania's money stock, the per capita money stock (paper money plus specie) could therefore not have exceeded £ 1.20 in sterling equivalent. If specie accounted for about 22.5 percent of the money supply—the average of the estimates from McCusker and Menard (1985) and Grubb (2004)—per capita holdings would be closer to £ 0.52 sterling. It is true that many English citizens could use money as a form of savings more easily than the colonists due to the presence of a still small but rapidly expanding set of country banks, and that their consumption possibilities in the market economy were wider, but it is hard to imagine that these differences would have created anywhere from a six- to thirteen-fold increase in the demand for money.

To make another comparison, fourteen Pennsylvania shillings in 1750 would be worth about $38 U.S. at the end of 2004.[11] This amount of currency would be insufficient for an individual in the United States today to complete weekly purchases without using checks and/or credit cards (i.e., instruments of a modern financial system), even if consumption possibilities were limited to those available to the colonists. Indeed, the U.S. monetary base (currency and coin) now exceeds $2,000 per person, and M1 (currency and checking deposits) exceeds $4,000 per person.

The per capita stock of paper money in New Jersey, given by the dashed line in figure 4.3, was more variable than that of Pennsylvania, but has the same downward trend from 1725 to the start of the French and Indian War. New York, given by the solid line, was more successful in monetizing between 1710 and 1760, but bills of credit per capita were still only £ 1.1 in sterling equivalent by 1750. Figure 4.3 suggests that, given reasonable

11. I obtained this estimate by multiplying £ 0.4 sterling in 1750 by the 6.15 percent total increase in English consumer prices between 1750 and 1900, converting to 1900 U.S. dollars using the exchange rate of $4.87/£, and multiplying the result by the eighteen-fold increase in U.S. prices that occurred between 1900 to 2004. I built a continuous index of English prices using U.S. Bureau of the Census (1975) by ratio-splicing the Schumpeter-Gilboy index for 1750 to 1819 (table 14.1.b, 719–20), with Rousseaux's index for 1820 to 1845 (table 14.3, 722), and the Sauerbeck-Statist index for 1846 to 1900 (table 14.4, 725).

conjectures about velocity of money and the amount of specie likely to have been in circulation, much of the middle colonies' transactions must have occurred outside of the formal monetary system.

4.5   Did Monetary "Founding Choices" Jump-Start the Early U.S. Economy?

The U.S. economy monetized much more rapidly after 1790. Data from Temin (1969) and Rousseau and Sylla (2005) illustrated in figure 4.4 indicate that the per capita money stock grew at an average annual rate of 0.8 percent per year from 1790 to 1850. Growth was even faster from 1790 to 1805—the first fifteen years after Hamilton's plans were enacted—reaching 1.7 percent per year, and rose rapidly after 1830. These estimates probably represent minimum quantities of money in that they do not account for issues by private banks and other undenominated (i.e., unmeasured) moneys, but the latter omission holds for the colonial estimates as well. In any event, as we measure it, with the exception of one year, the per capita stock always exceeded its 1790 level. The mean of the series from 1790 to 1850 is £ 2.1 per person. This is almost 50 percent above the highest level ever achieved in New York before the Revolutionary War, even assuming that specie accounted for 40 percent of the money supply.

At the same time, it is clear that the per capita money stock showed its largest advances after 1830—a time when the Second Bank of the United States lost much of its resolve to control monetary issues of state banks as

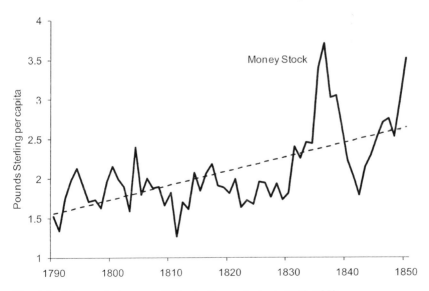

Fig. 4.4   Money stock per capita in sterling equivalents 1790–1850

its charter was allowed to lapse. A few comments seem appropriate here. First, the relative flatness of per capita money from 1790 to 1830 hides how extraordinary the advancement of the total money stock was given the rapid population growth that the nation was experiencing. For example, while per capita money was falling rapidly in the colonies (i.e., 1720–1750), total population was growing at an annual rate of 3.1 percent, just about the same rate achieved over the 1790–1830 period despite the much larger population base of 3.9 million in 1790 compared to 1.2 million in 1750. The fact that the money stock could even keep up with the population from 1790 to 1830 was quite an accomplishment in itself. Second, the acceleration in per capita money from 1830 to 1836 can be attributed to a number of factors unrelated to the demise of the Second Bank, most importantly, a rise in the specie stock that a ready banking system was able to multiply (Temin 1969).

But it was not so much growth in the amount of currency available for transactions that promoted the modernization of the U.S. economy as it was the way in which it grew, in particular, by increasing opportunities for entrepreneurs to obtain private sector credit through the banking system. Rather than having a system in which government officials and politicians controlled the money supply process and the direction of credit, banks were able to amass private capital and issue notes that could promote investment and foreign trade. This shift in emphasis to private sector credit helped to poise the nation for industrialization by 1815, a feat that would have been more difficult had the money supply remained under the control of state legislatures.[12]

Along with rapid monetization and the successful placement of public debt came the emergence of the nation's first securities markets. To the extent that these markets first arose to trade central bank shares and the restructured federal debt, they were also closely linked to founding choices and Hamilton's plan. Figure 4.5 shows the total money stock in 1840 dollars, as well as the number of securities listings from Rousseau and Sylla (2005) that appeared in the financial press of three major cities (New York, Philadelphia, and Boston) near the end of each calendar year. Both series show evidence of a "take-off" around 1815. The average growth rates of both series from 1790 to 1850 were about 4.5 percent per year, which is higher than the 1.9 percent average growth rate of real GDP for 1790 to 1850 reported by Berry (1988), or the 3.8 percent growth rate of the Millennial Edition GDP Series included in Carter et al. (2006), and implies rapid financial deepening.

---

12. Bank loans could grow rapidly though growth in the per capita money supply was modest. This is because, as Lamoreaux (1994) points out, the early U.S. banks had much more capital as a share of total liabilities on their balance sheets than later banks did, probably because these early banks were corporations and could attract large amounts of equity investment. So the connection between loans and money (or bank notes and deposits) was not as great as it would later be when banks were less leveraged. Sylla (2009) reports, for example, that the notes and deposits of New England banks averaged $22.7 million over the decade from 1825 to 1834 while their loans and discounts averaged $53.9 million!

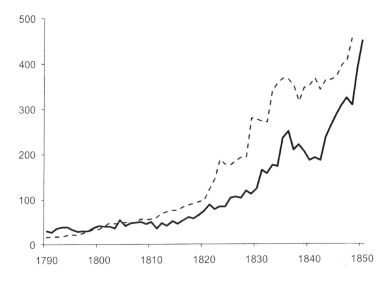

Fig. 4.5   **Monetary and financial aggregates, 1790–1850**

Fortunately, better data are available to measure development of the "modern" sector in the early Federal period than are available for the colonies, at least if we consider private domestic investment and foreign trade as broadly reflective of activity in that sector. Figure 4.6 shows foreign trade (U.S. Bureau of the Census 1975, series U1 and U8, 865–66) and private domestic investment (Berry 1988) for 1790 to 1850 after converting to constant 1840 dollars. These series also indicate an acceleration beginning around 1815, which is consistent with the rise of a modern sector at about this time. The similar rhythm of the financial and real aggregates suggest that the financial system established in the United States during the 1790s was ready to meet the demands of financing real economic activity just as the technologies of the first Industrial Revolution were arriving on the nation's shores.

Rousseau and Sylla (2005) and Rousseau (2006) explore the timing and causal direction of links between the financial and real sectors of the early U.S. economy between 1790 and 1850 with a set of vector autoregressive statistical models. They find strong evidence of unidirectional statistical causality from the money stock and the number of securities listings to the real values of investment and international trade. These results suggest that it was not so much that the financial sector responded to real economic opportunities, but rather that it enabled these opportunities to come to fruition.

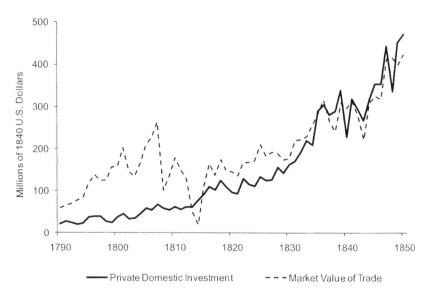

Fig. 4.6   Investment and international trade, 1790–1850

4.6   Conclusion

In this chapter I have advanced the proposition that the transition to the dollar and the move from a fiat to specie standard that came with it was a pivotal moment in the nation's early history. The shift was a marked improvement over the monetary systems of colonial America. The earlier systems were unable to monetize their respective regions due to an inability of colonial legislatures to increase the money supply adequately to support the volume of transactions for which it would have been useful. The legislatures could not do this because they feared the depreciation that would set in if the public's confidence in the backing were to weaken. The possibility of rapid depreciation, which was quite real to the colonists, discouraged them from holding paper money as a store of value and promoted the hoarding of specie when available. Most of the time, however, the colonists simply chose to forego long-term investments that required agglomerations of capital. This could not have been conducive to economic growth.

The federal Constitution of 1787, with its ban of state currency issues, was a positive step in that it established a specie standard and transferred monetary control to Congress by explicitly giving it the power to "coin money and regulate the value thereof." Secretary Hamilton then used an expansive interpretation of this short clause along with a "necessary and proper" clause to get the First Bank of the United States enacted, and then used the Bank as an example to promote more state banks. These actions were important not because the states would have been unable to administer issues of currency, but because the supply of money could then be tied more closely to the capital market and the provision of credit. Of course, this system did not share all of the features of today's monetary system, but the similarities outweigh the differences. In particular, while the central bank now controls a money supply backed only by the faith and credit of the United States, it is still the banks that multiply it through the provision of credit to businesses and households. And, though banks can and do sometimes become overly sanguine in their expectations surrounding the returns from their lending activities, this is not a new phenomenon, with the pattern of occasional setbacks followed by even greater advances repeating time and time again in the nation's history.

With the credit of the United States at an all-time low in the 1780s, the switch to a specie standard was at the time necessary to restore domestic and international confidence in the *system,* and this standard served the country well during the long transition to a point when it was no longer necessary. In this sense, it is no exaggeration to say that as the young United States pushed forward into an era of fiscal and monetary responsibility under a common political and monetary union spearheaded by the transition to the dollar, it embarked upon a financial revolution that shaped the early character of the nation and continues to shape it today.

References

Berry, T. S. 1988. Production and population since 1789: Revised GNP series in constant dollars. Bostwick Paper no. 6. Richmond, VA: Bostwick Press.
Bezanson, A. 1951. *Prices and inflation during the American Revolution: Pennsylvania 1770–1790.* Philadelphia: University of Pennsylvania Press.
Brock, L. V. 1975. *The currency of the American colonies, 1700–1764: A study in colonial finance and imperial relations.* New York: Arno Press.
———. 1992. The colonial currency, prices, and exchange rates. *Essays in history* 34. Available at: http://etext.virginia.edu/journals/EH/EH34/brock34.htm.
Calomiris, C. W. 1988. Institutional failure, monetary scarcity, and the depreciation of the continental. *Journal of Economic History* 48:47–68
Cameron, R. 1967. England, 1750–1844. In *Banking in the early stages of industrialization: A study in comparative economic history,* ed. R. Cameron, O. Crisp, H. T. Patrick, and R. Tilly. New York: Oxford University Press.
Carter, S. B., S. Gartner, M. Haines, A. Olmstead, R. Sutch, and G. Wright. 2006. *Historical statistics of the United States: Millennial edition.* Cambridge: Cambridge University Press.
Cole, A. H. 1938. *Wholesale commodity prices in the United States, 1700–1861: Statistical supplement, actual wholesale prices of various commodities.* Cambridge, MA: Harvard University Press.
David, P. A., and P. Solar. 1977. A bicentenary contribution to the history of the cost of living in the United States. *Research in Economic History* 2:1–80.
Gorton, G. 1996. Reputation formation in early bank note markets. *Journal of Political Economy* 104:346–97.

Grubb, F. 2004. The circulating medium of exchange in colonial Pennsylvania, 1729–1775: New estimates of monetary composition, performance, and economic growth. *Explorations in Economic History* 41:329–60.

Hammond, B. 1957. *Banks and politics in America: From the Revolution to the Civil War.* Princeton, NJ: Princeton University Press.

Jones, A. H. 1980. *Wealth of a nation to be: The American colonies on the eve of the Revolution.* New York: Columbia University Press.

Lamoreaux, N. R. 1994. *Insider lending: Banks, personal connections, and economic development in industrial New England.* New York: Cambridge University Press.

Lester, R. A. 1938. Currency issues to overcome depressions in Pennsylvania, 1723 and 1729. *Journal of Political Economy* 46:324–74.

Madison, J. 2009. The Federalist No. 44: Restrictions on the authority of the several states, New York packet, Friday, January 25, 1788. In *The Federalist papers*, ed. I. Shapiro, 227–33. New Haven, CT: Yale University Press.

McCallum, B. T. 1992. Money and prices in colonial America: A new test of competing theories. *Journal of Political Economy* 100:143–61.

McCusker, J. J. 1978. *Money and exchange in Europe and America, 1600–1775: A handbook.* Chapel Hill, NC: University of North Carolina Press.

McCusker, J. J., and R. R. Menard. 1985. *The economy of British America: 1607–1789.* Chapel Hill, NC: University of North Carolina Press.

McKinnon, R. I. 1973. *Money and capital in economic development.* Washington, DC: Brookings Institution.

Michener, R. 1987. Fixed exchange rates and the quantity theory in colonial America. *Carnegie-Rochester Conference Series on Public Policy* 27:233–307.

Michener, R., and R. E. Wright. 2005. State "currencies" and the transition to the dollar: Clarifying some confusions. *American Economic Review* 95:682–703.

Mihm, S. 2007. *A nation of counterfeiters: Capitalists, con men, and the making of the United States.* Cambridge, MA: Harvard University Press.

Perkins, E. J. 1994. *American public finance and financial services, 1700–1815.* Columbus: Ohio State University Press.

Rolnick, A., B. D. Smith, and W. E. Weber. 1993. In order to form a more perfect monetary union. *Federal Reserve Bank of Minneapolis Quarterly Review* 17:2–13.

Rose, A. K. 2000. One money, one market: The effect of common currencies on trade. *Economic Policy* 15 30: 7–46.

Rousseau, P. L. 2006. A common currency: Early U.S. monetary policy and the transition to the dollar. *Financial History Review* 13:97–122.

———. 2007. Backing, the quantity theory, and the transition to the U.S. dollar, 1723–1850. *American Economic Review* 97 (2): 266–270.

Rousseau, P. L., and R. Sylla. 2005. Emerging financial markets and early U.S. growth. *Explorations in Economic History* 42:1–26.

Sargent, T. J., and B. D. Smith. 1987. Irrelevance of open market operations in some economies with government currency being dominated in rate of return. *American Economic Review* 77:78–92.

Sargent, T. J., and N. Wallace. 1981. Some unpleasant monetarist arithmetic. *Federal Reserve Bank of Minneapolis Quarterly Review* 5:1–17.

Smith, B. D. 1985. Some colonial evidence on two theories of money: Maryland and the Carolinas. *Journal of Political Economy* 93:1178–211.

———. 1988. The relationship between money and prices: Some historical evidence reconsidered. *Federal Reserve Bank of Minneapolis Quarterly Review* 12:18–32.

Sylla, R. 2002. Financial systems and economic modernization. *Journal of Economic History* 62:277–92.

———. 2009. Comparing the UK and U.S. financial systems, 1790–1830. In *The origin and development of financial markets and institutions: From the seventeenth century to the present,* ed. J. Atack and L. Neal, 209–40. New York: Cambridge University Press.

Sylla, R., R. E. Wright, and D. J. Cowen. 2009. Alexander Hamilton, central banker: Crisis management during the U.S. financial panic of 1792. *Business History Review* 83:61–86.

Temin, P. 1969. *The Jacksonian economy.* New York: W. W. Norton and Company.

U.S. Bureau of the Census. 1975. *Historical statistics of the United States: From colonial times to 1970.* Washington, DC: Government Printing Office.

Van Fenstermaker, J. 1965a. *The development of American commercial banking: 1782–1837.* Kent, OH: Kent State University Press.

———. 1965b. The statistics of American commercial banking, 1782–1818. *Journal of Economic History* 25:400–14.

West, R. C. 1978. Money in the colonial American economy. *Economic Inquiry* 16:1–15.

5

Federal and State Commercial Banking Policy in the Federalist Era and Beyond

Howard Bodenhorn

5.1 Introduction

In his study of the development of American law, historian Lawrence Friedman (1993) reminded us that the Bill of Rights applies only to the federal government, not the states. Although the Virginia Declaration of Rights predated the Bill of Rights by thirteen years and provided its philosophical underpinnings, the direction of constitutional influence was from federal to state levels. Many states simply copied the first ten amendments to the federal Constitution when drafting their own. The hypothesis offered here is that the same federal-to-state line of influence is evident in early American banking law and policy. Pennsylvania, Massachusetts, Maryland, and New York chartered banks prior to Congress's charter of the Bank of the United States in 1791. Yet it was the Bank of the United States charter, not that of any of the previously chartered state banks, that served as a model for most subsequent bank charters. The choice to model charters after that of the Bank of the United States rather than those of the early state banks followed from contemporary concerns with political governance, and reflected the outcome of a wider debate about the nature of representative government. In addition, the decision to follow the Bank of the United States model notably influenced how banks were organized, operated, and governed.

Translating federal charters into state law was not seamless, and the debates were charged and rancorous. Although many contemporaries supported

Howard Bodenhorn is professor of economics at Clemson University and a research associate of the National Bureau of Economic Research.

I thank Farley Grubb, Richard Sylla, John Wallis, Eugene White, two anonymous referees, and participants at the NBER Founding Choices Conference for many helpful comments. I also thank Pam Bodenhorn for exceptional research assistance.

banks and finance, many late-eighteenth- and early-nineteenth-century Americans saw banking as something to be entered into with caution, if at all. Henry Clay, an otherwise ardent spokesman for pro-growth internal improvements such as roads, turnpikes, and canals, was less enthusiastic about banks. During Congressional debate in 1811, Henry Clay labeled the Bank of the United States a "splendid association of favoured individuals invested with exemptions and surrounded by immunities and privilege" (Dorfman 1946, 341). Clay's distaste for the bank sprang not just from a western agrarian's conception of banks as promoters of speculation and sharp dealing; rather, his distaste sprang from a more general view of the corporation as an instrument of oppression capable of robbing the country of its hard-won republicanism. Americans had fought a war to rid itself of aristocratic privilege. Corporations smacked of a return to a government sanction of privilege.

Early American firms were shaped by contemporary social conceptions of appropriate horizontal power relations inside the firm, and the Federalist era bank, as a corporation, was shaped by those conceptions (Lamoreaux 1997; Dunlavy 2006). But, the debate was more fundamental than how partners or shareholders would treat with one another. Contemporary Americans who had no direct stake in the business corporation took great interest in its internal governance because rules for how the elite—and make no mistake about it, the elite controlled America's earliest financial corporations—shared power within the corporate body politic spoke to their attitudes toward sharing power in the wider civic polity.

Incorporating a bank or other business enterprise in the Federalist period was contentious because of different beliefs about the nature of governance. Was governance to be plutocratic or democratic? It was within this debate that the first banks were established and this debate influenced how banks were governed, which ultimately influenced how banks did their business. The political debates surrounding the establishment of the Bank of North America (1782) and the Bank of the United States (1791) defined these banks and nearly every bank chartered thereafter up to the mid-1830s and beyond. Specifically, the liberal Bank of North America charter that imposed few meaningful restrictions on the bank's operation, accountability, or governance gave way to the Bank of the United States' more restrictive charter that sharply limited its operations, made it accountable to government, and defined many of its internal governance procedures. And, as all students of American history are aware, concerns with the role of the corporation within the polity, especially the large corporation, remained unresolved through Jackson's war on the second Bank of the United States, into the progressive era trust-busting, beyond the New Deal reforms, and up to the present. Debates over the establishment of the country's earliest banks cast light on the origins of modern concerns. Ultimately, eighteenth-century Americans wrestled with questions of appropriate internal governance, effective transparency, and prudent regulation that remain unresolved into the twenty-first century. This chapter traces four features of the Bank of the United States charter that found their way into many, if not most, state bank charters—charter term limits, partial state ownership, branch banking, and internal voting rules–and how those features influenced banking for the next half-century. Charter term limits and state ownership played havoc with federal and state banking policies because they made banks as much political as economic agents. Branch banking was not widely adopted, but where it was it generally performed fairly well. The advantages of branch banking became most apparent during panics and financial crises as banks and branches could support one another. The adoption of share voting rules that capped the votes of large shareholders encouraged small investors. This choice may have affected the ability of entrepreneurs to raise external capital and, ultimately, the pace of economic growth. Through his influence over the charter of the Bank of the United States, Hamilton's legacy reverberated through the antebellum era and beyond.

5.2 The Bank of North America: The Debate on Corporate Privilege Is Joined

The Bank of North America (BONA) was born of crisis. In the spring of 1781, the English army was moving easily through the South. The currency was depreciated to the point of near collapse, Congress had exhausted its fiscal resources, patriotic fervor had given way to frustration, and American morale sank lower by the day. Facing a grave situation, Congress centralized the army and other administrative departments. It also created the office of the superintendent of finance and appointed Robert Morris to the post. The new superintendent was the second most powerful figure in the reorganized government, second only to George Washington, and was granted almost complete control over fiscal policy (Rappaport 1970).

Morris entered his post with a sweeping vision of fiscal reform (Riesman 1987). Morris' public finance plan featured a bank as its centerpiece, a bank that was to provide assistance during the war and contribute to the country's postwar prosperity.[1] Rappaport (1970, 1996) contended that Morris unveiled his banking plan so quickly after assuming office that he must have contemplated it long before. We know that Hamilton, while still a member of Washington's staff, twice wrote to Morris with bank proposals. But Morris thought Hamilton's schemes too bold, too audacious—one called for a

1. Morris originally believed that the BONA's profits would be sufficient to retire the Congressional debt, and envisioned refunding the debt and financing it through a sinking fund made up of the bank's profits. Riesman (1987, 144) argues that Morris formulated this plan after reading the work of the English Whig Richard Price, who in 1772 formulated a comparable plan for extinguishing Britain's massive debt.

bank of $200 million capital—and proposed a more modest institution. Morris's plan called for a bank with just $400,000 in capital, divided into $400 shares. The difference between Hamilton and Morris on the bank was that Hamilton envisioned a bank as an arm of government that might serve commercial interests; Morris envisioned the bank as an arm of commerce that might serve the government. It did not occur to Morris that the government would own shares, perhaps because the government was effectively bankrupt, and more in need of capital than a supplier of it.

Congress chartered the bank on 31 December 1781, but lingering concerns over whether it actually had the power to do so led it to ask states to enact similar supporting legislation (Lewis 1882). Massachusetts, Rhode Island, Connecticut, New York, New Jersey, and North Carolina all passed enabling legislation. It was not until Morris petitioned the Pennsylvania legislature for a charter that serious concerns were raised. Critics feared the consequences of the original grant's concession of a perpetual charter and its right to amass up to $10 million in assets. The latter was troublesome because it held the potential for the establishment of a "monied aristocracy"; the former was equally troublesome because a perpetual charter placed the institution beyond subsequent legislative control. Neither argument gained traction and the bank received its charter.

Except for the profits earned in its early years, the BONA did not become noteworthy until 1785, when the bank's operations and its charter provoked a larger debate over the meaning of democracy and the corporation's place within it. In September 1785, less than four years after Congress had chartered it, the Pennsylvania Assembly repealed the bank's charter.

What had the bank done to turn the Assembly against it? To many legislators the better question was what hadn't the bank done. Hammond (1957, 53) listed the sundry charges leveled against the bank: it encouraged usury; it refused to lend on long terms to farmers; it refused to lend on mortgage security, again, to farmers; it insisted on punctuality in meeting one's debts to the bank; it allowed foreigners (which included not only Europeans, but individuals from neighboring states) to invest in the bank; and, it demonstrated favoritism toward certain borrowers, mostly shareholders. The bank's real sins, however, were its opposition to the chartering of a rival institution, its opposition to the state's emission of £100,000 in bills of credit, its refusal to accept notes issued by a £50,000 loan office, or land bank and, above all, its adoption of high-pressure lobbying practices against all three otherwise popular (and populist) measures.

Morris was quick to defend his bank and denied that its agents' actions in any way undermined democratic institutions. But his arguments failed to sway many critics because he was also quick to point out that it had been established on the idea that it could lend to whomever it saw fit. Reisman (1987, 148) observed that Morris was blind "to charges that the bank was a monopoly favoring some and not others" and he failed to grasp why others cared so deeply about the larger issues raised by the bank and its practices.

Care they did, and deeply, too. Although the bank's critics provided a laundry list of the bank's transgressions, many of which were fallacious, the legislative committee recommending the annulment of the bank's charter stated "that the accumulation of enormous wealth in the hands of a society who claim perpetual duration, will necessarily produce a degree of influence and power, which cannot be entrusted in the hands of any one sett [*sic*] of men whatsoever, without endangering the public safety" (Carey 1786, 52). Further, the bank, which was envisioned by Congress as an arm of government, was no longer dependent on that government, and thus without an effective check on its operations.[2] Because the bank's president, Thomas Willing, and other officers and supporters, including Morris, failed to take the legislature's annulment threat seriously, few arguments in support of the bank were offered until the matter was all but decided. The breadth of opposition to the bank took its supporters by surprise. The vote to annul was lopsided as legislators from every region of the state, including Philadelphia, voted against the bank. Outside the legislature, criticism came from all quarters. Farmers and mechanics opposed it because it confined its loans to mercantile firms. Mercantile firms on whom the bank did not bestow its favors opposed it for its favoritism.

The ink on the act annulling the charter was barely dry before plans to have the charter restored were put in motion. The election of Robert Morris and two of the bank's other directors to the Assembly, coincident with a mass petitioning campaign asking for reinstatement of the charter guaranteed that the issue would be revisited. Transcripts of the legislative debates offer a window into contemporary attitudes about republican government and whether it could survive economic and financial modernization. The foundational political disagreement centered not on favoritism in lending or the bank's opposition to a state loan office and the emission of bills of credit, but on the internal governance of the bank, which reflected wider concerns with the nature of republican governance writ large. If the corporation was, as Samuel Blodgett insisted, a "moneyed commonwealth" within a commonwealth, a "moneyed republic" within a republic, then the nature of corporate governance reflected on the possibilities and the pitfalls of political governance.[3]

What were the governance features inside the bank that so offended republican sensibilities? Two features of the bank's internal operations—one share-one vote and the absence of any mechanism to ensure the rotation in office for directors—became recurring themes of the debate. Assemblymen

2. The federal government had repaid its large loans to the bank by selling off the interest it took when Morris subscribed to $254,000 in stock on its behalf.
3. Blodgett is quoted in Dorfman (1946, 338).

Lollar and Smilie attacked the one share-one vote rule directly because it concentrated power, a practice that Smilie argued was "highly dangerous" because it would inevitably lead to "direct tyranny" by the large shareholders over the small (Carey 1786, 109). He raised the rhetoric further by drawing an analogy between the bank and the wider polity, asking whether members of the assembly would ever agree to vest power in any similarly small group of men through a voting rule that allocated votes by wealth.[4]

Greater wealth did not establish a basis for multiple votes in the polity, so there was no reason for it to do so within the corporation. Voting power determined by wealth, in fact, was likely to spill over into the polity. William Findlay, skilled debater, western Republican, lover of large beaver hats, and vocal opponent of the bank, provided an alarming vision of proportional voting rules. Liberal corporate charters, like that given the bank, created not little republics but "little aristocracies" that would ultimately "engross all the wealth, power, and influence of the state," and if made large enough would first monopolize land holding, then trade, and finally the government itself (Carey 1786, 66–9).

The failure of the bank's charter or bylaws to establish a system of rotation among the directors also smacked of privilege and aristocracy. It conjured up a vision of aristocrats with permanent, powerful positions. Even more troubling was that it conjured a "vision of placemen and tax gatherers [or, in this case, usurers] swarming the countryside . . . to support wealthy men in high places" (Reisman 1987, 157). Moreover, without established term limits "the bank will remain under the present directors, during their lives, which is a direct tyranny" (Carey 1786, 109).

In his defense of the bank, Robert Morris dismissed Republican concerns as "bugaboo" (Carey 1786, 58). Instead of allaying fears of concentrated power, he celebrated it. It might be true that the directors of the bank remained in office for long periods and were elected by "six or seven men, largely concerned in stock," but how else might it be? Would it be right for those with small numbers of shares to have power equal to those with many? "Voting according to property," Morris asserted, "is the only proper mode of election" (Carey 1786, 117). If the legislature was to tamper with the proportional voting rule inside the corporation, it may as well pass an agrarian law—contemporary code words for radical mass reallocation of land from rich to poor—and divide all property equally. Such would be the tyranny of

---

4. It is ironic that legislators voted into office by the fraction of the potential electorate who met the property requirement for voting spoke against voting rights allocated by wealth. It was the case, of course, that once a man met the property requirement, he received only one vote regardless of how many times over he satisfied the requirement. I thank Eugene White for pointing this out. Harris (2009) reported that it was the charter of the English East Indies company that established the one shareholder-one vote rule. It was only later that the voting rule was altered. The original Bank of England charter also imposed a one shareholder-one vote rule (Redlich 1968). Redlich argued that Americans were aware of the Bank of England rule and purposely adopted an alternative.

the small shareholders over the large and, ultimately, the poor over the rich. So Morris, too, believed the debate over internal corporate governance was about something deeper and more fundamental than corporate governance per se. If corporate governance, as constituted in the BONA charter at least, was a mirror in which to view the potentialities of republican governance generally, Morris liked what he saw inside the bank; his opponents feared it.

The BONA's proponents carried the day. The act repealing the charter was itself repealed, but the legislature imposed several new restrictions on the bank, among them a fourteen-year charter, and stricter limits on the amount and type of assets it might hold, most notably a restriction on land ownership except what was needed to operate the bank. The new charter did not overturn the one share-one vote rule, but under pressure the bank's shareholders adopted a bylaw that established an upper limit on the number of votes a single shareholder could cast.

To modern sensibilities, the late-eighteenth-century debate over the corporation seems a tempest in a teapot. To contemporaries, however, the concern was very real. Historians note contemporary beliefs that republics were inherently fragile. The risks were so great and the prospect of failure so ever present, that the institutions of modernity, including the corporation and all it represented, spelled its eventual but certain doom (Lewis 1993, 117). The modern conception of representative democracy as one in which multiple interest groups vie with one another in shaping policy had not yet revealed itself to late-eighteenth-century politicians, Federalist no. 10 notwithstanding. Most Americans, including those in power or aspiring to it, whether Federalist or Republican, believed in a "unitary, definable public good and common purpose that could be discerned and articulated by virtuous and selfless men" (Sharp 1993, 89). This approach became what later historians labeled the *politics of the absolute,* or the belief that there was a single, definable objective and that dissent emerged not from a legitimate and alternate view of the public good, but from a desire to undermine the republic and subvert the constitution (Elkins and McKitrick 1993).

An appreciation of the political debates of the 1780s matters because only in understanding it can later state banking policies be understood. Although modern political parties had not yet emerged by the time the original thirteen states started chartering banks, the battle lines were already sharply drawn. What would later be labeled "Federalist" or "Republican" found expression in the Pennsylvania debates transcribed by Carey. Moreover, Carey's decision to publish the transcripts put the debate on the national stage and provided the foundational arguments for two or three subsequent generations of banking proponents and critics alike. When Sullivan (1792) attacked the Massachusetts Bank, he expressed many of the same concerns in the same terms as those raised in the BONA debates. Like the revisions to the BONA charter in 1786, the Massachusetts Bank's charter was amended in 1792 in an attempt to place more effective limits on its corporate powers. That same year Massachusetts incorporated the Union Bank, the charter of which can only be read as a legislative attempt to balance the growing demand for commercial banking with democratic principles. Instead of dividing the Union Bank's capital stock into $400 (par) shares, as it had done with the Massachusetts Bank, its $800,000 capital was divided into $8 (par) shares to disperse shareholding as widely as possible. It was an everyman's bank and, therefore, neither as prone to insider favoritism nor as dire a threat to the republic.

5.3   Alexander Hamilton, the Bank of the United States, and Early State Banking Policy

Like Morris a decade earlier, when Hamilton assumed leadership of the Treasury, he was bedeviled by three questions of public finance: How would the government raise revenues? How would the government raise funds in anticipation of future revenues? And how would it transfer funds from the place of collection to the place of disbursement? Hamilton's answers comprised the three pillars of the Federalist financial revolution (Sylla 1998). Hamilton's plan included, among other features, the Bank of the United States (BUS).

Hamilton produced a number of documents in support of his plan, but it was his *Report on the Bank* that is considered groundbreaking (Cowen 2000; Wright and Cowen 2006), and it reveals a cognizance of the 1785 BONA debates. His *Report* did not represent Hamilton's first thinking about a bank. He had previously corresponded with Robert Morris about the desirability of a national bank, and he was the principal author of the Bank of New York's 1784 articles of association (Hammond 1957, Redlich 1968), several features of which found expression in the BUS charter.

Hamilton's plan for the bank began with a discussion of what the bank should not be. First, it should not be a land or mortgage bank. It was important that the national bank be a specie-based commercial bank that could realize and liquidate its assets promptly. Second, it should not be a wholly state-owned bank. Hamilton understood the importance of private interest and believed that the profit motive should guide its operations. Nevertheless, it was imperative that the government was a part owner so that it could receive dividends and exercise some direction or management. Third, the bank should not be without supervision. A vital element of Hamilton's plan was that some officer of the state, preferably the treasury secretary, should retain the right to conduct inquiries and inspect its books (Clarke and Hall 1832, 30).

The features of the 1791 BUS charter are provided in table 5.1, and can be usefully divided into *general* provisions, *regulations*, and *governance* rules. The general provisions include features such as the capitalization and share value described in Section 1, how, when, and where the shares would be

Table 5.1	Features of Bank of the United States charter originally proposed by Hamilton and adopted by Congress
Charter section	Provisions of the Bank of the United States charter (1791)
1	$10 million capital in $400 shares.
2	Individual subscriptions limited to 1,000 shares. Shares payable–1/4 in specie, 3/4 in 6% federal bonds–in four installments.
3	Bank granted corporate powers for 20 years and may hold up to $15 million in real and personal property.
4	Bank governed by 25 directors subject to annual reelection. President to be chosen from among the elected directors.
5	Bank may commence as soon as $400,000 in capital is paid in.
6	Directors have power to appoint managers and determine managerial compensation.
7.1	Prudent mean voting rule for shareholders. Only shareholders resident in United States could vote by proxy.
7.2	Only 3/4 of existing directors eligible for reelection.
7.3	Directors must be shareholders.
7.4	Directors will not be paid for services unless specifically approved by shareholders.
7.5	Board quorum is 7 directors.
7.6	Any 60 stockholders with a combined 200 shares could call a special meeting of stockholders.
7.7	Officers required to post performance bonds.
7.8	Bank may only own so much land as required for the conduct of business or that surrendered in judgment.
7.9	Bank's debts (banknotes) may not exceed $10 million. Directors are personally liable for any excess.
7.10	Bank may sell any of the public debt used to purchase shares, but it cannot buy additional bonds. Its trade will be limited to bills of exchange and specie. Interest charges limited to 6%.
7.11	Loans to state, federal, or foreign governments limited without express Congressional consent.
7.12	Stock transferrable by rules adopted by directors.
7.13	Debts signed by president and countersigned by cashier are negotiable and transferable.
7.14	Semiannual dividends payable from profits at discretion of directors.
7.15	Branch offices may be opened wherever directors see fit.
7.16	Secretary of treasury may inspect the bank's books at any time, not more often than once each week.
8	All officers and directors who trade or authorize trade in goods not allowed by charter are subject to treble damages.
9	All officers and directors who loan or authorize loans to governments in amounts in excess of limits are subject to treble damages.
10	Bank's notes are receivable for all debts to United States.
11	President of the United States may, at his discretion, subscribe to one-fifth of the bank's stock. The bank shall loan the amount to the government.
12	No other bank will be chartered by Congress during the term of the 20-year charter.

Sources: Hamilton's *Report* reprinted in Clarke and Hall (1832, 21–32). Bank of the United States charter reprinted in Holdsworth and Dewey (1910, 126–32).

subscribed and paid for (§2), the time limit of the charter (§3), the reserva-
tion of shares for the government (§11), and the promise to not charter a
competing bank for the duration of the BUS's charter (§12). Regulatory
provisions included such features as Section 7.8, which forbade the bank
from trading in real estate, Section 7.9 that limited its banknote issues, Section 7.10 that restricted its dealings in public debt, as well as Sections 8 and 9
that prescribed punishments for violations of these restrictions. Finally, and
perhaps, most importantly, the charter included several conditions—found
mostly in Sections 4 and 7—that established internal governance procedures
for the bank. Internal governance rules, as was evident in the BONA debates,
not only affected shareholders and managers, but influenced the perceptions
of outsiders.

The BUS charter became the model that many legislatures followed in
drafting state bank charters and, therefore, shaped the contractual relationship between hundreds of banks and the states in which they operated.[5]
The nature of these contracts determined how well banks performed their
intermediation functions and how they responded (or failed to respond) to
contemporary political and economic circumstances. This is not to diminish the BUS as an important agent of treasury's fiscal policy or independent monetary policy. Those features of the BUS have been explored elsewhere (Holdsworth and Dewey 1910; Timberlake 1978; Kaplan 1999; Sylla,
Wright, and Cowen 2009). What is less well appreciated is the fundamental
role the BUS—and by implication Hamilton—played in shaping state banking policy up to the adoption of free banking by several states after 1837.

The extent to which the BUS charter influenced state bank policy becomes
evident in table 5.2, which lists twenty-five features of the BUS charter and
their appearance in the charters of four banks organized prior to the establishment of the BUS in 1791, and four banks chartered thereafter. Some
variant of the most basic general provisions appear in the earliest bank
charters (or articles of association), including the total capital, the number
of shares, and the grant of corporate status. Few restrictions appear in the
pre-1791 charters. It is particularly notable that the earliest bank organizers
imposed relatively few internal governance rules on themselves. Compared
to the BUS charter, the governance rules were a patchwork and tended to the
innocuous, such as the requirement that directors stand for annual reelection.
It is notable that not one of the pre-BUS banks afforded shareholders the
right to call extraordinary meetings. Of course, banks might provide some
of the governance features not included in their charters through bylaws or
other internal operating rules, but bylaws provided a lesser guarantee that

5. Redlich (1968, 21) recognized this fact when he wrote: "the tendency to model charters
of newer banks on those of certain older ones led to integration. In fact some bank charters
became models to whole groups of banks in the same state and even elsewhere." Redlich was
correct, but he failed to trace the influence back to the BUS charter and how it shaped state
banking policy, or how it influenced financial sector performance.

Table 5.2   Bank of the United States charter provisions adopted by selected state banks

BUS features	Bank of North America 1781	Massachusetts Bank 1784	Bank of Maryland 1790	Bank of New York 1791	Hartford Bank 1792	Bank of Penn 1793	Bank of Baltimore 1795	State Bank of S.C. 1802
General provisions								
1. Capital stock			$300,000	$1m	$100,000	$3m	$1.2m	$800,000
2. Share values			$300	$500	$100	$400	$300	$100
3. Corporate status	✓	✓	✓		✓			
4. Term limit (years)				20		20	20	21
5. Reports to government		✓						✓
6. State ownership option					✓	✓	✓	✓
7. Monopoly charter				✓				
Regulations								
8. Nonbank assets limits	✓	✓						
9. Limit on trade in merchandise		✓		✓	✓	✓	✓	✓
10. Performance bonds					✓	✓	✓	✓
11. Debt limits				✓	✓	✓	✓	✓
12. Note redemption				✓		✓	✓	
13. Limits on government lending						✓	✓	✓[a]
14. Interest rate ceilings					✓			✓
Governance provisions								
15. Large board	12		12	13	9	25	15	15
16. Quorum			7		3	13	9	6
17. Annual reelection			✓	✓	✓	✓	✓	✓
18. Rotation in office				✓	✓	✓	✓	✓
19. Director citizenship			✓	✓	✓	✓	✓	✓
20. Directors determine executive compensation			✓	✓	✓	✓	✓	✓
21. Prudent mean voting								✓
21a. Votes for 25 shares	25	25	21	9	25	9	9	9
22. Proxy voting					✓	✓	✓	✓
23. % of shareholders necessary to call meeting						0.03	0.05	0.09
24. Semiannual dividends from profits				✓	✓	✓	✓	✓

[a] Lending limited to foreign, but not domestic governments.

investors would ever realize a return on their investment (Shleifer and Vishny 1997). Directors might change bylaws whenever they no longer suited the directors' purposes so that, compared to explicit charter provisions, internal rules were a second-best guarantee of shareholder rights.

The influence of the BUS charter on state banking policy becomes apparent when we consider the charters of post-BUS banks. Although the banks listed in table 5.2 were not randomly selected, they are indicative of the wide and long-lasting influence of the BUS charter. Nearly every charter imposed a time limit, required regular reports of condition to the government, and reserved some shares for the state. Every legislature reserved the right, most implicitly, to charter other banks. There are similar commonalities between the BUS and the state banks in the restrictions placed on banks' activities and in the basic corporate governance rules.

5.4   Hamilton's Legacy in the Near- and Long-Term

This section discusses the consequences of four notable features of the BONA debate and the BUS charter that influenced later charters: charter time limits, branch banking, government ownership, and prudent mean voting rules. In 1791, United States policymakers stood at a crossroads where they could adopt BONA-style charters or BUS-style charters. In the main, they opted for the BUS form, and that choice had notable long-term consequences. The following paragraphs illuminate the practical effects of those choices on financial stability and bank ownership.

5.4.1   Charter Time Limits

It is notable that, in his twenty-four point plan for a bank in his *Report*, Hamilton accepted a de facto term limit for the BUS (Clarke and Hall 1832, 31), when earlier in the document he dismissed the suggestion that the BONA become the national bank because in accepting its Pennsylvania charter it had "rendered [itself] a mere bank of a particular state, liable to dissolution at the expiration of fourteen years" (26). That it faced the prospect of another contentious rechartering debate in 1800 rendered the BONA unfit to be a national bank.

Why did legislatures impose term limits on banks? At least three reasons, two philosophical and one practical, present themselves. First, under the theory that a charter represented an inviolable contract between a state and a corporation, a perpetual charter was troublesome because it placed the corporation beyond effective legislative control. John Taylor of Caroline was not alone in his conviction that a corporation might hide behind its charter, outlive its original purpose, and threaten the republic (Conkin 1980, 65).[6]

---

6. The famous Dartmouth College case (*Trustees of Dartmouth College v. Woodward*, 4 Wheaton [1819]) had not yet been decided. In *Dartmouth College*, the Supreme Court of the

Second, a related though distinct objection to a perpetual charter is summarized in Jeffersopn's oft-quoted phrase that "the Earth belongs in usufruct to the living" (Sloan 1993). A fundamental tenet of contemporary Republican political philosophy held that each generation owed to its successors the freedom to make their own choices. Because it was easier to renew good laws than repeal bad ones, it was imperative that laws be written with limited duration. Even bad laws have a constituency, Jefferson observed. Automatic expiration approximately every twenty years would limit the pernicious effects of bad laws.[7] A third, more pragmatic, reason for charter term limits reflected the states' ongoing search for sources of revenue and the discovery by state assemblies that not only were prospective bankers were willing to pay for new charters, but existing bankers would pay for the renewal of existing charters (Schwartz 1947). Charter renewal generated income for state treasuries as banks were forced to pay, sometimes handsomely, to extend their charters.[8]

The most consequential legacy of charter time limits was that rechartering debates were often more rancorous and politically charged than the original chartering debates; so much so, in fact, that rechartering efforts sometimes failed. It is ironic that Hamilton's bank fell prey to the very concerns he expressed over transforming the BONA into a national bank—that the term limit on its charter made it susceptible to political intrigue and, ultimately, closure. Although its charter did not expire until 1811, the bank's proponents unsuccessfully initiated the recharter process in 1808. Although treasury secretary Albert Gallatin recommended recharter, the House bill was defeated 65 to 64, while the Senate deadlocked at 17 to 17 until Vice President Clinton, a political enemy of both Madison and Gallatin, cast the deciding negative vote (Cowen 2008).

Of the thirty-nine recorded congressional speeches on recharter, thirty-five revisited the constitutionality of the bank (Clarke and Hall 1832). Hammond (1957) questions the sincerity of these statements given that Jefferson and Madison's original constitutional concerns had been allayed by 1811 and Gallatin himself, once a foe of the bank, expressed confidence in it and

United States held that corporate grants were protected under the contract clause of the federal Constitution. Once granted, governments had limited power to amend charters. After Dartmouth, many states introduced clauses into bank charters that reserved the right of the state to amend them.

7. It is notable that Madison was less enthusiastic about regular rewriting of laws than Jefferson. Madison, in fact, viewed the prospect of rewriting laws every nineteen years with alarm (Sloan 1993, 300; see Madison to Jefferson, 4 February 1790). The difference in approach between the two probably reflects Madison's pragmatism born of his more extensive legislative experience. It was also the case that some present improvements were of sufficient magnitude that it was efficient to burden future generations with some of their costs.

8. In 1830 the Bank of Pennsylvania was required to lend the state $4 million at below-market rates to assist the state's ongoing canal building project. It was also forced to accept responsibility for maintaining the transfer books for the state debt, an uncompensated service that cost the bank an estimated $9,000 per year over the next two decades (Holdsworth 1928, 148–50).

lauded its utility to treasury operations. Others objected to foreign owner-ship, suggesting that British ownership of the bank undermined American republicanism. But this argument, too, was specious because foreign owners could not vote their shares and had little say in the bank's management. The BUS's most outspoken supporters were city bankers who made use of the BUS's branches to facilitate interregional remittances and recognized that it might serve as a lender of last resort in a crisis. Most state banks, however, were pleased with the BUS's demise because it meant the shuttering of its clearing and collection functions, which had served as a check on their own lending and note issues. The bottom line: because Hamilton succumbed to pressures to include a charter term limit, the bank was forced to close not from malfeasance, mismanagement, or misfortune, but rather from partisan motivations.

The mistake was repeated in the charter of the Second Bank of the United States and in a multitude of state bank charters. The story of President Andrew Jackson's war on the Second Bank of the United States is now so well known that it does not bear repeating here, but the twenty-year term limit written into the 1816 charter meant that the Second Bank's survival hung on whether the bank's supporters and, ultimately, its leader—Nicholas Biddle—might bargain with Jackson over the terms of the recharter (Ham-mond 1957; Schlesinger 1946). Neither Biddle nor Jackson was willing to compromise, and the war between these two mighty personalities resulted in the closing of a proto-central bank whose presence under Biddle's leadership may have mitigated the financial effects of the panic of 1837 (Temin 1969). A similar drama, albeit on a smaller stage, was replayed in Indiana in the early 1850s. A charter limit-induced political battle between free banking Democrats and more regulatory minded Whigs ended with the closing of the State Bank of Indiana, one the Old Northwest's best-managed banks (Esary 1912). One legacy, then, of the BUS charter was charter term limits. Such term limits, no matter how philosophically justified or expedient, generated unwarranted economic dislocations.

5.4.2   State Ownership

In reserving one-fifth of the shares of the BUS for itself, the federal gov-ernment became the largest residual claimant to the profits of the country's single largest enterprise. Several states followed suit. Virginia, for example, subscribed to shares in the Bank of Virginia, whose charter was modeled closely after the BUS charter. North Carolina and Kentucky later followed Virginia's example. In taking a direct ownership stake, the state ensured that it received a share of a bank's profits. It also provided the state with some say, through the appointment of directors, over the operations of the bank. Finally, if the state needed to borrow money, legislators believed that it might borrow more readily and on better terms from a bank in which it was a part owner (Esary 1912).

State ownership, established in Hamilton's Report as a fundamental mechanism of corporate governance, was not viewed by all contemporaries as desirable. Some believed that "there was no evil more to be dreaded, except war and pestilence, than a connection between government and banking" (Esary 1912, 267), and John M. Felder of South Carolina spoke of the "vile concubinage of banks and state" (Klebaner 1990, 42). Despite such concerns, by 1812 a majority of the states owned some bank stock; some states already did, or soon would, charter wholly state-owned banks.[9]

State-owned enterprises are typically justified in that they will correct a market failure and are expected to improve resource allocation and overall welfare (Atkinson and Stiglitz 1980). An alternative view holds that state-owned enterprises are created by politicians to pursue the goals and interests of politicians, not the community at large (Shleifer and Vishny 1994). If they fall under political control, state-owned enterprises become sources of inefficiency because they (mis)allocate resources to favored groups. The evidence on state ownership of banks in modern economies is not positive. State ownership is associated with lower rates of productivity and economic growth, less efficient private finance, greater credit risk and lower management efficiency, and lending not to credit constrained but to politically connected firms (La Porta, Lopez-de-Silanes, and Shleifer 2002; Sapienza 2004; Cornett et al. 2010).

Berg and Haber (2009), however, argue that the manifold problems that have emerged with state-owned enterprises, especially among banks in the twentieth century, may not have been as severe in the nineteenth century. The U.S. experience is best described as mixed. Vermont, for example, chartered a state-owned bank in 1806. By the time it was closed in 1812, it had suffered $200,000 ($3.7 billion in 2008 dollars) in losses and land owners paid additional assessments to reimburse creditors (Klebaner 1990; Root 1895). State-owned banks also failed, with significant losses to creditors, in Alabama, Georgia, Tennessee, and Illinois (see table 5.3).

Hamilton, of course, did not propose full state ownership; he proposed that the government take a 20 percent stake. But 20 percent may have been enough to establish effective control over the board, which rendered even those banks with less than 100 percent state ownership state banks (La Porta, Lopez-de-Silanes, and Shleifer 1999). The evidence in table 5.3 on the partly state-owned banks is not easily summarized either. Virginia's early experience may be indicative of the pitfalls surrounding mixed public and private banks. Chartered in 1804 and organized in 1805, it quickly became clear that the legislature was determined to exercise as much control over the Bank of Virginia (whose charter is as close to a copy of the BUS charter as any) as possible. Under the bank's charter, the state could vote all 3,000 of its

---

9. Dividends arising from these holdings, as well as bank taxes, represented a significant share of state revenues (Sylla, Legler, and Wallis 1987).

Table 5.3 Selected experiences with state bank ownership

State	Years	State ownership (%)	Failed	Notes
Maryland	1790–	15	N	Profitable, but required support of transportation infrastructure and banks generated low returns to shareholders.
Pennsylvania	1793–1857	20	Y	Bank of Pennsylvania profitable until asked to bail out state investments in Main Line Canal.
Virginia	1804–1865	20	N	Profitable, well managed; state divested in 1850s.
Vermont	1806–1811	100	Y	Land tax assessment to repay creditors.
Kentucky	1806–1821	20	Y	Undermined by state policies.
Delaware	1807–	20	N	Independent of state intervention, profitable.
North Carolina	1810–1835	20	Y	Cotton speculation soured and led to bankruptcy.
South Carolina	1812–1870	100	N	Profitable, focused on agricultural lending and avoided competition with private commercial banks.
Indiana	1816–1821	37	Y	Poor management led to charter revocation.
Mississippi	1818–	50	Y	Finances undermined by state's railroad investments.
Tennessee	1820–1832	100	Y	Taxpayers reimbursed bank's creditors.
Illinois	1821–1824	100	Y	Poorly managed and failed quickly.
Alabama	1823–	100	Y	Taxpayers reimbursed bank's creditors.
Georgia	1828–	100	Y	State lost "large amount"; taxpayers reimbursed bank's creditors.
North Carolina	1833–1863	40	N	Not well regarded by contemporaries.
Indiana	1834–1857	50	N	Profitable, well regarded, charter not renewed.
Missouri	1837–	50	N	Profitable, well managed.
Tennessee	1838–1868	100	N	Bank returned dividend to state, but struggled underwriting state railroad investments.

Sources: Root (1895); Starnes (1931); Duke (1895); Bryan (1899); Holdsworth (1928).

shares while the maximum number of votes afforded any other shareholder was limited to thirty. Additionally, the state treasurer was an ex officio member of the board. Thus, the state wielded inordinate power over the board.

In early January 1805, the Republican-dominated state assembly adopted, by a 124 to 14 vote, a resolution instructing the state treasurer to "procure a compleat [sic] preponderance of persons of sound [R]epublican principles" (Enquirer 1805) to the bank's board. The resolution, in fact, instructed the treasurer to ensure that the fourteen-member board of the Richmond branch have at least ten Republicans and that each thirteen-member board of the branches have nine Republicans. In the 1805 board elections, the state cast 3,000 of 5,107 ballots (even though it owned only 20 percent of the shares) and, not surprisingly, each branch had either nine or ten Republican directors. It is notable that in August 1805 the bank's share prices were depressed, and one newspaper attributed the low prices to shareholder uncertainty over the consequences of partisan boards. Despite the politicized nature of the bank's boards in its early days, the Bank of Virginia established a strong dividend record and survived to the Civil War (Starnes 1931). No systematic inquiry into the performance of state-owned banks in the nineteenth century United States exists, but if the modern record is indicative, the likelihood that they were a net benefit is low. On the other hand, evidence on failure rates implies that no easy conclusion can be drawn without a deeper understanding of the legal and political constraints under which each bank operated in each state. A handful of success stories in the nineteenth century certainly counters the charge that state-owned institutions are inherently flawed. The available evidence and existing interpretations are not inconsistent with the possiblity that economies in the early stages of development, such as Indiana, Tennessee, and Missouri circa 1835, faced some market failure that a well-run state bank mitigated.

5.4.3 Branch Banking

Alexander Hamilton was not of a single mind in his remarks on branching in the *Report*. At one point, he contended that branching was problematic and best avoided, but later in the document he remarked on the utility of branches. These statements were probably less symptomatic of inconsistency of thought than imprecision in expression: Hamilton favored branches, but only once the BUS was established and had developed the internal controls and managerial capabilities necessary to keep them in check. But *if* Hamilton was of two minds on branch banking, he was not alone among his contemporaries and several subesequent generations of United States bankers. Branch banking never gained a foothold in New England or the Mid-Atlantic region. Ironically, branch banking took hold and prospered south and west of Maryland, the home states of those Republicans most opposed to the size and scope granted the BUS in its charter.

Branch banking was attractive in the South and Old Northwest because large branch banks consolidated small, scattered pools of capital that may have been invested in undercapitalized financial institutions in the absence of larger, often state-sponsored branch banks. When scattered pools of private capital were supplemented with direct state investment, public confidence in many of these banks was enhanced, fears of "vile concubinage" notwithstanding. Confidence in the banks' abilities to meet their obligations encouraged the use of bank money, which reinforced the banks' intermediary abilities and encouraged the spread of the market. To the extent that developed, functioning markets are public goods, state sponsorship of banks in regions not yet fully within the orbit of such markets was an instance of state-sponsored enterprises solving a market failure (Friedman 2005).

One common justification for branch banking is that it provides opportunities for portfolio diversification, hence stability, unavailable to unit banks. Given the underlying economies of the states in which branch banking emerged—Virginia, North and South Carolina, Kentucky, Tennessee,

Ohio, and Indiana—it is not clear that branch banking facilitated anything other than geographic diversification. These were not economies with notable manufacturing, and even the mercantile sector was small compared to that in New England and the Mid-Atlantic. The fortunes of these banks was heavily dependent on shipments of cotton, grain, and other primary products. Bad weather and bad prices led to bad loans, no matter how the loans were spread among the branches.

The real advantage of branch banking in the antebellum South and West—interbank cooperation—became apparent in crises. Intrabank and interbank cooperation arose among branch banks during the panics of 1837 and 1857 (Bodenhorn 2003; Calomiris and Schweikart 1991). During the panic of 1837, for example, Kentucky's branch banks labored to maintain specie payments after their correspondents in Philadelphia and New Orleans had suspended them. Surprisingly, two of the state's largest banks—the Bank of Kentucky and the Northern Bank of Kentucky—were able to maintain their pre-panic levels of loans and circulation through the summer of 1837, even while they increased their specie holdings. When the Northern Bank was run in August 1837, it met the specie calls and survived the run mostly because its rival, the Bank of Kentucky, came to its aid. Interbank lending increased sharply in late summer 1837, and the Kentucky branch banks weathered the panic about as well as any state's system.

The State Bank of Ohio's branch and mutual guarantee features also allowed that system to survive the panic of 1857, even though the banks were heavy creditors of the failed Ohio Life Insurance and Trust Company. The State Bank avoided suspension and failure because its mutually insured branches cooperated with one another during the panic. Although the State Bank of Ohio was not a branch bank in the traditional sense, they formed a federation of banks under a common supervisory and regulatory board. Each bank was autonomously managed, but each was proportionately responsible for the liabilities of the thirty other members, which provided each with an incentive to monitor the actions of all others in good times. In a panic, this structure created incentives to assist others facing a run. During the panic, in fact, stronger banks supplied reserves to weaker or vulnerable banks. None of the State Bank's members failed, compared to the failure of nearly half of neighboring Indiana's independent banks.

Hammond (1957) commended Canadians for adopting charters closely modeled on that of Hamilton's BUS, charters that included the right to establish branches. Unlike the United States, where branching was confined to the less economically developed regions, branching in Canada was ubiquitous. In this feature, at least, "the handiwork of Alexander Hamilton . . . survives still in the Dominion [of Canada]" (Hammond 1957, 662). Although the Canadians embraced branch banking at the expense of oligopoly, the citizenry benefitted from greater stability and many fewer failures during panics and recessions (Bordo, Rockoff, and Redish 1994). It is well known that no Canadian bank failed during the Great Depression, though thousands of branches were closed. Branch closings, however, were not as destabilizing as bank failures.

Some of the states that followed Hamilton's lead and adopted branch banking in the nineteenth century anticipated the Canadian experience in that they reaped the benefits of greater stability and paid the costs of modestly higher interest rates (Bodenhorn and Rockoff 1992). Was the trade-off welfare enhancing? Consider the Indiana experience. When the branched State Bank of Indiana dominated in the early 1850s, borrowers were charged interest rates about 1.4 percentage points higher than borrowers in New York City (Bodenhorn and Rockoff 1992, 177). The State Bank had about $1 million in outstanding loans at any time in the early 1850s and the state had 988,000 inhabitants. If the bank's loans turned over about 2.5 times per year, the annual per capita interest rate costs of market power amounted to 3.6 cents. When the State Bank's charter lapsed and it was replaced by free banks, an average of two failed each year with annual losses of nearly $80,000 (Economopoulos 1988). With 1.35 million inhabitants in 1860, the annual per capita loss due to bank failure was 5.9 cents. For Indiana in the late antebellum era, at least, the cost of bank instability exceeded the cost of bank monopoly, unless the deadweight losses of monopoly exceeded the deadweight losses of instability-induced reduced money holdings. Branch banking, then, provided several benefits to bank customers, the most notable of which was greater stability. It is unclear whether Hamilton considered this a likely outcome, but it was certainly a valuable by-product.

5.4.4   Voting Rules

Voting rights, especially how votes would be cast and by whom, represented a critical governance feature outlined in the *Report* and in the BUS charter. Hamilton's *Report* and the BUS charter had three important voting rights clauses. First, foreign shareholders were excluded from voting their shares and exercising any direct control rights. Foreigners retained residual claims to profits, but were unable to influence management, at least through their voting power. "Due caution," wrote Hamilton, was called for in order to "guard against a foreign influence insinuating itself" into the bank (Clarke and Hall 1832, 28).

Second, item 11 of the *Report* recommended proxy voting. Hamilton recognized that liberal voting rights assured stockholders that managers could not substantially modify the terms of the stockholders' investment without their consent. Liberal voting rights limited managerial discretion and protected against expropriation (Baums 1997; La Porta et al. 1998). Of course, occasions might arise when substantial modifications to the charter contract might benefit stockholders, so gaining their consent was vital. Because shareholding was geographically dispersed and transportation costly, shareholder meetings at which corporate policy might be renegotiated would be prohibitively costly to organize and mediate. Proxy voting reduced the costs of gaining majority consent and effecting change in corporate policy. Charter clauses allowing proxy voting are missing from all pre-1792 charters. After the clause is included in the BUS charter, it becomes ubiquitous in state bank charters. In this instance, the BUS influence on state banking policy is unmistakable.

A system of voting rights that Hamilton labeled the "prudent mean" represented the third important governance feature included in the BUS charter that found its way into several state banking systems. The BONA debates highlighted the gravity with which contemporaries viewed corporate voting. "Like civic governance," wrote Dunlavy (2006), "corporate governance has many dimensions, but there are good reasons to single out voting rights as its foundation" (1354). Dunlavy (2006) classified voting rights along a continuum from "plutocratic" (one share-one vote) to "democratic" (one shareholder-one vote), with all manner of variation in between. Hamilton labeled one point along the continuum the "prudent mean," which he defined with the following voting rule:

> For one share, and not more than two shares, one vote; for every two shares above two, and not exceeding ten, one vote; for every four shares above ten, and not exceeding thirty, one vote; for every six shares above thirty, and not exceeding sixty, one vote; for every eight shares above sixty, and not exceeding one hundred, one vote; and for every ten shares above one hundred, one vote; but no person, co-partnership, or body politic, shall be entitled to a greater number than thirty votes. (Clarke and Hall 1832, 32)

Hamilton offered his prudent mean voting rule because he considered the one share-one vote rule adopted by the BONA "improper" and the one shareholder-one vote rule "not less erroneous" (Clarke and Hall 1832, 28).

The plutocratic rule of one share-one vote increased the likelihood that a few stockholders might take control of the bank and direct its resources to their advantage and to the detriment of minority shareholders. Concentration of about 20 percent of shares appears sufficient to take control of a modern corporation, and given the communication and transportation network circa 1800, 20 percent was surely enough to take effective control (La Porta, Lopez-de-Silanes, and Shleifer 1999). It was on this issue that Morris and Hamilton's visions of proper corporate governance diverged. In the BONA debates, Morris adamantly defended one share-one vote rules as the only available mechanism to protect large shareholders from the depredations of the minority. Hamilton was not only more concerned about the ability of large shareholders to subvert the corporation to the detriment of minority shareholders, but about political appearances. In advocating a prudent mean voting rule, Hamilton successfully walked a tightrope: he simultaneously undermined political objections to plutocratic voting rules, protected minority shareholders by affording them disproportionately large voting representation, and still encouraged large bloc investment by offering larger shareholders a greater measure of control over the bank's operations than a democratic one shareholder-one vote rule would have afforded.

Although one share-one vote rules were common by the end of the nineteenth century (Morris's view ultimately prevailed), at the beginning of the century most Americans remained wary of power vested with large shareholders under one share-one vote rules and, instead, adopted rules more akin to Hamilton's prudent mean (Dunlavy 2006). Lines 21 and 21a in table 5.2, again, reveal BUS influence on American corporate governance, at least for the first half of the nineteenth century. None of the pre-BUS charters adopted a prudent mean-type rule. Many, but not all banks, adopted it thereafter. As a measure of the limits placed on large stockholders, line 21a reports the number of votes a stockholder holding twenty-five shares was allowed to cast at a stockholder's meeting. While the Hartford Bank adopted the one share-one vote rule, the other banks adopted rules that gave a shareholder with twenty-five shares only nine votes—the same rule imposed on stockholders in the BUS. Variations quickly appeared: stockholders with twenty-five shares could cast eight votes at shareholder meetings in New Jersey, ten votes at meetings in New Hampshire, eleven votes in Ohio, twelve or thirteen in Missouri, but only six in Georgia. Connecticut developed no hard and fast rule, but rather responded to the organizers' wishes. Only two of the first ten banks chartered in Connecticut adopted prudent mean voting rules. The other eight adopted one share-one vote rules.

That some states adopted prudent mean voting while others adopted one share-one vote rules affords an opportunity to determine whether the prudent mean rule had any meaningful effect on shareholding. State bank commissioners occasionally published the names and shareholdings of bank shareholders in the antebellum era. These records were combined with voting rules included in bank charters. Data on sixty-nine banks from five states (Connecticut, Maine, New York, Pennsylvania, and Wisconsin) between the 1830s and 1850s show that the average concentration ratio for the twenty largest shareholdings (i.e., CR-20) was 0.79. That is, the twenty largest shareholders owned nearly 80 percent of the outstanding shares of the sample banks. The Herfindahl-Hirshman index (HHI) of share ownership was 1355.[10] The CR-20 and HHI values suggest fairly concentrated

---

10. The Herfindahl-Hirschman Index [(HHI) = $(1,000) \cdot \Sigma s_i^2$] can assume any value between 0 and 10,000. A value of 10,000 implies ownership by one shareholder. A value approaching 0 implies completely atomized ownership. The HHI values for the range between 75 and 10,000, and the standard deviation is 1,756.

bank share ownership: the mean of the sample was $125,000 in paid-in capital owned by sixty-seven shareholders.[11]

To better understand the association between the dispersion of share ownership and prudent mean voting rules, I regressed shareholder concentration measures against a prudent mean indicator variable, in addition to measures of the bank's age (more time for shares to either disperse or concentrate), nominal capital stock (larger banks had more available shares), and state dummy variables. The estimated coefficient on the prudent mean indicator coefficient when regressed on CR-20 was –0.24 (t-statistic = 5.80; $p < 0.001$), which implies that the twenty largest shareholders owned approximately one-fourth less of the outstanding shares of banks with prudent mean voting rules compared to banks with one share-one vote rules. When CR-20 was replaced with the HHI as the dependent variable, the coefficient on the prudent mean indicator variable was –216.4 (t-statistic = 1.7; $p < 0.10$). At the mean HHI a prudent mean voting rule reduced share owner concentration by about 12 percent of the standard deviation in HHI.

The sample is too small and the estimating technique too crude to draw causal inferences, but the size and significance of the association suggests that early nineteenth-century minority bank shareholders were concerned with majority shareholder expropriation. Minority shareholdings were much more common and represented a larger fraction of bank ownership when charters limited large shareholder control through prudent mean voting rules. More research is required, but the results suggest that if the organizers' principal concern was raising outside capital, they might prefer a prudent mean share voting rule to encourage dispersed ownership. If the organizers' principal concern was retaining control of the bank, they probably preferred a one share-one vote rule.

The corporate governance issues surrounding voting rules run deeper than horizontal power relations inside the firm, however. Although large bloc shareholding might improve managerial performance because large shareholders had greater incentives to monitor, nineteenth-century Americans also recognized that large bloc holdings come at a cost: large shareholders might adopt rules or policies that disadvantage or expropriate from small shareholders (Shleifer and Vishny 1986; Holderness and Sheehan 2000). It remains to be determined whether dispersed ownership, encouraged by prudent mean voting rules, or more concentrated ownership, encouraged by one share-one vote rules, resulted in more profitable, more prudent, more stable banks.

11. Using the turnover of shares as a proxy for dispersion of ownership, Wright (1999) concludes that shares were widely dispersed. The concentration ratios at points in time suggest otherwise. Of course, there is no consensus on the values of the various concentration measures that separate concentrated from dispersed ownership. Minguez-Vera and Martin-Ugedo (2007) contend that an average HHI of 1,500 for the modern Spanish publicly traded corporation is high, especially when compared to an average HHI of 570 for the modern British publicly traded corporation (Trojanowski and Renneboog 2002).

5.5   Conclusion

It is historically inaccurate to think about Federalist banking policy as a clearly articulated set of objectives, statutes, and administrative regulations. Federalist banking policy was an attitude and a loosely constructed approach to the establishment of, and control over, financial intermediaries. The clearest statement of that approach is found in Hamilton's *Report on a National Bank* and in the charter of the Bank of the United States. These were the documents that defined two generations of the contract between states and their banks. Although Hamilton was a student of history, as were many of his contemporaries, he had limited guidance in how to construct a bank and almost no guidance in constructing a system. It is clear that the Bank of England charter influenced Federalist approaches to banking (Andréadès 1909), but the politicians and the bankers of the time were making up much of the script as they went along.

This is not to say that the Federalists did not impose some structure on their banks, which later developed into a banking system. They imposed structure and order through the charters they granted. Federal policies became state policies because state legislators had the same concerns as the founders about the relationship between business and government and adopted the BUS charter as a model in creating state systems. It was an organic process and the model evolved over time, of course, but the Bank of the United States' DNA remains evident in state bank charters several generations removed from the 1791 original.

References

Andréadès, A. 1909. *History of the Bank of England.* Translated by Christabel Meredith. London: P.S. King & Son.
Atkinson, A. B., and J. E. Stiglitz. 1980. *Lectures on public economics.* London: McGraw Hill.
Baums, T. 1997. Shareholder representation and proxy voting in the European Union: A comparative study. Max Planck Institute. Working Paper.
Berg, A., and S. Haber. 2009. Always turkeys? Brazil's state owned banks in historical perspective. Stanford University. Working Paper.
Bodenhorn, H. 2003. *State banking in early America: A new economic history.* New York and Oxford: Oxford University Press.
Bodenhorn, H., and H. Rockoff. 1992. Regional interest rates in antebellum America. In *Strategic factors in nineteenth century American economic history: A volume to honor Robert W. Fogel,* ed. C. Goldin and H. Rockoff, 159–87. Chicago: University of Chicago Press.
Bordo, M. D., H. Rockoff, and A. Redish. 1994. The U.S. banking system from a northern exposure: Stability versus efficiency. *Journal of Economic History* 54 (2): 325–41.

Bryan, A. C. 1899. *History of state banking in Maryland.* Baltimore, MD: Johns Hopkins University Press.

Calomiris, C., and L. Schweikart. 1991. The panic of 1857: Origins, transmission, and containment. *Journal of Economic History* 51 (4): 807–34.

Carey, M. 1786. *Debates and proceedings of the general assembly of Pennsylvania: On the memorials praying for a repeal or suspension of the law annulling the charter of the Bank.* Philadelphia: Seddon & Pritchard.

Clarke, M., and D. A. Hall. 1832. *Legislative and documentary history of the Bank of the United States.* Washington, DC: Gales & Seaton.

Conkin, P. K. 1980. *Prophets of prosperity: America's first political economists.* Bloomington: Indiana University Press.

Cornett, M. M., L. Guo, S. Khaksari, and H. Tehranian. 2010. The impact of state ownership on performance differences in privately-owned versus state-owned banks: An international comparison. *Journal of Financial Intermediation* 19: 74–94.

Cowen, D. 2000. *The origins and economic impact of the first bank of the United States, 1791–1797.* New York and London: Garland Publishing, Inc.

———. 2008. First Bank of the United States. EH.Net Encyclopedia. Ed. R. Whaples. Available at: http://eh.net/encyclopedia/article/cowen.banking.first_bank.us.

Dorfman, J. 1946. *The economic mind in American civilization, 1606–1865.* New York: Viking Press.

Duke, B. W. 1895. *History of the Bank of Kentucky, 1792–1895.* Louisville: John P. Morton & Co.

Dunlavy, C. 2006. Social conceptions of the corporation: Insight from the history of shareholder voting rights. *Washington & Lee Law Review* 63:1347–88.

Economopoulos, A. J. 1988. Illinois free banking experience. *Journal of Money, Credit and Banking* 20 (2): 249–64.

Elkins, S., and E. McKitrick. 1993. *The age of Federalism.* New York: Oxford University Press.

Enquirer. 1805 (January 8). Richmond, Virginia.

Esary, L. 1912. *State banking in Indiana, 1814–1873.* Bloomington, IN: Indiana University Bulletin, vol. 10, no. 2.

Friedman, B. M. 2005. *The moral consequences of economic growth.* New York: Vintage Books.

Friedman, L. 1993. *Crime and punishment in American history.* New York: Basic Books.

Hammond, B. 1957. *Banks and politics from the Revolution to the Civil War.* Princeton, NJ: Princeton University Press.

Harris, R. 2009. Law, finance and the first corporations. In *Global perspectives on the rule of law.* Ed. J. J. Heckman, R. L. Nelson, and L. Cabatingan, 145–72. Abingdon: Routledge-Cavendish.

Holderness, C. G., and D. P. Sheehan. 2000. Constraints on large-block shareholders. In *Concentrated corporate ownership,* ed. R. K. Morck, 139–75. Chicago and London: University of Chicago Press.

Holdsworth, J. T. 1928. *Financing an empire: History of banking in Pennsylvania.* Chicago and Philadelphia: S. J. Clarke Publishing Company.

Holdsworth, J. T., and D. R. Dewey. 1910. *The first and second Banks of the United States.* Washington, DC: Government Printing Office.

Kaplan, E. S. 1999. *The Bank of the United States and the American economy.* Westport, CT and London: Greenwood Press.

Klebaner, B. J. 1990. *American commercial banking: A history.* Boston: Twayne Publishers.

Lamoreaux, N. 1997. The partnership of organization: Its popularity in early-nineteenth-century Boston. In *Entrepreneurs: The Boston business community, 1700–1850,* ed. C. E. Wright, and K. P. Viens, 269–95. Boston: Massachusetts History Society.

La Porta, R., F. Lopez-de-Silanes, and A. Shleifer. 1999. Corporate governance around the world. *Journal of Finance* 54 (2): 471–517.

———. 2002. Government ownership of banks. *Journal of Finance* 57:265–301.

La Porta, R., F. Lopez-de-Silanes, A. Shleifer, and R. W. Vishny. 1998. Law and finance. *Journal of Political Economy* 106 (6): 1113–55.

Lewis, J. 1993. "The blessings of domestic society": Thomas Jefferson's family and the transformation of American politics. In *Jeffersonian legacies,* ed. P. S. Onuf, 109–46. Charlottesville: University Press of Virginia.

Lewis, L., Jr. 1882. *A history of the Bank of North America: The first bank chartered in the United States.* Philadelphia: J. B. Lippincott & Company.

Minguez-Vera, A., and J. F. Martin-Ugedo. 2007. Does ownership structure affect value? A panel data analysis for the Spanish market. *International Review of Financial Analysis* 16 (1): 81–98.

Rappaport, G. D. 1970. *The sources and early development of the hostility to banks in early American thought.* PhD diss. New York University.

———. 1996. *Stability and change in revolutionary Pennsylvania: Banking, politics, and social structure.* University Park: Pennsylvania State University Press.

Redlich, F. 1968. *Molding of American banking.* New York: Johnson Reprint Company.

Riesman, J. A. 1987. Money, credit, and Federalist political economy. In *Beyond confederation: Origins of the Constitution and American national identity,* ed. R. Beeman, S. Botein, and E. C. Carter II, 128–61. Chapel Hill: University of North Carolina Press for the Institute of Early American History.

Root, L. C. 1895. States as bankers. *Sound currency* 2 (10): 221–52.

Sapienza, P. 2004. The efefcts of government owenership on bank lending. *Journal of Financial Economics* 72:357–84.

Schwartz, A. J. 1947. The beginnings of competitive banking in Philadelphia, 1782–1809. *Journal of Political Economy* 55 (5): 417–31.

Sharp, J. R. 1993. *American politics in the early republic: The new nation in crisis.* New Haven, CT and London: Yale University Press.

Shleifer, A., and R. Vishny. 1986. Large shareholders and corporate control. *Journal of Political Economy* 94:461–88.

———. 1994. Politicians and firms. *Quarterly Journal of Economics* 109 (4): 995–1025.

———. 1997. A survey of corporate governance. *Journal of Finance* 52 (2): 737–83.

Schlesinger, A. M., Jr. 1946. *The age of Jackson.* Boston: Little Brown.

Sloan, H. 1993. "The Earth belongs in usufruct to the living." In *Jeffersonian legacies,* ed. P. S. Onuf, 281–316. Charlottesville: University Press of Virginia.

Starnes, G. T. 1931. *Sixty years of branch banking in Virginia.* New York: Macmillan.

Sullivan, J. 1792. *The path to riches: An inquiry into the origins and use of money; and into the principles of stocks and banks.* Boston: P. Edes.

Sylla, R. 1998. U.S. securities markets and the banking system, 1790–1840. *Review* 1998 (May): 83–98.

Sylla, R., J. B. Legler, and J. J. Wallis. 1987. Banks and state public finance in the new republic: The United States, 1790–1860. *Journal of Economic History* 47 (2): 391–413.

Sylla, R., R. E. Wright, and D. J. Cowen. 2009. Alexander Hamilton, central banker:

Crisis management during the U.S. financial panic of 1792. *Business History Review* 83:61–86.

Temin, P. 1969. *The Jacksonian economy.* New York: W.W. Norton & Co.

Timberlake, R. H., Jr. 1978. *The origins of central banking in the United States.* Cambridge and London: Harvard University Press.

Trojanowski, G., and L. Renneboog. 2002. The managerial labor market and the governance role of shareholders control structures. Social Science Research Network. Working Paper. Available at: http://papers.ssrn.com.

Wright, R. E. 1999. Bank ownership and lending patterns in New York and Pennsylvania, 1781–1831. *Business History Review* 73 (1): 40–60.

Wright, R. E., and D. J. Cowen. 2006. *Financial founding fathers: The men who Made America rich.* Chicago: University of Chicago Press.

6

The Other Foundings
Federalism and the Constitutional Structure of American Government

John Joseph Wallis

6.1 Introduction

One of the distinctive features of American society from the Revolution onward was the sustained development of the polity and the economy. Economic development can be measured in rising per capita income, but more important aspects were the development of an integrated and well-organized market economy, the development of the most important forms of business organization—the partnership and the corporation—and the consolidation of secure property rights in land and moveable wealth. Economic development was matched by political development through a broader suffrage, the emergence of political parties at the state and national level, hotly contested but generally fair elections, a reliable legal system, and increasing ability to guide government decisions through democratic institutions. Economic, political, and general historians have always suspected that the two development processes were intimately connected. Economists have come to understand quite clearly that modern economic development is not possible without modern political development, and vice versa, if not quite understanding how they are connected. The United States should offer a rich laboratory for understanding the dynamic interplay of economics and politics.

Traditionally, however, questions about social dynamics in the early republic have been framed by the founding choices made at the national level. The ability of the founders to construct a democratic republic capable of defending and expanding its territorial sovereignty, providing security of property and persons to its citizens, and, until 1861, ensuring relative stabil-

John Joseph Wallis is a professor of economics at the University of Maryland, and a research associate of the National Bureau of Economic Research.

ity of government institutions and policies constituted a bedrock for the subsequent development of American society. The national history has strongly influenced our attempts to understand American development since, from 1790 to 1860, national government structures and policies basically stayed the same. The national Constitution was amended just twice between 1791 and 1865.[1] Policies with respect to public lands, taxation, the military, and internal improvements (transportation) were often hotly debated but underwent no fundamental change. Policies regarding patents, banks, and international trade did change, but not dramatically so, even though arguments about policies were intensely argued as well. While history focuses on the arguments, one major implication of the founding choices were unexpectedly stable national government policies.

Interplay is the result of action and reaction. If economic and political development are connected, then political actions should lead to economic consequences and economic actors should change their behavior and, in turn, pressure political actors to make political changes. Unlike the static national government policies, state governments were deeply involved in actions, new experiments, and fundamental changes that affected the economy from 1776 through 1860. State political development was, in turn, affected by economic changes. Historians have always known that a history written from the perspective of the national government is important, but incomplete, because most of the political policies affecting economic development in the new nation originated at the state level. The assumption has often been that the interplay between capitalism and democracy at the state level followed the same pattern as at the national level. Indeed, it is often implicitly assumed that the national level dominated the interaction between economics and politics because of the central importance of national constitutional guarantees for security of property and contract.

This chapter argues the opposite: if we want to understand the relationship between political and economic development in the United States, then we need to understand American history at the state level. It was at the state, not the national, level that the critical interplay between political and economic development, between democracy and capitalism if you will, occurred between the 1780s and 1840s and on into the late nineteenth century. The chapters in this volume by Howard Bodenhorn and Robert Wright look closely at banking and corporations, two areas of the economy in which the states were the primary government actors that exerted profound influence over the economy. Symmetrically, the growing economy also posed profound questions for democracy. Early Americans feared that their new democracies would not be sustainable. It was by no means clear that governments could promote development without corrupting democracy.

---

1. The Bill of Rights was ratified in 1791, the 11th amendment in 1795 concerned states and judiciary, and the 12th amendment in 1804 was a technical modification in the presidential election system; the 13th amendment banned slavery in 1865.

The states led the process of political and economic development. The first three sections of the chapter document the rapid and continuous state constitutional change, the persistent expansion of democracy at the state level, and the relative inaction at the federal level. Then we turn to the fears of early Americans that the energetic promotion of economic development threatened new democratic institutions by using public power to promote private interests that would derail and corrupt the political process. On the economic side, fundamental changes were made in the nature of business organizations, both partnerships and corporations; the nature and regulation of entry into markets, including financial markets; the ability of private firms to draw on capital from public sources; and the structure of taxation. On the political side, fundamental changes were made in constitutional provisions that specified the kind of economic activity state and local governments could engage in directly, government relationships with private organizations; the methods, procedures, and limits on the creation of government debts; and, ultimately, on the kinds of laws state governments could pass. Understanding how Americans gradually learned, over time, to create more powerful and productive private economic organizations at the same time that they secured the democratic process from being unduly influenced by those organizations is the fundamental story of this chapter.

The national government faced the same challenges as the states but was unable to deliver significant investments in finance and transportation. The emphasis placed here on state governments does not imply that states played a more important role than the national government in the development of early nineteenth century America: both were important. The role of states has, however, been slighted by historians of all types and redressing the balance is important. Understanding how America promoted political and economic development is impossible if we ignore the states because we get an incomplete picture of how American institutions changed. Equally important, there has long been both a (raw) political and (sophisticated) theoretical explanation of American development neatly conveyed in the motto of *The United States Magazine and Democratic Review,* a standard bearer of the Jacksonian Democrats, published from the late 1830s into the 1850s: "The best government is that which governs least." The intense political debate about how active a role the national government should take, epitomized by the struggle between the Democrats and Whigs in the 1830s and 1840s but present from 1790 through to the Civil War, by and large resulted in a relatively inactive national government. Undue focus on the national government can lead to the simple conclusion that American development was the result of inactive and quiescent government.

Almost all of the important constitutional development in the United States between 1787 and 1865 occurred at the state level, changes that can be documented in the state constitutions. Presenting that evidences makes up the bulk of this chapter. A continuous interplay between the people's desire to promote economic development and secure democracy produced a long record of institutional change. When the pieces are lined up correctly, it is easy to see the tension and interplay. In the simplest terms, Americans feared that organized economic or political groups posed a threat to democracy, the fear of faction so persuasively described by Madison in Federalist Paper no. 10. At the same time, Americans wanted to promote economic development (although there were enormous differences about how that should be done) and saw the creation of economic organizations as the best way to achieve those ends. The tension was particularly acute in the area of financial and transportation infrastructure. The states figured out how to resolve the tension. Their constitutional flexibility and innovation shows clearly when we look at the right places in our history.

6.2   Constitutional Change

Between 1800 and 1900, the national government amended its Constitution four times, once to correct a defect in the procedures for electing the president and vice-president and three times in the wake of the Civil War. During the same period, thirty states wrote new constitutions when they entered the Union, and sixty-four existing state constitutions were revised for a total of ninety-four complete constitutions. States also amended their constitutions hundreds of times during the century.

Table 6.1 lists the dates of state constitutions, new and revised, for states in existence up to 1850. States are grouped by region: New England, Mid-Atlantic, South, Southwest, Northwest, and the trans-Mississippi West. The columns reflect roughly twenty-year time periods, except for the 1860s and 1870s, which were particularly active constitutional times. There are four main points to take away from the table.

First, states actively reconsidered constitutional arrangements in the nine-teenth century. Of all the states in the table, only Massachusetts and New Hampshire did not revise their constitution at least once between 1800 and 1900. In addition, only South Carolina, North Carolina, Georgia, Alabama, Missouri, Arkansas, Texas, and California did not revise their constitution at least once between 1800 and 1860.

Second, after a wave of constitution making and revising in the 1790s, New England states were much less active. Connecticut and Rhode Island operated with revised versions of the colonial charters until writing new constitutions in 1818 and 1843, respectively. Vermont was the only other state to revise its constitution in 1836, and the Vermont changes were relatively small. Although New England states did amend their constitutions, the region as a whole stands apart from the rest of the country when it comes to constitutions. New Englanders were willing to change laws, with-

Table 6.1   New or revised state constitution dates

State	1776–1799	1800–1819	1820–1839	1840–1859	1860–1869	1870–1879	1880–1899
CT	1662	1818					
MA	1780						
NH	1776,1785,1792						
RI	1663			1843			
VT	1777,1786,1793		1836				
DE	1776,1792		1831				1897
NJ	1776			1844			
NY	1777	1821		1846			1894
PA	1776,1790		1839			1874	
MD	1776			1851	1864,1867		
SC	1776,1790				1861,1865,1868		1896
VA	1776		1830	1850	1864	1870	
GA	1777,1789,1798				1861,1865,1868	1877	
NC	1776				1868		
KY	1792,1799			1850			1890
TN	1790,1796		1834			1870	
AL		1819			1861,1865,1868	1875	
MS		1817	1832		1861,1868		1890
LA		1812		1845,1852	1861,1864,1868	1879	1898
OH		1802		1851			
IN		1816		1851			
IL		1818	1848			1870	
MI			1835	1850			
WI			1848				
IA			1846	1857			
MN				1857			
MO			1820		1865	1875	
AR			1836		1864	1874	
TX			1845		1866,1869	1876	
CA			1849			1879	

out changing their underlying constitutions, where other states found it necessary, or advisable, to change their constitutions and the laws. New England exceptionalism appears often in what follows.

Third, the most active period for constitutional revision stretched from the early 1830s through the early 1850s. States in the South and in New England were less likely to revise their constitutions in this period; all other states replaced their constitutions at least once. It was in the 1840s, in particular, that changes in constitutional provisions with respect to the economy and public finance changed that later spread through the rest of the country.

Fourth, the 1860s and 1870s were a period of intense constitutional revision in South. This was triggered by secession in 1861 and 1862, the return of states to the Union in 1865 and the period of reconstruction up to 1877, and a third wave of Southern constitutional reaction to reconstruction constitutions after 1877. Many of the constitutional reforms of the 1840s were adopted in Southern constitutions under reconstruction, and those provisions were generally not removed in later Southern constitutions.

In short, states actively considered and reconsidered their constitutional arrangements throughout the nineteenth century. They were not content to rest on the laurels of their revolutionary constitutions. As we will see, after changing their constitutions in the early nineteenth century to make them more democratic, by widening the suffrage and making officials more responsive to direct selection by voters, they engaged in another round of constitutional changes that reflected the changing relationship of their democratic polities to their growing economies.

6.3 Suffrage and Democracy

Control over elections in the early republic was left completely up to the states. Table 6.2 reports restrictions on suffrage at the state level. All of the original states, with the exception of New Hampshire and Vermont, imposed either property or tax paying requirements for voting in the 1770s. Kentucky imposed no requirements (except color) when it entered in 1792, Tennessee had a property requirement when it entered in 1796, and Ohio had a tax paying requirement when it entered in 1802. Ohio was the last new state to impose property or tax paying requirements when it entered the Union; every state after that allowed free, white, male, adult suffrage in their initial constitutions. Existing states began opening suffrage by reducing or eliminating requirements, as shown in the table. By 1855, only Rhode Island, New York, and South Carolina still imposed a property requirement and, as Keyssar notes (2000, appendix A.3), Rhode Island exempted native-born citizens from the requirement, New York's property restrictions applied only to African Americans, and South Carolina offered a residency alternative to the property qualification.

The movement toward free, white, male suffrage was matched by a movement toward direct election of state officials. By the 1850s, almost all the states elected their governors by direct popular vote; only half had done so in their original constitutions. States moved to eliminate extralegislative bodies with the power to review laws or propose constitutional amendments, such as the Council of Revision in New York or the Council of Censors in Pennsylvania and Vermont.

Beginning in the 1830s, states also began selecting judges by popular election, taking the power of appointment and approval from legislatures and governors. Table 6.3 lists the years when states considered electing judges, sometimes accepting and sometimes rejecting the idea (taken from Shugerman 2008).

After independence, American states moved steadily toward more democratic institutions: wider suffrage and a direct selection of more government office holders through popular election.

Table 6.2   **Suffrage requirements**

State	1776–1799	1800–1819	1820–1839	1840–1859	1860–1869
CT	T,P			1845 0	
MA	P		1821 P0, T		
NH	0				
RI	P			1842 P-,T	
VT	0				
DE	T				
NJ	P	1807 T,P		1844 0	
NY	P	1804 P-	1821 P0		Note property requirements still applied to blacks after 1821.
PA	T		1838 T		
MD	P	1801 P0			
SC	P,T	1810 P, T0			
VA	P	1804 P-	1830 P	1850 0	
GA	T				
NC	P,T		1835 P-,T	1854 P0, T	
KY	0				
TN	1796 P		1834 P0		
AL		0			
MS		0			
LA		1812 T			
OH		1802 T		1851 0	
IN		0			
IL		0			
MI		0			
WI		0			
IA		0			
MN		0			
MO		0			
AR		0			
TX		0			

Notes: "P" denotes a state with a property requirement for voting; "T" denotes a state with a tax paying requirement for voting. The first appearance of state gives a "P," "T," or "0" to denote whether a state had either provision or none when it became a state (or in 1800). Successive appearances, moving from left to right, indicate whether a state continued the requirement, "P" or "T"; reduced the requirement "P-" or "T-" or eliminated one or both of the requirements: "P0," "T0," or "0." The dates were taken from Keyssar (2000).

6.4   Federal Inactivity

Between 1790 and 1860, the federal government spent only $60 million on transportation improvements and chartered two banks.[2] Over the same period state and local governments spent over $450 million and chartered thousands of banks. Why was the federal government unable to make transportation investments? The federal government not only stood to gain from

2. The argument in this section is developed in full in Wallis and Weingast (2005).

Table 6.3   Timeline for judicial elections

Year	Elections	Against elections
1777	The territory of VT for lower courts	
1812	GA for "inferior" courts	
1816	IN for associate circuit court judges	
1832	MS (C)	
1833		
1834		MO (A), TN (C)
1835		NC (C), GA (A)
1835–1936	MI for circuit judges (C)	
1837		
1838		PA (C)
1839–1843		
1844	IA for lower courts (C)	NJ (C)
1845		TX (C), LA (C), MO (C)
1846	NY (C)	
	WI (C)	
1847	IL (C)	
1848–1850	PA (A)	
1848	AR for circuit court judges (A)	
1849	CA (C)	
1850	MO (A)	
	OH (C)	
	KT (C)	
	MI (C)	
	TX (A)	
	AL, CT, and VT for circuit court judges (A)	
	VA (C)	
1851	MD (C)	NH (C)
	IN (C)	
1852	LA (C)	
1853	TN (C)	MA (C)
	FL (A)	
1857	MN (C)	
	IA (C)	

Source: Taken from Shugerman (2008).
Note: C = convention; A = amendment(s).

tying the nation more closely together through a system of transportation, the federal government could be expected to be a more efficient provider of such investments. The federal government was larger, in fiscal terms, with well-established domestic and international credit (after the 1790s), and the federal government could internalize the external benefits of transportation investments. When New York built the Erie Canal, many of the benefits of the canal accrued to residents of the Ohio River Valley in Ohio, Indiana, and Illinois who were able to ship their good to the eastern seaboard via the canal. All of those benefits could, in principle, have been internalized by a national system of internal improvements.

The problem wasn't lack of effort. As Goodrich (1960) and Larson (2000) both document, Congress continually wrestled with proposals to involve the federal government in transportation projects.[3] Even Thomas Jefferson, in his second inaugural, suggested that a national system of transportation improvements be considered, leading to the famous Gallatin plan. Gallatin was Jefferson's secretary of the Treasury, and his proposed system of eight major and several minor projects would have tied the nation together, both north and south, and east and west, at an estimated costs of only $25 million. Why was Gallatin's plan rejected? Democracy.

The major obstacle was the competing interests of geographic areas: the unwillingness of one area to incur costs for projects that would benefit other areas. For example, in the debate over the building the Cumberland Road, which the federal government was obligated to build because of promises it made when Ohio was admitted to the Union (so there was no constitutional question that the road was going to be built), the issue was where the road would be located. Throughout the debates over siting the road, geographic rivalries stood in the way of the adoption of specific route. One Maryland congressman declared that Pennsylvania seemed more inclined "to put a mountain in the middle of the Cumberland road than to repair it."[4] Opposition to the Maryland route, for example, came primarily from Pennsylvania and Virginia. When sectional rivalries dominated the debate, as they sometimes did, it was the rivalry between the East and West that mattered, not the North and South.[5]

How were these centrifugal forces inherent in democracy to be overcome? One way was to charter a privileged corporation to provide the public good so that taxes would not have to be raised on anyone. This mitigated the opposition of regions that paid taxes but received little or no benefits. Both the first and second Banks of the United States were created by giving a charter to a small group of investors and guaranteeing them control over federal financial business. The federal government investment in the stock of both banks was financed by loans from the banks themselves. No federal taxes were raised to create or invest in the banks; in fact, both banks paid a nice dividend regularly into the federal treasury. But both Banks generated an enormous amount of political opposition based on fears that the Banks were powerful configurations of private interests that would use their power

3. Nettels (1924) found 117 grants by Congress that funded federal transportation projects and discusses a large number of bills that were proposed but failed of passage. Feller (1984) details the long association of proposals to use revenues from public land sales with attempts to obtain federal financing for internal improvements.

4. See Goodrich (1960, 45). See Larson (2001, 54–57).

5. "[John Quincy] Adams's charge that the national program was overthrown by what he called 'the Sable Genius of the South' is therefore a great over-simplification" Goodrich (1960, 46). Nettels (1924) focuses on the importance of the West's growing voting power and awareness of their collective interests as the key factor that forced a decision about the national government's role in transportation improvements early in the Jackson administration.

to dominate the polity: the first Bank at its origins in the 1790s, the second Bank when its charter was renewed in 1832.

Fears over organized economic interests, articulated clearly in Washington's farewell address, suggest that the struggles over the Banks were a good indicator of the stiff opposition that any nationally chartered corporation would face in Congress. Building transportation infrastructure by creating privileged corporations appeared to be beyond the capacity of the federal government. Alternatively, the federal government could borrow the money and hope that revenues from the transportation improvement would repay the bonds (that was how the transcontinental railroads were financed), but there was little support for peace time federal borrowing in the early nineteenth century.

The importance of geographic and fiscal factors is illuminated by the two types of transportation investments that could command a majority of votes in Congress and were successfully pursued by the federal government. The first type was funding small, geographically diverse projects continued on an annual basis. Every state got something. Lighthouse construction began with the first Congress in 1790, with the addition of roads in 1802, rivers in 1824, harbors in 1824, and the first "rivers and harbors" bill in 1826.[6] Small omnibus lighthouse, roads, and rivers and harbor legislation account for $41 million of the $60 million in federal transportation expenditures between 1790 and 1860. Funding for small and scattered rivers and harbors type of transportation projects was continuous and, with the exception of Jackson's 1830s vetoes, never frustrated by the president.

The second important federal initiative, and the second most important in fiscal terms, began in 1802 with the enabling act admitting Ohio to statehood. This act set aside 5 percent of land sales revenues in Ohio for the "building of public roads" to and within the state of Ohio.[7] The Ohio legislature asked that 3 percent of the funds be expended inside Ohio and Congress agreed. The "2 percent" fund for roads leading to Ohio began to accumulate, and in 1805, Congress authorized a survey of the route for the National, or Cumberland, Road. Construction began in 1808, continued into the 1850s, and accounted for $6.8 million in expenditures.[8] Similar land funds in other states, along with grants of acreage to states, account for $10 million in expenditures. Together, rivers and harbor improvements and state

6. See Goodrich (1960, 40). See Malone (1998) and Senate Executive Document 196, 47th Congress, 1st Session, "Statement of the Appropriations and Expenditures for Public Buildings, Rivers and Harbors, Forts, Arsenals, Armories and Other Public Works from March 4, 1789 to June 30, 1882." Malone's book analyzes the information in the report. He comes up with a total of $54 million on transportation expenditures. Our calculations total $60 million. We have chosen to go with our total and have been unable to determine from where Malone derived his $54 million total.
7. The arrangement was an explicit deal in which Congress agreed to build roads to and within Ohio in return for Ohio's promise not to tax federal lands for five years after they were sold to private individuals. See Larson (2001, 54–55).
8. See Goodrich (1960, 24–26).

land funds amounted to $58 million of the total of $61 million in federal transportation investments in the antebellum period.

River and harbor projects worked in a democracy because they provided something for everyone. Each state was able to get its share of rivers and harbor appropriation. If a state wanted to it could bargain away its river and harbor money for some advantage in another piece of legislation. The land funds built roads out of out of land sales revenues. Presumably these funds paid for themselves, as land sales in the states who received the funds would be more vigorous because the roads were being built.

Confirmation of such political forces were at work can be found in three successful attempts to get Congress to pass funding for a general system of transportation improvements that were eventually vetoed or nullified by presidents. Henry Clay of Kentucky shepherded each bill through Congress, in 1816, 1831, and 1841. The first bill, the Bonus Bill, was tied to the $2 million bonus the second Bank of the United States paid for its charter and the expected flow of dividends from the bank stock the federal government owned. Clay and Calhoun proposed that a fund be established with the money to distribute among the states to finance transportation projects. After Congress got through with Clay and Calhoun, the fund had been changed to a formula: each state would get a share of the bonus (or dividends) equal to its share in the Congressional allocation (two senators + representatives). Small states would get slightly more per capita than large states, but there would be no discretion in the allocation of funds. Something for everyone. President Madison unexpectedly vetoed the Bonus Bill on his last day as president.

In 1831, and again in 1841, Clay pushed bills through Congress allocating the residual revenues from federal land sales, after the costs of administering the public land process, to the states on a Congressional allocation formula. The 1831 bill was part of the compromise that ended the Nullification Crisis, but Andrew Jackson double-crossed Clay and pocket vetoed the distribution bill. The 1841 legislation was part of the Land Act of 1841, which made preemption the general federal land policy from that time forward. The distribution provision would lapse if tariffs were raised beyond a specific level, and President Tyler scotched the deal by raising tariffs.

The presidential vetoes are remarkable in light of the Ohio enabling act. Similar provisions were included in the enabling acts of every state that entered the Union after Ohio.[9] The Ohio enabling act clearly authorized the federal government to redistribute funds from one revenue source, sale of public lands, to another expenditure purpose, public roads (that were not post roads, which were explicitly authorized in the Constitution). The

---

9. Terms of the other enabling acts varied slightly but contained the same principles. See Gates (1968). The Michigan enabling act in 1837 did not contain fund provisions.

Ohio act authorized the construction of public roads within one state, with the consent of the state. As president Madison had signed enabling acts for states that implemented exactly the same type of legislation that Madison vetoed in the Bonus Bill, Madison and Jackson vetoed the Bonus and Distribution bills as unconstitutional, despite those bills containing exactly the same procedures and policies as the state enabling acts.

Despite the strong and persistent calls for a national transportation system, the operation of democratic forces at the federal level prevented much from being done. What was done amounted only to a collection of small and scattered projects.

6.5   Democratic Dilemmas

The United States has, since the first state constitutions were written in 1776, always been a republic, which James Madison defined as "a government in which the scheme of representation takes place." If by democracy we mean, as Madison defined "a society consisting of a small number of citizens who assemble and administer the government in person," then the United States has never been a democracy, except perhaps in some of its local governments. If a democratic republic is a society with a government made up of representatives and offices, where selection of representatives and office holders is by direct election of all duly certified citizens, then the United States started out as a republic with some democracy and gradually evolved into a democratic republic. Democracy could be dangerous. As Madison's definition of democracy in the Federalist papers continued, democracy "can admit of no cure for the mischiefs of faction. A common passion or interest till, in almost every case, be felt by a majority of the whole; a communication and concert, results from the form of government itself; and there is nothing to check the inducement to sacrifice the weaker party, or an obnoxious individual."[10] Would a democratic republic be any better?

Madison laid out the dangers of tyranny by the majority in Federalist Paper no. 10 and how an extended republic could mitigate the dangers of faction. He clearly stated that such fears were justified by the experience of the states up until 1787:

> Complaints are every where heard from our most considerate and virtuous citizens, equally the friends of public and private faith, and or public and personal liberty, that our governments are too unstable; that the public good is disregarded in the conflicts of rival parties; and that measures are to often decided, not according to the rules of justice, and the rights of the minor party, but by the superior force of an interested and overbearing majority. However anxiously we may wish that these complaints had no

---

10. See Hamilton, Jay, and Madison (2001, 46) in the Liberty Press's reprint of the Gideon edition of the Federalist Papers.

foundation, the evidence of well known facts will no permit us to deny that they are in some degree true.[11]

The charge that the original state constitutions set up governance institutions that were too democratic, that they allowed too much control to rest in the hands of legislatures without sufficient checks and balances, has flavored our view of early state constitutions ever since.[12] Because most of the constitutional changes discussed in this chapter limited or modified the capacity or procedures of state legislatures, this explanation needs to be kept in mind.

On the other side, Madison and the founders also feared tyranny of the minority. Tyranny of the minority was rooted in fears of faction, which Madison defined as "a number of citizens, whether amounting to a majority or minority of the whole, who are united and actuated by some common impulse of passion, out of interest, adverse to the rights of other citizens, or to the permanent and aggregate interests of the country" (Hamilton, Jay, and Madison 2001, 43). Factions were groups, however organized, that pursued their own interests to the detriment of the larger society (so whether a group was a faction or not was, to a certain extent, in the eye of the beholder). Earlier republics were not democracies, but contained competing groups of people, usually powerful people, whose interests needed to be kept in balance to prevent civil war, violence, and tyranny.

The key to good government was mixing the interest of different groups so that the interest of each group would keep any one group from seizing control and tyrannizing the excluded groups.[13] Polybius, Aristotle, Machiavelli, Harrington, and Montesque had all written how a mixed government could balance competing factions and prevent tyranny. In eighteenth-century Britain, these ideas coalesced into what came to be known as Whig or Commonwealth theory. In the Whig's view, the British constitution protected the interests of British citizens because of a balance between the interests of the

11. The quote is from page 42. In the penultimate paragraph of Federalist Paper no. 10, he again warned that "factious leaders" had kindled a flame in their states, but that "a rage for paper money, for an abolition of debts, for an equal division of property, or for any other improper or wicked project, will be less apt to pervade the whole body of the union, than a particular member of it" (48).

12. Gordon Wood (1969) bought Madison's argument that the state constitutions gave too much unchecked power to legislatures, although Marc Kruman's (1997) argument that state constitutions were as keenly aware of the power of government and of legislatures in particular, seems persuasive to me.

13. As Quentin Skinner (1998, 49) noted, in the late eighteenth century, tyranny represented a very clear state of affairs:

"These writers are no less insistent, however, that a state or nation will be deprived of its liberty if it is merely subject or liable to having its actions determined by the will of anyone other than the representatives of the body politic as a whole. It may be that the community is not as a matter of fact governed tyrannically; its rulers may choose to follow the dictates of the law, so that the body politic may not in practice be deprived of any of its constitutional rights. Such a state will nevertheless be counted as living in slavery if its capacity for action is in any way dependent on the will of anyone other than the body of its own citizens."

one, the few, and the many represented in the king, the House of Lords, and the House of Commons. The Whig's charged that the British constitution was being corrupted over the course of 1700s by an expansion of royal authority and influence in the House of Commons. The king and his ministers used the granting of economic privileges, stock in the Bank of England, shares of the national debt, pensions, and offices to members of Parliament in return for their political support. A political faction (the king) used the granting of economic privileges to suborn the independence of Parliament and obtained complete control of the government. The inevitable result would be tyranny. So went at least part of the justification for the American Revolution.[14]

One result of this way of thinking about how government worked was that the Founding Fathers feared the dangers to liberty presented by organized interests in general and, in particular, any close links between political parties (or factions) and economic corporations. They were paranoid—to use Bailyn's phrase—about the possibility that political factions would use organized interest as a tool to subvert democracy. These fears were not merely muttered under the breath of a few elite members of the Constitutional Convention, they were broadcast wholesale from the 1770s up through the 1850s. The founders worried that political factions would use the creation of economic and other privileges to create interests that could be used to dominate the government. They were much more concerned that politics would corrupt economics than our modern concerns that economics would corrupt politics.[15]

Other chapters in this volume trace the development of political parties, the business corporation, banks, and the financial system in general. Given their deep fear of organized interests, of parties and corporations, as threats to liberty and democracy, it is curious that by 1850, the United States came to have the world's first mass political parties, ten times more corporations than Britain and France combined, and the first institutions that allowed free and open access to the corporate form.[16] Something had to give somewhere before 1850. Ideas about factions and governments must have changed, but there is little evidence of these changes in the national debates or national policies.

A key to understanding the American experience is to realize that Ameri-

<hr/>

14. The classic statement of this hypothesis about the causes of the Revolution is in Bailyn (1967). For Whig thinking in Western political thought, see Pocock (1975), for Whig thinking in Britain, see Robbins (1959); and for a general survey of Whig thought in America, see Shalhope's review articles (1972, 1982).

15. In an earlier paper (Wallis 2006), I used the term "systematic corruption" to denote Whig fears that a faction would use political manipulation of the economy to secure political power, in contrast to the modern notion of "venal corruption" in which economic interests distort the political process to obtain economic benefits.

16. For estimates and counts of the number of corporations for the United States, see Wright (2008); for Britain, Harris (2000); for France, Freedeman (1979) and the comparative work of Guinnane, Harris, Lamoreaux, and Rosenthal (2007) and Lamoreaux and Rosenthal (2005, 2006).

cans did not really understood how democracy would actually work in 1776 or 1787. No one could have understood how democracy worked because no democracy on the scale of the United States had ever existed before. As Americans tried to use their governments to accomplish widely shared goals, like increasing the value of land through investments in transportation and finance, aspects of how democracy worked became apparent to them. In order to create transportation and financial infrastructure, Americans needed to create small, well-organized groups. Given their predisposition to fear organized interests, the creation of such groups raised alarms and fears that the government was being corrupted, systematically corrupted in the sense that the organized economic groups would serve as tools for assembling a political majority. How those fears were relieved through changes in the constitutional structure of state governments is the story of this chapter.

6.6 Democracy and Development: The Example of Canals

Let me begin with the example of a canal. Canals dramatically reduced overland transportation costs. Because farm products could be shipped to market much more cheaply, the construction of a canal into a region without existing water transportation raised the farm gate price of farm products and increased the value of farm land commensurately.[17] Given the wide distribution of land ownership in the United States, many people were interested in building canals. But it wasn't easy for a democratic republic to build a canal. Canals were geographically specific investments. Only people living in close proximity to the canal received direct benefits. Yet if a state attempted to build a canal, all taxpayers potentially had to pay higher taxes. Because most voters expected higher taxes and little or no benefits from the canal, they and their representatives voted against the canal.

Scenarios like this played out in the band of northern states that attempted to build canals in the 1810s, 1820s, and 1830s, stretching from New York, Pennsylvania, Maryland, and Virginia on the eastern seaboard and west into Ohio, Indiana, and Illinois. Canal proponents were concentrated among people who stood to benefit directly from the canal, typically because they owned land on or near the canal. Canal opponents were either people who stood to lose directly from the canal or people who worried that their taxes would increase. For example, in New York, opposition to the Erie Canal included farmers on Long Island who opposed building a canal into western New York that would increase competition, but also merchants in New York City who feared higher taxes. The second group turned out to be spectacularly wrong about the Erie Canal, which helped make the fortune of New York merchants.

---

17. For estimates of the impact of transportation costs on the price of land, see Coffman and Gregson (1998), Craig, Palmquist, and Weiss (1998), and Wallis (2003).

One possible solution to the impasse was to follow the existing European pattern of chartering a privileged corporation to undertake the project. The corporation might be given a monopoly on transportation services along the canal route, help in obtaining property through eminent domain proceedings, favorable access to credit, and perhaps guarantees of limited public funds. In return for their privileges, shareholders in the private company would endeavor to build and operate the canal. The interests of the private actors was coordinated with the public welfare through granting privileges. No taxes needed to be raised, muting opposition from potential taxpayers. The deal could be even sweeter for taxpayers if the corporation promised to grant an ownership share to the state. Rather than paying taxes, voters might enjoy a stream of dividends from the canal. Something like this arrangement was how New Jersey encouraged the construction and operation of the Camden & Amboy Railroad connecting New York and Philadelphia.[18]

Another possibility was for those who benefitted most from the canal to offer to pay a higher share of the taxes. This is how the deadlock over the Erie Canal was ultimately resolved in New York in 1817, the counties along the canal route agreed that to pay a property tax surcharge in the event that the canal fund ran out of money (Miller 1962). In Ohio, Indiana, and Illinois, part of the deal leading to the passage of legislation committing the state to borrow money and build a canal(s), was a change in property taxation. All three states had previously levied a per acre tax on land (graduated by the value of land), which meant that farm land bore the largest burden of the tax. In Indiana, for example, most settled farm land in the 1830s was in the southern part of the state along the Ohio river. Southern farmers opposed the Wabash and Erie Canal, which served the western and northern part of the state. The farmers had the most land to tax and the least to gain from the canal. In 1836, Indiana moved to an ad valorem property tax, which shifted the burden of taxation from farm land more towards towns and urban areas (who were agitating for the canals). Under the ad valorem tax system, land nearer the canal bore a greater share of the tax burden. Indiana set out on its mammoth system of internal improvements in January of 1836, the same month they switched to the ad valorem property tax.[19]

A third option was not to raise taxes at all. The positive experience of the Erie Canal, which began construction in 1817 and before its completion in 1825, was already returning a steady revenue to the state of New York (which owned and operated the canal). Other states began funding canal projects in the anticipation that revenues from the canal would eventually be available to service bonds issued to cover construction costs. By borrowing a bit more than the cost of building the canal, the state could use borrowed funds to

18. For the Camden & Amboy story, see Cadman (1949).
19. For events in Indiana and Illinois, see Wallis (2003); for Ohio, see Scheiber (1969).

pay bond interest in the early years of the project, then redeem the bonds when the canal came on line. This method of financing did not entail raising taxes, but it did entail the taxpayers incurring a contingent obligation to repay the bonds if canal profits did not materialize. Taxpayers also stood to gain, however, because any canal profits left over from servicing canal bonds would go into the general fund of the state and enable other taxes to be reduced. This is what had happened in New York, which was able to eliminate the state property tax in the 1820s as revenues from the Erie Canal came on line. This method of financing canal construction through borrowing and anticipating canal revenues was used in Pennsylvania and Maryland in the 1820s, and interestingly by New York in the 1830s when it decided to expand its canal network.[20]

The central feature of all these finance schemes was to shift the benefits and burdens of government policy in ways that affected voters directly. Only if a majority of the voters, or their representatives, felt that they benefitted from the canal when both benefits and taxes were taken into account could legislation funding a canal pass a state legislature. This is how democracy actually worked.

Canals, railroads, and banks were all potentially large investments that state governments could make. Many local groups sought to promote economic development through local promotion (see Majewski 2000), but only a state could charter a corporation. The financial resources of local governments were limited, particularly in frontier areas in the West. The pressures on state governments to deliver these important public goods was high, but so were the dangers. First, as discussed, Americans were always suspicious of organized economic interests in the form of a corporation. The manipulation of economic interests through corporate chartering to advance the fortunes of a political faction was an essential danger to a republic in Whig political theory. The opportunity to trade privileges for tax revenues, however, proved to be enticing for American voters and taxpayers. Borrowing offered an even greater danger. A faction might convince voters and taxpayers to extend state credit, either to a private corporation or a public entity, to build or finance an investment in which most of the benefits would go to the minority faction in the hopes that the same minority would bear the burden of repaying the debt.

Second, it turned out that democracies were neither capable of correctly evaluating the costs and benefits of such proposals, nor was democracy particularly good at turning down such proposals. Whether improvement efforts were the result of corruption, excessive optimism, or naïvete, by the 1830s, American states found themselves deeply engaged in such projects. After 1839, their large debts came back to haunt states and taxpayers.

20. The standard work on government transportation investments is in Goodrich (1960), which is now supplemented by Larson (2001).

6.7   What States Did

With the coming of independence, the United States turned its economic focus and energies of the country inward. The major economic opportunities were within the United States, not outside of it, and the most important and potentially profitable investments were in transportation and finance. The process of opening the West required enormous resources. The role of states in finance and transportation far outstripped the national government in importance. The financial system that arose between 1790 and 1860 was based on banks not only chartered by state governments, but in some cases owned by state governments. Nine out of every ten dollars spent on public transportation investment came from state and local governments. Banking was always under the control of state governments, with the exception of the two Banks of the United States, and it was not until 1863 that the national government took an active role in chartering and regulating banks. State governments were at the center of the development process.

There were no banks in America before the Revolution. States began chartering banks in the 1780s and 1790s. By the 1830s, there were over 600 state chartered banks with a capital of over $400 million dollars.[21] A corporate charter often, although not always, endowed the bank with limited liability, which was important to bankers whose profits came mainly from borrowing money in the form of bank notes. The legal ability to issue bank notes soon became a privilege that required a bank charter. The first bank charters in the eastern states often gave the state ownership shares in the bank as part of the cost of obtaining the charter. Massachusetts, New York, Pennsylvania, Maryland, Virginia, and South Carolina all came to hold a financial interest in banks in this way. Most early banks were chartered as public utilities. The rational ran along the traditional European lines: the charter was an explicit exchange of a privilege for a public service. That dividends on bank stock were an important element in the revenues of state governments in the East was an added bonus.[22] These banks were often opposed by antibank or anticorporation groups, but they were fiscally attractive. Because the banks generated revenues, they lowered state taxes.

Once a state acquired an ownership interest in one bank, it faced conflicting incentives when asked to charter a second bank. The profitability of a bank depended, in part, on competition. As more banks were chartered, rates of return on the capital invested in individual banks declined. Existing banks opposed the formation of new banks, but states were constantly asked to open new banks, particularly in developing areas where financial systems were primitive (for example, the western parts of New York and

21. Fenstermaker (1965) provides detailed information on the chartering of state banks before 1837.
22. Sylla, Legler, and Wallis (1987) and Wallis, Sylla, and Legler (1994) provided information on state banks and their importance to state revenues.

Pennsylvania in the 1810s.) States that held large amounts of stock in existing banks were less likely to charter new banks, as happened in Pennsylvania. Other states, like Massachusetts, decided to sell their bank stock and
tax bank capital. States that taxed bank capital tended to have many more,
and smaller, banks (Wallis, Sylla, and Legler 1994). The interaction of a
state's fiscal interest and the way states regulated bank entry through their
chartering policies is an early example of the interaction between political
and economic forces.

   By the 1810s, all of the states on the eastern seaboard were promoting or
involved in banking in some way. In places like New York, Philadelphia, Baltimore, and Boston, many groups of businessmen aspired to have a bank. In
these places, states could sell bank charters and receive substantial revenues
from doing so. In per capita terms, there were more banking services in the
northeast than in the rest of the country: more bank notes per capita, more
bank credit, more bank capital, and so on.[23] Moving west and south from
the northeast, however, the size and sophistication of commercial centers
decreased (the exception was New Orleans), the number of banks decreased,
the number of farmers increased, but the need for banking services did not
decline. States in the South and West wanted banks just as much as New
Englanders, but the low density of population, the high share of farmers,
and the geographic concentration of crops meant that banking was riskier.
Banks in Mississippi, for example, made loans on cotton, both directly to
farmers to plant crops and by discounting bills of exchange to facilitate getting the crop to market. If the cotton crop failed or cotton prices collapsed,
all the banks in Mississippi were in trouble. The ability to diversify banking
risk in Mississippi was limited, unlike banks in major eastern commercial
centers with many opportunities to diversify. The same was true in the northwest, where markets for wheat, corn, and other grains dominated.

   Economic conditions determined political options. Conditions in the
South and West were less conducive to banking, and potential bankers
were not willing to pay states for charters. States responded in two way.
First, states invested their own funds in banks, providing bankers with larger
amounts of public capital (eastern states usually received bank stock as part
of the charter process, and did not put state funds *into* the bank.) States did
not raise current taxes to invest in banks, however. Typically states chartered
banks and then bought stock in the bank, paying for their investment by
issuing state bonds, which were given to the bank. The banks were, suppos-
edly, responsible for servicing the state bonds.

   Second, because states held large ownership shares in the banks, there
were fewer banks, and the banks tended to be larger. Table 6.4 gives the
number of banks, total capital, and capital per bank for five regions in 1837.
Western states had many fewer banks. Ohio and Louisiana were the only

---

23. See Bodenhorn (2000, 63, 2003).

Table 6.4   Banks and bank capital and state investments in banks in 1837

State	Banks (1)	Capital (2)	Capital per bank (3)	Bank debt (4)	State investment share of capital (5)	Bank debt, share all debt (6)
ME	55	5,226,700	95,031			
NH	27	2,839,508	105,167			
VT	6	510,000	85,000			
MA	123	37,074,690	301,420			
RI	62	9,837,171	158,664			
CT	31	8,744,697	282,087			
NY	98	37,101,460	378,586			
NJ	25	4,142,031	165,681			
PA	49	23,750,338	484,701			
DE	4	818,020	204,505			
MD	21	10,438,655	497,079			
DC	7	2,204,415	314,916			
VA	5	6,731,200	1,346,240			
NC	3	2,525,000	841,667			
SC	10	8,636,118	863,612			
GA	16	11,438,828	714,927			
FL	4	2,046,710	511,678	1,500,000	73%	100%
AL	3	7,572,176	2,524,059	7,800,000	103%	72%
LA	16	36,769,455	2,298,091	22,950,000	62%	97%
MS	9	12,872,815	1,430,313	7,000,000	54%	100%
TN	3	5,092,665	1,697,555	3,000,000	59%	42%
KY	4	7,145,326	1,786,332	2,000,000	28%	27%
MO	1	250,000	250,000	2,500,000	100%	100%
IL	2	2,014,760	1,007,380	3,000,000	149%	26%
IN	1	1,585,481	1,585,481	1,390,000	88%	12%
OH	32	9,247,296	288,978			
MI	9	1,400,000	155,556			
Total	627	293,015,515	467,329			
Regional shares or Averages						
New England	48%	22%	211,292			
Mid-Atlantic	33%	27%	384,583			
South Atlantic	6%	11%	825,733			
Southwest	5%	21%	2,009,907			
Northwest	8%	7%	441,691			

states west of the Appalachians with more than ten banks, and they were the two oldest and most-developed western states by the 1830s. Most frontier states had four or fewer banks.[24] Southern states in general had larger banks than northern states, but banks overall were much larger in the West than in the East. Banks in the southwest had ten times the average capital of banks in New England.

The last three columns of the table provide some insight into state investment in banks in the West. Column (4) gives the amount of state debt incurred to invest in banks up 1837. Only states in the frontier South and West borrowed money to invest in banks. Column (5) gives state investment

24. The numbers for Mississippi and Michigan are larger because of the creation of banks in 1835 and 1836.

as a share of total bank capital. With the exception of Kentucky, Ohio, and Michigan, state governments provide more than half of bank capital in each of these states.[25] State involvement was critically important to the development of banks in the south and west. Column (6) gives the share of all state borrowing that went to investments in banks. We'll return to this shortly.

The First and Second Banks of the United States were extremely important to the development of American financial systems. They spanned the country with their branches, provided a uniform paper currency, and stabilized the conduct of national financial activities. But they were not the only, or even the most important, elements of the banking system that developed in the early nineteenth century. By 1836, state chartered banks had ten times the capital of the Second Bank. When the Second Bank lost its charter, it was quickly rechartered as the Bank of the United States of Pennsylvania. The banking system continued to develop without a national bank, and there is no reason to believe that the banking system would not have developed before 1836 if there had not been a national bank, although the system would have looked somewhat different.

State involvement in transportation investment has as a long history as well. By the 1780s, states were chartering private companies, providing subsidies, and purchasing stock in canal, bridge, road, and turnpike companies.[26] Virginia chartered the Potomac Company and the James River Company in 1785 and the Dismal Swamp Company in 1790. In 1792, New York chartered two companies, the Western Inland Lock Navigation Company and the Northern Inland Lock Navigation Company, to open canals to Lake Ontario in the west and at the St. Lawrence in the north via Lake Champlain. Maryland chartered the Chesapeake and Delaware canal in 1799. By 1811, Pennsylvania had spent $825,000 to build turnpikes. Massachusetts also invested in turnpikes. Unlike their investments in banks, however, transportation projects were rarely profitable investments for state governments. For a few brief years around 1805, it appeared the national government might get involved in transportation. Jefferson's second inaugural message led Congress to ask the Secretary of the Treasury, Albert Gallatin, to prepare a report laying out a possible system of internal improvements. Gallatin's famous report proposed a network of canals that would have connected the disparate parts of the country at a cost of over $20,000,000. Most of the projects envisioned in the report were eventually carried out in one form or another by state or private interests, but the national government spent very little on transportation before the 1820s.

Despite national inaction, there was widespread support for internal improvements. In 1811, the New York legislature authorized the issue of

---

25. The 148 percent figure in Illinois is the result of a large state investment in 1837, which occurred after the figure on bank capital was collected in January. The same is true for Alabama.

26. The classic history of government involvement in transportation remains Goodrich (1960) which has been supplemented by Larson (2001).

$5,000,000 in state bonds to build a canal, a plan sidetracked by the outbreak of the War of 1812. Virginia created a Board of Public Works in 1816. In 1817, after failing to receive national support, New York embarked on the largest infrastructure project of its time, the Erie Canal. The canal turned out to be a phenomenally successful investment. Completed in 1825, it soon returned funds to the state over and above maintenance costs and interest payments. Now it appeared canals could prove as profitable as banks. The pattern of state transportation investment, after the Erie success, was influenced by two factors.

The first was geography. States with access to ocean transportation did not need to build canals, although they often improved their rivers and built short canals to bring their interior regions into contact with ports. The real payoff was the construction of interregional canals, like the Erie, that reached into the northwestern interior. In the late 1820s Ohio, Pennsylvania, and Maryland started canals, all with hopes they would pay for themselves and return a handsome dividend to the state treasury. Virginia, South Carolina, and Georgia contemplated projects that would open up routes into Tennessee and Kentucky.

The second factor was the youth of western states. Indiana became a state in 1816, Mississippi in 1817, Illinois in 1818, Alabama in 1819, and Missouri in 1820. Indiana was the largest of those states in 1820, with a population of just 147,000. It was not until the early 1830s that western populations, swelled by rapid population inflows, and western state budgets, spurred by the rapidly expanding economy and the boom in national land sales, enabled these young states to contemplate transportation investments of their own. In 1836 and 1837, Indiana, Illinois, and Michigan started new canal and railroad systems. In the same years, New York, Ohio, and Pennsylvania committed to expanding their existing systems. Rising western populations raised land prices; rising land prices stimulated public land sales; increased sale of public land raised the property tax base; and states began to think they could afford to build better transportation systems, which would further raise land prices, increase land sales, and expand the property tax base. The direction of causation in this story is difficult to disentangle, but all the factors came together to produce a major economic boom in the 1830s.

Again, the development of transportation investment reflects the interaction of economics and politics. Both Goodrich and Larson tend to view the timing of state investments as dependent on federal policy, arguing that states only took up the challenge of building canals when it became clear that the federal government would not. But there is little support for their view. Before the War of 1812, almost all of the non-New England states either actively engaged in transportation investments or were contemplating them. The early model, again, was the European model, with state chartering of privileged private corporations. That model failed in the 1790s to produce results. States had begun to consider alternatives before the war. After the war, state investment picked up again, notably in New York. The Erie Canal example (1817) forced states on the eastern seaboard to move; Pennsylvania and Maryland borrowed and began construction on their canals in 1825; Maryland was also involved in the Baltimore and Ohio railroad.

States farther west, Indiana, Illinois, and Michigan, were simply not in an economic position to begin transportation investments until the 1830s. There was neither a population nor tax base in place. In 1835 and 1836 alone, public land sales in Indiana amounted to twice the taxable acreage in 1834. The land boom represented a fiscal windfall for these states, and they began investments soon afterward: Indiana in 1836, Illinois and Michigan in 1837.

The boom affected southwestern states as well, but southern states were not in need of major transportation investments. Their already navigable rivers ran to the sea. In the South, banks dominated state investments. Louisiana invested $23 million in banks beginning in 1824. Alabama, Georgia, and Florida made substantial investments in the early 1830s, while Mississippi and Arkansas committed millions to banks in 1837 and 1838. More than half of the banking capital in each of these states by 1837 came from state investment, and almost all of the debt in these states was issued for the purpose of investing in banks (see table 6.4).[27] In most southern banks, it was the banks, and not the states, that had the obligation to service the bonds. Southern voters were willing to support banks, but they had no anticipation that they would have to pay any taxes to obtain those banks. The history of banking in the east suggested that bank investments were profitable. Northwestern states needed banks, too; Illinois and Indiana made significant investments in their state banks.

States had always borrowed money to finance long-term capital projects. But the pace of state borrowing increased dramatically in the 1830s. State debts expanded from a few million in 1820, to $80 million in 1830, and to $200 million in 1841. The relative size of some of the state debts is truly amazing. In 1836, Indiana, with a population of roughly 600,000 and a state budget of $50,000 a year, authorized a bond issue of $10,000,000 in 5 percent bonds. Interest payments on the bonds alone would come to $500,000 a year, ten times the entire state budget of 1836. Michigan, with a population of no more than 200,000 and state revenues of $17,000 in 1836, authorized a bond issue of $5,000,000 of 5 percent bonds in 1837.[28] Total and per capita state debts outstanding in 1841 are given for each state in table 6.5.

In 1837, the American economy was hit by a financial panic, and in 1839, a depression began that lasted until 1843. Many of the transportation and

27. Arkansas became a state in 1837, and the first act of the state legislature was to create a bank capitalized by state bonds.
28. Information on state finances in the 1830s and 1840s is available at Inter-University Consortium for Political and Social Research (ICSPR), Richard Sylla, John Legler, and John Wallis "Sources and Uses of Funds in State and Local Governments, 1790–1915: [United States]," Data set 1993-05-13.

Table 6.5   Total state debt and debt per capita in 1841, and whether a state defaulted

State	Total debt ($)	Debt per capita ($)	Default?
FL	4,000,000	74.07	Yes
LA	23,985,000	68.14	Yes
MD	15,214,761	32.37	Yes
IL	13,527,292	28.42	Yes
AK	2,676,000	27.31	Yes
MI	5,611,000	26.47	Yes
AL	15,400,000	26.06	No
PA	33,301,013	19.32	Yes
MS	7,000,000	18.62	Yes
IN	12,751,000	18.59	Yes
NY	21,797,267	8.97	No
MA	5,424,137	7.35	No
OH	10,924,123	7.19	No
WI	200,000	6.45	No
SC	3,691,234	6.21	No
TN	3,398,000	4.10	No
KY	3,085,500	3.96	No
ME	1,734,861	3.46	No
VA	4,037,200	3.23	No
MO	842,261	2.19	No
GA	1,309,750	1.90	No
NH	0	0.00	No
CT	0	0.00	No
VT	0	0.00	No
RI	0	0.00	No
NC	0	0.00	No
NJ	0	0.00	No
DE	0	0.00	No

Note: Debt in 1841 and 1880 taken from 1880 Census.

banking projects of the western states were abandoned. Indiana, Illinois, Michigan, Arkansas, Louisiana, Mississippi, Florida (still a territory), Maryland, and Pennsylvania stopped paying interest payments on their state bonds in 1841 and 1842. Mississippi and Florida formally repudiated their debts, while Louisiana, Arkansas, and Michigan ultimately failed to repay part of the money they had borrowed. Indiana and Illinois worked out a deal with their creditors. Maryland and Pennsylvania quickly resumed payments on their bonds and, in the end, repaid all of the principal and most of the back interest. New York, Ohio, and Alabama narrowly avoided default.

It is tempting to think of the "canal" boom of the 1830s as the result of naïve western states optimistically thinking they could borrow to build canals, railroads, and banks and live off the dividends and tolls. Such a view is inconsistent with the history. States had been deeply involved in the creation of banks and transportation companies since the 1780s. In the case of banks, state involvement had proven profitable. States who owned stock in banks received substantial and steady dividends, and those states that taxed banks earned a hefty share of state revenues from bank revenues. In the case of transportation, until the Erie Canal, state investments had rarely been directly profitable, but there is little reason to doubt that the overall returns to the state treasury in terms of higher property tax revenues on increased land values made these good investments.[29] What happened after 1839 was an unexpected economic depression. Just as the land and economic boom in 1835 and 1836 was fed, in part, by the anticipation of state investments in transportation and finance, the bust was caused, in part, by the realization in 1839 that many states would have trouble repaying their debts.

6.8   How States Reacted

There is no doubt about why states defaulted. As table 6.5 shows, nine of the ten states with the largest per capita debts defaulted, and Alabama, Ohio, and New York narrowly avoided default. State legislatures throughout the country were asking "how did we get into this mess?" and "how can we prevent this from happening again?" Although conditions in every state were unique, the answers given in the 1840s shared a common theme that echoed the fears of systematic corruption that had been heard since the Revolution. States felt that they had gotten into trouble because they allowed small, well-organized groups to exert a disproportionate influence in the legislative process. These groups were able to sway democratic legislators and voters to support their schemes because they promised a significant return to the state in the form of a bank, canal, or railroad, and at the same time promising taxpayers that they would not have to foot the bill.

Was this kind of corruption a real problem? Or was the language of corruption (of systematic corruption) so dominant in political discourse that Americans expressed their concern over how democracy worked in terms that focused attention on small privileged groups when the serious problems lay elsewhere? A complete answer to the questions involves detailed examination of each state, something I can't venture to do here, but some general observations seem warranted.

There were cases of systematic corruption. The clearest examples occurred in chartering banks in the South, particularly in Real Estate Bank of Arkansas and the Union Bank of Mississippi.[30] These were cases where a small group had obtained privileges from the state and resources in the form of state bonds, had used the distribution of those economic resources to build

29. For a paper that estimates the effect of railroad construction on land values and property tax revenues in the late nineteenth century, see Heckelman and Wallis (1997), and for a direct measure of canal construction on land values in Indiana in the mid-1830s, see Wallis (2003).
30. For an overview of banking in the South, see Schwiekart (1987); for banking in Mississippi, see Bentley (1978); Brough (1970), and Kilbourne (2006); for Alabama, see Brantley (1961); for Arkansas, see Worley (1950); for an overview of the corruption question in Southern banking, see Wallis (2008).

or enlarge a political coalition, and then had defaulted on the state, leaving taxpayers and bondholders holding the bag. Systematic corruption played a significant role in explaining why Arkansas and Mississippi didn't just default on interest payments for a time, but repudiated their bonds.[31] The manipulation of bank chartering by Martin Van Buren and the Albany Regency in New York in the 1820s and 1830s borders on systematic corruption as well (Bodenhorn 2006).

In most cases, however, states had not been hoodwinked. Deliberation over whether to build canals was usually a multiyear process, involving different groups and interests, many of whom had full opportunity to put their case before the people and the legislature. Bank chartering policy evolved over a number of years and was also the subject of an extended public debate (Wallis, Sylla, and Legler 1994). The debates were so long lasting that they formed the basis for informal (or formal in some cases) political parties and organizations. The Albany Regency was a consciously designed political machine that used control of bank chartering as an element in funding the party machinery.[32] There were canal Democrats in New York, bank Democrats in Indiana, and the canal faction and the railroad faction in Pennsylvania (Holt, 1999). In most states, the ongoing debate over internal improvements and banking provided the structure and interest for the formation of durable patterns of interests that were often reflected in nascent political parties.

In Whig theory, political parties were an anathema to republican government. George Washington's farewell address notably pointed to factions and parties as one of the greatest dangers the new nation faced. Even as Madison and Jefferson organized a political party to oppose the Federalists and their Bank of the United States, in the 1790s, they did all that they could to deny that they were actually forming a party. Madison, in particular, struggled with the legitimacy of party.[33] The Whig party formed in the 1830s to oppose the Jacksonian Democrats, along battle lines laid out by Jackson's veto of the second Bank of the United States rechartering and Jackson's opposition to a national system of internal improvements. One of the strongest arguments in the Whig arsenal was Jackson's conscious development of a political party, something still regarded as inherently systematically corrupt in the political debates of the 1830s. It was no accident that the fault lines in the first two prominent party struggles at the national level, between the Federalists and Republicans in the 1790s and between the Democrats and Whigs in the 1830s and 1840s, concerned political promo-

31. The Arkansas constitution still contains a provision preventing the state from ever repaying the "Holford bonds."

32. Bodenhorn (2006) is the most recent investigation into New York banking. Benson (1961) uses the Albany Regency and the adoption of free banking in 1837 as his test case for understanding Jacksonian democracy. Hofstadter (1969) places Martin Van Buren at the center of the process by which Americans realized that parties were not inherently corrupt, but instead an inherent part of a democratic society. Leonard (2002) expands on Hofstadter's themes and provides a better understanding of how Van Buren and his contemporaries viewed parties.

33. Madison wrote a series of articles about parties in the early 1790s; see Sheehan (1992).

tion of economic development through government involvement in banks and transportation projects.

Factions and parties were inherently corrupt in Whig theory. As suffrage widened and state governments became more democratic, pressure on state governments to deliver economic infrastructure intensified. Successful early examples of banking and canal investments raised expectations that those favorable results could be duplicated in other states. Promoters and supporters of projects formed natural alliances from which to build political coalitions and parties.[34] Partisans on both sides, those for or against the bank, canal, or railroad, claimed at the top of their lungs that the other side was corrupt, that the other side was forming a political party to subvert democracy.

The clinching feature that often culminated debates about internal improvements turned out to be taxes. Promoters who could figure a way to package their proposal in a way that did not involve raising current taxes or that shifted tax burdens away from project opponents and toward project supporters, for example, New York, were often able to craft the final compromise that enabled them to build a coalition sufficient to win legislative support. Americans complained in the 1840s that unscrupulous promoters had promised them canals and railroads for nothing, banks and financial services for free, and that somehow they had been tricked into assuming obligations unknowingly. They cried corruption, but what they had really learned was that an unstructured democracy with simple majority rule decision-making processes was liable, indeed invited, decisions to be made that looked good ex ante but subsequently turned out to be very expensive.

When states went on their internal improvements borrowing binges in the 1820s and 1830s, they were not acting naïvely. They based their forward looking expectations on a half century of experience with financing bank and transportation projects.[35] As Americans have learned again in 2008 and 2009, when a financial crisis hits, investments that looked good and were good can suddenly turn disastrous. Something similar happed after 1839. Rather than blaming the crisis on bad men, states blamed the basic structure of democratic decision making and so moved to make changes in the way politics and economics interacted. The new institutions dealt with taxation, borrowing, the creation of organizations (largely corporations), and the structure of legislation. The states responded to the crisis by making fundamental changes in their state constitutions that altered their simple democracies into governance structure with considerably more subtlety and sophistication.

---

34. Ershkowitz and Shade (1971) examine party differences over a range of issues in early nineteenth-century state legislatures. Banking and corporation chartering were two of the most divisive issues, internal improvements somewhat less so.

35. Wallis (2003) examines Indiana, which was one of the largest borrowers in the 1830s, and shows that with very reasonable expectations the state could expect to repay its debts.

The simplest solution to preventing another crisis like the early 1840s from happening again was prohibiting government debt altogether. Goodrich (1950) took his ironic title "The Revulsion Against Internal Improvements" from Henry Adams's suggestion that was what occurred in the 1840s. But the point of Goodrich's paper was that the wave of constitutional reforms in the 1840s did *not* stop states, and certainly not local governments, from continuing to pursue internal improvements in the 1850s and after the Civil War. States did not close off the possibility of financing internal improvement projects by borrowing. Instead, they required that any legislative authorization to borrow new funds be matched with an immediate increase in taxation that had to be approved by the voters, what today are called bond referendums. The primary aim of the procedural debt restrictions was to pair tax increases with borrowing. Debt provisions affected the procedures by which debt could be issued rather than imposing absolute limits on borrowing.

The first complete debt clause was Article 4, Section 6, Part 4 of the New Jersey Constitution of 1844.[36]

> The legislature shall not, in any manner, create any debt or debts, liability or liabilities, of the State which shall, singly or in the aggregate with any previous debts or liabilities, at any time exceed one hundred thousand dollars, except for purposes of war, or to repel invasion, or to suppress insurrection, unless the same shall be authorized by a law for some single object or work, to be distinctly specified therein; which law shall provide the ways and means, exclusive of loans, to pay the interest of such debt or liability as it falls due, and also to pay and discharge the principal of such debt or liability within thirty five years from the time of the contracting thereof, and shall be irrepealable until such debt or liability, and the interest thereon, are fully paid and discharged; and no such law shall take effect until it shall, at a general election, have been submitted to the people, and have received the sanction of a majority of all the votes cast for and against it, at such election; and all money to be raised by the authority of such law shall be applied only to the specific object stated therein, and to the payment of the debt thereby created. This section shall not be construed to refer to any money, that has been, or may be, deposited with this State by the government of the United States.

The New Jersey restrictions were repeated, with alterations, in other states. New Jersey limited "casual" debt to $100,000.[37] Issue of more debt than that

---

36. A procedural restriction was included in the Rhode Island constitution of 1842, but it simply required the consent of the people before the state could borrow more than $50,000. Its essence, but not its details, are the same as in New Jersey. All references to constitutions in the paper are to Thorpe, *Federal and State Constitutions,* as corrected by John Joseph Wallis in the NBER/University of Maryland State Constitution Project (see www.stateconstitutions .umd.edu).

37. The language of the New Jersey clause follows closely the language of an amendment proposed to the New York constitution in 1842. Adoption of the 1842 amendment was delayed until the New York constitutional convention in 1846. See the discussion in Gunn (1988).

required legislation that specified the purpose of the debt, and the "ways and means," that is, the tax revenues, to service the debt within thirty-five years (such legislation was "irrepealable"). The legislation authorizing the debt issue could not take effect until it was approved by a majority of the voters in a general election. The key element in the procedural restrictions was the requirement that the "ways and means" shall be provided. Legislation authorizing the bond issue had to include new taxes sufficient to service the debt, and the new taxes had to be approved by the voters. In New York and Iowa, "ways and means" was replaced with "direct annual tax," that is, a property tax. In most states, the property tax would be the tax used to provide revenues.

Table 6.6 gives the year when states adopted procedural debt restrictions of some type. By 1900, only Delaware, Vermont, Connecticut, New Hampshire, Massachusetts, Rhode Island, and Arkansas did not have debt restrictions. New England states were, again, different in this regard. Of the twelve states that revised their constitutions between 1840 and 1851, every state but Virginia adopted procedural restrictions on debt issue.[38]

Procedural restrictions on debt issue dramatically changed the political process for approving debt issues. By requiring voters to raise their own taxes immediately before any bonds could be issued, the debt provisions ensured that a political coalition encompassing at least half the voters had to be put together to secure passage. The next step was to prevent a political coalition from manipulating interests by creating special privileges for small groups.

The initial wave of constitutional changes directed at special privileges in the 1840s focused on corporations. A requirement that mandated legislatures pass general incorporation acts, was tied with a restriction, and in some cases prohibition, on special incorporation. General incorporation was a administrative procedure that enabled individuals to get a corporate charter by filing the appropriate paperwork and paying a fee. Special incorporation was any charter issued by the legislature.[39] Most (though not all) states required general incorporation and prohibited special incorporation. In some states, special incorporation was explicitly prohibited: "The General Assembly shall pass no special act conferring corporate powers" (Ohio, 1851, Article 13, Section 1). In other states, special incorporation was prohibited "except for municipal purposes, and in cases where in the judgment of the Legislature, the objects of the corporation cannot be attained under general laws" (Wisconsin, 1848, Article 11, Section 1). In these states, the prohibition on special corporations was implicit. New York initially con-

38. Indiana banned all debt issue, while Ohio, and Michigan banned new debt issue for internal improvements. Issues in Virginia revolved around the apportionment of political power between the western and eastern parts of the state.
39. Many acts of special incorporation did not create corporations that were special in any way; many corporate charters were virtually identical. What was special about special incorporation was the legislative grant.

Table 6.6   When states adopted constitutional provisions regulating the issue of
                   state debt

New Jersey	1844
Texas	1845, 1876
Louisiana	1845,1879
New York	1846
Maine	1848
Wisconsin	1848
Illinois	1848,1870
California	1849,1879
Michigan	1850
Kentucky	1850
Ohio	1851
Indiana	1851
Maryland	1851,1867
Iowa	1857
Oregon	1857
Minnesota	1857
Pennsylvania	1858,1873
Kansas	1859
Nevada	1864
Nebraska	1866,1875
South Carolina	1868,1873,1884
Florida	1868,1875
Tennessee	1870
Virginia	1870
West Virginia	1872
Missouri	1875
Mississippi	1875
Alabama	1875
North Carolina	1876
Colorado	1876
Georgia	1877
Idaho	1889
Wyoming	1889
Montana	1889
Washington	1889
North Dakota	1889
South Dakota	1889
Utah	1895

Note: Delaware, Vermont, Connecticut, New Hampshire, Massachusetts, Rhode Island, and
Arkansas did not have a procedural debt restriction in 1900.

sidered a ban on special incorporation, but in the end, adopted language
similar to Wisconsin because of the need to specify special terms in charters
for municipalities and, on occasion, the need to grant specific powers of
eminent domain to transportation or communication companies.[40] Banks

40. See New York Constitution, 1846, Article 8, Section 1: "Corporations may be formed
under general laws; but shall not be created by special act, except for municipal purposes, and

were inextricably linked with corporations in the constitutions. While some states banned banks outright, most states required that banks be incorporated under general laws approved by the voters (free banking).[41] Table 6.7 gives the years that states adopted constitutional provisions making general incorporation acts mandatory.

As the table shows, the New England states were, again, the exception. General incorporation acts were legislative acts, not constitutional acts. The constitutional provisions only required that the legislature pass a general incorporation act. The first general incorporation act appears to have been passed by New York in 1783; it was an act to incorporate churches.[42] New York adopted general incorporation for manufacturing companies in 1810. Massachusetts established a general regulatory act for banks, which essentially established general incorporation for banking by 1820. I do not want to imply that general incorporation was an invention of the 1840s; it was clearly not. New England states managed to effect general incorporation through legislation and never found it necessary to mandate general incorporation in their constitutions. But most states found such a mandate necessary.

The third major change also had earlier precedents but first appeared in 1851, when Indiana adopted a constitutional provision prohibiting the state legislature from passing special legislation to benefit individuals, in seventeen different categories. Some of the categories concerned legislation that affected individual persons, like acts granting divorces to individuals and changing the names of individuals. But others acts reflected more general concerns: setting judicial venues, locating highways, regulating county and township business, providing for the support of common schools or of school funds. Table 6.8 presents the dates for prohibitions on special laws. Some states adopted prohibitions on special laws for specific purposes earlier than 1851, the "partial" restrictions listed in the table. Full restrictions varied somewhat in their content across states, and not every state adopted them, including many states in New England.

6.9   Conclusions

The history of state constitutional development often treats the constitutional changes that began in the 1840s as a continuation of the trend toward limiting the discretion of state legislatures that began in the 1780s with the

---

in cases where in the judgment of the Legislature, the objects of the corporation cannot be attained under general laws. All general laws and special acts pursuant to this section, may be altered from time to time or repealed." See the discussion in Gunn (1988, 231–2).

41. States also began asserting their absolute authority to govern corporations, even after they had granted corporate charters, special or general: "All general laws or special acts, enacted under the provisions of this section may be altered or repealed by the Legislature at any time after their passage" (Ohio, 1851, Article 13, Section 1).

42. See Seavoy (1982). There is some doubt about the first general act and whether it was in Massachusetts; see Handlin (1943), Handlin and Handlin (1945, 1969), and Maier (1992, 1993).

Table 6.7   Dates that states adopted mandatory general incorporation laws in their constitutions

Existing states		New states	
State	Year	State	Year
Louisiana	1845	Iowa	1846
New York	1846	Wisconsin	1848
Illinois	1848	California	1849
Michigan	1850	Minnesota	1858
Maryland	1851	Oregon	1859
Ohio	1851	Kansas	1861
Indiana	1851	West Virginia	1863
Missouri	1865	Nevada	1864
Alabama	1867	Nebraska	1867
North Carolina	1868	Colorado	1876
Arkansas	1868	North Dakota	1889
Tennessee	1870	South Dakota	1889
Pennsylvania	1874	Montana	1889
New Jersey	1875	Washington	1889
Maine	1875	Idaho	1890
Texas	1876	Wyoming	1890
Georgia	1877	Utah	1896
Mississippi	1890	Oklahoma	1907
Kentucky	1891	New Mexico	1912
South Carolina	1895	Arizona	1912
Delaware	1897		
Florida	1900		
Virginia	1902		
Vermont	1913		

Source: Evans (1948, table 5, 11).
Note: As of 1940, only Massachusetts, New Hampshire, Rhode Island, and Connecticut did not require general incorporation laws in their constitutions.

adoption of the second national constitution.[43] Because the changes clearly did limit state legislatures, it is impossible to argue with the general point.

This perspective, however, misses two very important developments in early nineteenth century America. First, on several dimensions, state constitutions and political institutions were becoming more democratic, not less. The excesses of democracy led James Madison to press for a national veto over state laws at the constitutional convention in 1787. The institutions that led to the excesses had certainly become stronger, not weaker, over the course of the early nineteenth century. The suffrage had been broadened considerably. Direct election of governors and judges increased the ability of the electorate to effect changes in policy through the ballot box. Before

43. Tarr (1998) makes this point and provides a useful summary of the literature on state constitutions.

State	Full	Partial
Indiana	1851	
Iowa	1857	1846
Nevada	1864	
Maryland	1864	1851
Florida	1868	1839, 1869
Texas	1869	
Illinois	1870	1848, 1872
West Virginia	1872	
Pennsylvania	1874	
New Jersey	1875	1844
Colorado	1876	
Louisiana	1879	1845
California	1879	1849
Minnesota	1881	
Washington	1889	
North Dakota	1889	
Wyoming	1889	
Montana	1889	
Idaho	1889	
South Dakota	1889	
Mississippi	1890	
Kentucky	1891	
New York	1894	
Utah	1895	
South Carolina	1896	
Alabama	1901	1861
Oklahoma	1907	
New Mexico	1911	
Arizona	1912	
Georgia		1865
Michigan		1835, 1909
Kansas		1859
Maine		1875
North Carolina		1835, 1916
Delaware		1831
Arkansas		1868, 1951
Rhode Island		1951

Table 6.8   When state adopted restrictions on "special laws" in their constitutions

the mid-1830s, state constitutions were regularly modified to widen the scope of democracy, not to narrow it.

Americans were continually learning about how democracy worked. The interplay between politics and economics at the state level continually evolved as states chartered and invested in banks, chartered and invested in transportation enterprises, and responded to the demands of voters that they pursue policies that brought prosperity and higher land values to the average citizen. State politics were intense, and internal improvement debates pitted those who would gain against those who would pay. The nature of the democratic process itself led to legislative compromises in which taxes often were not raised at all, or deferred to some hopeful future.

The trade-off of lower taxes in return for granting special privileges to small groups was not a new dilemma in the United States. European governments had faced those trade-offs for centuries. As the first democracy with widespread popular inclusion, however, the United States had to wrestle with how to balance different options for providing public goods that were an important element in a growing economy. American states made two basic choices. First, they attempted to remove the possibility of avoiding taxes, forcing voters being wooed by the benefits of government policies to also take into account the costs of those policies. Second, they opened access to public support for organizations to everyone without approval of the legislature. General incorporation came for businesses, but it also came for churches, schools, municipal governments, and eventually for political parties as well.

As much as guarantees of contract and property, these institutions enabled the American economy to grow and the American polity to develop. None of these changes were preordained or prefigured by the national Constitution in 1787. We must not overlook that the free, open, and competitive economy Americans managed to create by allowing anyone to form an organization and enter into almost any line of business, was not a given in early America. The early history of banking and transportation enterprises illustrate privilege, not open access. Nor should we forget that an important reason for opening economic access was to solve a political problem of making democracy work better, not to promote economic growth in an abstract sense. Economics and politics went together; it was an integral part of the American genius for building institutions.

References

Bailyn, Bernard. 1967. *The ideological origins of the American Revolution.* Cambridge, MA: Harvard University Press.
Benson, Lee. 1961. *The concept of Jacksonian Democracy: New York as a test case.* Princeton, NJ: Princeton University Press.
Bentley, Marvin. 1978. The State Bank of Mississippi: Monopoly bank on the frontier (1809–1830). *Journal of Mississippi History* 40:297–319.
Bodenhorn, Howard. 2000. *A history of banking in antebellum America.* Cambridge: Cambridge University Press.
———. 2006. Bank chartering and political corruption in ante-bellum New York: Free banking as reform. In *Corruption and reform,* ed. Claudia Goldin and Ed Glaeser, 231–57. Chicago: University of Chicago Press.
Brantley, William H. 1961. *Banking in Alabama, 1816–1860.* Privately Printed.

Brough, Charles. 1970. *The history of banking in Mississippi.* Mississippi Historical Society Publications. Oxford: Mississippi Historical Society.

Cadman, John W. 1949. *The corporation in New Jersey: Business and politics, 1791–1875.* Cambridge, MA: Harvard University Press.

Coffman, Chad, and Mary Eschelbach Gregson. 1998. Railroad development and land values. *Journal of Real Estate Finance and Economics* 16 (2): 191–204.

Craig, Lee, Raymond Palmquist, and Thomas Weiss. 1998. Transportation improvements and land values in the antebellum United States. *Journal of Real Estate Finance and Economics* 16 (2): 173–90.

Ershkowitz, Herbert, and William G. Shade. 1971. Consensus of conflict? Political behavior in the state legislatures during the Jacksonian Era. *Journal of American History* 58 (3): 591–621.

Evans, George Heberton. 1948. *Business incorporations in the United States, 1800–1943.* NBER, Baltimore: Waverly Press.

Feller, Daniel. 1984. *The public lands in Jacksonian politics.* Madison, WI: University of Wisconsin Press.

Fenstermaker, J. Van. 1965. *The development of American commercial banking, 1782–1837.* Kent, Ohio: Kent State University.

Gates, Paul Wallace. 1968. *History of public land law development.* Washington, D.C.: GPO.

Goodrich, Carter. 1950. The revulsion against internal improvements. *Journal of Economic History* 10:145–69.

———. 1960. *Government promotion of American canals and railroads.* New York: Columbia University Press.

Guinnane, Timothy W., Ron Harris, Naomi R. Lamoreaux, and Jean-Laurent Rosenthal. 2007. Putting the corporation in its place. *Enterprise and Society* 8 (Sept.): 687–729.

Gunn, L. Ray. 1988. *The decline of authority.* Ithaca, NY: Cornell University Press.

Hamilton, Alexander, John Jay, and James Madison. 2001. *The federalist.* Edited by George W. Carey and James McClellan. Indianapolis: Liberty Fund Press.

Handlin, Oscar. 1943. Laissez-faire thought in Massachusetts, 1790–1880. *Journal of Economic History* 3:55–65.

Handlin, Oscar, and Mart Flug Handlin. 1945. Origins of the American business corporation. *Journal of Economic History* 5 (1): 1–23.

———. 1969. *Commonwealth: A study of the role of government in the American economy, Massachusetts, 1774–1861.* Rev. ed. Cambridge, MA: Harvard University Press.

Harris, Ron. 2000. *Industrializing English law.* New York: Cambridge University Press.

Heckelman, Jac, and John Joseph Wallis. 1997. Railroads and property taxes. *Explorations in Economic History* 34:77–99.

Hofstadter, Richard. 1969. *The idea of a party system.* Berkeley, CA: University of California Press.

Holt, Michael F. 1999. *The rise and fall of the American Whig party.* New York: Oxford University Press.

Keyssar, Alexander. 2000. *The right to vote: The contested history of democracy in the United States.* New York: Basic Books.

Kilbourne, Richard Holcombe Jr. 2006. *Slave agriculture and financial markets in antebellum America: The Bank of the United States in Mississippi, 1831–1852.* London: Pickering and Chatto.

Kruman, Marc W. 1997. *Between authority and liberty: State constitution making in revolutionary America.* Chapel Hill: University of North Carolina Press.

Lamoreaux, Naomi R., and Jean-Laurent Rosenthal. 2005. Legal regime and contractual flexibility: A comparison of business's organizational choices in France and the United States during the era of industrialization. *American Law and Economics Review* 7 (Spring): 28–61.

———. 2006. Corporate governance and the plight of minority shareholders in the United States before the great depression. In *Corruption and reform: Lessons from America's economic history,* ed. Edward L. Glaeser and Claudia Goldin, 125–52. Chicago: University of Chicago Press.

Larson, John Lauritz. 2001. *Internal improvement: National public works and the promise of popular government in the early United States.* Chapel Hill, NC: University of North Carolina Press.

Leonard, Gerald. 2002. *The invention of party politics: Federalism, popular sovereignty, and constitutional development in Jacksonian Illinois.* Chapel Hill, NC: University of North Carolina Press.

Maier, Pauline. 1993. The Revolutionary origins of the American Corporation. *William and Mary Quarterly* 50 (1): 51–84.

———. 1992. The debate over incorporations: Massachusetts in the early Republic. In *Massachusetts and the new nation,* ed. Conrad Wright. Boston: Massachusetts Historical Society.

Majewski, John. 2000. A house dividing: Economic development in Pennsylvania and Virginia before the Civil War. New York: Cambridge University Press.

Malone, Laurence J. 1998. *Opening the West: Federal internal improvements before 1860.* Westport, CT: Greenwood Press.

Miller, Nathan. 1962. *The enterprise of a free people: Aspects of economic development in New York State during the Canal Period, 1792–1838.* Ithaca, NY: Cornell University Press.

Nettels, Curtis. 1924. The Mississippi Valley and the Constitution, 1815–1829. *The Mississippi Valley Historical Review* 11 (3): 332–57.

Pocock, J. G. A. 1975. *The Machiavellian moment: Florentine political thought and the Atlantic Republican tradition.* Princeton, NJ: Princeton University Press.

Robbins, Caroline. 1959. *The eighteenth-century commonwealthman.* Cambridge, MA: Harvard University Press.

Scheiber, Harry N. 1969. *Ohio Canal era: A case study of government and the economy, 1820–1861.* Athens, OH: Ohio State University Press.

Schweikart, Larry. 1987. *Banking in the American South from the age of Jackson to Reconstruction.* Baton Rouge, LA: Louisiana State University Press.

Seavoy, Ronald E. 1982. *The origins of the American business corporation, 1784–1855.* Westport, CT: Greenwood Press.

Shalhope, Robert E. 1972. Toward a Republican synthesis: The emergence of an understanding of republicanism in American historiography. *William and Mary Quarterly* 29 (1): 49–80.

———. 1982. Republicanism and Early American historiography. *William and Mary Quarterly* 39 (2): 334–56.

Sheehan, Colleen A. 1992. The politics of public opinion: James Madison's "Notes on Government." *William and Mary Quarterly* 39 (4): 609–27.

Shugerman, Jed. 2008. *The people's courts: The rise of judicial elections and judicial power in America.* Unpublished Manuscript.

Skinner, Quentin. 1998. *Liberty before liberalism.* New York: Cambridge University Press.

Sylla, Richard, John B. Legler, and John Joseph Wallis. 1987. Banks and state public finance in the New Republic. *Journal of Economic History* 47 (2): 391–402.
Tarr, Alan. 1998. *Understanding state constitutions.* Princeton, NJ: Princeton University Press.
Thorpe, Francis Newton. 1906. *Federal and State Constitutions.* Washington, DC: Government Printing Office.
Wallis, John Joseph. 2003. The property tax as a coordination device: Financing Indiana's mammoth system of internal improvements. *Explorations in Economic History* 40 (3): 223–50.
———. 2005. Constitutions, corporations, and corruption: American states and constitutional change, 1842 to 1852. *Journal of Economic History* 65 (1): 211–56.
———. 2006. The concept of systematic corruption in American economic and political history. In *Corruption and reform,* ed. Edward L. Glaeser and Claudia Goldin, 23–62. Chicago: University of Chicago Press.
———. 2008. Answering Mary Shirley's question or: What can the World Bank learn from American history? In *Political institutions and financial development,* ed. Stephen H. Haber, Douglass Cecil North, and Barry R. Weingast, 92–124. Stanford, CA: Stanford University Press.
Wallis, John Joseph, Richard Sylla, and John Legler. 1994. The interaction of taxation and regulation in nineteenth century banking. In *The regulated economy: A historical approach to political economy,* ed. Claudia Goldin and Gary Libecap, 121–44. Chicago: University of Chicago Press.
Wallis, John Joseph, and Barry R. Weingast. 2005. Equilibrium impotence: Why the states and not the American National Government financed infrastructure investment in the antebellum era. NBER Working Paper no. 11397. Cambridge, MA: National Bureau of Economic Research.
Wright, Robert E. 2008. Corporate entrepreneurship and economic growth in America, 1790–1860. Paper presented at the Economic History Association meetings.
Wood, Gordon S. 1969. *The creation of the American republic, 1776–1787.* Chapel Hill: University of North Carolina Press.
Worley, Ted R. 1950. Control of the Real Estate Bank of the State of Arkansas, 1836–1855. *Mississippi Valley Historical Review* 37 (3): 403–26.

III

Business Organization and the Factors of Production

7

Rise of the Corporation Nation

Robert E. Wright

What is done in England by combination, unless it be the
management of municipal concerns, is most generally done
by a combination of individuals, established by mere articles
of agreement. On the other hand, what is done here by the
co-operation of several persons, is, in the greater number of
instances, the result of a consolidation effected by an express
act or charter of incorporation. . . . We cannot but be impressed with a deep sense of the importance of this law in our
own country . . . In no country have corporations been multiplied to so great an extent, as in our own. If a native of Europe, who has never traversed the wide barrier which sepa-
rates him from us should be informed, even with tolerable
accuracy, of the number of Banking Companies, Insurance
Companies, Canal Companies, Turnpike Companies, Manufacturing Companies &c. . . . that are diffused throughout
these United States, and fully invested with corporate privileges, he could not be made to believe that he was told the
truth.
—Angell and Ames 1832, v–vi, 35

Robert E. Wright is the Nef Family Chair of Political Economy in the Division of Social
Sciences at Augustana College in Sioux Falls, South Dakota.
This chapter was written with the aid of research grants from the National Science Foundation (SES-0751577) and the Berkley Center for Entrepreneurial Studies at New York University's Stern School of Business, where the author taught from 2003 until 2009 when the chapter
was drafted and revised. The author thanks Eric Hilt, Doug Irwin, Pauline Maier, Richard
Sylla, John Wallis, and the NBER (July 2008) and Dartmouth (May 2009) conferees for their
perceptive comments on earlier versions of the chapter. All errors of omission and commission,
however, remain the sole responsibility of the author.

By breaking away from Great Britain and forming a new system of government, the founding generation transformed the institutional basis of their
young nation's economy. No longer rigidly tied to Britain's empire or laws,
Americans were free to build upon their colonial and British heritages and
to adapt the best features of the old world to the unique circumstances of
the new. They strove to imitate what worked well, improve what did not,
develop what remained inchoate, and jettison what failed miserably. The
multifaceted economic transformation they engineered spawned the world's
largest, richest, and most dynamic economy.

The development of the for-profit business corporation was one of the
most original and important aspects of the new nation's institutional transformation (Dodd 1954, 1, 195; Angell and Ames 1832, v, vii; Seavoy 1982,
46–47; Hurst 1970, 8; Arner 2002, 24).[1] Before the Revolution, American
business corporations were few, small, and largely inconsequential.[2] The
weight of imperial regulations and unenlightened and uninspired British
corporate law, which imposed relatively high costs on would be incorporators while offering little in the way of benefits (Banner 1998, 1–121; Dodd
1954, 195–97; Anon. 1835, 10), induced most colonial entrepreneurs to
choose other business forms, including sole proprietorships, partnerships,
and the unincorporated joint stock firm (Livermore 1939). Table 7.1 shows
that after the Revolution, and particularly after ratification of the Constitution (Baldwin 1903, 449–65; Davis 1917, 4–8, 22–25, 31–32), U.S. corporations rapidly grew in number. By 1801, the institutional groundwork for
further growth and development—some 20,000 specially chartered corporations with about $6 to $7 billion of authorized capital would be created
by 1860—had been laid. As the head quote suggests, within a generation,
America became the world's leader in corporate development, including the
number of corporations and the sophistication and flexibility of its innovative corporate law (Maier 1993, 52; Dodd 1954, 198; Anon. 1829, 94;
Cochran 1974).

Although debates about existing corporations or the efficacy of the corporate form played little role in its adoption, the Constitution was a formative
element in the rise of the corporation nation. Many Americans, especially
those in the more market-oriented coastal areas, readily perceived that the
new frame of government struck the right balance between the lethargy of

1. Municipal governments, churches, and sundry nonprofit associations often took the corporate form and have been studied in some detail elsewhere. Here the concern is with "corporations formed with the primary object of securing pecuniary gain or avoiding pecuniary loss,
for the benefit of the members" (Davis 1917, 3). A minor class of business corporations, the
corporation sole, or a corporation consisting of a single individual, is also not discussed here as
it was seldom used (Kent 1894, 2:273). For more on other types of corporations, see McCarthy
(2003), Angell and Ames (1832, v), and Seavoy (1982, 9–38).
2. They were not annulled by the Revolution, "for the dismemberment of empire, it is well
settled, caused no destruction of the civil rights of individuals or corporate bodies." At least
one, the Philadelphia Contributionship, survives to this day (Angell and Ames 1832, 504; Davis
1917, 10; Gower 1956).

the Articles of Confederation and the tyranny of British monarchy and that it contained sufficient checks and balances to ensure political stability. With policy uncertainty minimized and public goods like protection of life, liberty, and property relatively well-assured, the latent energies of entrepreneurs were unleashed (Wright 2008, 75–122). "A laudable spirit of emulation" soon suffused the nation, including both the "*Agricultural* and *Commercial* States of the Union," the citizens of which began to undertake "the improvement of their respective territories, and transportation of their produce to the proper markets, by means of INLAND NAVIGATION and good ROADS" financed by banks and protected from loss by insurance companies (Anon. 1798a, 1).

The actions of early entrepreneurs bear out their words. In the 1780s, few established business corporations but the number of nonbusiness corporations such as municipal governments, churches, and voluntary associations expanded rapidly. Evidently, independence alone was sufficient to induce Americans to associate, but not until the Constitution was in place were they willing to invest significant sums of their own money in risky, large-scale enterprises. Cross-country comparisons cast additional light on the Constitution's crucial role in increasing investment. Entrepreneurs in Florida, Louisiana, California, Texas, and other parts of North America did not embrace business corporations until they became subject to the Constitution or, in the case of Canada, until they came to be governed by a similarly well-constructed frame of government (Wright 2008, 237–46).

According to historian Pauline Maier (1993, 51), "social and economic development could have been accomplished in other ways," without relying heavily on the corporate form. That is undoubtedly true, but the rate of such development would almost certainly have been slower. Entrepreneurs establishing for-profit businesses possessed strong incentives to choose the most efficient form of business organization in order to minimize project costs. Restricting access to the corporate form would have prevented the formation of some businesses entirely and decreased the efficiency of others. Without the corporate form, Americans would have paid more for their banks, bridges, canals, harbor facilities, roads, waterworks, and other improvements; waited longer before enjoying them; or extracted less quantity and quality output from them. The founding choice, to leave corporation formation decisions to state governments and entrepreneurs, ensured that early Americans could form corporations at relatively low cost in terms of time and money. Eventually, it ensured that they could do so on demand for a nominal fee.

This chapter shows that few corporations formed before the Constitution but many after it. It explains the proliferation of the corporate form from a cost-benefit perspective. Limited liability, entity shielding, perpetual secession, transferable shares, and the other privileges of the corporate form allowed corporations to achieve large size relative to other forms of busi-

Table 7.1   **Corporations chartered before 1801**

Jurisdiction	Colonial	1776–1789	1790	1791	1792	1793	1794	1795	1796	1797	1798	1799	1800	Total
Connecticut	2	1	0	0	3	0	0	7	2	9	9	2	9	44
Delaware	0	0	0	0	0	1	0	0	1	0	0	0	0	2
Georgia	0	0	0	0	0	0	0	0	0	0	0	1	0	1
Kentucky	0	0	0	0	0	0	1	0	0	0	0	1	0	1
Maryland	0	3	1	2	1	1	1	4	3	0	4	1	0	21
Massachusetts	1	5	0	1	8	5	5	8	11	15	8	7	7	81
National	0	1	0	0	0	0	0	0	0	0	0	0	0	2
New Hampshire	0	0	0	0	4	1	2	8	3	4	1	3	3	29
New Jersey	0	0	0	1	1	0	0	2	1	2	0	3	2	12
New York	0	0	1	1	3	1	0	0	0	3	6	7	5	27
North Carolina	0	0	1	0	1	0	0	1	0	0	1	0	0	9
Pennsylvania	2	1	0	1	2	5	3	1	5	1	4	0	0	22
Rhode Island	3	0	0	1	2	0	3	1	2	0	0	2	7	20
South Carolina	0	4	0	0	0	0	1	0	1	3	0	2	0	10
Vermont	0	0	0	1	0	0	1	2	1	4	0	4	5	18
Virginia	0	6	0	0	2	1	1	6	1	0	2	0	1	20
Total	8	21	3	9	27	15	17	40	31	41	35	33	39	319

Type														Total
Banks	0	2	1	3	8	3	0	5	2	0	0	2	3	29
Bridge	0	3	0	1	10	6	7	13	6	14	6	3	2	71
Canal	0	12	1	3	7	5	2	8	12	5	5	3	2	65
Insurance														
Fire	1	2	0	1	0	0	2	3	0	1	3	0	1	14
Marine	0	0	0	0	0	0	2	2	0	2	3	5	5	19
Manufacturing	0	1	1	1	0	0	1	0	1	1	0	0	1	7
Mapping	0	0	0	0	0	0	0	0	0	0	0	0	0	1
Mining	0	1	0	0	0	0	0	1	0	0	0	0	0	1
Pier/wharf	2	0	0	0	0	0	0	0	0	0	1	0	0	4
Trading	2	0	0	0	0	0	0	0	0	0	0	0	0	2
Turnpike	0	0	0	0	1	0	3	6	6	10	11	15	21	73
Viticulture	0	0	0	0	0	1	0	0	0	0	0	0	0	1
Water utility	3	0	0	0	1	0	0	2	4	8	6	4	4	32
Total	8	21	3	9	27	15	17	40	31	41	35	33	38	319

Sources: Baldwin (1903); Davis (1917); sundry state session laws, acts and resolves, and statutes at large were also consulted, as were state archival records and published charters and bylaws when available.

Notes: I count original charters only, not laws reviving existing charters or laws that merely validate corporations already chartered by another state. I was able to verify almost all of the charters found by Davis (1917). I include one organization that he dismissed as a charity but removed another (very charity-like) organization that he believed to be a for-profit corporation. I found one turnpike in Connecticut not listed in Davis. Future research may uncover additional charters, but it is highly unlikely that any significant number of business corporations chartered prior to 1801 have been missed. Of the 319 business corporations tracked in the table, I found positive evidence that fifteen of them never began operations. For most others, ample evidence from subsequent laws, newspaper notices, letters, and other contemporary sources exists. No systematic effort, however, has been made to verify the operation of the other corporations. Most early corporations performed only one activity. A few, however, engaged in two or more activities, for example, bridges and turnpikes or fire and marine insurance. They are categorized in this chart according to what appears to have been their primary activity.

ness organization. Large size allowed corporations to exploit economies of scale; gain market power; and undertake projects too large, complex, or long term for other types of organizations to complete. The biggest cost of the corporate form was agency problems, especially between stockholders and employees, including managers. Early corporations also faced political risks associated with the widespread misconception that their "special privileges" threatened the nation's political institutions and that corporations constituted pernicious "monopolies," careful deconstruction of which term shows that Americans were concerned with issues of market power and structure. Corporations struggled with those and related problems but reduced them enough to allow for tremendous growth of both the corporate form and the economy.

7.1   A Cost-Benefit Approach

The 3,884 entrepreneurs involved in forming U.S. corporations in the 1790s opted for the corporate form when the net benefits (all benefits minus all costs) of incorporating exceeded the net benefits of forming a sole proprietorship, partnership, or other type of business organization.[3] For some lines of business, like commercial banking and insurance, the net benefits of incorporation almost always outweighed the net benefits of other business forms.[4] For other lines, particularly manufacturing, noncorporate forms sometimes offered higher net benefits. A few early Pennsylvania iron manufacturers incorporated their firms, for example, but until the mid-nineteenth century, most did not; tanners generally eschewed the corporate form throughout the nineteenth century (Paskoff 1983, 91–131; Ellsworth 1972, 399–402). In the 1790s, taxation was low and hence not a major consideration for entrepreneurs deciding whether to incorporate (Heath 1954).

The two main costs of incorporation included internal agency conflicts between majority and minority shareholders, shareholders and bondholders, and shareholders and managers as well as the costs of obtaining a charter from state legislatures. The latter cost was increased by political animosities stemming from commercial rivalry as well as anticorporate prejudices

---

3. This is the count of all persons named in early acts of incorporation as incorporators or stock subscription agents. Many individuals were involved in more than one corporation, but undoubtedly many others were involved in corporation formation who were not explicitly mentioned in legislation, which did not always provide the names of incorporators.

4. This analysis answers the questions raised by Handlin and Handlin (1945). The same net benefit framework can also be used to analyze why entrepreneurs chose the particular form of incorporation that they did. For-profit corporations came in three major varieties, joint-stock, mutual, and mixed. Stockholders owned joint-stock corporations; depositors, policyholders, or other types of customers owned mutuals. Mixed business corporations were partly owned by stockholders and partly by customers. In the 1790s, most American corporations took the pure joint-stock form, but several insurers opted for the mutual form.

inherited from the old world and the deepest recesses of the human psyche. Until well into the nineteenth century, incorporation required the formal sanction of government, at times subjecting early incorporators to intense political pressures. Those costs declined over the first half of the nineteenth century as anticorporate sentiment waned (without disappearing) and state legislatures rendered the chartering process faster and cheaper (Anon. 1835, 9–10; Evans 1948).

The biggest benefit of incorporation was the almost singular ability of corporations to raise large, long-term pools of capital. Demand for long-term corporate securities, both bonds and equities, stemmed from six major sources: (a) the corporation's power of perpetual succession; (b) its ability to sue and be sued in its own name; (c) limited liability and entity shielding; (d) various technical advantages of corporate over more complex and convoluted partnership law; (e) the sale of call options in the primary (issuance) market; (f) the existence of liquid secondary markets. In other legal aspects of business, from general contracts to the employment of agents, corporations could generally do, within the confines of their charter, whatever sole proprietors or partnerships could do (Angell and Ames 1832, 376; Anon. 1835, 11–12; Anon. 1829, 94). So when large sums of capital were necessary and the costs of obtaining a charter were minimal, entrepreneurs usually opted for incorporation.

Quantifying with precision how much development of the corporate form aided the growth of the early U.S. economy presents insurmountable empirical barriers. That the corporate form helped the economy, rather than hurting it or serving a neutral role, is, however, undeniable. As explained in the preceding, entrepreneurs usually sought incorporation because they wanted to establish and operate large businesses more cheaply than they could by forming proprietorships or partnerships. Large business enterprises helped economic growth in at least three ways. First, in many lines of business, they lowered production costs by exploiting economies of scale. Second, large size allowed for greater vertical integration where appropriate. Third, by holding out the promise of market power, they stimulated entrepreneurship and hence helped to drive technological innovation. To the extent that it was too costly or even impossible to operate large businesses without a corporate charter, incorporation aided the economy (Cochran 1974).

7.2   Counting Costs

Obtaining a corporate charter in early America was far from costless. Those costs varied over time, place, and type of business but clearly declined over time and just as clearly were from the start lower than in Europe. Moreover, the costs of obtaining incorporation compared to the costs of forming other types of businesses are easily overestimated. The costs of governing corporations or, in other words, of limiting the internal agency problems that they faced, were considerable. Again, though, those costs tended to decrease over time and, compared to the agency costs of partnerships, are easy to overestimate.

7.2.1 Obtaining a Charter

In the United States in the 1780s and 1790s, as elsewhere in the world in the eighteenth century, so-called special incorporation was the norm. Obtaining a corporate charter required passage of a statute or, in other words, a law that explicitly granted corporate privileges to a specific group and that detailed the corporation's name, location, and vocation, and that sometimes stipulated its authorized capital, the number and duties of its directors, stockholder voting rights and liability, and other corporate characteristics. "Corporations," Zephaniah Swift correctly asserted in 1795, "can be created only by act of assembly" (Swift 1795, 225).

Many, perhaps most, entrepreneurs were able to win a charter quickly and cheaply by petitioning the legislature of the state in which they wished to conduct business (Hurst 1970, 46–47; Blandi 1934, 92). Paper, pen, publicity, and postage, as well as the time needed to collect signatures and shepherd a bill through the legislature, constituted the biggest outlays. Other enterprisers expended large amounts of time, effort, and money, including the cost of lobbyists and bribes, before gaining charter (Cadman 1949, 7–12). Costs increased, but usually were not doubled, when a corporation, like a toll bridge over the Delaware River (separating New Jersey from Pennsylvania), needed to obtain a charter from two states. Additional costs were incurred if a corporation needed to update its charter, a frequent occurrence (Cadman 1949, 13–14). Those costs varied with the ambitiousness of the suggested amendment(s) but apparently were seldom prohibitive as in many states the number of charter revisions equaled or exceeded the number of new charters granted.

Every experience was unique, but some generalizations can be made. Generally, entrepreneurs who sought to compete with the state, either directly or because the state owned shares in existing enterprises, found it costlier to obtain a charter than ones who did not threaten the state's coffers. Likewise, enterprises that seemed to offer more direct net public benefits found incorporation relatively cheaper (Livermore 1935, 674–87; Dodd 1954, 44; Gunn 1988, 106; Seavoy 1982, 5–7; Hurst 1970, 15; Heath 1954, 323–24). Toll bridge companies, for example, found it cheaper to gain legislative sanction than, say, mining companies. Turnpikes created public benefits but sometimes encountered political resistance because they could invoke the dreaded power of eminent domain (Majewski 2000, 85–86). Smaller enterprises, all else constant, had an easier go of it than larger ones. Most important, the costs of obtaining a charter trended downward over time in most states as anticorporate angst subsided and more legislators sought to aid business interests (Moss 2002, 53–84). Legislators also became more efficient by copying existing charters, creating charter blanks and blanket corporation laws, and, eventually, passing general incorporation acts that depoliticized the chartering process (Dodd 1954, 3, 269–70; Gunn 1988, 110, 227; Seavoy 1982, 5; Cadman 1949, 12).

Those gains were partially offset, however, by increased imposition of bonuses or other taxes on new and existing corporations (Livermore 1935, 676–77; Dodd 1954, 30–31, 45–46, 266–68; Angell and Ames 1832, 257–74; Blandi 1934, 72–81; Cadman 1949, 389–404). Large increases in the number of corporate charters granted in the first half of the nineteenth century were a function of both an increased number of entrepreneurs seeking incorpora-tion and the decreased cost of producing charters. (In economic parlance, more charters were obtained due to a rightward shift of the incorporation demand curve and a rightward shift of the incorporation supply curve.)

Regardless of time or place, legislators faced limits on the costs that they could impose on entrepreneurs, who enjoyed at least three other major options. One was to bide time and try again at the next session. The Bank of New York took that approach. Another was to set up operations in a more pliable state. The Society for the Establishment of Useful Manufactures, for example, opted for New Jersey after its legislature expressed support for the project (Cadman 1949, 32–33).[5] Likewise, the Jersey Bank nominally oper-ated in Jersey City but kept an office on Wall Street where it conducted most of its business. Later, it incorporated in New York to avoid a New Jersey tax on bank capital (Anon. 1804b; Dreikorn 1949, 22).

A third option was to organize as an unincorporated joint-stock associa-tion, a sort of charter by private contract rather than government sanction. Precedent for this included British common law joint-stock associations in general and various colonial joint-stock associations, including colonial land companies and the Philadelphia Linen Manufactory, in particular (Dodd 1954, 366–67; Davis 1917, 5, 258–62; Livermore 1939). Established during the long debt deflation that followed the French and Indian War, the organizers of the linen manufactory formed a joint-stock company by solic-iting subscribers to articles of association or agreement that tried to replicate the main features of the corporation via contract (Anon. 1764). Initial and subsequent stockholders signed articles of agreement providing for election of directors and other internal governance procedures. Creditors, too, had to sign a contract stipulating that the association's stockholders were not personally liable for its debts.

Contracting costs and the legal risks of unincorporated status were high enough to induce most associations to seek a charter until one was obtained (Swift 1795, 225; Moss 2002, 80–83; Angell and Ames 1832, 23, 46, 373; Hurst 1970, 14; Livermore 1939, 272–94). Nevertheless, a significant number

---

5. By the 1830s, such practices were rampant: "When they could not get charters from our own legislature, they procured them from other states" (Taylor 1833, 16).

of entrepreneurs resorted to this expedient. The Bank of New York operated
for some seven years as a joint stock association (Davis 1917, 44–45). Massachusetts's Essex Bank was also in operation for about seven years before
obtaining a charter (Davis 1917, 78, 98). The option was removed for banking associations, however, when states passed laws forbidding unincorporated entities from engaging in commercial banking, or at least the note issue
aspect of it (Dodd 1954, 205–6). That did not stop other types of companies
from starting operations as associations, however. The New York Insurance
Company began operations in 1796 under article of associations before
gaining a formal charter in 1798 (New York Insurance Company 1796). The
following year, the Marine Insurance Office of Baltimore formed under articles of association, its 400 shares snapped up by thirty-six area merchants
(Marine Insurance Office 1799). The Mutual Assurance Company of New
York began operations under articles of association in 1787; not until 1798
did it obtain the official sanction of the New York legislature (Mutual Assurance Company 1787). The Stamford Mutual Insurance Company likewise
began its existence unincorporated, its members bound by a "constitution"
dated February 20, 1797 (Stamford Mutual Insurance Company 1797). The
Hamilton Manufacturing Society began operations a year before receiving
its charter in 1797, and the Salem Iron Factory Company began operations
in 1796, four years before obtaining its charter (Seavoy 1982, 61–62; Davis
1917, 279). Numerous other companies held direct public offerings of stock
(DPOs) in anticipation of obtaining a charter, a practice generally upheld by
the courts (Dodd 1954, 78–80; Davis 1917, 33). The Warren Insurance Company and the Washington Insurance Company (both of Rhode Island), for
example, held direct public offerings (DPOs), elected directors, and enacted
bylaws before the Rhode Island legislature enacted their charters (Warren
Insurance Company 1800; Washington Insurance Company 1800).

The existence of such associations pressured governments to liberalize
chartering provisions lest they lose control of the process and the power
and taxes it brought. Considerable anticorporate sentiment among voters, however, constrained legislators from too liberally doling out charters
(Davis 1917, 303–9). Antimarket and antimonopoly biases may be inbred,
a constant condition of the human psyche, but historical circumstances
sometimes exacerbated those natural predilections (Caplan 2007, 34). The
Mother Country's experience with monopolies, behemoths aligned with the
government ostensibly designed to promote state ends while simultaneously
enriching stockholders, directors, and managers, usually at the expense of
consumers, further biased Americans against early corporations (Hovenkamp 1988, 1:595).

7.2.2   Anticorporate Angst

In 1796, a British wit defined a corporation as "an infamous relic of the
ancient feudal system; a tyrannical, exclusive monopoly, generally consisting

of gluttons, idiots, and oppressors; brutes in a human form" (Pigott 1796, 15). Harsh words indeed but by no means out of line with the sentiments of learned British scholars (Anon. 1785, 11–12; Davis 1917, 6). "One great cheque to industry in England," brilliant political economist David Hume was said to have asserted, "was the erecting of corporations, an abuse which is not yet entirely corrected." University of Glasgow professor Adam Smith also disdained most corporations, which he believed caused two major problems, internal agency conflicts and monopoly (Arner 2002, 38–42). Agency costs arose from the fact that managers followed their own interests, which were often distinct from those of stockholders. "Being the managers rather of other people's money than of their own," Smith argued, managers did not watch over the business "with the same anxious vigilance with which the partners in a private copartnery frequently watch over their own" (Smith 1937, 700). Outside of banking, insurance, and large public works like canals and water utilities, joint-stock companies were ill-advised, Smith believed. For most corporations to be profitable, he argued, the government had to provide them with monopoly privileges (Smith 1937, 699–716), another "great enemy to good management" and economic efficiency (Smith 1776, 1:184).

Monopoly for Smith came in two varieties, international trade restrictions and companies with considerable domestic market power (Smith 1776, 2:31, 243). Both varieties were lucrative, Smith pointed out, so "merchants and manufacturers are always demanding a monopoly against their countrymen" (Smith 1776, 2:50). Business interests often won their monopolies by making government "subservient" to their interests. "They will," he explained, "employ the whole authority of government, and pervert the administration of justice, in order to harrass [sic] and ruin those who interfere with them in any branch of industry . . . they may chuse to carry on" (Smith 1776, 2:252–54). That made it costly or, in extreme cases, impossible for competitors to emerge (Smith 1776, 2:42). Able to quash competition with political force instead of innovation, monopolies grew fat, indolent, and inefficient.

Smith also argued that monopoly trade restrictions "must, in almost all cases, be either a useless or a hurtful regulation" (Smith 1776, 2:36) "All the original sources of revenue, the wages of labor, the rent of land, and the profits of stock," he argued, "the monopoly renders much less abundant than they otherwise would be" (Smith 1776, 2:219). That was damning testimony indeed, but not everyone agreed with Smith, especially monopolists and their apologists. Thomas Pownall, for example, told Smith that although he had "seen some errors in the extension of the measure, further than is expedient or necessary, yet I do not see the malignancy of the principle of monopoly; nor while I have lived amidst the daily proofs of the relative advantage which it gives to the mother country, by its colonies" over other foreign powers (Pownall 1776, 7). In America, however, the nuance of the parent was lost; monopoly was evil, plain and simple.

The wrenching separation from the mother country helps to explain the especially deep antipathy toward monopoly voiced during the Early Republic. Complaints of Britain's trade restrictions, its so-called monopoly of trade, suffused the imperial crisis (Smith 1776, 2:222; Anon. 1780, 74, 77; Ramsay 1785, 9, 372; Price 1785, 50; Franklin 1794, 161; Winterbotham 1795, 423), particularly the tea troubles (Donoughue 1964, 22). After the Revolution, hatred of Britain continued unabated, with frequent allusion to her "love of monopoly" (Findley 1794, 107; Baldwin 1903, 464–65). Anything smacking of monopoly was tainted and, in some states, unconstitutional (Anon. 1790, 89–90). Tennessee's constitution stipulated "that perpetuities and monopolies are contrary to the genius of a free state, and shall not be allowed" and other state constitutions did likewise (State of Tennessee 1796, 26; A Farmer 1792, 20). In 1787, for example, a New Yorker noted that there were two ways "by which a monopoly may be effected; one proceeding from the authority of the state, and the other by means of an association, which as it acquires artificial strength from the collective wealth, is enabled to surpass, and eventually to defeat, the efforts of enterprising individuals." Because the state "happily denies the power to sanction a monopoly," the commentator noted, "the only question that can arise is, how far the government ought to exercise its power to prevent one" (Anon. 1787a, 2). Some New Yorkers even sought to amend the U.S. Constitution to prohibit the federal government from granting monopolies (Baldwin 1903, 464).

Monopoly also had dire political implications for early Americans. Perhaps Thomas Paine summed it up best when he wrote: "As property honestly obtained is best secured by equality of rights, so ill-gotten property depends for protection on a monopoly of rights. He who has robbed another of his property, will next endeavour to disarm him of his rights, to secure that property" (Paine 1795, 26). For many early Americans, corporations smacked too much of aristocracy, of hereditary privilege (Maier 1993, 66). They saw corporations as permanent monoliths because they did not yet appreciate the rapid change in ownership that the joint-stock form and liquid secondary markets made possible. Nor did they yet understand that middling and poorer sorts could, and would, own corporate equities (Maier 1993, 69–70; Wright 2002).

Distrust of monopoly ran so deep in the 1790s that some Americans opposed patents because "they conceive them to be *monopolies*" (Barnes 1792, 27). Learned Vermont jurist Nathaniel Chipman called "a system of monopoly, one of the greatest evils in civil policy" (Chipman 1793, 214). While he tolerated them "in a limited degree, for the improvement of arts, and the encouragement of genius," New York jurist James Kent also castigated monopolies because they fostered "inequalities of power and property," inviting indolence, damping enterprise, and facilitating corruption (Kent 1795, 20). Like Smith, Kent also considered mercantilism a form of monopoly because it gave artificial market power to the center at the expense of the periphery (Anon. 1798b, xvi–xxiii).

In addition to using "monopoly" to describe restrictive international trading systems like mercantilism, early Americans used the term to describe domestic market structures. Economists now think of competition as a spectrum, with perfect Smithian competition at one end and monopoly at the other. In between lay monopolistic competition, oligopoly, duopoly, contestable monopolies, and other types of imperfect markets (Lee 1990, 17–31). Early Americans, by contrast, labeled any market power, anything that was not pure competition, monopoly. They simply did not have the terminology to express the notion of market power in any other way. Use of the word monopoly in English dates to at least the sixteenth century. By the mid-eighteenth century, if not earlier, its meaning in some contexts strayed from the strict definition of the exclusive possession or control of a good to any persons or groups that could influence price, quantity, or quality (Rolt 1756, 541–44). Duopoly, oligopoly, monopolistic competition, and market power, by contrast, were not widely used until the twentieth century.[6] The broad definition of monopoly explains why early Americans regularly used it to describe market structures that clearly were not characterized by a single dominant firm.[7]

When early Americans used the word monopoly they sometimes meant precisely the same thing we mean by it today, an industry dominated by a single large producer ([Bard][1835?], 1). Clearly, however, they sometimes simply meant market power, as evidenced by more discerning writers who qualified their use of the term with phrases like "exclusive," "complete," "partial," "almost," "principles of," "spirit of," "sort of," "partaking of the nature of," and so forth (Hurst 1970, 30, 43; Anon. 1804a, 17). Baker John White, for example, explained to the Massachusetts legislature that for centuries the number of bakers allowed to bake in Great Britain had been limited by the bakers themselves.[8] That policy, he argued, was "attended with the same consequences, as a monopoly, though in a less degree" (White [1791?], 2). An anonymous writer in 1791 noted that traders could collude to bring "trade near to an open, or at least a concealed, monopoly." "They will have momentary power," he argued, but soon they will suffer "a weakness as great as their short-lived splendour was dazzling" (Anon. 1791a,

---

6. *The Oxford English Dictionary;* Hovenkamp (1988); Readex's *Archive of Americana,* searchable full-text of most early American newspapers, broadsheets, pamphlets, and books; and Thomson's *Making of the Modern World,* searchable full-text of the Goldsmith-Kress collection, record no valid hits of their use in America prior to 1820. Monopoly, however, appears in thousands of entries.

7. According to Duer (1819, 14), the following definition of monopoly was "of common use and known import": "Monopolies are sole grants of any trade or occupation, or of exclusive privileges, which ought to be common."

8. Ireland had a similar institution, designed, the bakers claimed, to ensure they "could obtain a living Profit" (Baker 1756, 4).

43–44). Economists today recognize this as a failed attempt to create a cartel. Similarly, Philadelphians long complained about a law that mandated that all auctions within the city be conducted by a single vendue master (A Plain Dealer 1786, 2). In 1790, the legislature responded by appointing a second vendue master. "A Philadelphia Merchant" objected, noting that "this, to be sure, may be a temporary *palliative;* but can never effect a *radical cure* of the evils attendant on a monopoly of this business. For if a *monopoly* be dangerous and liable to abuse, the same objection may be made against confining it to *two*" (A Philadelphia Merchant 1790, 2).

In early tariff debates, legislators also used monopoly loosely, as economists use the term market power today. In 1789, for example, George Gale (1756–1815, F-MD) thought a nine cent levy on beer too dear because it "would give the brewers here a monopoly." Thomas Fitzsimons (1741–1811, F-PA) and Tench Coxe both spoke of breaking the "monopoly" European nations enjoyed in the Eastern trade (Lloyd 1789, 1:65, 96; Coxe 1792, 23). Similarly, in 1797, "An Inhabitant" of New York complained that numerous "small grocers and hucksters" monopolized the market for food. "Not a vessel or boat" laden with food, he complained, was "not bought up in large quantities for the purpose of retail—whereby" consumers were forced to pay "of those retailers at the advance from 25 to 100 per cent" (An Inhabitant 1796, 3).

More to the point here, critics assailed early U.S. corporations as evil monopolies even when the institutions sought or obtained nothing close to full market power. Critics often portrayed banks as monopolies, for example, even as they proliferated and even though they did not claim the exclusive right to make loans, accept deposits, or even issue notes. Although it helped America to win its independence by serving as a quasi-central bank during the final phase of the Revolution, the Philadelphia-based Bank of North America came under intense political fire that in 1785 led to the revocation of its Pennsylvania charter.[9] Bank critic William Findley admitted that "whether the bank is a monopoly in the strict legal sense of the word" was an open question. But "in the common sense," he claimed, it was "a monopoly, and being so in its nature, it must be so in its effects." That made it "inconsistent with not only the frame, but the spirit of our government." "By taking advantage of a scarcity of money, which they have it so much in their power to occasion," he claimed, the bank's directors and stockholders "may become sole lords of the soil" (Anon. 1786b, 3:98). Apparently, like some other early bank critics, Findley believed the bank could control the money supply and interest rates and hence, to a considerable degree, land prices (Anon. 1785, 9; Anon. 1827).

9. Massachusetts and New York chartered it in early 1782, but it had no physical operations in either place. Congress also chartered it, but many believed its actions were unconstitutional (Davis 1917, 36–43).

The Bank of North America's founder, merchant-speculator-politician Robert Morris, retorted that there was no chance that the bank's stockholders could form a "monopoly" because they were numerous and diverse and the market for the bank's stock was active. In fact, he argued, the bank prevented monopoly in other areas of the economy by extending credit to numerous entrepreneurs. Finally, market forces, not the bank, determined the money supply (Anon. 1786c, 3; Anon. 1804a, 10; Platt 1811, 5). The Bank of North America won recharter in 1787 but over time became just one state-chartered commercial bank among many (Davis 1917, 43–44). The problem had never been the bank itself but rather the lack of competition. One critic of the bank argued that "it will not be denied to be a monopoly, if it has sufficient influence to make head against all attempts at establishing a similar institution" (Anon. 1786b), an allusion to a failed attempt to establish another bank in Philadelphia in late 1783 and early 1784 (Davis 1917, 40–42). Rather than destroy the bank, and perhaps the nation's struggling economy with it, the solution was to grant additional bank charters. "The establishment of another bank," many realized, would produce "a speedy and power influence towards producing" desirable ends, like a flourishing economy. Competition would squelch the "untowardness of men's passions" more readily and thoroughly than direct government regulation could (Citizens 1792).

The Bank of North America's successor as the national government's bank, the Bank of the United States (BUS), also found itself assailed as a monopoly even though it clearly was no such thing in the strict sense of the term. Even some shareholders of the Bank of North America called the new bank a monopoly (Webster 1791, 14)! John Taylor claimed that the BUS allowed a small number of people to monopolize "the bulk of the circulating medium." Apparently, he feared the bank would be able to influence both interest rates and the price level by increasing or decreasing the quantity of money in circulation (Taylor 1794, 11, 73–75, 80). Although the BUS dwarfed existing banks early on, it steadily lost market share because its capital remained fixed while state banks multiplied rapidly. Moreover, its monetary liabilities (notes and deposits) were convertible on demand into gold or silver, firmly tethering the money supply and interest rates to world markets.

Nevertheless, claims of the Bank's monopoly persisted. "Was it necessary that the advantages arising from the deposits of public money," William Findley asked, "should be given as a monopoly to one institution, and government deprived of a competition of proposals?" (Findley 1794, 78, 93). George Jackson (1757–1831, R-VA) also considered the BUS "a monopoly of the public monies" (Anon. 1791b, 2:754). In fact, it was not even that because the Treasury Secretary could and did deposit monies elsewhere for various reasons. But most public funds went into it and under the broader definition of monopoly then current that was enough. For the same reason, Peletiah Webster could credibly complain of the "monopoly of bank-influence in the hands of a few stockholders" of the BUS (Webster 1791, 14).

Disappointed loan applicants who blamed Federalist-controlled banks for extending discounts based on political preference further fueled claims of monopoly (Anon. 1793, 3; Anon. 1796). In sooth, those denied loans should have blamed excess demand for loans at the maximum rates allowed by law for their misfortune. After the incorporation of more banks, including some which lent extensively to Republicans, monopoly charges faded. "A necessary competition," one observer claimed after the Manhattan Company began banking operations, "has annihilated the despotism of banking monopoly" (Philander 1800, 3; Anon. 1800b, 1). Some nonbank corporations, particularly manufacturing companies, may have also enjoyed considerable local market power simply due to the high transportation costs that prevailed in parts of the early nation, particularly the South. In those situations, allowing additional corporations to form in the affected region provided the necessary relief (Bateman and Weiss 1981, 143–56).

Paradoxically, then, Americans' morbid fear of monopoly engendered corporation proliferation, and not only in banking (Maier 1993, 67). In his 1791 report on manufacturers, Treasury Secretary Alexander Hamilton claimed that opponents of "the expediency of encouraging manufactures in the United States" argued that "a virtual monopoly will be given" to those aided "and an enhancement of price, the inevitable consequence of every monopoly" would soon follow. Hamilton responded, correctly, that "the internal competition, which takes place, soon does away every thing like monopoly, and by degrees reduces the price of the article to the *minimum* of a reasonable profit on the capital employed" (Hamilton 1791, 2, 27). That did not stop George Logan, dressed in the rhetorical garb of "A Farmer," from arguing in 1792 that the Society of the Establishment of Useful Manufacturers would injure manufacturing because no man would "think of giving seven years of the prime of his life to acquire the knowledge of any profession in which he may be supplanted by a junto of monied men, under the immediate patronage and protection of Government" (A Farmer 1792, 20). Logan exaggerated and missed Hamilton's point. For the most part, early charters merely enabled corporate entrepreneurs to compete against other economic entities. Market forces dictated which businesses won and which lost. Sometimes, as in marine insurance, corporations came out on top. Other times, as in manufacturing, a variety of business forms persisted for generations.

Early corporations may have enjoyed the presumption of monopoly, as Supreme Court Justice Joseph Story later held, but in fact few charters contained explicit promises of monopoly rights (Hovenkamp 1988, 1:610; Hurst 1970, 35; Cadman 1949, 224–28). In 1799, New Jersey granted a corporation the exclusive right to sell maps of the state for fifteen years. It clearly thought of the monopoly as akin to a patent or copyright as the mapmaker's intellectual property, the extensive surveys required to create the first copy of the map, could easily be lost to a mere copyist (New Jersey 1799, 652–54). For similar reasons, bridges and other transportation companies were often promised a local monopoly of so many yards or miles for a period of years in order to protect their capital investment.

In most instances, however, government protection of monopoly rights was neither necessary nor desired (Davis 1917, 320). Where monopoly was granted, or where a degree of natural monopoly was thought to exist, state governments regularly capped tolls, interest rates, or dividends (Cadman 1949, 234–38). Nevertheless, criticism of corporations continued, their "monopoly" powers associated with special privileges. Corporations "are founded on the right claimed by government, to confer privileges and immunities on one class of citizens, not only not enjoyed by the rest, but at the expense of the rest," Jeffersonian political economist Thomas Cooper complained (Hovenkamp 1988, 1:634; Gunn 1988, 110–11). Noncorporate firms often complained bitterly about corporate competition, but their complaints were rarely heeded. When the first chartered marine insurers appeared, for example, premiums dropped, inducing individual underwriters to protest vigorously. By reducing premiums, one apologist argued, showing little regard for his clients, the new corporations did nothing but invade "the fair profits of private industry" (Mercator 1793). State legislators generally refused to arrest progress by giving in to the cries of those being fairly defeated in the marketplace because it would have been politically costly for them to do so.

In the nineteenth century, disdain for special privileges and favors dramatically reduced the cost of obtaining a charter by ushering in the age of general incorporation (Hurst 1970, 30–34). That anticorporate angst eventually led to the creation of *more* corporations should not be surprising because most Americans hated only other people's monopolies. Their own monopolies and corporations were just fine, as evidenced by the fact that many of the people who wailed against some corporations were stockholders or directors in others (Maier 1993, 52–53, 74; Davis 1917, 306–7). "There is scarcely an individual of respectable character in our community," two jurists noted in the early 1830s, "who is not a member of, at least, one private company or society which is incorporated" (Angell and Ames 1832, 35).

7.2.3   Governing the Gargantua

From political economist Adam Smith to mining observer George Taylor, critics noted that internal agency problems within corporations were endemic (Taylor 1833; Hurst 1970, 48). George Logan argued in 1792 that corporate managers were "uninterested Agents" that aggrandized themselves at the expense of shareholders (Maier 1993, 72–73). Corporations certainly faced internal agency problems, but so too did partnerships, especially ones that tried to achieve large scale. Partners were fully liable for each other's debts, so they had to monitor the activities of other partners closely. Adding partners added capital but also monitoring costs. Partnerships coped with that trade-off the best they could, usually by limiting their size and number of partners, but at times they succumbed to internal squabbling, shirking, and even theft. Forewarned of agency internal conflicts, entrepreneurs and legislators were forearmed. As a result, the governance of early U.S. corporations, although far from perfect, was remarkably good.

Legislators put some features of early corporate governance into place mainly to protect the public from potentially rapacious companies. Limitation of corporate charters to a specific number of years and explicit provision of their right to repeal or amend charters led the list, but to some extent, maximum capitalization, voting rules, and mandatory director rotation also were thought to protect society from the influence of a few great rich aristocrats (Maier 1993, 75–77; Hurst 1970, 47; Bonney 1857, 6). Such strictures, however, were also important mechanisms of internal corporate governance.

Some early corporate charters provided shareholders with one vote for each share they owned, respectively, as is typical today. Other charters, however, stipulated that each shareholder received one vote, regardless of the number of shares he or she owned. Others mandated what Alexander Hamilton called a "prudent mean," a voting rule between the extremes of one person, one vote and one share, one vote. The idea was to balance the power of large and small shareholders, so that each felt protected from the others. Voting was by secret ballot, so stockholders could exercise their franchise and "avoid the odium and violence of party prejudice" (Angell and Ames 1832, 195; Coxe 1786, 3–6).

According to historian Colleen Dunlavy (2006, 1:354; 2004, 72–79), under the common law, shareholders received one vote per person unless the corporate charter stipulated otherwise.[10] Because most early charters did not discuss voting rules, most corporations provided each shareholder with one vote, she concludes. As an empirical matter, however, three-quarters (238 of 319) of early charters did, in fact, explicitly mandate voting rules. (The other eighty were either completely silent on the matter or were so poorly worded that no determination of the voting rule could be made with confidence.) About one-third (ninety-eight) of early charters explicitly granted shareholders one vote per share without limitation. Approximately one in five (sixty-four) stipulated that shareholders should receive one vote per

10. Dunlavy's claim rests on Cadman (1949, 307) and Kerbel (1987, 47), both of which rest on a single case, *Taylor v. Griswold* (misspelled by Kerbel as Griswald), 14 *New Jersey Law* (1834), 224. However, Ratner (1970, 3–11) argues persuasively that the common law had no fixed rule regarding voting rights when they were not made explicit in corporate charters. The rule apparently held for municipal corporations and other corporations without a capital stock and hence no shares; the court's only reference to American law was a flawed inference from Angell and Ames (1832, 237). Kerbel was aware of Ratner's article but dismisses it, claiming that Ratner "forms part of a very limited minority," without proffering evidence for that claim and without critiquing the article's substance.

share up to some limit, like five, ten, or fifty votes. About the same number (sixty-seven) provided for some prudent mean voting rule. Less than 3 percent (nine) explicitly stipulated one vote per person (Davis 1917, 323; Blandi 1934, 65–66; Cadman 1949, 307–11). Most of those were mutuals that had no shares upon which to base voting rights (Virginia 1788, 19–21). Of the early nation's 319 corporations, thirteen were mutuals, six of which stipulated one vote per member, two of which provided for one vote per policy, and five of which were silent on voting rules. It makes sense that voting in those mutuals would have been based on the one vote per member or per policy models. But would such a voting scheme have been the default for joint-stock corporations?

Evidence of Dunlavy's legal claim is inconclusive. The author of an important 1829 article noted that "it has long been perceived that the common law of corporations was not adequate to govern these numerous institutions" (Anon. 1829, 94). The authors of the earliest treatise of U.S. business corporation law did not discuss the issue directly. They did note, however, that "important changes, both silent and declaratory, have been made in this country as regards the law of private corporations" (Angell and Ames 1832, vii). In other words, British common law precedents did not always hold in America de facto, a point to which we shall return in the following regarding limited liability. It appears likely that when charters were silent on the issue of stockholder voting rights, the corporate bylaws would control. Some charters, especially earlier ones, made this quite explicit. Delaware, for example, empowered the directors of the Bank of Delaware to exercise "such powers, for the well-governing and ordering the said corporation, and the affairs and business thereof . . . as have been, or shall be fixed, described and determined by the rules, laws, regulations, and ordinances of the said corporation" (Delaware 1797, 1:236–39). Similarly, voting rules were explicitly established in the corporate bylaws of the Sixth Massachusetts Turnpike Corporation, chartered in June 1799. More generally, early jurists made it clear that "where the mode of electing corporate officers is not prescribed by charter, or immemorial usage, it may be wholly ordained by by-laws" (Angell and Ames 1832, 195).[11] Almost without exception, bylaws that were not contrary to the charter or the constitution or laws of the state of incorporation were valid (Davis 1917, 317).

In a corporation controlled by one or more large interests, minority shareholders could invoke other means of protection, including calling for third-party inquiries into the corporation's activities and depressing stock prices by voting with their feet, selling off their shares in one of the nation's numerous equities markets (Wright 2002; Wright et al. 2004; Dunlavy 2006,

---

11. See also Kent (1894, 2:294), who wrote: "If this be not done to the requisite extent in the act or charter creating the corporation, it is in the power of the corporation itself, by its by-laws, to regulate the manner of election, and the requisite proof of the qualifications of the electors, in conformity with the principles of the charter."

1:356). Regardless of voting rules, courts generally worked to assure that stockholder meetings and corporate elections were transparent and fair. They insisted, for instance, that meetings be adequately advertised, that quorums be achieved before binding decisions could be made, and that treasury stock (shares owned by the corporation itself) could not be voted (Dodd 1954, 67–70; Angell and Ames 1832, 69–71).

Moreover, minority stockholders did not need as much protection then as they do now because charters constrained the activities of early corporations or, to be more precise, their managers (Hovenkamp 1988, 1:664; Berle and Means 1932, 122), a point upheld by early case law (Dodd 1954, 42–43; Angell and Ames 1832, 60; Kent 1894, 2:299; Cadman 1949, 318–26). "If a company be formed . . . to supply water," jurist James Kent explained, "the nature of their business does not raise a necessary implication that they should have power to make notes, and issue bills; and there must be express authority to enable them to do it" (Kent 1894, 2:300). So when the Potomack Company ran out of cash in 1799, it turned to its stockholders for ideas about how to raise more. When their ideas did not produce enough to finish an important series of locks, the managers suggested increasing the company's capital by levying an additional $100 on shares that were already fully paid in. Before they could do so, however, they had to win the consent of most shareholders, engineer a buyout of holdouts, and obtain legislative approval (Keith et al. 1799). Similarly, in October 1798, the stockholders of the Middlesex Canal met to consider whether "the *Directors* shall be authorized to hire *Money* to finish the *Canal* the year ensuing" (Middlesex Canal 1798). The directors of New York's canal and lock companies, by contrast, thought nothing of mortgaging the completed parts of the works to raise cash to finish its route when stockholders proved reticent to pay for their shares quickly enough (Western and Northern Inland Lock Navigation Companies 1796, 6). While directors in some companies could borrow without the explicit approval of stockholders, corporations that offered additional shares (equity) for sale generally had to offer them to existing stockholders first, so stockholders could protect their pro rata equity and voting position if they wanted to (Angell and Ames 1832, 312–15; Berle and Means 1932, 123, 133).

Such restrictions on managerial discretion were important because, by the 1790s, U.S. capital markets were quite sophisticated. In 1794, for example, the Schuylkill and Susquehanna Canal Company issued a convertible preferred stock. Holders were to receive 6 percent per annum, payable quarterly, plus their proportionate share of any dividends paid to common stockholders. They also had the option of converting their preferred shares into common stock if the company issued more of the latter during the thirteen-year contract period (Anon. 1794). Rapacious managers (or majority stockholders) could have used such instruments to bilk investors. Charter restrictions, however, limited the scope of scams as did other requirements, such as that any major change be approved by stockholders and that dividends be paid out of operating profit and not capital (Berle and Means 1932, 124, 135).

Stockholder activism also kept managers and majority stockholders in check. Stockholders in the 1790s did not spend all their waking hours monitoring their investments, but they were certainly more activist than investors were in the 1930s, when Adolf Berle and Gardiner Means complained that ownership and control had separated, that managers called the shots while rationally apathetic shareholders looked on (Wright et al. 2004; Berle and Means 1932, 76, 112–16). In 1800, for example, stockholders in the Hartford and New Haven Turnpike monitored management by appointing a committee of three men, Heman Swift, Epaphroditus Champion, and Jonathan O. Moseley, to inspect the road. The trio dutifully submitted a detailed forty-nine-point report urging the directors, due to the "immense importance" of the road, to make improvements like lowering all grades to at least 5 degrees, filling in low-lying areas, improving drainage, and building up walls and banks (Hartford and New Haven Turnpike Road Company 1800).

Dividend policies—the presumption was that profits would be paid to stockholders at regular intervals—also aided in governance by denying managers the means of undertaking self-serving or untoward activities (Davis 1917, 326). Because they were not supposed to be paid out of capital, only out of profits, dividends were also important pieces of information for stockholders and would-be investors (Cadman 1949, 320). Early stockholders could be very well informed about the status of the corporation if they wished to be. Full public disclosure was a product of the late twentieth century and was not obviously superior to the early form disclosure took, which was selective and private. In 1799, for example, the president and directors of the Potomack Company wrote stockholders a circular letter detailing the company's accomplishments, challenges, operations, and financial situation. Tellingly, the directors noted that they thought it "incumbent" upon themselves to provide stockholders with accurate and timely information (Keith et al. 1799). It was indeed incumbent upon them to provide information to stockholders who requested it because they were clearly just the owners' elected agents (Berle and Means 1932, 126). Stockholder rights to information were not unrestricted (especially in the case of banks) or uniform, but generally stockholders could view the corporation's books at frequencies ranging from annually to continuously (Cadman 1949, 319).

Corporations could also go public with information if they wished. In 1792, Philip Schuyler, president of the Northern and Western Inland Lock Navigation Company, decided he had to publish the reasons that construction progress on the canal was slow (Schuyler 1793). A few years later, the company again went public with its troubles, though perhaps more to curry political favor than to attract additional private investment (Western and Northern Inland Lock Navigation Companies 1796). Early corporations also often published their charters and bylaws. The Bank of the United

States did so, for example, likely to show potential investors that the directors had constructed elaborate rules and regulations designed to keep shareholders safe and big dividends flowing (Bank of the United States [179?]). Numerous other companies did likewise.[12]

Because early stockholders usually asserted their rights as owners, many early directors were careful to keep their interests in mind when making important decisions. The directors of the Schuylkill and Susquehanna Company, for example, declined to enter into a contract with the state of Pennsylvania to build a canal around Conewago Falls because they thought the risk too high to impose on their stockholders. So instead they spun off a company specifically organized to do the work. And good thing, too, as the cost of the locks alone far surpassed the initial allowance (Anon. 1798a, 6–7; Western and Northern Inland Lock Navigation Companies 1796, 5–6; Davis 1917, 153).

None of this is to say that early directors were mere marionettes. They could, and did, push back when stockholders were obviously biased or just plain delusional. For example, Schuyler patiently explained to shareholders that it would not be prudent to run up expenses simply because the company's charter allowed it to make dividends of 15 percent "on all their expenditures." "This appears plausible in theory," he granted, "but may and probably will be found fallacious on actual experiment" because tolls (to wit, company revenues) would not be sufficient to pay such high dividends for many years. Tolls would have to be less than the cost of overland transportation, otherwise the river improvements "would have no beneficial object to the community" and the area's population, while growing, would not be sufficient to generate high revenue for some years. Maintenance expenses also had to be factored in, he noted. He concluded that completing the improvements "on a scale more extensive than what is indispensibly [sic] necessary, would be injurious to the reputation of the company" by forcing it to charge high tolls. "It ought to be the invariable pursuit of the company," he opined, "so to conduct its operations as that its interests and those of the community may go hand in hand" (Anon. 1792, 15–16).

In the first few decades of the nineteenth century, some corporate managers discovered ways of circumventing the early corporate governance safe-

12. Examples include Bank of Rhode Island, Bank of the United States, Boston Marine Insurance Company, Company for Opening Inland Navigation between the Santee and Cooper Rivers, Conewago Canal Company, Insurance Company of North America, Kennebec Bridge, Lehigh Navigation Company, Locks and Canals Over Merrimack River, Manhattan Company, Massachusetts Fire Insurance Company, Massachusetts Mutual Fire Insurance Company, Massachusetts State Bank, Middlesex Canal, Mutual Assurance Company of the City of New York, Mutual Assurance Company of Philadelphia, Mutual Fire Insurance Company of Boston, New Hampshire Bank, Newport Insurance Company, New York Insurance Company, Providence Insurance Company, Providence Mutual Insurance Company, Salem Marine Insurance Company, Sixth Massachusetts Turnpike Company, Stamford Mutual Insurance Company, Susquehanna Canal, Warren Insurance Company, and Washington Insurance Company.

guards discussed in the preceding. Some economically disruptive financial panics and high-profile business failures resulted but so too did counter-measures that were effective at least for a time (Kamensky 2008; Hilt 2008, 2009). Maintaining close alignment of the incentives of stockholders, managers, and society remains a challenge to this day (Acharya and Richardson 2009). Nevertheless, then as now it appears that many more corporations succumbed to competitive pressures and recessions than to managerial malfeasance.[13]

7.3   The Benefits of Big

Big businesses suffered from internal agency problems, but, as discussed in the preceding, not intractable ones. Large size also brought big benefits, including market power (control over input costs and output prices), economies of scale (horizontal integration leading to the lower per unit costs typically associated with larger production facilities), and vertical integration (including more of the production and distribution process within the business, rather than purchasing inputs or distribution services in the market). Each strategy required that businesses grow to a large size relative to traditional firms. Although proprietorships and partnerships occasionally grew to great size, it was costly for them to do so. Proprietors had to generate equity capital themselves. They could borrow but usually only for short periods and rarely for more than a few years. Bonds and mortgages could run for decades, but after a year or two, they usually became callable, to the great risk of the borrower. Moreover, creditors frowned upon highly leveraged operations due to interest rate and, in this prelife insurance environment, mortality and morbidity risks. Unless they controlled their own banks, few entrepreneurs would or could venture big by borrowing or by using only their own funds and those of a few close compatriots (Lamoreaux 1994; Heath 1954, 322). Large size almost demanded incorporation. "The multiplication of corporations, and the avidity with which they are sought," wrote Kent, "have arisen in consequence of the power which a large and consolidated capital gives them over business of every kind" (Kent 1894, 2:271–72).

Corporate market power sometimes flowed directly from government decree. More often, however, it stemmed from relative size and an early form of branding. The Beverly Cotton Manufactory, for example, obtained a trademark for its seal, which it affixed to its products like its soon famous Beverly corduroys (Davis 1917, 271–72). After the Bank of Alexandria organized and launched successful operations it appealed to the state legislature not for exclusive banking privileges in Northern Virginia but rather for an

---

13. More research in this area is warranted. Suffice it to say here that there were no major corporate governance failures until the few small banks described by Kamensky (2008).

increase of its capital and for the right to issue notes of less than $5 denomination for the "convenience of the planters, farmers, and mechanicks," especially in "country places" where small change was often in short supply. Small notes earned seigniorage but also spread the bank's name and fame far and wide (Herberts et al. 1793).

To attract large sums of capital, long-term or "locked in" debt and equity, entrepreneurs turned to the corporate form, which offered investors five major advantages over other types of organization (Blair 2003, 387–455; Hurst 1970, 44). First and foremost, corporations enjoyed perpetual succession (Williston 1888, 117; Kent 1894, 2:268). That did not mean that corporations were guaranteed to survive forever or even that their charters extended to the end of days. In fact, a few early corporate charters were perpetual, but most were limited to a specific number of years (Livermore 1935, 676–77; Angell and Ames 1832, 4, 501–14). Also, in most states, corporations could dissolve of their own accord (Angell and Ames 1832, 507–10). Rather, succession meant that shareholders and managers could come and go without forcing the dissolution of the enterprise, that "the body continues the same, notwithstanding the change of the individuals who compose it" (Maier 1993, 54; Angell and Ames 1832, 1, 21, 58–59). Succession provided a big advantage over partnerships, which had to dissolve and reform whenever a partner joined or left the firm. It was also advantageous in some lines of business where customers had to account for the mortality, morbidity, and credit risks posed by sole proprietors. During the 1790s, for example, incorporated marine insurance companies increasingly took market share away from old style brokers, making particularly rapid gains during the Quasi-War against France. Corporations were more likely to pay claims than individuals because they had larger capitals and were more robust in the face of shocks like yellow fever epidemics. Moreover, they proved just as good as individual underwriters at combating adverse selection and moral hazard, the two great banes of insurers (Kingston 2007).

Corporations were also afforded the presumption of state noninterference. Those that did not begin operations in a prompt manner could have their charters revoked by the government after due process. Sometimes charters explicitly specified how long the corporation had to begin operations; other times, the matter was left up to later negotiation (Angell and Ames 1832, 510–12; Kent 1894, 2:312; Davis 1917, 227). In no instance countenanced by early jurisprudence, however, could government capriciously seize, terminate, or substantially alter the charter of a business corporation unless it explicitly reserved the right to do so in the charter (Hovenkamp 1988, 1:659–60; Dodd 1954, 26–28; Angell and Ames 1832, 504; Kent 1894, 2:306). The glaring exception, Pennsylvania's revocation of the Bank of North America's charter, was never tested in court because the bank was satisfied to secure a new, albeit less generous, act of incorporation in 1787. Massachusetts took the less objectionable path of modifying the charter of its first bank, the Massachusetts Bank, over time as it became clear that the original charter was not up to best practices (Dodd 1954, 201–2; Davis 1917, 43, 310–13).

Second, a corporation could also sue and be sued in its own name (Angell and Ames 1832, 207–36). (In the late eighteenth and early nineteenth century, corporation names were more flexible than today. As Angell and Ames noted, "the name of a corporation, frequently consists of several words, and the transposition, interpolation, omission, or alteration of some of them may make no essential difference in their sense" [Angell and Ames 1832, 55, 123].) Thanks to a New York Supreme Court decision in 1799, corporations could sue without exhibiting their charters or listing the names of shareholders (Angell and Ames 1832, 382). Subsequent jurists deftly dodged some legal niceties about the definition of "person" and "citizen" to ensure corporations close to full and equal access to federal courts and courts in states where the corporation was not domiciled (Dodd 1954, 35–41, 48–57). That made it cheaper for a corporation to collect debts owed to it than a similarly sized copartnership, which had to sue in the name of all partners. To sue or be sued the partnership needed the active participation of all the principals, which was often inconvenient and always costly. Partly for that reason, most early American partnerships had four or fewer members, usually all resident in the same city, and often related by birth or marriage.[14] All else constant, creditors also recovered debts from corporations more easily than they could from partnerships (Sylla and Wright 2003, 1:xii–lii).

Of course, all else was not always, or even usually, constant. Corporations were much more likely to extend limited liability to its owners than partnerships were. Limited liability, the third great advantage of the corporate form, ostensibly injured corporations' ability to borrow but greatly aided its ability to attract equity financing (Manne 1967, 262; Baskin and Miranti 1997, 139). The unique structure of the primary or issuance market for shares constituted the fourth advantage of the corporate form, and the creation and perpetuation of active secondary markets in corporate equities was the fifth. All three receive more detailed discussion in the following.

7.3.1   Limited Liability and Entity Shielding

In only two cases, the Hamilton Manufacturing Society of New York and the Salem Iron Factory Company of Massachusetts, did early charters mandate full stockholder liability (Davis 1917, 279, 318). In the Maryland Insurance Company, stockholders were made proportionally liable for the corporation's debts. (In other words, if a shareholder owned 10 percent of the outstanding shares when the company went bankrupt, he or she would have to pay 10 percent of any of its debts remaining unpaid after its assets

---

14. "It is uncommon for a partnership to consist of more than three or four individuals; two is the most usual number" (Anon. 1829, 110). See also Hilt and O'Banion (2009).

had been liquidated.) In their classic article on the origins of the business corporation, Oscar and Mary Handlin baldly assert that corporate charters by default mandated full stockholder liability. In other words, unless a charter explicitly provided otherwise, in the event of corporate bankruptcy, creditors could recover all they were due from any stockholder or stockholders. Because most early charters did not contain an explicit clause limiting shareholder liability (Blandi 1934, 39; Cadman 1949, 327), sixteen expressly provided unqualified limited liability for shareholders, while another sixteen imposed full liability on directors or shareholders only if certain financial ratios were exceeded, the Handlins reasoned, limited liability must have been of only "slight importance" to early stockholders (Handlin and Handlin 1945, 8–10).

More recent research questions the Handlins' analysis. According to the new view, stockholder liability in the early United States was limited de facto. In other words, unless explicitly altered by statute, investors and observers widely considered shareholder liability to be limited to the par value of the stock owned by each (Arner 2002, 53–56; Dodd 1954, 66, 84–93; Perkins 1994, 373–76; Moss 2002, 59; Heath 1954, 316; Anon. 1829, 104). Bank historian Bray Hammond (1957, 654) put it best when he wrote: "The exemption of stockholders from personal liability became established in subterranean fashion with almost no formal advocacy and with very little formal recognition." Contemporaries also understood that, unless their charters explicitly provided otherwise, corporations could not assess stockholders for more than the par value of their shares so liability for solvent corporations was inherently limited (Angell and Ames 1832, 302–3). Moreover, the Handlins themselves admitted that whatever its legal status, liability was not tested in the courts because most early corporations did not impose losses on creditors (Handlin and Handlin, 1945, 16–17; Hurst 1970, 51; Davis 1917, 294). Legal scholar Edwin Dodd (1954, 12) concurred, noting that reported case law on corporations in America prior to 1800 was extremely scanty. After several corporations failed following the War of 1812, courts finally definitively ruled that absent an explicit charter clause to the contrary, the limited liability of stockholders was assumed. Thereafter, limited liability clearly became ensconced in the American corporate scene. In Massachusetts, Georgia, and some other states, however, double, treble, proportional, and even full liability for shareholders in certain types of corporations, sometimes banks but more often mining and manufacturing companies, was often explicitly mandated (Hovenkamp 1988, 1:651–56; Howard 1938; Livermore 1935; Dodd 1954, 364–437; Angell and Ames 1832, 357–64; Cadman 1949, 325; Heath 1954, 316–21; Anon. 1829, 95–102).

Evidence supporting the new view of de facto limited liability in the 1790s abounds. When commenting on the repeal of the charter of the Bank of North America, Robert Whitehill noted that he was "not surprised" the stockholders were "so solicitous to procure another charter for the bank.

While it has no charter, their private circumstances are liable to account for any deficiencies" (Anon. 1786a, 3:95). The Bank apparently agreed, obtaining a charter from Delaware, just in case (Baldwin 1903, 459; Davis 1917, 11, 43). Before it received the official sanction of the state, the Bank of New York had some difficulties attracting investors who feared that they could be held personally responsible for the bank's debts should it fail.[15] In 1793, "Mercator" argued against the incorporation of a marine insurer on the grounds that the stockholders would receive limited liability, a gift that would provide it unfair advantage over individual underwriters. America's earliest corporate law treatise unequivocally stated that "no rule of law" was "better settled, than that, in general, the individual members of a private corporate body are not liable for the debts, either in their persons or in their property, beyond the amount of property which they have in the stock" (Angell and Ames 1832, 349). Adam Smith also unequivocally noted that in partnerships "each partner is bound for the debts contracted by the company to the whole extent of his fortune," but in a joint-stock corporation "each partner is bound only to the extent of his share" (Smith 1937, 699). "The estate and rights of a corporation belong so completely to the body," a nineteenth-century commentator argued, "that none of the individuals who compose it can dispose of any part of them." Therefore, the commentator continued, "what is due to the corporation is not due to any of the individuals who compose it, and *vice versa*" (Glenn 1846, 511).

Early widespread adoption of limited liability (de facto or de jure) helped the U.S. economy to steer clear of a trap that ensnared the British economy in the latter half of the nineteenth century. Corporate creditors disliked limited liability because it limited the pool of income and assets from which they could demand repayment. They responded by insisting that directors or prominent shareholders pledge their personal estates as well or by charging a risk premium on corporate bonds. In the United States, most corporate shareholders enjoyed de facto limited liability, so those who wished to lend to American corporations had little recourse. Competition among lenders kept risk premiums or demands for personal collateral low; there was no presumption that a company with limited liability was weak. In Great Britain, by contrast, corporations could choose their liability status. Higher quality firms typically chose full liability, while lower quality ones typically chose limited liability, or so bond investors widely believed. Full liability corporations, therefore, found it much cheaper to borrow than limited liability ones did, inducing many firms to maintain their full liability status and raising the cost of capital for others, whether justly or not. That may explain in part why Britain's economy lagged behind that of the United States and other

15. Alexander Hamilton's attempt to build limited liability into the bank's articles of association was never tested because the bank never failed. In fact, it still operates today.

countries where limited liability developed and proliferated more rapidly (Nosal and Smart 2007).

Scholars sometimes argue that limited liability merely transferred risk to creditors. It certainly did; that was the point. Those scholars go too far, however, when they conclude that limited liability was inconsequential. It actually reduced risk. Lenders and other creditors were senior to stockholders and their liability, as it were, was always limited to the amount of their loan. In other words, in case of default or bankruptcy, they had first dibs on the corporation's assets and had no fear of being called on for more. With full liability, each shareholder had to worry about paying all of the corporation's debts, however remote that possibility might be. Buying a share with full liability was a bit like buying a lottery ticket where one might by chance draw the obligation of paying off the winner! Not many people would prize such a dubious opportunity (Anon. 1829, 105–7, 115–16). Limited liability leveled the playing field. Stockholders were still junior; they bore the residual risk of bankruptcy. With limited liability, however, they no longer had to factor in the probability of losing all their assets. That undoubtedly had a large, positive impact on share demand and liquidity, lowering the cost of equity capital (Angell and Ames 1832, 23–24, 371–72). Limited liability was, therefore, a Pareto improvement because it made some groups better off (stockholders, the corporation itself) while rendering no one worse off (because creditors were free to increase the cost of credit to reflect limited liability).[16]

Limited liability protected shareholders when a corporation failed. Entity shielding, by contrast, protected the corporation from the bankruptcy of one or more of its stockholders and, by extension, protected shareholders from each other. Thanks to entity shielding, neither the corporation nor its shareholders needed to know or care about the identity of its investors. That, in turn, allowed corporations to accept anyone who bought their stock without vote or cavil (Angell and Ames 1832, 62, 239). That, of course, increased the liquidity of equities and hence demand for them both at the time of issuance (the primary market) and thereafter (the secondary market). Partnerships also enjoyed some entity shielding, but the corporate shield was much more robust (Hansmann, Kraakman, and Squire 2006; Bodenhorn 2006).

7.3.2   Primary Markets

Most early U.S. corporations were start-ups, new companies with little or no operational history (Davis 1917, 33). Early corporate entrepreneurs were able to go public before beginning operations for four reasons. First, even the nation's largest cities were geographically and socially compact. Entre-

---

16. The only exception would be involuntary creditors, like tort victims, but such cases were rare in the eighteenth and early nineteenth centuries. They are more common today but are probably best handled through other, possibly government-sponsored, means (Moss 2002, 74–75, 81, 84).

preneurs and potential investors knew each other, often quite well, or at least knew of each other. In fact, most early corporate securities sales were direct public offerings (DPOs) rather than initial public offerings (IPOs). In other words, corporations sold securities directly to the public, not via investment banks. To do so, they advertised the time and place of subscription, and sometimes their general business plans, by word of mouth, broadsides, and newspaper advertisements.[17]

Second, DPOs were largely unregulated, allowing entrepreneurs to engage in selective disclosure, as in private placements today. Selective disclosure mitigated one of the major costs of full disclosure public offerings. Some investors could learn important details of the business plan while others, suspected competitors, were told little, perhaps only the names of the people who had already subscribed (Manne 1967, 260). Entrepreneurs were loath to withhold that information because a list of good names could jumpstart demand as smaller investors looked to follow the "smart" money. "From the respectability of the characters who already subscribed," a New York paper noted of a 1792 canal DPO, "we have reason to congratulate our fellow-citizens in the prospect of the respective subscriptions being speedily and substantially filled." The paper was a little too sanguine but the number of subscriptions did jump despite the monetary stringency caused by the Panic of 1792 (Davis 1917, 160–63).

Third, a culture of activist corporate governance, prudent mean stockholder voting rules, and legal restrictions against corporate activities that served to mitigate agency problems protected the rights of minority stockholders. Early corporations clearly wanted, and needed, all of the equity investment they could get. Strong protection of the rights of small stockholders, many of whom were women, minors, and men of middling means, was, therefore, paramount.[18]

Fourth, early U.S. corporations in their DPOs typically sold de facto call options on shares rather than the shares themselves (Dodd 1954, 74). Subscribers initially made a down payment, as low as a dollar or two per share. The Bank of Rhode Island, for example, took at subscription just $5 for every $200 par value share (Rhode-Island Bank 1795, 2). After the company organized, corporate officers called in all or part of the par value of the share in installments. The $10, $25, $50, $100, or $1,000 par value per share was not fully paid in until some weeks, months, or years after the corporation began business, giving investors some idea of its operations before they were "all in." The Middlesex Canal, for example, called in its capital stock in

17. For examples of printed advertisements of general business plans, see Anon. [1782?]; Thomson and Morris (1781); Anon. (1799, 19–20). For an example of personal solicitation of stock, see Appleton (1858, 8).
18. "A corporation may consist of both men and women, provided, its institution is not repugnant to the condition and modesty of women" (Angell and Ames 1832, 51, n1). See also Wright (2000, 2002, 2008).

100 different assessments ranging from $2.50 to $10 per share (Davis 1917, 172). Subscribers usually could walk away by selling their options to other investors.[19] The most (in)famous of these markets for "scrip" was that of the Bank of the United States. The sub*scrip*tion in any joint-stock corporation was tradable but not necessarily easily so if money market conditions tightened or the company faced operational difficulties (Davis 1917, 52, 60–61, 80). If no buyer could be found, subscribers generally could forfeit their shares (Angell and Ames 1832, 327). Directors had considerable discretion regarding when and if they called for installments and what happened to shareholders who did not pay up. The directors of the Charles River Bridge, for example, gave fifteen days' grace after which it levied interest at "Five per Cent. per Month." After four months, unpaid shares "and all the Monies he has before advanced" were forfeited to the corporation (Austin 1785). It was extremely difficult, however, for corporations to force subscribers to pay for their shares, hence the de facto call option nature of the obligation (Angell and Ames 1832, 293–302).

Unincorporated joint-stock associations selling de facto options faced legal barriers. They could not sue delinquent members because courts saw them as both a plaintiff and a defendant; members could voluntarily withdraw from the association (Dodd 1954, 66, 80). Chartered companies, by contrast, could and did sue subscribers who missed installment payments on their shares when they formally agreed to pay all their installments on time or suffer explicit penalties (Dodd 1954, 65–66). When faced by a mass defection of stockholders, the Delaware and Schuylkill Canal Company asked the courts to enforce just such an agreement. The directors and leading stockholders (presumably those who had fully paid up) argued that share forfeiture would not serve the company because its works were already well underway. "All those immense sums of money, already advanced will be totally lost," they argued, "and the wreck of the canal, exhibit a lasting monument of folly; and even prevent other enterprises worthy of great minds." They seemed to worry about their ability to collect, however, so they also argued that if delinquent stockholders would only examine the canal's affairs they would see that the investment was still solid (Anon. 1800a, 8). When some still refused to pay, Pennsylvania courts upheld forfeiture of shares purchased in the secondary market and fines for original subscribers (Dodd 1954, 75–76; Angell and Ames 1832, 310). Similarly, work on an early New York canal halted when stockholders failed to meet directors' calls "either because they had not the means to supply such advances, or from an apprehension of the impracticability of succeeding in the operation." An

19. See, for example, the stock transfer ledgers of the Upper Appommatox Company, Virginia Historical Society, especially the transfer from John Hurt to Henry Moss on 20 May 1797 and the transfer from Thomas Read to John Haskins on 15 January 1803.

infusion of government funds bolstered confidence in the project, however, and the canal was eventually completed (Western and Northern Inland Lock Navigation Companies 1796, 3).

Assured that they could sell their shares for a fair market price whenever they needed to, early Americans usually purchased share options in DPOs with alacrity, providing corporations with the equity capital that they needed to commence and continue large scale operations (Davis 1917, passim).

7.3.3   Secondary Markets

Liquidity of ownership stakes was another advantage because it allowed stockholders to increase, decrease, or maintain their holdings in specific enterprises as they saw fit and to borrow money by posting shares as collateral (Manne 1967, 264; Heath 1954, 319, 322). Liquidity also provided stockholders with the opportunity to "vote with their feet." Selling out freed individual investors from situations they did not like and, if enough shareholders felt similarly, decreased share prices and hence the cost of takeover by a new control group (Manne 1967, 265–66). Most judges realized this and generally used the power of the bench to ensure the full and easy transferability of corporate shares (Banner 1998, 230–36; Dodd 1954, 114–20; Angell and Ames 1832, 316–48). Thanks to those rules, equities of major corporations, including the Bank of the United States, traded in European capital markets like London (Angell and Ames 1832, 326; Sylla, Wilson, and Wright 2006). Courts also made it relatively easy for people to hypothecate equities or, in other words, to use them as collateral for loans.

Corporate securities ownership was not limited to the rich, or even the well-to-do. Many people of middling means bought a share or two in local banks, turnpikes, and other corporate enterprises (Baldwin 1903, 463; Banner 1998, 129–30). Most early U.S. corporations had scores or hundreds, rather than just a few shareholders. Ninety-one different people invested in the Charles River Bridge in 1785; fifty different people purchased the 120 shares offered in the Malden Bridge Company in 1787 (Charles River Bridge Company 1785; Anon. 1787b). At one point in the 1790s, 309 different entities, mostly individuals but also a few corporations, partnerships, and nonprofit organizations, owned shares in the Bank of Pennsylvania (Bank of Pennsylvania [179?]).

In a few cases, surviving corporate records allow us to detail changes in stock ownership (Wright 2002; Davis 1917, 300). In other cases, the existence of liquid secondary markets can be inferred with confidence from the regular publication of stock prices in contemporary newspapers (Sylla, Wilson, and Wright n.d.). Finally, we know from the large size and frequent trading of U.S. government bonds that the financial infrastructure requisite to trade any corporate security—brokers, dealers, exchanges, and the like—were in place by the early 1790s (Wright 2008; Wright n.d.).

7.4   Corporations and Economic Growth

A vigorous spirit of enterprise was not unknown in colonial America (Doerflinger 1986), but it was much more muted and limited than the spirit of entrepreneurship that swept the nation, including even agrarian Virginia, after passage of the Constitution (Crothers 1999). Part of the spirit stemmed from the realization that Americans needed services, particularly financial ones, no longer easily available from Britain (Dodd 1954, 196–97). Another part arose from the improved protection of property rights afforded under the Constitution (Wright 2008). Much of the new entrepreneurial spirit gravitated toward relatively large scale projects. "Not until the new government under our present Constitution came into active operation in the spring of 1789," wrote historian Simeon Baldwin (1903, 449–50) over a century ago, "was a fair field open for the permanent investment of capital in large operations with the assurance of safety as could command general public confidence."

Some large scale enterprises could be successfully undertaken without creating a corporation. Not all toll bridges were owned and operated by corporations, for example. Numerous bridges in Virginia were owned and operated by proprietorships or partnerships. In New Jersey in 1791, the government auctioned off the right to build bridges and collect tolls over the Passaic and Hackensack rivers to the highest bidder, the person or firm that would accept the shortest lease period (Tuthill 1791). Interestingly, however, some of those firms later incorporated and New Jersey later chartered numerous bridge companies (Davis 1917, 207; Cadman 1949, 44–45). Similarly, a small group of entrepreneurs in South Carolina discovered it was far too expensive for them to clear Pine Tree Creek as thoroughly as they hoped. In order to finish the project, they prayed to be incorporated so that investors could be "admitted upon equal and safe terms." The legislature agreed, giving rise to the Pine Tree Creek Navigation Company in late 1797 (South Carolina 1797, 129–32). Entrepreneurs heading up larger enterprises, including larger bridges and river improvements, knew from the start that they needed to incorporate in order to attract enough long-term capital to make a go of it. Without the corporate form, entrepreneurs would have been forced to find more costly ways of raising capital or to forego larger or riskier projects completely.

Entrepreneurs did not generally risk their time, reputation, fortunes, and, in an age of debtors' prisons, their freedom, without the prospect of considerable gain. Large projects held out two inducements to early entrepreneurs, market power and scale economies, which combined spelled the opportunity for large profits (high prices coupled with low costs). While entrepreneurs struggled to grow rich, Adam Smith's invisible hand took over, rendering their selfish greed socially beneficial as they created new technologies, developed new industries, and made production processes more efficient. Taking a broader view, the rise of the corporation nation helped to ensure that the United States developed and maintained a system of "good capitalism," a healthy mix of smaller startups and efficient, well-established industrial giants. While not without its flaws, such a system is far better for economic growth, and hence individuals and their governments, than the various forms of "bad capitalism" that flourished elsewhere (Baumol, Litan, and Schramm 2007).

Modern management is generally considered a product of the second half of the nineteenth century. That may be true, but already by the 1790s, corporate managers were learning how to run large enterprises efficiently (Cochran 1974), some by applying experience gained on the larger plantations and manors (Kamoie 2007, 136–40). After some initial difficulties, banks by 1800 were generally very well managed (Davis 1917, 34–108; Bodenhorn 2000, 2002). Less is known about the management of insurance companies, but there is little reason to question their competence (Davis 1917, 231–46). They were astute enough, for example, to urge state and local governments to construct lighthouses, install navigation buoys, and pass basic fire safety legislation (U.S. Treasury Department 1798). Bankers and insurers made mistakes to be sure, but anyone conversant with recent events knows that they remain far from infallible (Acharya and Richardson 2009).

Canals and turnpikes were often completed late and over budget, but that is not uncommon even today (LePatner, Jacobson, and Wright 2007). Early canal and turnpike companies often made a hash of things for two main reasons. First, large-scale construction experts, particularly experienced engineers, were few. At least two of those who emigrated from Europe, John Senf and Pierre L'Enfant, were more like artsy architects than solid civil engineers (Davis 1917, 144–45; Wright 2010). Second, laborers, even the unskilled, were expensive and uppity, and supervision was often lax (Davis 1917, 126). Even though they paid efficiency wages, the Potomac Company found that its laborers manifested a "turbulent and insubordinate spirit" so strong that "the work that was directed to be done was either entirely omitted or but partially performed." Attempts to bolster the labor force with indentured servants and slaves backfired as tensions between the three types of laborers mounted and many servants fled. Gunpowder began to go missing and neighbors complained of ill treatment (Davis 1917, 127–28). Conditions eventually improved on that and other projects but labor-management difficulties persisted.[20]

When things got tough, early American managers tended to squabble

---

20. Some readers, especially those of a theoretical bent, may wonder how a firm could pay efficiency wages but still end up with unwilling workers. The key, of course, was poor management. Workers, like other people, will try to get away with as much as possible. If managers are unable or unwilling to monitor workers and fire shirkers, the wage level will be immaterial to worker productivity.

amongst themselves rather than work together to fix the problem. On the Potomac Canal, for example, the assistant managers regularly bickered, quarreled, and hurled insults at each other in an apparent attempt to curry favor with the company's directors (Davis 1917, 129–30). Early managers usually learned on the job, but they did learn. Instead of repeating the woes of the Potomac Company, the James River Company used slaves exclusively or contracted jobs out to smaller firms (Davis 1917, 137–40).

Cost-estimation techniques, though still primitive by later standards, also improved with experience. The Cooper and Santee River canal in South Carolina ended up costing three times its original estimate (Davis 1917, 146). Such overruns prompted one early observer to advise doubling engineer estimates "in order to provide against contingencies" (Anon. 1798a, 7). Another committee explained that "in works of this kind [canal construction] where many men are employed, worthless characters will introduce themselves notwithstanding every attention to prevent it; accidents will intervene, tending to retard the business." It, therefore, padded its cost estimate of £72,350 by £7,650, which was a little more than the 10 percent padding suggested by experienced British engineer William Weston (Western and Northern Inland Lock Navigation Companies 1796, 20). Perhaps more important, the committee noted that tolls would be less than the "market rate of interest" (approximately 7 percent) on £80,000 so "the Stockholders will be sufferers" unless the legislature cut the company some slack regarding the width and depth of the canal (Northern Inland Lock Navigation Company 1792, 12–14). Architects also warned of massive cost overruns, "especially in buildings of a public nature" (Kamensky 2008, 108).

Early directors had some idea about how to keep expenses down. A committee of the Western Inland Lock Navigation Company, for example, realized that it needed to delegate considerable operational power to a single strong manager, someone who could engage in comprehensive planning so "that supplies may be prepared, without incurring that extra expence which ever attends collections made on the spur of the occasion." "To find such a character," the committee admitted, "is certainly not very easy" but at least they were looking (Schuyler 1792, 19; Davis 1917, 162–63). The Middlesex Canal Company apparently found one because its extensive works—over twenty-seven miles of canal, twenty locks, seven aqueducts, and over two score bridges—came in only slightly over budget, despite the fact that like many early canals it at first built economically inefficient wooden locks instead of more expensive but much more durable stone ones (Davis 1917, 172–73).

After much time and expense, some canal companies eventually got the job done, bestowing the benefits of cheaper and faster transportation to the farmer, merchant, and manufacturer alike. By 1799, for example, the Potomac Company had made it possible for boats laden with 100 barrels of flour to navigate the Potomac River from George's Creek to the tidewater with only a single portage around the Great Falls (Keith et al. 1799). The canal at Conewago Falls in Pennsylvania also worked well when finally completed, reducing the amount of time it took to negotiate the falls fully laden from many hours and dollars to about a half an hour (Anon. 1798a, 6–7; Western and Northern Inland Lock Navigation Companies 1796, 5–6). By 1800, the James River Company had improved the navigation of its namesake some forty-five miles. By 1816, that figure had grown to 300 miles, at the cost of only $1,200 per mile, a figure low enough to allow it to pay handsome dividends (Davis 1917, 139–40). From South Carolina to Massachusetts, other canals, most owned and operated by corporations, eventually opened for business, greatly aiding the size and efficiency of local and regional markets (Rothenberg 1992).

Bridges usually fared quite well. Even the large ones typically constructed by corporations were easy to build and manage relative to canals. (Smaller ones were handled by local road crews, individual proprietors, turnpikes, and so forth.) Damaging floods and ice were their biggest foes. Like canals, bridges aided the economy and improved market efficiency by lowering transaction costs. Far better to traverse a bridge than to ford an icy river or wait for the ferryman, especially along important thoroughfares like the York road that connected Manhattan to Philadelphia via New Jersey (Davis 1917, 186–215).

Far better, too, to travel a well kempt turnpike than rutty local roads. Larger and more difficult to construct and keep in good repair than bridges but easier to build and maintain than canals, turnpikes not surprisingly generally suffered more financial, engineering, labor, and other problems than bridges but fewer than canals. Most new turnpikes successfully raised cash via DPOs, completed their roads, and remained in business for decades. Some were financially successful, but many found it difficult to collect enough tolls to cover the cost of road repair and gatekeepers (Davis 1917, 216–27, 292–93).

Some early manufacturers also struggled. Management and labor difficulties plagued the Society for the Establishment of Useful Manufacturers, for example, eventually bringing it to its financial knees. But it later recovered and other manufacturers got on well from the start. America in 1800 was still a nation of farms and plantations, but industrial output was growing fast and would continue to do so throughout the nineteenth century (Davis 2004). Many manufacturing concerns were still small, ranging from a corner of a farmhouse with a spinning wheel or a small nail forge to a mill employing a dozen hands. Much of the *growth* in manufacturing, however, was aided by corporations (Davis 1917, 255–82). Growth in other modern sectors, including mining, transportation, and financial services, was also largely attributable to the net benefits entrepreneurs discovered, laying mostly latent, in a hoary institution inherited from the old world.[21] By 1801, thousands of entrepreneurs interested in pursuing relatively complex, large-scale, and long-term projects found that the benefits of the corporate form outweighed the costs of obtaining a charter and aligning the incentives of stockholders, employees, and other stakeholders. By the Civil War, over 100,000 more calculated likewise. Some corporations sputtered and failed but others created the machines, transportation networks, and financial and other services that ultimately transformed the U.S. economy into the world's largest and most dynamic.

References

Acharya, Viral, and Matthew Richardson. 2009. *Restoring financial stability: How to repair a failed system.* Hoboken, NJ: John Wiley and Sons.
A Farmer. 1792. *Five letters addressed to the yeomanry of the United States.* Philadelphia: Eleazar Oswald.
Angell, Joseph, and Samuel Ames. 1832. *A treatise on the law of private corporations aggregate.* Boston: Hilliard, Gray, Little & Wilkins.
An Inhabitant. 1796. That a monopoly is baneful cannot be controverted. *New York Minerva,* September 15.
Anon. 1764. *Whereas the number of poor.* Philadelphia: n.p.
Anon. 1780. *The history of the origin, rise, and progress of the war in America between Great Britain and her colonies.* Boston: Thomas and John Fleet.
Anon. [1782?] *Proposals for a Bank.* Boston: n.p.
Anon. 1785. *Remarks on a pamphlet entitled "Considerations on the Bank of North America."* Philadelphia: John Steele.
Anon. 1786a. Friday, March 31, 1786, A.M. *Pennsylvania Evening Herald,* April 15.
Anon. 1786b. General Assembly, Friday, March 31, 1786, A.M. *Pennsylvania Evening Herald,* April 19.
Anon. 1786c. Philadelphia, December 28. Conclusion of the debates in the General Assembly the 13th inst. on the subject of chartering the Bank of North America. *Pennsylvania Packet,* December 28.
Anon. 1787a. Albany, June 14. *New Hampshire Mercury,* June 28.
Anon. 1787b. *Subscribers to Malden-Bridge.* Boston: n.p.
Anon. 1790. *Minutes of the grand committee of the whole convention of the Commonwealth of Pennsylvania.* Philadelphia: Zachariah Poulson Jr.
Anon. 1791a. *Of commerce and luxury.* Philadelphia: T. Lang.
Anon. 1791b. USA Congress, House of Representatives, Tuesday, February 1. *Gazette of the United States,* February 19.
Anon. 1792. *The report of a committee appointed to explore the western waters in the state of New York.* Albany: Barber and Southwick.
Anon. 1793. Branch bank. *Boston Independent Chronicle,* January 10.
Anon. 1794. *Plan for raising by loan a sum of money.* Philadelphia: n.p.

21. Micklethwait and Wooldridge (2003) miss America's crucial contribution to corporation formation and proliferation. Contemporary foreigner observers, by contrast, knew that America was the original corporation nation (Murat 1833, 337–38).

Anon. 1796. *A letter to certain bank directors, from a merchant.* Philadelphia: n.p.
Anon. 1798a. *Account of the Conewago Canal, on the river Susquehanna.* Philadelphia: Whitehall Press.
Anon. 1798b. *Transactions of the Society . . . for the Promotion of Agriculture, Arts, and Manufactures.* Albany, NY: Loring Andrews.
Anon. 1799. *By laws of the Sixth Massachusetts Turnpike Corporation, for establishing a turnpike road, from Amherst to Shrewsbury.* Worcester, MA: Mower & Greenleaf.
Anon. 1800a. *Extracts from the resolutions of the stockholders of the Delaware and Schuylkill Canal Navigation.* Philadelphia: n.p.
Anon. 1800b. New York, February 15. *Greenleaf's New York Journal,* February 15.
Anon. 1804a. *Observations on the principles and operation of banking with strictures on the opposition to the Bank of Philadelphia.* Philadelphia: Helmbold.
Anon. 1804b. *To the honourable, the legislature of the state of New York, in Senate and Assembly convened. The memorial of the subscribers, merchants, tradesmen, and inhabitants of the City of New York.* [New York?]: n.p.
Anon. 1827. *Letter on the use and abuse of corporations.* New York: C & G Carvill.
Anon. 1829. Manufacturing corporations. *American Jurist* 3:92–118.
Anon. 1835. *What is a monopoly? Or some considerations upon the subject of corporations and currency.* New York: George P. Scott.
A Philadelphia Merchant. 1790. To the editor of the *Federal Gazette. Philadelphia Federal Gazette,* March 30.
A Plain Dealer. 1786. Philadelphia, September 7, 1786, Mr. Printer. *Pennsylvania Mercury,* September 15.
Appleton, Nathan. 1858. *Introduction of the power loom and origin of Lowell.* Lowell, MA: B. H. Penhallow.
Arner, Douglas. 2002. Development of the American law of corporations to 1832. *SMU Law Review* 55:23–57.
Austin, John Jr. 1785. *Charles River Bridge.* [Boston?]: n.p.
Baker. 1756. *A vindication of the case of the corporations of bakers.* Dublin: A. McCulloh.
Baldwin, Simeon E. 1903. American business corporations before 1789. *American Historical Review* 8:449–65.
Bank of Pennsylvania. [179?] *List of stockholders.* Philadelphia: E. Oswald.
Bank of the United States. [179?] *The acts of incorporation, bye-laws, rules and regulations of the Bank of the United States.* n.p.
Banner, Stuart. 1998. *Anglo-American securities regulation: Cultural and political roots, 1690–1860.* New York: Cambridge University Press.
[Bard, William?]. [1835?] *An inquiry into the nature and utility of corporations, addressed to the farmers, mechanics, and laboring men of Connecticut.* [New York?]: n.p.
Barnes, Joseph. 1792. *Treatise on the justice, policy, and utility of establishing an effectual system for promoting the progress of useful arts, by assuring property in the products of genius.* Philadelphia: Francis Bailey.
Baskin, Jonathan, and Paul Miranti. 1997. *A history of corporate finance.* New York: Cambridge University Press.
Bateman, Fred, and Thomas Weiss. 1981. *A deplorable scarcity: The failure of industrialization in the slave economy.* Chapel Hill, NC: University of North Carolina Press.
Baumol, Will, Robert Litan, and Carl Schramm. 2007. *Good capitalism, bad capitalism, and the economics of growth and prosperity.* New Haven, CT: Yale University Press.

Berle, Adolf, and Gardiner Means. 1932. *The modern corporation and private property*. New York: Harcourt Brace.

Blair, Margaret. 2003. Locking in capital: What corporate law achieved for business organizers in the 19th Century. *UCLA Law Review* 51:387–455.

Blandi, Joseph. 1934. *Maryland business corporations, 1783–1852*. Baltimore, MD: Johns Hopkins Press.

Bodenhorn, Howard. 2000. *A history of banking in antebellum America: Financial markets and economic development in an era of nation-building*. New York: Cambridge University Press.

———. 2002. *State banking in early America: A new economic history*. New York: Oxford University Press.

———. 2006. Partnership, entity shielding and bank credit. Clemson University. Working Paper.

Bonney, Charles C. 1857. *Speech of Charles C. Bonney, of Peoria, against an act entitled an act to incorporate the Illinois River Improvement Company*. St. Louis: n.p.

Cadman, John. 1949. *The corporation in New Jersey: Business and politics, 1791–1875*. Cambridge, MA: Harvard University Press.

Caplan, Bryan. 2007. *The myth of the rational voter: Why democracies choose bad policies*. Princeton, NJ: Princeton University Press.

Charles River Bridge Company. 1785. At a meeting of the proprietors. Boston: n.p.

Chipman, Nathaniel. 1793. *Sketches of the principles of government*. Rutland, VT: J. Lyon.

Citizens. 1792. *To the honorable the legislature*. [Richmond, VA?]: n.p.

Cochran, Thomas. 1974. The business revolution. *American Historical Review* 79 (1): 449–66.

Coxe, Tench. 1786. *Thoughts concerning the Bank of North America*. Philadelphia: n.p.

———. 1792. *Reflexions on the State of the Union*. Philadelphia: Mathew Carey.

Crothers, A. Glenn. 1999. Banks and economic development in post-Revolutionary northern Virginia, 1790–1812. *Business History Review* 73:1–39.

Davis, Joseph H. 2004. An annual index of U.S. industrial production, 1790–1915. *Quarterly Journal of Economics* 119 (1): 177–215.

Davis, Joseph S. 1917. *Eighteenth century business corporations in the United States*. Cambridge, MA: Harvard University Press.

Delaware. 1797. *Laws of the State of Delaware*. New Castle, DE: Samuel and John Adams.

Dodd, Edwin Merrick. 1954. *American business corporations until 1860, with special reference to Massachusetts*. Cambridge, MA: Harvard University Press.

Doerflinger, Thomas. 1986. *A vigorous spirit of enterprise: Merchants and economic development in revolutionary Philadelphia*. Chapel Hill, NC: University of North Carolina.

Donoughue, Bernard. 1964. *British politics and the American Revolution: The path to war, 1773–75*. London: Macmillan.

Dreikorn, Wilbur. 1949. The history and development of banking in New Jersey. MA thesis, Rutgers-ABA.

Duer, William Alexander. 1819. *A reply to Mr. Colden's vindication of the steam-boat monopoly*. Albany: E. and E. Hosford.

Dunlavy, Colleen. 2004. From citizens to plutocrats: Nineteenth-century shareholder voting rights and theories of the corporation. In *Constructing corporate America: History, politics, culture*, ed. Kenneth Lipartito and David Sicilia, 66–93. New York: Oxford University Press.

———. 2006. Social conceptions of the corporation: Insights from the history of shareholder voting rights. *Washington and Lee Law Review* 63 (1): 347–88.

Ellsworth, Lucius. 1972. Craft to national industry in the nineteenth century: A case study of the transformation of the New York State tanning industry. *Journal of Economic History* 32:399–402.

Evans, George Jr. 1948. *Business incorporations in the United States, 1800–1943*. New York: National Bureau of Economic Research, no. 49.

Findley, William. 1794. *A review of the revenue system adopted by the first Congress under the Federal Constitution*. Philadelphia: T. Dobson.

Franklin, Benjamin. 1794. *The life of Dr. Benjamin Franklin, written by himself.* Philadelphia: Benjamin Johnson.

Glenn, S. F. 1846. Corporations. *DeBow's Review.*

Gower, L. C. B. 1956. Some contrasts between British and American corporation law. *Harvard Law Review* 69:1369–1402.

Gunn, L. Ray. 1988. *The decline of public authority: Public economic policy and political development in New York, 1800–1860*. Ithaca, NY: Cornell University Press.

Hamilton, Alexander. 1791. *Report of the Secretary of the Treasury of the United States on the subject of manufactures*. Philadelphia: Childs and Swaine.

Hammond, Bray. 1957. *Banks and politics in America: From the Revolution to the Civil War.* Princeton, NJ: Princeton University Press.

Handlin, Oscar, and Mary F. Handlin. 1945. Origins of American business corporation. *Journal of Economic History* 5:1–23.

Hansmann, Henry, Reinier Kraakman, and Richard Squire. 2006. Law and the rise of the firm. *Harvard Law Review* 119:1336–1403.

Hartford and New Haven Turnpike Road Company. 1800. *We the subscribers.* Hartford, CT: n.p.

Heath, Milton. 1954. *Constructive liberalism: The role of the state in economic development in Georgia to 1860*. Cambridge, MA: Harvard University Press.

Herberts, Thomas, et al. 1793. *To the honorable the speakers.* Alexandria, VA: n.p.

Hilt, Eric. 2008. When did ownership separate from control? Corporate governance in the early nineteenth century. *Journal of Economic History* 68:645–85.

———. 2009. Rogue finance: The Life and Fire Insurance Company and the Panic of 1826. *Business History Review* 83:87–112.

Hilt, Eric, and Katharine O'Banion. 2009. The limited partnership in New York, 1822–1858: Partnerships without kinship. NBER Working Paper no. 14412. Cambridge, MA: National Bureau of Economic Research.

Hovenkamp, Herbert. 1988. The classical corporation in American legal thought. *Georgetown Law Journal* 76:1593–690.

Howard, Stanley E. 1938. Stockholders' liability under the New York Act of March 22, 1811. *Journal of Political Economy* 46:499–514.

Hurst, James. 1970. *The legitimacy of the business corporation in the law of the United States, 1780–1970.* Charlottesville, VA: University Press of Virginia.

Kamensky, Jane. 2008. *The exchange artist: A tale of high-flying speculation and America's first banking collapse.* New York: Viking.

Kamoie, Laura. 2007. *Irons in the fire: The business history of the Tayloe family and Virginia's gentry, 1700–1860.* Charlottesville, VA: University of Virginia Press.

Keith, James, et al. 1799. *Entrusted as we are.* Georgetown, VA: n.p.

Kent, James. 1795. *Dissertations, being the preliminary part of a course of law lectures.* New York: George Forman.

———. 1894. *Commentaries on American law.* 4 vols. New York: Banks and Brothers.

Kerbel, Jeffrey. 1987. An examination of nonvoting and limited voting common shares—Their history, legality, and validity. *Securities Regulation Law Journal* 16:37–68.

Kingston, Christopher. 2007. Marine insurance in Philadelphia during the Quasi-War with France, 1795–1801. Amherst College. Working Paper.

Lamoreaux, Naomi. 1994. *Insider lending: Banks, personal connections, and economic development in industrial New England.* New York: Cambridge University Press.

Lee, C. H. 1990. Corporate behaviour in theory and history: I. The evolution of theory. *Business History* 32:17–31.

LePatner, Barry, Timothy Jacobson, and Robert E. Wright. 2007. *Broken buildings, busted budgets: How to fix America's trillion-dollar construction industry.* Chicago: University of Chicago Press.

Livermore, Shaw. 1935. Unlimited liability in early American corporations. *Journal of Political Economy* 43:674–87.

———. 1939. *Early American land companies: Their influence on corporate development.* New York: Commonwealth Fund.

Lloyd, Thomas. 1789. *The Congressional Register.* New York: Harrison and Purday.

Maier, Pauline. 1993. The revolutionary origins of the American corporation. *William and Mary Quarterly* 50:51–84.

Majewski, John. 2000. *A house dividing: Economic development in Pennsylvania and Virginia before the Civil War.* New York: Cambridge University Press.

Manne, Henry G. 1967. Our two corporation systems: Law and economics. *Virginia Law Review* 53:259–84.

Marine Insurance Office. 1799. *Whereas it is contemplated.* Baltimore, MD: n.p.

McCarthy, Kathleen. 2003. *American creed: Philanthropy and the rise of civil society, 1700–1865.* Chicago: University of Chicago Press.

Mercator. 1793. For the *Federal Gazette. Federal Gazette,* January 15.

Micklethwait, John, and Adrian Wooldridge. 2003. *The company: A short history of a revolutionary idea.* New York: Modern Library.

Middlesex Canal. 1798. *At a meeting of the Middlesex-Canal Corporation, held at Charlestown, on the 16th day of October, 1798.* Boston: n.p.

Moss, David. 2002. *When all else fails: Government as the ultimate risk manager.* Cambridge, MA: Harvard University Press.

Murat, Achille. 1833. *A moral and political sketch of the United States of North America.* London: Effingham Wilson.

Mutual Assurance Company. 1787. *The deed of settlement of the Mutual Assurance Company for insuring houses from loss by fire in New York.* New York: William Morton.

New Jersey. 1799. *New Jersey session laws.* n.p.

New York Insurance Company. 1796. *Articles of association.* New York: Childs.

Northern Inland Lock Navigation Company. 1792. *A report of the committee appointed by the directors of the Northern Inland Lock Navigation Company.* New York: W. Durell.

Nosal, Ed, and Michael Smart. 2007. Limited liability and the development of capital markets. Federal Reserve Bank of Cleveland Working Paper no. 07-03.

Paine, Thomas. 1795. *Dissertation on first principles of government.* Philadelphia: E. Conrad.

Paskoff, Paul. 1983. *Industrial evolution: Organization, structure, and growth of the Pennsylvania iron industry, 1750–1860.* Baltimore, MD: Johns Hopkins University Press.

Perkins, Edwin. 1994. *American public finance and financial services, 1700–1815.* Columbus, OH: Ohio State University Press.

Philander. 1800. For the *American Citizen:* To the cartmen of New York. *American Citizen,* April 29.

Pigott, Charles. 1796. *A political dictionary: Explaining the true meaning of words.* New York: Thomas Greenleaf.

Platt, Jonas. 1811. *Mr. Platt's speech on the bill for establishing the Western District Bank.* n.p.

Pownall, Thomas. 1776. *A letter from Governor Pownall to Adam Smith.* London: J. Almon.

Price, Richard. 1785. *Observations on the importance of the American Revolution and the means of making it a benefit to the world.* London: n.p.

Ramsay, David. 1785. *The history of the Revolution of South Carolina from a British province to an independent state.* Trenton, NJ: Isaac Collins.

Ratner, David. 1970. The government of business corporations: Critical reflections on the rule of "one share, one vote." *Cornell Law Review* 56:1–56.

Rhode-Island Bank. 1795. *Charter of the Rhode-Island Bank.* n.p.

Rolt, Richard. 1756. *A new dictionary of trade and commerce.* London: T. Osborne and J. Shipton.

Rothenberg, Winifred. 1992. *From market-places to a market economy: The transformation of rural Massachusetts, 1750–1850.* Chicago: University of Chicago Press.

Schuyler, Philip. 1792. *The report of a committee appointed to explore the western waters in the state of New York.* Albany: Barber and Southwick.

———. 1793. *To the stockholders in the Northern and Western Lock Navigation Companies.* [Albany, NY?]: n.p.

Seavoy, Ronald. 1982. *The origins of the American business corporation, 1784–1855: Broadening the concept of public service during industrialization.* Westport, CT: Greenwood.

Smith, Adam. 1776. *An inquiry into the nature and causes of the wealth of nations.* London: W. Strahan and T. Cadell.

———. 1937. *An inquiry into the nature and causes of the wealth of nations.* New York: The Modern Library.

South Carolina. 1797. *South Carolina session laws.* n.p.

Stamford Mutual Insurance Company. 1797. *The constitution of Stamford Mutual Insurance Company.* New York: J. Harrisson.

State of Tennessee. 1796. *Constitution of the State of Tennessee.* Philadelphia: Thomas Condie.

Swift, Zephaniah. 1795. *A system of the laws of the state of Connecticut.* Windham, CT: John Byrne.

Sylla, Richard, Jack Wilson, and Robert E. Wright. 2006. Trans-Atlantic capital market integration, 1790–1845. *Review of Finance* 10:613–44.

———. n.d. Early U.S. Securities Prices, 1790–1860. http://eh.net/databases/early-us-securities-prices.

Sylla, Richard E., and Robert E. Wright, eds. 2003. *The history of corporate finance: Development of Anglo-American securities markets, financial practices, theories and laws.* 6 vols. London: Pickering and Chatto.

Taylor, George. 1833. *Effect of incorporated coal companies upon the anthracite coal trade of Pennsylvania.* Pottsville, PA: Benjamin Bannan.

Taylor, John. 1794. *An enquiry into the principles and tendency of certain public measures.* Philadelphia: Thomas Dobson.

Thomson, Charles, and Robert Morris. 1781. *To the public.* [Philadelphia?]: n.p.

Tuthill, Samuel, et al. 1791. *Contract for erecting bridges.* Elizabethtown, NJ: n.p.

U.S. Treasury Department. 1798. Letter from the Secretary of the Treasury, to accompany his report on the petitions of sundry inhabitants of the town of Newport. Philadelphia: n.p.

Virginia. 1788. *Virginia session laws.* n.p.

Warren Insurance Company. 1800. *The charter of the Warren Insurance Company in Warren (R.I.) established for the purpose of insuring on vessels, and all other objects of risque.* Warren, RI: Nathaniel Phillips.

Washington Insurance Company. 1800. *Charter of the Washington Insurance Company in Providence.* Providence, RI: B. Wheeler.

Webster, Peletiah. 1791. *An address to the stockholders of the Bank of North America on the subject of the old and new bank.* Philadelphia: Joseph Crukshank.

Western and Northern Inland Lock Navigation Companies. 1796. *Report of the directors of the Western and Northern Inland Lock Navigation Companies.* New York: George Foreman.

White, John. [1791?] *To the honourable the Senate, and the House of Representatives, of the Commonwealth of Massachusetts.* Boston: n.p.

Williston, Samuel. 1888. History of the law of business corporations before 1800. *Harvard Law Review* 2:149–66.

Winterbotham, William. 1795. *A geographical, commercial, and philosophical view of the present situation of the United States of America.* Philadelphia: Tiebout and O'Brien.

Wright, Robert E. 2000. Women and finance in the early national U.S. *Essays in History* 42. http://etext.virginia.edu/journals/EH/EH42/Wright42.html.

———. 2002. *The wealth of nations rediscovered: Integration and expansion in American financial markets, 1780–1850.* New York: Cambridge University Press.

———. 2008. *One nation under debt: Hamilton, Jefferson and the history of what we owe.* New York: McGraw-Hill.

———. 2010. *Corporations and the economic growth and development of the antebellum Ohio River Valley.* Ohio Valley History 9: 47–70.

———. n.d. U.S. Government bond trading database, 1776–1835. http://eh.net/databases/govtbond/.

Wright, Robert E., Wray Barber, Matthew Crafton, and Anand Jain, eds. 2004. *History of corporate governance: The importance of stakeholder activism.* London: Pickering and Chatto.

8

U.S. Land Policy
Founding Choices and Outcomes, 1781–1802

Farley Grubb

Independence brought a vast amount of land within the grasp of the new nation—land unsettled by nonindigenous Americans. Choices had to be made regarding which governments had jurisdiction over these lands, how these lands would be used to benefit those governments as well as the public, and how these lands would be transferred to white settlers. Conflicts over which governments had jurisdiction over these lands created the first crisis of disunion. The choice that resolved this crisis led to other choices on how to use these lands to salvage the nation's financial position. How the government would transfer these lands to the public also required choices over lot sizes, shapes, prices, and methods of sale. Between 1781 and 1802, these land policy choices were truly founding choices in that they had lasting effects on the economic and political trajectory of the nation.

This short chapter cannot adequately address all the land policy controversies that arose in the founding era. Instead, the focus will be on the key choices that affected economic development for which economic analysis can enhance our understanding. The essay begins by documenting the conflicting claims over the trans-Appalachian territories post-Revolution. As a condition of political unity, states without land claims required states with claims to cede them to the national government for the benefit of all. Adopting the U.S. Constitution as drafted in 1787 may not have been possible without this prior solution to western land claims. The timing and amount of lands ceded to the national government from 1781 through 1802 is also documented, with the total being roughly 222 million acres worth

Farley Grubb is a professor of economics at the University of Delaware, Newark, and a research associate of the National Bureau of Economic Research.

The author thanks the other authors of this volume and Max Edling, William Fischel, and Tom Weiss for helpful comments on earlier drafts, and Tracy McQueen for editorial assistance.

about $215 million by 1802. The U.S. Federal Government was born land
rich and land-asset-value rich.

The national government's choices over how to use its lands are addressed
next. The public, Founding Fathers, and states all expected the ceded lands
to be used to satisfy the debts incurred fighting the Revolution. A government budget constraint model linking revenue and spending flows with
stocks of land assets and debt is developed to show the options available
for using land assets to service the national debt, that is, (a) swap all the
land at once for as much debt as possible or (b) sell the land slowly over
time at good prices with the proceeds pledged to redeeming debt principal.
The Federal Government was solvent when land prices were valued at their
long-run constant-dollar equilibrium price but insolvent if valued at prices
likely to prevail if all the land was dumped onto the market at once. In 1790,
option (b) became the founding choice, which, in turn, helped salvage the
government's credit position.

Finally, the essay describes the choices made regarding how the land
would be sold, that is, lot sizes and shapes, and discusses the economic benefits of these choices. The Land Ordinances of 1784, 1785, and 1787 that
were carried forward largely intact after the adoption of the Constitution
are discussed. The choices made in these ordinances enhanced the value
and, thus, the sale price of the land. The rectangular property grid imposed
on land buyers rationalized land boundaries making property rights more
secure. The required purchase of minimum lot sizes far larger than the typical farm reduced the cost of surveying and allowed purchasers to capture the
positive externalities of their initial development efforts. The chapter ends
with a brief epilogue summarizing the results and linking the subsequent
Louisiana Purchase in 1803 directly to the founding choices made regarding
the initial land cessions to the national government.

8.1   The First Crisis of Disunion: Who Should Get the Spoils of War?

With George Rogers Clark's victories over the British in the Ohio territories and the pending triumph of the American Revolution, British claims and
restrictions over the trans-Appalachian territories were removed, and these
lands fell into the hands of the revolutionaries.[1] This transfer was codified in

1. Being the victor in the French and Indian War (Seven Year's War), Britain acquired in
1763 French Canada and French claims to the upper Ohio and Mississippi regions—claims
that conflicted with those of several British colonies whose royal charters encompassed some of
these lands. With the Proclamation of 1763, Britain declared British treaties with the Indians in
these regions superior to any made by the American colonies and forbade, with a few exceptions,
further white incursions into these lands. American colonists worked to evade this proclamation, which they viewed as an attempt by prominent Englishmen to execute their own land
patents in the region. Prominent Americans formed land companies and moved to lay claim to
these regions. With the 1774 Quebec Act, the British also attached the lands west of the Alleghenies and north of the Ohio River to the colony of Quebec for administrative purposes and to
reaffirm the Proclamation of 1763—in part to counter the American land company incursions
into these regions (Friedenberg 1992, 104–42; Livermore 1939, 74–122; Sakolski 1932, 1–28).

1783 with the Treaty of Paris that recognized U.S. sovereign independence from Britain, but not without effort and controversy. For example, Spain sought surrender of U.S. claims to the eastern Mississippi region and to free navigation of the Mississippi River through New Orleans in exchange for aid during the Revolution and trade concessions to the Americans, mostly to northern shippers, after the Revolution. These Spanish intrigues were fended off by the southern states, effectively stopping northern commercial interests and their political allies in Congress from trading away these navigation rights and land claims. In addition, U.S. efforts to claim Canadian lands were dropped in the final 1783 treaty.[2]

The new lands acquired in the Treaty of Paris represented a vast territory stretching from the Appalachian Mountains to the Mississippi River between the southern shores of the Great Lakes and Spanish Florida. Which government should get these lands? Initially several states, for example, Massachusetts, Connecticut, Virginia, North Carolina, South Carolina, and Georgia, claimed these lands based on old colonial grants and Indian treaties. Many of these claims were overlapping. Other states, for example, Maryland, Delaware, Pennsylvania, New Jersey, Rhode Island, and New Hampshire, were hard pressed to make claims to these lands.[3] See figure 8.1. Conflicting land claims created discord among the states. For example, as early as 1775, Connecticut claims to the Wyoming Valley in Pennsylvania were brought before an otherwise busy Continental Congress by Pennsylvania for redress—an issue Congress failed to resolve fully even by 1785. Similarly, from 1780 through 1786, a jurisdictional dispute between New Hampshire, Massachusetts, and New York was brought before Congress for redress.[4]

Of greater concern were state claims to the trans-Appalachian territories. Many of these claims overlapped creating potential discord; see figure 8.1. In addition, states that did not have claims feared that the states that did have such claims would become economically and politically dominant. The sheer size of these enlarged states would give them economic power, and any move toward a representative national government based on population or land area would give them political dominance. States without western land

2. See Adams (1960, 3:209–19); Dougherty (2001, 139–40); Friedenberg (1992, 203–12); Henretta et al. (1987, 186, 218, 228, 231); Jensen (1981, 8–18, 171–73); Ford et al. (1904–1937, 13:239–44, 263–65, 329–30; 14:955–67; 15:1084–85; 18:900–902, 935–47, 1070–71; 19:151–54; 21:853–54; 22:207–8, 219–20; 24:243–51; 26:23–29; 27:489–89, 529–30, 687–90, 705–6, 616–24; 30:85–87; 31:469–84, 509–10, 537–52, 565–70, 574–613; 32:184–204, 210, 216–20; 34:319, 527, 534–35).

3. See Donaldson (1884, 30–88); Feller (1984, 3–4); Henretta et al. (1987, 201, 227–28); Jensen (1981, 8–18, 25–26, 44–45, 64); Ford et al. (1904–1937, 6:946, 1076–79, 1082–83; 17:806–8; 18:915–14; 22:184, 191–94, 223–32; 23:694–96; 25:554–64).

4. See Donaldson (1884, 4, 85); Jensen (1981, 330–36); Ford et al. (1904–1937, 3:321, 335–36, 435, 439–40; 5:656; 13:821, 827–28; 20:770–72; 21:823–24, 838–39, 892–93, 1115–16; 22:57–60, 108–13, 166–73, 186–88, 282–86, 389–92; 23:461; 24:7–32; 26:45, 283–27; 27:532–36, 547–50, 603–5, 666–72; 29:721, 725–31, 777; 30:196–97; 31:636–69, 653–54).

Fig. 8.1   Western lands claimed and then ceded to the U.S. Federal Government by the thirteen original states, 1784–1802

Sources: Stephenson (1934, 248). For similar maps, see Friedenberg (1992, 199); Henretta et al. (1987, 201); Hughes and Cain (2007, 94); and Tindall (1988, 266).

claims brought these concerns to Congress. If a solution could not be found, disunion was likely.

The Articles of Confederation were drafted and approved by Congress and sent to the states for ratification in November of 1777 (Ford et al. 1904–1937, 9:906–28). Ratification, which required unanimous consent of the states, was held up until the land issue was resolved. For example, by 1780, Maryland was still refusing to ratify the Articles of Confederation until this issue was solved by the states claiming western lands ceding them to the national government for "the general benefit." The problem of western land claims was viewed in Congress in 1780 as the "only obstacle to final ratification of the articles of confederation."[5]

States without claims to western lands pressed states with such claims to cede their claims to the national government. In 1779, congressmen from Delaware and Maryland asserted that the western territories were "gained from the King of Great Britain, or the native Indians, by the blood and treasure of all, and ought therefore to be a common estate, to be granted out on terms beneficial to the United States." In 1780, congressmen from New York asserted that the ". . . uncultivated territory within the limits or claims of certain States ought to be appropriated as a common fund for the expenses of the war. . . ." A congressional committee in 1780 argued that these lands were "essential to public credit and confidence . . . and so necessary to the happy establishment of the federal union . . ." and that they could not "be preserved entire" by the claiming states "without endangering the stability of the general confederacy. . . ." Later in 1780, Congress resolved that all lands so ceded by the states to the national government "shall be disposed of for the common benefit of the United States. . . ."[6]

An important controversy over state land cessions was the status of claims made by land speculators to lands north of the Ohio River based on their acquisition of Indian deeds. Many of these speculators were prominent individuals from states that had no claims to the western territories. Virginia insisted that such claims be voided. Virginia did not want to surrender these lands to the general public just to have them fall directly into the hands of prominent New York and Philadelphia land speculators. The political battle in Congress between these land speculators and Virginia held up the major land cessions until 1784 when Virginia got its way. By contrast, speculative land claims by Virginians in Kentucky and by North Carolinians in Tennessee were held valid. As such, Kentucky and Tennessee lands never really came under alienable Federal possession. These regions were the first two trans-Appalachian states to join the union—in 1792 and 1796, respectively. Last, Virginia and Connecticut retained sizable portions of their cession of Ohio as their "western and military reserves" to satisfy their commitments during the Revolution to pay their soldiers in land bounties.[7]

As these conditions were hammered out, states one by one from 1781

---

5. See Donaldson (1884, 61–64); Feller (1984, 3–5); Gates (1968, 50–57); Jensen (1981, 8–18, 25–26); Ford et al. (1904–1937, 17:806–8).

6. See Donaldson (1884, 61–64); Gates (1968, 50–57); Jensen (1981, 8–18, 25–26); Ford et al. (1904–1937, 17:806–8).

7. See figure 8.4; Adams (1960, 3:214–19); *American State Papers: Public Lands* (1834, 1:1, 12, 17, 112, 164, 193–99, 283); Donaldson (1884, 67–70, 82, 86–87); Feller (1984, 3–5); Friedenberg (1992, 143–221, 248–60, 275–83); Gates (1968, 50–57); Jensen (1981, 8–18, 25–26, 44–45, 64, 112–14, 171–73, 330–36, 350–59); Ford et al. (1904–1937, 17:806–8; 18:914–16; 21:1057–58, 1076–78; 22:184, 191–94, 223–32; 25:554–64; 26:110–17; 28:234–36; 34:133, 270–71, 331–34, 476); Livermore (1939, 74–122); Sakolski (1932, 1–123); Tindall (1988, 268). Negotiations over the future status of Kentucky and Tennessee as separate states also slowed the Virginia and North Carolina land cessions.

through 1802 ceded their western lands to the national government. The commitment to so cede these lands in 1781 opened the door to the final ratification, by Maryland, of the Articles of Confederation (Ford et al. 1904–1937, 19:208–24). These lands did not come into the alienable possession of the Federal Government all at once. It took over two decades to complete the transfer (Donaldson 1884, 30–88). Table 8.1 lists the timing and amount of land ceded by the states to the national government. Figure 8.2 shows the cumulative total alienable acres from 1784 to 1802, net of overlapping claims and past sales, in the possession of the national government. By the 1787 Constitutional Convention, the question of who would possess the spoils of war—the western lands—had been settled, though the Georgia cession was yet to be executed. The new national (federal) government representing all the nation's citizens would own, control, and determine the distribution of these lands. It seems unlikely that the Constitution as written in 1787 could have been created if not for this prior solution to the problem of western land claims.

The shift in the sectional balance of power between the southern, middle, and northeastern states that would have likely breached the union in the early

Table 8.1   Land cessions to the Federal Government by the 13 original states, 1781–1802

Year	State	Acres	Notes
1781	New York	202,187	Jointly claimed by Massachusetts.
1784	Virginia	229,917,493	Some acres jointly claimed by other states, excludes Kentucky, and includes lands reserved in Ohio to Virginia.
1785	Massachusetts	34,560,000	Jointly claimed by other states.
1786	Connecticut	25,600,000	Jointly claimed by other states, but with 3,800,000 of Ohio held back as a reserve.
1787	South Carolina	3,136,000	Solely claimed
1790	North Carolina	26,679,600	Mostly Tennessee which had already been alienated and so is typically not counted.
1802	Georgia	56,689,920	Solely claimed.
Gross total		376,785,200	Simple sum.
Net total ceded to the national government[a]		221,989,787	Minus overlapping claims, the North Carolina cession, and Virginia and Connecticut reserve lands in Ohio.

Sources: Figure 8.1; American State Papers: Public Lands (1834, 1:1, 12, 17, 112, 164, 193–99); Donaldson (1884, 11, 86–88); Gates (1968, 57); Grubb (2007b, 146–47); Hibbard (1939, 13); Historical Statistics of the United States (1975, 1:428); Ford et al. (1904–1937, 19:208–13; 26:110–17, 142–43, 315–17; 28:271–75, 280–84, 382–87, 408–10; 30:159–60, 307–08, 310–11; 31:654–55; 33:466–77, 692–93; 34:320–06).
[a]The net total is not consistently estimated across the sources; see Grubb (2007b, 147).

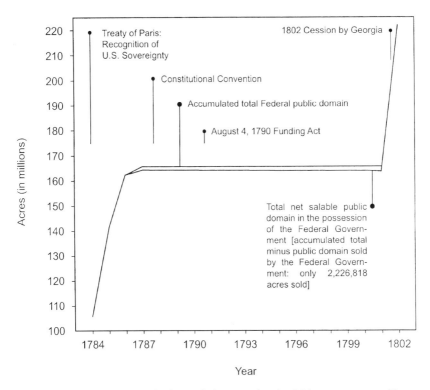

Fig. 8.2   Total and net (total minus sales) accumulated salable acres possessed by the Federal Government
Source: Derived from Grubb (2007b, 146–47).

decades of the Republic (if, for example, states like Virginia were allowed to retain all their western lands) was averted by the cession of these lands to the national government. The sectional conflict within the national government was shifted to competition over the admission of new states carved out of these territories—a peaceful though spirited competition that would only devolve into a breach in the union some seventy years later.

Between 1784 and 1802, the national government acquired a treasure trove of assets amounting to 222 million acres of potentially salable land lying between the Mississippi River, the Great Lakes, Florida, and the current western borders of the original 13 states (see figure 8.1). Congress adopted the Constitution in 1789, replacing the Articles of Confederation with this new government. The new Constitution reaffirmed congressional control over the ceded western lands. Article IV, section 3, paragraph 2 of the Constitution stated, "The Congress shall have Power to dispose of and make all needful Rules and Regulations respecting the Territory or other property belonging to the United States . . ." The Supreme Court would later determine that this power vested in Congress was without limitation

(Donaldson 1884, 13; Gates 1968, 73–4). The new Federal Government was born land rich!

8.2   What Was the Value of These Federally Owned Land Assets?

Establishing the total asset value of the lands held by the Federal Government matters because these lands were to be used in some fashion to service the debts incurred fighting the Revolution, which amounted to $80 million in interest-bearing bonds in 1792. To do this, an average price per acre of the public domain held by the Federal Government is needed. This is hard to come by as land is very heterogeneous, and sales in this period were small and sometimes selective—meaning possibly unrepresentative. Given a true average nominal price, that price still has to be adjusted for inflation and deflation. Between 1784 and 1802, prices experienced large swings so that comparing values over time cannot be done in just nominal or current prices (Bezanson, Gray, and Hussey 1936, 392–3; Grubb 2003, 1782–83). Given a true inflation-adjusted constant dollar average price of an acre, consideration must also be given to what might happen to that price if the Federal Government tried to sell all its land at once versus trying to sell it slowly over time. The Federal Government was such a large landholder that trying to sell a substantial amount at once would likely depress the price. Given these formidable problems, presenting a range of estimates based on some likely average prices is the best that can be done.

Figure 8.3 presents four estimates of the value of the net salable public domain in the hands of the Federal Government in constant dollars over time. Each estimate is based on a different average nominal price for an acre of land that was reported in a different year. Because land is heterogeneous, only the sale or pricing of reasonably large tracts can give some reassurance that the average price observed is close to a true average price. Only one estimate in figure 8.3 uses an actual sale price from the period, while the other three use official published prices, two set by Congress and one used by the Treasury Secretary, Alexander Hamilton.

Land had to be surveyed before being sold at public auction. Surveying and selling the public domain, including administration expenses, cost between three and six cents an acre. These costs were to be paid by the purchaser. Fees for application, registration, and patenting of land were around half a cent an acre and were also to be paid by the purchaser (Donaldson 1884, 189–90, 192, 197, 201–2).[8]

---

8. Carstensen (1963, xviii) and Hughes and Cain (2007, 98–99) indicate that the cost of acquiring, surveying, and selling the land exceeded the revenue received from land sales. Their source is Donaldson (1884, 17–21, 517–27). However, Donaldson's estimates show that this assessment arises from decisions made post-1830 to purchase new lands and especially to increase spending on Indian affairs (around 85 percent of the total cost), while at the same time revenues from land sales were reduced via giving land to railroads and homesteaders. The cost of surveying and selling the land was a trivial component by comparison. Pre-1830, and especially pre-1813, virtually all the value of its original cession lands was captured by the

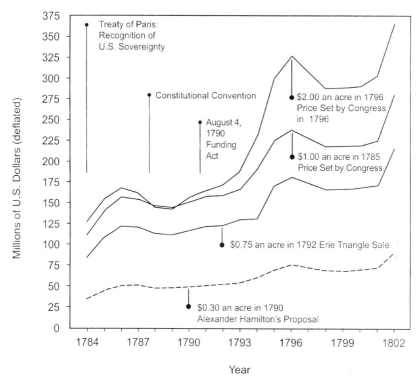

Fig. 8.3 **Constant dollar value of salable Federal Government land assets, 1784– 1802: Various estimates**
Source: Derived from Grubb (2007b, 148–51).
Notes: The estimates multiply the total acres of salable public domain remaining in the Federal Government's possession each year from figure 8.2 by the nominal price per acre for the year that the respective nominal price was mentioned. From the year when the nominal price was stated, each estimate then inflation-adjusts the price to other years using the Bezanson, Gray, and Hussey (1936, 392–93) price index renormalized to the year the nominal price was given.

The official minimum price set by Congress (which was not strictly adhered to) for purchasing the public domain which had to be purchased in large tracts—a minimum purchase of a 640 acre lot—was $1.00 per acre in 1785 and raised to $2.00 per acre in 1796 (Davis et al. 1972, 104–5; Donaldson 1884, 196–98; Robbins 1942, 15–16). If these prices are inflation adjusted from the year they were enacted, they are almost equal at $1.00 per acre in 1785 dollars.[9] In 1781, Pelatiah Webster (1969, 93) also placed the average

---

United States when sold. For example, spending on Indian affairs pre-1813 amounted to less than one cent, and pre-1830 to about one cent, per acre of the public domain.
9. Interestingly, the sale of the Chickasaw Trust Lands in the central Southern states from 1836 through 1850 (4,025,395 acres for $3,326,404) yields an average nominal price of $0.83 an acre, which, when deflation-adjusted back to 1785, would be approximately $1.00 an acre (Gates 1968, 186; Bezanson Gray, and Hussey 1936, 392). Similarly, the bounty warrants for land given

value at one silver dollar per acre. The time series of real prices based on the nominal $2.00 per acre enacted in 1796 yields the highest overall price series among the official prices enacted by Congress.[10]

The fact that total land sales were not large through 1802 (see figure 8.2) suggests that these official prices may be on the high side. The slowness of sales, however, may have been due to the need to survey the lands before they could be put up for auction (the basic survey scheme not being fully established until the Land Acts of 1796 and 1800) and to several states who retained significant western and northern lands pricing their lands just under that set by the Federal Government. The difficulty of achieving unison of action under the Articles of Confederation also inhibited Congress' ability to adequately curb Indian hostilities in the West, stop squatters from occupying the public domain, dislodge the remaining British in the northern territories, and prevent Spanish blockades of the Mississippi River in the South. These inabilities may have, in turn, depressed the value of western lands until these weaknesses in the Federal Government were remedied by the adoption of the Constitution in 1789. To be conservative, the 1785 price of $1.00 per acre or the 1796 price of $2.00 per acre (inflation-adjusted) will be used here only to illustrate a possible upper-range estimate of the value of the public domain.[11]

The lowest price series based on a large actual sale of the public domain and used here in figure 8.3 as the best-guess estimate of the value of the public domain is for the Erie Triangle land transfer to Pennsylvania in 1792—202,187 acres for $151,640, or an average price of $0.75 an acre. In the same inflation-adjusted range is the average price of all public domain sold prior to 1800 (1,281,860 acres for $1,050,085, i.e., $0.82 an acre), the 23 July 1787 act that temporarily reduced the minimum price to $0.67 an acre, and

---

as compensation to veterans of the Revolution, War of 1812, and Mexican-American War when thrown onto the land market between 1848 and 1853 sold for an average of $0.85 an acre, or approximately $1.00 an acre in 1785 dollars (Lebergott 1985, 199–200).

10. Under the credit payment system inaugurated in 1800, the United States sold through 1813 a total of 4,520,933 acres and received $7,316,615 in actual cash or $1.62 an acre with $2,114,136 still owed; see Feller (1984, 12). Deflated back from 1813, $1.62 an acre in 1813 is the same as $1.01 an acre in 1785 (Bezanson, Gray, and Hussey 1936, 392).

11. See Adams (1960, 3:155); *American State Papers: Public Lands* (1834, 1:72–3); Davis et al. (1972, 102–3); Donaldson (1884, 189–90, 197, 201); Dougherty (2001, 175); Feller (1984, 9–10); Gates (1968, 128); Henretta et al. (1987, 221–24); Hibbard (1939, 41); Hughes and Cain (2007, 95–96); Jensen (1981, 414); Ford et al. (1904–1937, 30:230–31, 262; 31:685–86; 32:213, 231, 238–41; 34:331); Puls (2008, 200, 246); Robbins (1942, 9); and figure 8.4. A 13 February 1786 congressional report noted "with great satisfaction, the prospect of extinguishing a part of the domestic Debt, by sale of the western Territory of the United States; but [that] a considerable Time must elapse before that Country can be surveyed and disposed of . . ." (Ford et al. 1904–1937, 30:65). In 1788, Congress budgeted $4,000 for surveying western lands and $20,000 for Indian treaties—to extinguish Indian land claims. By comparison, $228,427 was budgeted for the Civil and Military Departments, $58,000 for invalid pensions, and $16,000 for contingencies (Ford et al. 1904–1937, 34:389, 438). When lands did finally go up for auction, some claim that they were worth more than the minimum price set by the government but that collusion among the bidders prevented prices from being offered that were above the minimum (Lebergott 1985, 199).

the proposed one million acre sale of Ohio territory to John Cleve Symmes in 1788 at $0.67 an acre (figure 8.4; Donaldson 1884, 17, 197–98; Hibbard 1939, 51, 55, 100; Ford et al. 1904–1937, 34:480; Rutland 1973–1983, 10:218). The 1792 estimate of $0.75 an acre (inflation-adjusted) yields a total value for the public domain in the Federal Government's possession in 1802 (after the Georgia land cession) of $215 million dollars.[12]

This best-guess estimate is surprisingly close to contemporary guesses. In an essay published in Philadelphia on 25 April 1781 (republished there in 1791), Pelatiah Webster (1969, 493, 497) claimed the government had about 200 million acres of good land that could be sold and valued it at about one silver dollar per acre on average. He also did not think that the "profit from our western lands, when disposed of according to my plan, so very distant as many may imagine." In 1792 Jedidiah Morse, the "father of American geography," estimated that Congress had 220 million acres of "unappropriated western territory" to dispose of which had been "pledged as a fund for sinking the continental debt" (Jensen 1981, 111; Morse 1792, 35).

Last, in part for heuristic purposes, a low estimate of $0.30 an acre is also reported in figure 8.3. This price does not come from an actual sale but is the price Alexander Hamilton used to calculate how much of the national debt could be extinguished by swapping it for western lands in his "Report on Vacant Lands" sent to Congress 22 July 1790. Hamilton also mentioned a price of $0.20 an acre in his January 1790 "Report on Public Credit" (*American State Papers: Public Lands* 1834, 1:1–5; Donaldson 1884, 198–99; Syrett 1961–1972, 6:90–91, 504). The logic Hamilton used to deduce these prices, however, is arbitrage inconsistent.[13] Assuming Hamil-

---

12. Pennsylvania paid for the Erie Triangle with U.S. public securities, a mixture of 6 percent, 3 percent, and deferred bonds, all taken at face value (par). Albert Gallatin rated the 6 percent bonds at par, but the 3 percent and deferred bonds at 60 and 75 percent of par, respectively (Adams 1960, 100, 197). Using these discounts, the total paid was $119,268 or $0.59 an acre. Inflation-adjusted to 1802 this yields a total value for the public domain of $177 million. Gallatin's assessment, however, is arbitrage inconsistent and so the adjusted values should be used with caution.

13. Hamilton was not proposing a price, but using what he thought would be the true market price. He combined two observations to deduce his true land price (Syrett 1961 1972, 6:91). First, the public domain had been sold for $1.00 an acre, which could be paid either in specie or in public debt at its face value. Second, the public debt had been trading for $0.20 to $0.30 specie per dollar of face value in the mid-1780s. Thus, Hamilton deduced that an acre of land was worth in specie $0.20 to $0.30 and not $1.00. This deduction, however, is arbitrage inconsistent if specie and public debt at face value were both used to buy land—which they were, see *American State Papers: Public Lands* (1834, 1:73); Donaldson (1884, 17, 201); Hibbard (1939, 41). Either anyone paying specie for land at $1.00 an acre was a fool or anyone selling their public debt for $0.30 of specie per dollar of face value was a fool. Hamilton's logic also ignores the appreciation effect that substantial land-for-debt sales would have on the market price of debt. The *Massachusetts Centinel*, 19 May 1787, reasoned that substantial land sales "must give an immediate rise to the current value of the securities of the United States, which are received in payment for lands as specie." Jensen (1981, 384) concluded, ". . . it was the unsettled land of the United States that seemed the best justification for speculation in American [war] debt." However, only about 1 percent of the interest-bearing debt had been pledged to be swapped for land by 1789 with most of these swaps not consummated until the early 1790s. These pre-1790 sales were also for the most part restricted to large negotiated swaps between Congress and

⬚ Ohio Special Grants and Reserves

Fig. 8.4   Example of lands not ceded to the Federal Government but retained by the states, plus some early prospective land sales, grants, and reserves, in the Ohio Territory
Sources: Hibbard (1939, 53). See a similar map in Sakolski (1932, 100).

ton was not stupid implies that his price estimates meant something else or were intended to achieve some other political purpose than simply reporting the true expected long-run equilibrium average constant-dollar price of an acre of public domain. Hamilton's rhetorical argumentation often has such

land companies (Grubb 2007a, 281; Donaldson 1884, 197–99, 201; Gates 1968, 69–71; Hibbard 1939, 41–55; Jensen 1981, 354–59; Ford et al. 1904–1937, 34:371–73, 565–66). As such, competitive land auctions did not get the chance to drive security prices up to par before the 4 August 1790 Funding Act solved the security-funding problem causing their prices to reinflate to face value. In conclusion, something is not right with Hamilton's logic, and his land price estimates should be used with caution (Grubb 2007b, 150).

a disingenuous tone that it is difficult to grasp its true meaning (Ratchford 1941, 52).

In his reports, Hamilton was talking about the possibility of selling or swapping most or all of the public domain at once to extinguish the national debt. Such a large sale or transfer of land in a short time interval would depress its market price. Thus, Hamilton's $0.30 an acre price could represent a guess about what would happen to the price of land if the Federal Government tried to unload all its land too quickly. Trying to gauge the effect on the market price of such a massive land dump is difficult, and Hamilton's estimate, as shown in figure 8.3, will be taken here as a best guess of this.[14]

Given the estimates in figure 8.3, how dollar-asset land rich was the Federal Government? The national debt between 1792 and 1802 hovered around $80 million, and tax revenues per year ranged between $4 and $15 million (Gordon 1998, 206; Grubb 2007a, 281; *Historical Statistics of the United States* 1975, 2:1104). Using the Erie Triangle estimate (inflation-adjusted and securities discounted), the value of the public domain in the possession of the Federal Government was over $95 million in 1786 and over $147 million in 1796. The Federal Government was not just born land rich, it was born dollar-asset rich! Paul Wallace Gates concluded (1968, 56), "The transfer of these territories probably did more than anything else at the time to give prestige to the government."

8.3   What Should Be Done with These Federally Owned Land Assets?

States considered that the lands they had ceded to the national government were to be used to satisfy the debts incurred to gain independence. This was the prominent theme in the congressional debates over ceding western lands to the national government, and after 1780, Congress continued to link its ceded land assets with the national debt (Donaldson 1884, 60–81; Gates 1968, 61–62, 124; Jensen 1981, 58). For example, on 5 September 1782, a congressional committee favored "ceding of the western lands, to be sold to 'discharge the national debt'" (Hibbard 1939, 33). A 1786 congressional report recommended that, "The whole product [from sales of western lands] . . . is [to be] appropriated for the payment of the principal and interest of the national debt, and no part thereof can be diverted to other purposes" (Ford et al. 1904–1937, 30:65).

Prominent Founding Fathers echoed this theme. In a letter to Nathaniel Chipman, 22 July 1788, dealing with how the national war debt might affect

---

14. The effect of throwing such a large amount of land onto the market at once might be gauged from the Bounty Act of 1847, which awarded 68 million acres of land warrants to war veterans. About 85 percent of these warrants were thrown onto the market for cash between 1848 and 1853 and traded for about $0.85 per acre. The government's minimum price per acre at that time was $1.25. As such, the effective market price was about two-thirds of the minimum government price for an acre of the public domain (Lebergott 1985, 199–200).

Vermont's federal tax obligations if it joined the union, Alexander Hamilton said, "The public debt, as far as it can prudently be provided for, will be by the Western lands and the appropriation of some general fund" (Syrett 1961–1972, 5:186). In a 19 June 1788 letter to Marquis de Lafayette, George Washington remarked, "When the people find . . . the burdens of war shall be in a manner done away by the sale of western lands . . . these blessings will be referred to the fostering influence of the new government. Whereas many causes will have conspired to produce them" (Fitzpatrick 1939, 29:522–26).

In the 1780s, the expectations of both the public and among the Founding Fathers, as well as the political mandates accompanying the land transfers from the states, were that the lands so transferred to the Federal Government were to be used to pay for the cost of the War for Independence (Feller 1984, 6; Jensen 1981, 246, 359, 384). But exactly how this should be done was not made clear. What choices existed for satisfying such expectations and mandates?

8.4   How Are a Government's Debts and (Land) Assets Related?

A government's debts and (land) assets are related through its budget constraint that connects its cash flows to its capital stocks. The government's yearly tax revenue (T_i) minus its yearly expenditures (G_i) must equal the change (Δ) in its contemporaneous stock of net capital assets ($A_i - D_i$), where A are salable capital assets—for example, inventories of specie, bank stock, and land, and D are the face value of its debt liabilities—for the United States after 1790, principally callable perpetuities with the principal payable only at the government's discretion.[15]

$$T_i[(t \cdot I_i) + O_i] - G_i\{[(1 - k_i) \cdot R_g \cdot D_i] + E_i\} = \Delta(A_i - D_i)$$

For the Federal Government after 1790, the principal tax revenue (T_i) came from a tariff (t) on current imports (I_i), with O_i representing all other

15. Debt liabilities (D) include both interest-bearing bonds (B) and non-interest-bearing fiat paper money (M), i.e. $D = B + M$. The Federal Government did not issue new M after 1779 and the new U.S. Constitution, by convention vote in 1787, prohibited the Federal Government from issuing new M thereafter (Farrand 1966, 2:308–10; Grubb 2006a, 43–44, 60–62). As such, only the B portion of D factors into G. Paying down or retiring any of the face value of the principal, either of B or M, without liquidating assets, however, would still require a current-year budget surplus ($T - G > 0$). As part of the debt restructuring plan of 1790, the Federal Government effectively and irrevocably defaulted on the remaining M issued prior to 1780 that was still outstanding in 1790 (Grubb 2007a). As such, distinguishing between B and M in the model is not necessary. The Federal Government's salable capital assets at a point in time (A_i) are what they are given the current asset prices in the marketplace at that point in time. If D is held constant, then a government budget surplus or deficit must change A_i (ΔA_i) as measured in those current market prices. Now, A can change over time due to changes in asset prices in the marketplace. That does not alter the fact that whatever A is at a given point in time (A_i) it will be changed (ΔA_i) by a current government budget surplus or deficit when D is held constant. A changing over time due to asset price appreciation or depreciation in the marketplace only enhances or reduces, respectively, the government's ability to sustain a given budget deficit in a particular year out of contemporaneous asset sales or its ability to use those contemporaneous assets as leverage for issuing more D at reasonable R_g to sustain that given budget deficit.

current-year tax revenues such as from the whiskey tax. As such, Federal tax revenues would not be affected in the near term by the speed or extent of land transfers to the public. Yearly expenditures (G_i) comprised the interest on the face value of the Federal Government's stock of interest-bearing debt ($R_g \cdot D_i$) not in default ($1 - k_i$), where k_i is the default rate ($0 \le k_i \le 1$), with E_i representing all other current-year (such as military) expenditures.

When the government has a budget surplus ($T_i - G_i > 0$), it has excess revenue and, assuming that it is not in default on its interest payments (i.e., that $k_i = 0$), it must either increase its stock of assets ($A_{i+1} > A_i$) at current market prices or pay down and retire some of the principal on its debt ($D_{i+1} < D_i$). When the government has a budget deficit ($T_i - G_i < 0$), then the shortfall in revenue must be covered either by selling some assets ($A_{i+1} < A_i$) at current market prices or borrowing more ($D_{i+1} > D_i$) or increasing its default on its interest payments ($k_{i+1} > k_i$). If an important goal of the government is to protect its creditworthiness by keeping $k_i = 0$, then increasing k is not an option but a last resort. If the government has no assets (A), then it has to increase its debt liabilities (D). However, increasing D via interest-bearing liabilities raises G in the future [$(R_g \cdot D_{i+1}) > (R_g \cdot D_i)$], which puts increased pressure on the budget to stay in deficit ($T_{i+1} - G_{i+1} < 0$), particularly given that in this period the Federal Government's ability to raise taxes in the near future was tightly constrained; that is, it is likely that per capita $T_i \ge T_{i+n}$. This scenario puts the government in an unsustainable long-run position, putting pressure on the government to increase k, that is, to default in the near future (Taylor 1950, 5). This pressure on future k would be incorporated into current expectations and so lead to an increase in R_g today, thus further constraining the government's ability to escape its current budget deficit anytime soon and further increasing the likelihood of a near-future default.

This last scenario fits the United States in the late 1780s as James Madison explained it to Thomas Jefferson on 24 October 1787:

> Such is the state & prospect of our fiscal department that any new loan however small, that should now be made, would probably subject us to the reproach of premeditated deception. The balance of Mr. Adams' last loan will be wanted for the interest due in Holland, and with all the income here, will, it is feared, not save our credit in Europe from further wounds. It may well be doubted whether the present Govt. can be kept alive thro' the ensuing year, or untill the new one may take its place. (Rutland 1973–1983, 10:218; Swanson 1963, 36)

As such, the government's contemporaneous net asset position ($A_i - D_i$), and expected position in the near future, should be important factors in assessing its creditworthiness. A positive net asset position functions as a safety valve that could potentially relieve the pressure to default when the budget unexpectedly falls into deficit. It is not the actual current revenue or contemporaneous cash flow from the sale of A that matters to assessing the government's creditworthiness but A's potential salability to cover or back the government's current and future debt position. As a sovereign entity, the Federal Government could not be forced to liquidate its assets to pay off its debts when in default. Nevertheless, default is costly to sovereign entities in terms of lost reputation, a lowered credit rating, and reduced access to borrowing in the future—a cost that the sale of assets could avert.

Between 1781 and 1790, the U.S. Federal Government made almost no interest or principal payments on the domestic portion of its debt (Taylor 1950, 2). In effect, $k = 1$ over the recent past so that even when the Federal Government started paying interest in full ($k = 0$) after 1790, its reputation for paying the interest on its debt would likely not fully recover until sometime after 1790—until after it had established a firm track record for always meeting interest payments. Expected budget surpluses did not look promising after 1790—even after the new Constitution gave the Federal Government an independent power to levy taxes directly on the public (Taylor 1950, 5). The government's revenue expectations were in doubt given its inability to prevent smuggling and enforce tariff (t) payments; in doubt given fluctuations in tariff revenues (the main source of tax revenue) due to ubiquitous fluctuations in foreign trade (I_j); and in doubt given questions about the government's ability to raise other taxes (O_j) considering the public's willingness to engage in violent large-scale tax revolts, for example, Shay's Rebellion 1786 to 1787, the Whiskey Rebellion 1794, and Fries' Rebellion 1798.[16]

All three rebellions were tax revolts that involved calling out the regular army on a substantial scale to confront its own citizens. The Whiskey Rebellion witnessed the only time a sitting U.S. president as commander-in-chief has taken the field at the head of an army. The Founding Fathers were aware that public resistance was a constraint on raising new taxes. In late 1789, James Madison, Congressman from Virginia, wrote to Alexander Hamilton, the Secretary of the Treasury, that, "In my opinion, in considering plans for the increase of our revenue, the difficulty lies, not so much in the want of objects as in the prejudices which may be feared with regard to almost every object. The Question is very much What further taxes will be *least* unpopular?" (Syrett 1961–1972, 5:439).

Hamilton may have also doubted the government's ability to raise enough revenue to meet expenses. In late 1789, as Secretary of the Treasury he broached the possibility of quietly approaching the French to see ". . . if the installments of the Principal of the debt [the U.S. owed France] could be suspended for a few years, [as] it would be a valuable accommodation to the U.S." (Syrett 1961–1972, 5:426, 429). Letters between Hamilton, as Secretary of the Treasury overseeing the tariff revenue tax, and his port agents often alluded to the problem of smuggling, the difficulty of enforcing the tariff, and the difficulty of collecting tariff revenues. As one customs officer put it in late 1789, "The difficulties that have occurred in the Execution of the laws

---

16. See Bouton (1996); Dougherty (2001, 103–28); Edling and Kaplanoff (2004); Richards (2002); Syrett (1961–1972, 17:2–6, 9–58, 61–72, 77–78); Szatmary (1980); Tindall (1988, 320–21, 333–34).

respecting the Customs have been infinite, and present themselves daily. The System itself is the most complicated and embarrassing of anything that has employed my attention . . . [and] the Owners pay with reluctance . . . others not at all without compulsion; and the law provides none" (Syrett 1961–1972, 5:422, 427, 459–64; 17:6–7).

The first full year of tariff revenues, 1 October 1789 through 30 September 1790, yielded $1,903,709. This sum was less than half of what was needed to pay the interest on the nation's $77 million interest-bearing debt, let alone meet any other expenses of government (Syrett 1961–1972, 6:87; 9:3). Hamilton expected revenue shortfalls from the tariff to continue and suggested new taxes, such as the Whiskey Tax. This in turn sparked the 1794 Whiskey Rebellion (Tindall 1988, 301, 320; Syrett 1961–1972, 7:225–36). The yearly value of imports fluctuated greatly between 1789 and 1811, making tariff revenues uncertain and difficult to forecast (North 1966, 19-32, 228). This was due in part to the problem the United States had, as a new nation, establishing trade treaties with foreign powers (Tindall 1988, 316–18, 330–31). In 1786, James Madison decried ". . . the present anarchy of our commerce . . ." and Hamilton expressed a similar sentiment in 1794 in a letter to President Washington (Rutland 1973–1983, 8:502–3; Syrett 1961–1972, 16:261–79). The next Secretary of the Treasury, Oliver Wolcott, in his communication to Congress on 14 December 1796 regarding implementing new direct taxes, recounted the past volatility and future uncertainty of tariff revenues that were in part due to the unpredictable course of European wars (Wolcott 1796). Albert Gallatin, who would be Secretary of the Treasury under Thomas Jefferson, reached a similar conclusion in 1796 regarding past and expected future deficits and the risk of constantly covering such through new loans (Adams 1960, 3:100–101, 105).

The annual Federal budget actually incurred deficits between $1.4 and $2.1 million in 1792, 1794 to 1795, and 1799, and came close to being in deficit in 1793, 1798, and 1800 (Gordon 1998, 206; *Historical Statistics of the United States* 1975, 2:1104). These deficits were not unanticipated. Creditors had to be concerned about the effects these deficits would have on the Federal Government's ability to meet its future debt obligations purely from current tax revenues. As such, the net asset position of the Federal Government ($A_i - D_i$) in this period may have been especially important to establishing and sustaining the government's creditworthiness. A positive net asset position would have been viewed as a safety valve to the pressure of increasing k to balance budget shortfalls in a world where the government's yearly tax revenue capacity was still in doubt.

8.5   But How Should the Public Domain Be Used to Support the National Debt?

The preceding budget constraint model suggests that there were two basic options for using the public domain to support the national debt. The first option would be to sell or swap land (A) for debt (D) as quickly as possible, thereby reducing D to zero or as close to zero as possible. This would take pressure off the budget by reducing the current yearly expenditure of (G_i) by reducing ($R_g \cdot D_i$). In essence, this would be like starting with a clean slate by clearing the books of as much old war debt as possible. The second option would be only to sell the land (A) when a good price could be had to pay down D and in the meantime hold the land in reserve as backing for D—a safety valve for when yearly tax revenues might fall short and meeting the interest payments on D purely out of current revenues was in doubt. Gallatin articulated these two options in his *Sketch of the Finance* in 1796 (Adams 1960, 3:155–56).

8.5.1   Option One

Between 1784 and 1790, there was much discussion and some plans, both executed and yet to be executed, to sell or swap the public domain for national government debt (A for D). The idea of liquidating war debts via land transfers was not strange. For example, one essayist argued in the *Salem Gazette,* reprinted in the *Pennsylvania Gazette,* 22 June 1785, "Our national debt is small, our resources almost untouched, and our means of discharging it, . . . nearly inexhaustible . . . The sale of vacant lands, the property of the continent or state, should not be strained for the highest price, but be immediately sold for the most they would readily bring" (Jensen 1981, 246). In the state cessions of lands to the national government, some states reserved lands for paying their soldiers and war debts; for example, Virginia and Connecticut held on to sizable chunks of Ohio as their "western and military reserve" lands; see figure 8.4. Congress itself had offered land bounties to soldiers as inducements to enlist during the Revolution. In addition, land companies sought to acquire large yet-to-be-surveyed tracts of the public domain in part hoping to exchange war debt obligations for said lands. In 1787, the Ohio Company offered to purchase one and one-half million acres and the Scioto Company another five million acres of the public domain from Congress. In 1788, Judge John Cleves Symmes made a similar offer for two million acres between the Great and Little Miami Rivers, see figure 8.4. Exchanging or selling land for war debt was a prominent theme and seen by many as the solution to the national government's financial distress.[17]

The Founding Fathers were aware of and talked about these possibilities. For example, on 23 October 1787, Edward Carrington wrote to Thomas Jefferson in reference to the land sale schemes just mentioned:

17. See Adams (1960, 3:221); Donaldson (1884, 17, 82–85); Friedenberg (1992); Gates (1968, 62, 70–71); Hibbard (1939, 10–14, 44–55); Jensen (1981, 32, 352–56, 359, 384–85); Ford et al. (1904–1937, 6:946; 17:808; 25:681–94; 32:155–57, 242–43, 276, 345–56, 350–51, 376–77; 33:692–97, 701–2; 34:80–81, 177, 181–82, 213–17, 247–42, 331–34, 371–73, 467–68, 473–74, 476, 540–42, 565–66); Livermore (1939, 74–214); Robbins (1942, 10–11); Sakolski (1932, 1–191); Sumner (1968, 2:251–70).

This mode of sale will relieve the U.S. of much expense, and the progress of the sales promise to be sufficiently rapid to give our people early relief from the pressure of the domestic debt. I am inclined to believe that some successful experiment might be made for the sale [of] a part of the territory in Europe, and have suggested a trial with a few [of the Seven] Ranges of the surveyed Townships. (Boyd 1953–1955, 12:256–57; figure 8.4)

James Madison wrote to Jefferson on 24 October 1787 on the same issue and, after talking about the woeful state of national government finances and borrowing prospects, said:

Upwards of 100,000 Acres of the surveyed lands of the U.S. have been disposed of in open market. Five million of unsurveyed have been sold by private contract to a N. England Company, at 2/3 of a dollar per acre, payment to be made in the principal of the public securities. A negotiation is nearly closed with a N. Jersey Company for two million more on like terms, and another commenced with a Company of this City for four million. (Rutland 1973–1983, 10:218)[18]

William Findley, congressman from Pennsylvania, claimed that proposals for large sales of the public domain were still being made in 1790. He said that:

Flint and Parker had agreed to purchase three millions of acres. To the second session of the New Congress, Scriba made proposals for four or five millions. And Hannibal William Dobbyne proposed to take more than all the others, and to settle it with people from Ireland. These proposals were referred to the secretary of the treasury [Hamilton], while he was privately preparing the funding system: but *he never reported on them.* . . . If the proposals of Messrs. Parker, Dobbyne, and others, which were offered before the funding system was originated, had been accepted, it is a moderate computation to suppose that fifteen millions of dollars would have been redeemed. (Taylor 1950, 62)

Hamilton, himself, in his 1790 "Report on Public Credit" proposed one plan whereby a full third of the national debt would be extinguished by swapping it for land (Syrett 1961–1972, 6:91–92).

The problem with this option—to sell all the land as quickly as possible to reduce D by as much as possible—was that dumping a lot of land on the market at once would likely reduce its price significantly. At $0.75 an acre in 1790, or even at $0.50 an acre, there was enough land to completely pay off the interest-bearing debt, but if the price was driven down to Hamilton's estimated $0.30 an acre there was not enough so that afterward $A = 0$ but

---

18. Of the last three sales mentioned, the first two were only partially executed and not paid for until after 1792 and the last sale failed to be executed; see *American State Papers: Public Lands* (1834, 1:59–60, 63, 66–68, 73, 115, 236–37); Donaldson (1884, 17, 201); Hibbard (1939, 43–55); Livermore (1939, 134–46).

$D > 0$ (Grubb 2007a, 280–84).[19] Under such an outcome, there would be no asset cushion or safety valve for the Federal Government to utilize. As such, the government's creditworthiness could easily unravel. The Federal Government would also lose leverage over populations in the territories regarding issues of local governance and new state formation if it sold all its land at once.

8.5.2   Option Two

If the public domain could be pledged to back the national debt only, that is, held in reserve to meet budget deficit emergencies only—with the interest on the national debt paid out of current revenues, and the public domain only sold slowly over time at good prices with these proceeds dedicated to retiring debt principal, then the creditworthiness of the Federal Government might be more safely ensured. The basic idea was not strange. The linkage of land assets to the "backing" of public financial instruments was deeply rooted in the American experience. Colonial governments formed land banks where a subject's land served as collateral for loans of government paper money. A colony's paper bills of credit were understood to be backed or collateralized not by specie but by the mortgaged land assets of the colony.[20]

Financiers understood the importance of a "pledge" of security by the government to the backing of its debts to foster public confidence in its debt position. For example, William Bingham, a director of the *Bank of North America,* in a letter to Alexander Hamilton, U.S. Treasury Secretary, on 25 November 1789 explained (Hamilton had solicited advice on how to fund the national debt from leading financiers and politicians such as Bingham):

> The Credit of the Funds [the national debt] must essentially depend on the permanent Nature of the Security; & if that is not to be relied on, they will fall in value, the disadvantage of which, Government will experience by the payment of an exorbitant Interest, whenever it is compelled to anticipate its revenues, by the Negotiation of domestic Loans. . . . If we offer a less Substantial Security, we must Submit to a consequent Depreciation in the Value of our Funds. . . . A Government should therefore pledge every security it can offer, to engage the Confidence of the public

19. In 1790, if all the public domain was exchanged for interest-bearing public debt at $0.30 per acre that would still leave D = $28 million ($77 million in debt [D] minus $49 million in land [$A$]). Such a move would also mean that the Federal Government may have had a harder time distinguishing between interest-bearing debt (B), $77 million in face value in 1790, and non-interest-bearing debt (M), another $81 million in face value in 1790. Directly swapping land (A) for debt principal (D) makes the interest-bearing distinction between types of D irrelevant. As such, the government would have found it harder to default with impunity on its non-interest-bearing debt (M) in 1790 (the Continental Dollars still outstanding) as they in fact successfully did. See Grubb (2007a, 280–84).

20. See Grubb (2006b); Kemmerer (1939); Perkins (1994, 44–46); Rabushka (2008); Ratchford (1941, 10–12, 18, 21–22).

Creditors, which, if once impaired, the pernicious Effects can be felt in all its future Dealings. (Syrett 1961–1972, 5:540–41)

Bingham's reference to "security" of a "permanent nature" would seem to mean government capital assets. And the only capital assets the Federal Government possessed at this time in any substantial quantities were its western lands.

Financiers in Congress and among the Founding Fathers also understood the importance of pledging land as security in order to secure loans (Jensen 1981, 222). In 1784, Congress considered the "vacant territories" in its possession to be a "capital resource" (Ford et al. 1904–1937, 26:315–16). Congress' Board of Treasury recommended in 1786 that the proceeds of the first half-million acres of its western territories surveyed and put up for sale be pledged as "Collateral Security" for a current loan of $500,000 to the national government (Ford et al. 1904–1937, 31:893). They understood that lands were capital assets that affected credit.

Along a similar vein, Hamilton in July of 1782 wrote, "The disposal of the unlocated lands will hereafter be a valuable source of revenue, and *an immediate one of credit.*" (Syrett 1961–1972, 3:105—italics added) As Secretary of the Treasury he said in his January 1790 "Report on Public Credit":

It is presumable, that no country will be able to borrow of foreigners upon better terms, than the United States, because none can, perhaps, afford so *good security.* Our situation exposes us less, than that of any other nation, to those casualties, which are the chief causes of expense; our incumbrances, in proportion to our real means, are less, though these cannot immediately be brought so readily into action, and our progress in resources from the early state of the country, and *the immense tracts of unsettled territory,* must necessarily exceed that of any other. The advantages of this situation have already engaged the attention of the European money-lenders . . . (Syrett 1961–1972, 6:89—italics added)

Option Two became the founding choice. With the 4 August 1790 Funding Act, Congress restructured its debt position by turning all its interest-bearing national debt into callable perpetuities with the yearly interest paid out of current-year revenues. The public domain was pledged to back that debt. In particular, the proceeds from any sale of the Federal Government's western lands were dedicated to retiring the national debt. There was no rush, no pressure, and no mandate to reduce D via land sales immediately. The salient feature of the act with respect to the use of the public domain reads:

That the proceeds of the sales which shall be made of lands in the western territory, now belonging, or that may hereafter belong, to the united states, shall be, and are hereby appropriated towards sinking or discharging the debts, for the payment whereof the United States now are, by virtue of this act may be, holden, and shall be applied solely to that use, until the said debts shall be fully satisfied. (United States Congress, *The Debates and Proceedings in the Congress of the United States*, 2:2251)

Hamilton sent this act to William Short, U.S. agent in Europe—principally Holland—for securing U.S. loans, who reported that "the acts of Congress were well known here." Dutch bankers who advised and interacted with Short in 1790 would also engage in American land speculation within the next two years as the Holland Land Company (Livermore 1939, 205–14; Syrett 1961–1972, 7:6, 176, 178). The importance of this part of the funding act is revealed in Hamilton's notes that he prepared 1 December 1790 to aid President Washington in his second annual message to Congress. Therein, Hamilton's states as his first item:

> Confidence that measures for the further support of the public Credit and for the payment of the interest and gradual extinguishment of the principal of the public debt will be pursued with zeal & vigour. And that as one mean to this a plan for the sale of the Western lands will be adopted, which will give them the effects intended, appropriating them to the sinking fund . . . (Syrett 1961–1972, 7:172–72)

The importance of land-backed debt can also be seen in William Short's May 1791 letter to Hamilton where he suggests in reference to potential European lenders that "It is possible also that it might be an agreeable circumstance to them to render them bonds for these loans or any part of them receivable in the land office of the U.S. for the purchase of lands agreeable to the prices fixed by law. This is only an idea which occurs as being an additional security against depreciation." In August 1791, Hamilton answered Short with "There can be no objection to making the bonds . . . receivable in payment for lands at the price or prices which *shall* be fixed by law . . ." (Syrett 1961–1972, 8:325, 9:2).

Contemporaries knew how much land the Federal Government had, knew its approximate value, and believed the government had pledged the public domain and had the potential to sell chunks of it if necessary to cover and service the national debt. It is the pledge to back and eventually redeem that debt with land assets, rather than any promise to quickly sell those assets to retire the debt right away, that mattered most.[21] Contemporaries could also observe the Federal Government following through on this pledge. Some of the first monies from land sales post-1790 going into the sinking fund created

---

21. For more on the land-to-debt linkage, see Grubb (2007b, 136–41); Robbins (1942, 15); Taylor (1950, 40); Syrett (1961–1972, 5:526); and the United States Congress, *The Debates and Proceedings in the Congress of the United States*, 1:647–54 (13 July 1789); 2:1345–47 (22 February 1790); 4:1314 (15 December 1794), 1017–18 (23 December 1794); and 5:60 (18 February 1829). Even by 1832, congressmen still referred to the requirement of applying the proceeds from the sale of public lands first to payments on the national debt, and only after the national debt was paid off could they use the proceeds for some other use (United States Congress, *The Debates and Proceedings in the Congress of the United States*, 5:1452 [27 December, 1832], 1475–78 [4 January 1832]). See also Jensen (1981, 414).

by the 1790 Funding Act to redeem public debt were from the 1792 Erie Tri-angle land sale to Pennsylvania (Adams 1960, 3:113, 197). By the mid-1790s, the Federal Government may have been seen as a good credit risk in spite of its recent checkered past of defaulting on its debt payments because by the early 1790s it had acquired enough land assets and had credibly committed those land assets to fully backing and then eventually redeeming its debt. The Federal Government's land assets made it solvent.

8.6   How Should the Land Be Controlled, Distributed, and Sold?

American Indians occupied much of the western lands ceded by the states to the national government. Land was to be sold by the national govern-ment, not by the Indians. As such, the Federal Government via treaty and coercion acquired land cessions from Indians when needed, amounting to about 22 million acres between 1795 and 1802 (Lebergott 1985, 211); see figure 8.5. Federal Government policy was to prevent hostilities between Indians and white settlers, but when conflicts arose, the government was often powerless to stop them. When the government did have the power, it was seldom tolerant of Indian resistance. The de facto policy was to treat Indians like bears and wolves. They were on the land and could be a dan-gerous nuisance if they did not voluntarily vacate lands coveted by white settlers. In case of hostile resistance, like bears and wolves, Indians were to be forced out or killed. This was often done by local militias, but sometimes by Federal military involvement.[22]

In 1786, Virginia delegates proposed that Congress "destroy [the Indi-ans] if they do not make concessions" in the Ohio territories. In a letter to General Josiah Harmar in 1790, General Henry Knox, Secretary of War, in reference to hostilities by the Indians in the Ohio region said, "No other remedy remains, but to extirpate, utterly, if possible, the said banditti." After a few military setbacks, General "Mad Anthony" Wayne with a force of about 2,600 men broke Indian power over the region at the battle of Fallen Timbers near the mouth of the Maumee River in 1794, thus securing the Ohio and Indiana territories for the U.S. government. The template was

22. See *American State Papers: Public Lands* (1834, 1:21–22, 63, 66, 146, 173); Ford et al. 1904–1937, 5:616–17; 6:1076–79; 1082–83; 25:681–94; 26:134–35, 152–54, 275; 27:453–65, 625–26, 658; 28:88, 118–20, 136–39, 159–62, 172–74, 330–33, 423–26, 431–32; 29:735–37, 806, 822; 30:133–35, 185–95, 257–58, 340, 342–43, 346–53, 368–81, 425–29; 31:490–93, 562–63, 656–58, 760; 32:66–69, 237–38, 266–69, 327–32, 347–49, 365–76; 33:385–91, 407–8, 410–11, 454–63, 477–81, 504–5, 696–97, 707–14; 34:59–60, 108, 124–26, 139–40, 160, 164–65, 267–69, 299–300, 326–27, 342–45, 368–71, 411–14, 423–25, 476–79). The number of militia and Federal troops deployed in battles against the Indians was relatively small and inconsequential in terms of costs and efforts. Being under 2,600 men and often under 1,000 men, their numbers were smaller than the troops employed in major battles during the Revolution, the War of 1812, the Mexican War, and the Civil War. Their numbers were on the order of the forces deployed to crush Shay's Rebellion in 1787 (Dougherty 2001, 107–21; Gates 1968, 59–61; Henretta et al. 1987, 227–30, 239, 243–45; Jensen 1981, 357–59; Puls 2008, 205–9; Tindall 1988, 318–19).

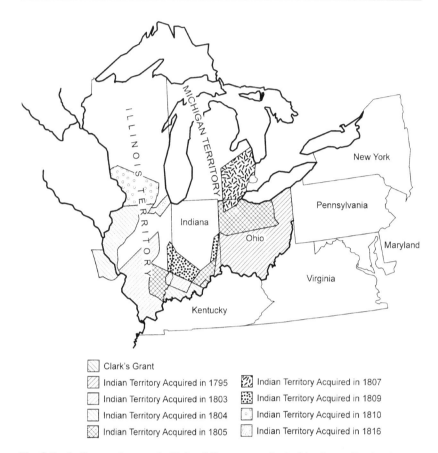

Fig. 8.5   Indian cessions to the Federal Government in the Northwest Territories, 1789–1816
Source: Robbins (1942, 23).

set for Federal Government dealings with Native Americans for decades to come.[23]

For whites, the public domain became a fact in 1784 with the Virginia cession. Between then and 1787, Congress confirmed its authority over the ceded lands and established the basic principles and policies of land distribution and governance for decades to come. This was accomplished by the passage of three great ordinances—the Ordinance of 1784, the Ordinance of 1785, and the Northwest Ordinance of 1787—initiated under Thomas Jefferson and then carried forward by others in Congress—with the 1785

---

23. See Dougherty (2001, 107–12); Gates (1968, 59–61); Henretta et al. (1987, 227–30, 239, 243–45); Hibbard (1939, 41–42); Jensen (1981, 357–59); Puls (2008, 205–9); Tindall (1988, 318–19).

and 1787 Ordinances superseding the 1784 Ordinance. These ordinances codified many of the intentions stated by Congress as early as 1780 regarding the ceded territories. They established conditions and procedures in the territories for moving from direct federal rule through democratic self-government and finally to the formation and admission as new states into the union under terms of equality of representation with the original thirteen states in Congress. They outlined potential new states. When new states were admitted to the union, however, they did not get possession of the remaining public domain within their borders. The Federal Government retained possession of its unsold lands regardless. This gave the Federal Government continuing leverage over fledgling states. Finally, a provision in the Ordinance of 1784 to ban slavery in all the lands west of the Alleghenies after 1800 was lost in Congress by a single vote, but the subsequent Northwest Ordinance of 1787 was able to prohibit slavery in the territories north of the Ohio River along with life-leases and quitrents.[24]

The 1785 and 1787 Ordinances divided the Northwest Territories into uniform townships measuring six miles square. These townships were subdivided into thirty-six one-mile square sections—one square mile being equal to 640 acres. One section out of every thirty-six was reserved "for the maintenance of public schools." These lands were to be surveyed using the "magnetic needle" to establish "true meridian" boundaries and then sold fee-simple into private ownership through competitive public auctions.

24. See Davis et al. (1972, 102–6); Donaldson (1884, 63–88, 146–63); Feller (1984, 6–9); Gates (1968, 59–74); Henretta et al. (1987, 202, 214, 224–25); Hughes and Cain (2007, 92–98); Jensen (1981, 348, 352–55); Ford et al. (1904–1937, 26:118–21, 247–52, 255–60, 274–79, 324–30; 27:446–53; 28:251–56, 298–303, 309–17, 335–40, 342–43, 370–81; 30:133–35, 230–31, 255–57, 262, 390–94; 32:281–83, 314–20, 334–43; 34:95–100, 107, 243–46, 277–81, 297–99, 301–3, 306–10); North and Rutten (1987, 25–27); Tindall (1988, 267–70). On 19 April 1784, Congress voted on whether the language banning slavery in all the western territories ceded to the national government should remain in the 1784 Land Ordinance. Votes in Congress were by state, and a majority of the thirteen states were needed to pass the motion. Delaware and Georgia were not present, and New Jersey only had a single delegate present, who while voting "yes" being this state's only delegate present meant, by rule, that New Jersey's vote would not count. That left ten states of which seven were needed to pass the motion. Not only did the six states north of Delaware vote for the motion, but every single delegate from those states (thirteen in total) voted for it. This was, however, one state short of the seven needed for a majority. The motion failed. Maryland, Virginia, and South Carolina voted "no" with every single delegate except Thomas Jefferson from those states (seven in total) voting against the motion. North Carolina was divided with Williamson for and Spaight against. The motion would have passed (received seven state "yes" votes) if any one of the following had happened: one more New Jersey delegate would have attended and voted yes; Spaight from North Carolina would have voted yes; either Hardy or Mercer from Virginia would have voted yes; or Delaware delegates would have been present and voted yes. Finally, if the motion had been worded in the reverse, namely if the motion would have been to remove the words banning slavery from the original draft of the 1784 Land Ordinance, then that motion too would have failed and the ban would have stayed. When the vote is reversed, only three states would have cast yes votes—four short of the majority needed to pass such a motion, and so the ban would have stayed in the ordinance. The razor's edge margins by which the historical trajectory of the nation could have been dramatically and fundamentally changed on 19 April 1784 is a rather sobering consideration (Ford et al. 1904–1937, 26:247).

Settlement was to be a lawful, patterned, and orderly process with secure property rights given to individual owners.

This rectangular pattern of property division and ownership, possibly derived from Dutch, Roman, and some New England precedents, was a rationalization of land-boundary structures. It contrasted sharply with the traditional "metes and bounds" land-boundary configurations found in England and in much of colonial and post-Revolutionary America, such as in Virginia and Maryland. Under metes and bounds, land boundaries typically followed natural contours and breaks, such as creeks, ridge lines, swell impressions, and so on, which in turn led to irregular land-plot shapes and sizes. The choice to replace metes and bounds with rectangular land boundaries had economic advantages. Rectangular patterns reduced survey costs (the government had to survey land before selling it); reduced boundary disputes between land owners by making boundaries clear, unchanged by natural events (e.g., naturally shifting river beds), and easy to adjudicate; and reduced odd lot sizes and shapes that were hard to use and sell. All these advantages increased the overall value of the public domain and, hence, what price the government could command when sold. It did this in part by enhancing the value of an average acre to a private property owner by rationalizing land market transactions with less idiosyncratic qualities to boundaries, thereby creating firmer property rights.[25]

The 1785 and 1787 Ordinances also established minimum acreage sizes for public land sales, that is, 640 acres. In 1800, it was reduced to 320 acres, and in 1804, it was reduced again to 160 acres, where it stayed through 1819. Why was such a large minimum purchase requirement chosen? The average farm size in the northern United States in 1800 was only 125 to 150 acres (Lebergott 1985, 185). As such, a 640 acre plot, or even a 320 acre plot, was several times the size of the typical farm. Therefore, the minimum acre purchase requirement did not reflect some natural economies of scale in farming for this period.

The choice to require these large minimum acre purchases may have been due to economic advantages gained by the government. For example, this requirement reduced survey costs. It allowed more land to be surveyed in a given space of time and so brought land under the auctioneer's gavel more quickly. Surveying a square of 640 acres would amount to "chain" or "pace" measuring four miles of distance. By contrast, if the government divided the 640 acres into four 160-acre squares or into sixteen 40-acre squares, then surveying would amount to chain or pace measuring six and ten miles of distance, respectively. In addition, more corner boundary markers would need to be established—four for one 640-acre square, nine for four 160-acre squares, and twenty-five for sixteen 40-acre squares.

---

25. See Adams (1960, 3:222); Davis et al. (1972, 102–6); Donaldson (1884, 189–90, 197, 576–78, 615–16); Feller (1984, 6–8); Henretta et al. (1987, 224–25); Libecap and Lueck (2009).

The large minimum acre purchase requirement may have served another economic function, namely allowing purchasers to capture the externality effects of land improvements the purchaser implemented on adjacent acres. In a frontier region where much of the land is initially unoccupied, the value of a particular acre depends on the degree of development of adjacent acres. Selling large lots, much larger than the typical farm, meant that the purchaser would be able to reap some of the spillover value on adjacent acres of his land improvements within his purchased allotment. He could capture that externality effect, being now capitalized into the value of that land, by selling those adjacent acres in the marketplace. If land were sold in smaller lots, buyers would not necessarily know who would own the adjacent lands or what would be done with them. As such, buyers could not gauge the true value of any particular small lot that they were considering for purchase from the government. Large minimum tract sales may have been a way to make sure that initial development externalities could be internalized by the purchaser and so maximize the sale price the government could command at auction.

Finally, the 1785 and 1787 Ordinances also established the minimum price per acre, payment credit conditions, and methods of sale. Minimum prices per acre were discussed in the preceding and appear to reflect a rough guess as to what the deflated long-run equilibrium value of land was given the pace of settlement. The method of sale was to be at competitive public auction venues in the relevant districts where the land was, with the lands sold for fee-simple ownership to the highest bidder above the minimum price. In 1785, only immediate payment was accepted, but over time, the upfront portion was reduced and the length of credit extended. In 1787, payment requirements were amended to one-third upfront and the rest in three months. In 1796, they were further amended to one-half paid within thirty days and the remainder in one year. After 1800, they were amended even further to one-fourth paid within thirty days and the balance over four years including 6 percent interest. The credit system often suffered from abuse, corruption, and nonpayment. The auction system occasionally suffered from corruption and noncompetitive manipulation at the local level. The credit part of this system ended in 1820 with a return to upfront payment only.[26]

The new Constitution affirmed Congress in possession and jurisdiction over the western ceded territories and in its intention to create new states out of said territories. It also protected the border sovereignty of existing states and guaranteed all states, new and old, republican forms of government (Article IV, sections 3 and 4). Congress under the Constitution carried the structure of the Land Ordinances of 1784, 1785, and 1787 created under

26. See Davis et al. (1972, 102–6); Donaldson (1884, 189–90, 197, 576–78); Feller (1984, 8–13); Gates (1968, 59–72, 121–43); Henretta et al. (1987, 224–25); Hughes and Cain (2007, 92–100).

the Confederation forward largely intact, making only minor modifications periodically thereafter.[27]

8.7 Epilogue

Choices made over land policy in the founding era had a lasting impact on the nation. They established the Federal Government as the largest land owner in North America, a role in which it has continued to the present day. The western lands from the Appalachian Mountains to the Mississippi River had been more or less peaceably and successfully transferred from the original thirteen states to the national government. The national government established rules whereby these lands could be acquired by citizens and new states could be formed. The rights to property had been clearly defined. Land would be distributed by the auctioneer's gavel for cash and credit in fee simple ownership to competing citizens and to soldiers who earned their land warrants through service to the nation. There would be no "colonies" of eastern states in the western territories, no life-leases, no quitrents, and, in the Northwest Territories, no slavery. There would be no landed aristocracy given large tracts of the public domain based on nobility of birth, political power, or private treaties with Native Americans. By 1800, some 387,000 Americans lived in the trans-Appalachian territories, about 7.3 percent of the U.S. population, and two new states carved out of these territories (Kentucky and Tennessee) had been formed and admitted to the union. The sectional conflict over power within Congress that threatened to dissolve the union at the end of the Revolution was transformed into a contest over new state formation and admission, a peaceful conflict that would last at least a half century before devolving into civil war (Henretta et al. 1987, 202, 204, 214, 221–29; *Historical Statistics of the United States* 1975, 1:8, 24–37).

The Federal Government was born land rich and asset-value rich. It chose to use its land assets to back the national debt, pledging the proceeds from land sales to be used, by law, only to redeem the national debt and nothing else. This land policy helped stabilize the national government's financial position and put the United States on a sound credit footing by the mid-1790s. The national debt was finally paid off in 1834, and Congress debated what it could now do with its remaining land. Freed from the 1790 Funding Act restriction, Congress could either continue to sell its land but now use the revenues on other projects, or Congress could devise some other land-transfer schemes that did not involve getting significant revenues from land

27. See Davis et al. (1972, 104); Donaldson (1884, 13); Feller (1984, 7); Gates (1968, 73–74). For the debates on these issues at the 1787 Constitutional Convention, see Farrand (1966, 1:22, 28, 117, 121, 202, 206, 226–27, 231, 237, 245; 2:39, 47, 133, 159, 188, 220, 313, 316, 321, 324, 454–66, 470, 628; 3:119–20, 223–27, 404).

sales, such as homesteading, land grants for transportation development, and the creation of national parks.

These early land policy choices led directly and immediately to one unanticipated outcome that dramatically altered U.S. history. By 1800, the Spanish or French obstruction of American navigation through New Orleans threatened not only the value of U.S. western lands, but posed the threat of these areas breaking away to form a separate country or merging with nearby Spanish or French colonies. To retain the loyalty of these western citizens and the value of these lands, Thomas Jefferson sought free navigation of the Mississippi River and the purchase of New Orleans from Napoleon—the current owner. An unexpected change in fortune led the French to offer the whole Louisiana territory to the United States on relatively cheap and easy terms. The 1803 Louisiana Purchase more than doubled the size of the United States with almost all these lands falling under Federal jurisdiction and control to be administered following the policies laid down in the 1780s and 1790s. While not without constitutional controversy—it is unclear that Congress has the power to purchase foreign territory—the end result continued the Federal Government's land possession and management role into the twentieth century (Henretta et al. 1987, 231–34; Lewis 1998, 12–32; Tindall 1988, 347–52).

References

Adams, Henry. 1960. *The writings of Albert Gallatin.* Vol. 3. New York: Antiquarian Press.
American State Papers: Public Lands. Vol. 1. Washington, DC: Government Printing Office. (Orig. pub. 1834).
Bezanson, Anne, Robert D. Gray, and Miriam Hussey. 1936. *Wholesale prices in Philadelphia, 1784–1861.* Philadelphia: University of Pennsylvania Press.
Bouton, Terry. 1996. Tying up the revolution: Money, power, and the regulation in Pennsylvania, 1765–1800. PhD diss., Duke University.
Boyd, Julian P. 1953–1955. *The papers of Thomas Jefferson.* Vols. 7–12. Princeton, NJ: Princeton University Press.
Carstensen, Vernon, ed. 1963. *The public lands.* Madison, WI: University of Wisconsin Press.
Davis, Lance E., Richard A. Easterlin, William N. Parker, Dorothy S. Brady, Albert Fishlow, Robert E. Gallman, Stanley Lebergott, Robert E. Lipsey, Douglass C. North, Nathan Rosenberg, Eugene Smolensky, and Peter Temin. 1972. *American economic growth: An economist's history of the United States.* New York: Harper & Row.
Donaldson, Thomas. 1884. *The public domain.* Washington, DC: Government Printing Office.
Dougherty, Keith L. 2001. *Collective action under the Articles of Confederation.* New York: Cambridge University Press.
Edling, Max M., and Mark D. Kaplanoff. 2004. Alexander Hamilton's fiscal reform:

Transforming the structure of taxation in the early Republic. *William and Mary Quarterly* 61:713–44.

Farrand, Max, ed. 1966. *The records of the Federal Convention of 1787.* Vols. 1–4. New Haven, CT: Yale University Press.

Feller, Daniel. 1984. *The public lands in Jacksonian politics.* Madison, WI: University of Wisconsin Press.

Fitzpatrick, John C. 1939. *The writings of George Washington.* Vol. 29. Washington, DC: U.S. Government Printing Office.

Ford, Worthington C., Gaillard Hunt, John C. Fitzpatrick, and Roscoe R. Hill, eds. 1904–1937. *Journals of the Continental Congress, 1774–1789.* Vols. 1–34. Washington DC: Government Printing Office.

Friedenberg, Daniel M. 1992. *Life, liberty, and the pursuit of land: The plunder of early America.* Buffalo, NY: Prometheus.

Gates, Paul Wallace. 1968. *History of public land law development.* Washington, DC: Zenger.

Gordon, John Steele. 1998. *Hamilton's blessing.* New York: Penguin.

Grubb, Farley. 2003. Creating the U.S.-dollar currency union, 1748–1811: A quest for monetary stability or a usurpation of state sovereignty for personal gain? *American Economic Review* 93:1778–98.

———. 2006a. The U.S. Constitution and monetary powers: An analysis of the 1787 Constitutional Convention and the constitutional transformation of the U.S. monetary system. *Financial History Review* 13:43–71.

———. 2006b. *Benjamin Franklin and the birth of a paper money economy.* Philadelphia, PA: Federal Reserve Bank of Philadelphia. http://www.philadelphiafed.org/publications/economic-education/ben-franklin-and-paper-money-economy.pdf.

———. 2007a. The net worth of the U.S. Federal government, 1784–1802. *American Economic Review: Papers and Proceedings* 97:280–84.

———. 2007b. The spoils of war: U.S. Federal government finance in the aftermath of the war for independence, 1784–1802. In *War, state and development. Fiscal-military states in the eighteenth century,* ed. Rafael Torres Sanchez, 133–56. Pamplona, Spain: EUNSA.

Henretta, James A., W. Elliot Brownlee, David Brody, and Susan Ware. 1987. *American history to 1877.* Chicago: Dorsey.

Hibbard, Benjamin Horace. 1939. *A history of the public land policies.* New York: Peter Smith.

Historical statistics of the United States: Colonial times to 1970. 1975. Washington, DC: U.S. Department of Commerce.

Hughes, Jonathan, and Louis P. Cain. 2007. *American economic history.* 7th ed. New York: Pearson Education.

Jensen, Merrill. 1981. *A new nation.* Boston: Northeastern University Press.

Kemmerer, Donald L. 1939. The colonial loan-office system in New Jersey. *Journal of Political Economy* 47:867–74.

Lebergott, Stanley. 1985. The demand for land: The United States, 1820–1860. *Journal of Economic History* 45:181–212.

Lewis, James E. Jr. 1998. *The American union and the problem of neighborhood: The United States and the collapse of the Spanish Empire, 1783–1829.* Chapel Hill, NC: University of North Carolina Press.

Libecap, Gary D., and Dean Lueck. 2009. The demarcation of land and the role of coordinating institutions. NBER Working Paper no. 14942. Cambridge, MA: National Bureau of Economic Research.

Livermore, Shaw. 1939. *Early American land companies.* New York: Commonwealth Fund.

Morse, Jedidiah. 1792. *The American geography.* 2nd ed. London: John Stockdale.

North, Douglass C. 1966. *The economic growth of the United States, 1790–1860.* New York: Norton.

North, Douglass C., and Andrew R. Rutten. 1987. The Northwest Ordinance in historical perspective. In *Essays on the economy of the old Northwest,* ed. David C. Klingaman and Richard K. Vedder, 19–31. Athens, OH: Ohio University Press.

Perkins, Edwin J. 1994. *American public finance and financial services, 1700–1815.* Columbus, OH: Ohio State University Press.

Puls, Mark. 2008. *Henry Knox: Visionary general of the American Revolution.* New York: Palgrave Macmillan.

Rabushka, Alvin. 2008. *Taxation in colonial America.* Princeton, NJ: Princeton University Press.

Ratchford, B. U. 1941. *American state debts.* Durham, NC: Duke University Press.

Richards, Leonard L. 2002. *Shay's Rebellion: The American Revolution's final battle.* Philadelphia, PA: University of Pennsylvania Press.

Robbins, Roy M. 1942. *Our landed heritage: The public domain, 1776–1936.* Princeton, NJ: Princeton University Press.

Rutland, Robert A., ed. 1973–1983. *Papers of James Madison.* Vols. 8–14. Charlottesville, VA: University Press of Virginia.

Sakolski, A. M. 1932. *The great American land bubble.* New York: Harper & Brothers.

Stephenson, Nathaniel Wright. 1934. *A history of the American people.* New York: Charles Scribner's Sons.

Sumner, William Graham. 1968. *The financier and the finances of the American Revolution, Vols. 1–2.* New York: Augustus M. Kelly. (Orig. pub. 1891).

Swanson, Donald F. 1963. *The origins of Hamilton's fiscal policy.* Gainesville, FL: University of Florida Press.

Syrett, Harold C., ed. 1961–1972. *Papers of Alexander Hamilton.* Vols. 2–17. New York: Columbia University Press.

Szatmary, David. 1980. *Shay's Rebellion: The making of an agrarian insurrection.* Amherst, MA: University of Massachusetts Press.

Taylor, George Rogers, ed. 1950. *Hamilton and the national debt.* Boston: D.C. Heath.

Tindall, George Brown. 1988. *America: A narrative history.* 2nd ed. New York: Norton.

United States Congress. 1834–1856. *The debates and proceedings in the Congress of the United States, Vols. 1–5.* Washington, DC: Gale & Seaton.

Webster, Pelatiah. 1969. *Political essays on nature and operation of money, public finances, and other subjects.* New York: Burt Franklin. (Orig. pub. 1791).

Wolcott, Oliver Jr. 1796. Direct taxes. *American state papers: Finances.* Vol. 1:414–17. Washington, DC: Government Printing Office. (Orig. pub. 1832).

9

Free Labor and Slave Labor

Stanley L. Engerman and Robert A. Margo

9.1 Human Capital

Policies regarding the level and growth rate of the stock of human capital were among the important decisions to be made at the founding of the new nation. At the start, the ratio of land to labor was extremely high; to make effective use of available land, it was necessary to attract more labor. Indeed, land itself would serve as a means of attracting labor. The changing ratio of the labor input to the settlement of what became the United States was influenced by legislation as well as by natural forces. The major sources of labor supply were the following:

- Rates of natural increase of the population, (the difference between fertility and mortality) for European descendents as well as Native Americans and slave labor.
- Immigration from abroad:
  - Free whites, free or subsidized as individuals, in families, and in other groups
  - Indentured labor, of white individuals from England and elsewhere in Europe, trading labor time for a set number of years for transport costs
  - Convict labor
  - Slaves from Africa
- Native Americans as slaves or free workers

Stanley L. Engerman is the John H. Munro Professor of Economics and a professor of history at the University of Rochester, and a research associate of the National Bureau of Economic Research. Robert A. Margo is a professor of economics and chair of the department of economics at Boston University, and a research associate of the National Bureau of Economic Research.

The basic forms of human capital, in addition to physical labor, were determined by the following:

- Education
- Medical and health practices
- Migration—internal and external
- On-the-job training at employment

9.2   Settling the Colonies

Before 1492 and the start of the European settlement of the Americas, the European population density was relatively high, while that of the Americas was quite low.[1] Within the Americas, population density differed significantly. In the regions including Mexico and the Andean areas, the density was considerably higher than in mainland North America, where the number of Native Americans was very low and where European settlement was less concentrated (Denevan 1976, 291). The populated areas of Latin America had sophisticated societies with developed agriculture, military force, and slavery. Even after the demographic collapse, due primarily to the introduction of European diseases to a population not previously exposed to these diseases, these areas still had a disproportionate large share of the population of the Americas. After the decline in population, the population density in the Americas became even lower compared to Europe than it had been prior to Columbus's arrival (see table 9.1).

The European settlement of the Americas took place in several steps. Over time, different countries led the way in terms of numbers and political controls. Spain and Portugal were the initial settling nations, leading the nations of Northwest Europe by about one century, going to the most populated and richest areas of the Americas and introducing African slaves into Brazil and Spanish America. It was only after 100 years of the Iberian settlements that the British, French, and Dutch arrived in the Americas, generally into the still available areas of the Caribbean and mainland North America. The French and Dutch sent few Europeans—the Dutch being considerably more heavily involved in the East Indies—and about 90 percent of the migrants to the Dutch and French colonies were slaves purchased in Africa (Eltis 2001; Engerman and Sokoloff 1997, 2002; Craven 1965). After their late start, the British ultimately had the largest number of immigrants, the structure by race and status varying by geographic regions. The colonies in the West Indies attracted few white workers for sugar production and came to depend on attracting a large number of slaves from Africa, to become

1. The estimated population density in 1500 for Europe was about twenty times that of the Americas, and that of Latin America about thirteen times that of North America (McEvedy and Jones 1978). The estimates for the Americas is low compared to most other sources. For some related estimates, see Inikori (2002, 158–60).

Table 9.1   The estimated distribution of the Aboriginal American population,
                   c. 1492

North America (the United States, Canada, Alaska, and Greenland)	4,400,000
Mexico	21,400,000
Central America	5,650,000
Caribbean	5,850,000
Central Andes	11,500,000
Lowland South America	8,500,000

Source: Denevan (1976, 291).

primarily sugar producers. This immigration stream was largest in the first half-century of British migration, when British migration to the West Indies exceeded that to the mainland, but then this migration to the mainland exceeded that to the West Indies. Unlike the British migration to the British West Indies, the migration to the mainland of the whites exceeded that of slaves, even in the southern colonies. This pattern of predominant white migration was unusual for the pre-nineteenth century Americas, making the thirteen British colonies a rather unique region.

As with their counterparts, the British colonies were interested in generating income for the home country, and accomplishing this meant acquiring a larger population of productive individuals. This could be achieved by several measures—purchases of slaves from Africa, enslavement of Native Americans, attracting free white workers to come by various forms of subsidies, by arrangement for indentured servants, or by acceptance of convicts. Given the great abundance of land relative to the size of the population, land was often used as the primary means of attracting population. The scarcity of land in Europe made this an attractive measure for Europeans. To take advantage of available land to provide benefits to possible migrants by ownership of small farms was, however, not the policy that the British introduced in a number of areas, which initially followed European landholding patterns. The Spanish and Portuguese provided large grants to settlers. The French in Quebec carried over the seigniorial system from France, while several of the British American colonies followed the precepts of the manorial system from England (Engerman and Sokoloff 2005). These systems, in the thirteen colonies and Canada, however, soon ended, with a movement to smaller, owner-operated farms.

Colonies with a high initial and ongoing ratio of land to labor characterized most of the Americas, but they were not the only type of colony settled by Europeans at the time. Outside of the American colonies, colonies such as India and the East Indies had quite high population densities, so high that there was no need to attract more labor and no need to adopt liberal land policies to attract new workers (Engerman and Sokoloff 2005). Many colonies in Asia and Africa had similarly high population densities, suggesting that rather different land policies would be applied in various parts of the world and also that the political systems imposed by the Europeans would differ.

With the limited number of Native Americans to enslave or use as free labor in North America, and the inability to pay the high prices for slaves that Latin American and Caribbean sugar producers could, because of the limited number of slaves sent by Africans in the transatlantic slave trade, the British North Americans had to depend upon white British laborers to provide their labor force (Galenson 1981). In Great Britain, the main concern in much of this period was with overpopulation, so that transatlantic migration was encouraged. Spain, on the other hand, was concerned with the changes in its domestic population and introduced constraints on migration to the new world, while outmigration to the Americas from France and the Netherlands, for various reasons, was also relatively small (see Elliott 2006, particularly 255–91).

British outmigration in the seventeenth and eighteenth centuries took two major forms. There was some free migration, often of religious groups, to the colonies, but more important in numbers, accounting for about three-quarters of migrants, most often to the southern and middle Atlantic states, were the many indentured servants. There were also limited numbers of redemptioners from Germany after 1720 (see Galenson 1981; Smith 1947; Wokeck 1999; Baseler 1998; and Grubb 1985a, 1985b, 1992). These indenture contracts generally were for four to seven years, and during this period the laborers could be bought and sold. There were, at times, subsidies paid in land or cash to the initial purchasers of these servants, and at the end of the indenture period, the laborers were at times given "freedom dues" of land or cash to establish themselves as free workers or landowners. To encourage transportation of free or indentured labor, the colonies could provide land grants, tax exemptions, acceptance of religious tolerance, financial assistance, and easier terms of naturalization and voting privileges; all to make transatlantic settlement more desirable. Not all migrants were considered acceptable, some colonies having restrictions based on religion, generally Catholic and Quaker, and against public charges, such as poor and indigent immigrants, as well as paupers and criminals. These would be excluded or else required some security or bond. Another source of immigrants from England, often unpopular but amounting to about 50,000, mainly to southern states, were British convicts who served out their term of labor in the colonies (Ekirch 1987). Several colonies limited convict imports, and, after the Revolution, when the colonies were given the opportunity to continue to receive British convicts, this offer was refused by the new republic, leading to the larger, longer-term shipment of convicts to Australia.

Two other forms of labor were used. Native Americans were sometimes enslaved, but these were limited in numbers and were not regarded as a major labor source (Lauber 1913; Gallay 2002; Chapin 2005). Unlike in Latin America, where Native Americans were the major component of the labor force, even though not generally legally enslaved, few Native Americans in North America were members of the general labor force, either as slaves or as free workers. Beside white Europeans, slaves purchased from Africa or, earlier, from the West Indies, were of considerable importance in the South. Slave labor was legal in all the colonies, but the major constraint on the numbers arriving was the limited profitability to their owners relative to that obtained from the slaves in the West Indies and Brazil. The crops in North America, commonly grains and livestock, did not have the profitability of those in the rest of the Americas. While slaves were legal in all the Americas and all regions did have some slaves, the overall share of slave arrivals in North America was only about 5 percent of all slaves in the Americas, and the use of slave labor in production there was smaller than elsewhere (Curtin 1969; Eltis 2001). Slave labor was of primary importance for crops grown on larger than family-sized farms, but those in the U.S. South were much smaller than the sugar plantations in Latin America.[2] The British North American colonies, at the end of the seventeenth century, produced mainly tobacco; then, in the middle of the eighteenth century, there was an expansion into rice production in South Carolina, and, then, of greatest importance, cotton throughout the South in the nineteenth century, the latter development presumably not anticipated by the founders.

There was a significant difference between the rates of growth of the population in the North American colonies and those elsewhere in the Americas (Klein 2004, 10–106; Engerman and Sokoloff 1997). Free whites and black slaves in North America had rates of natural increase that were exceptionally high by any standard, and this meant that their population numbers greatly exceeded the number of immigrants received. Thus, the major increase of the labor force over time came about from the natural increase of the arrivals rather than from the number of immigrants. Without this high rate of natural increase, the growth of the labor force would no doubt have been considerably lower. The United States thus had a much larger share of population—white and black—than its share of immigrants and came to demographically dominate the Americas. To Malthus, the North American white population grew at close to what was thought to be the maximum possible for a people under favorable conditions—available land and circumstances permitting relatively early and frequent marriages—without leading to a demographic crisis (Malthus 1960–1961). The U.S. slave population, unlike other slave populations, also grew at a very rapid rate, with many surviving children per female, whereas in the Caribbean and Brazil, it was necessary to maintain imports of slaves to keep its population from falling. Such a decline of a slave population was never an issue for North America.

As a new area of colonization, with considerable amounts of still unset-

2. There is a rather extensive literature on this topic, but see in particular Menard (2001) and McCusker and Menard (1991). See also, in regard to the role of diseases, Coelho and McGuire (1997).

tled land, a basic concern of early settlers was to increase the number of potential producers, either as workers or as landowners. Coming relatively late to the settlement process, over a century behind Spain and Portugal, and even for British North America, late compared to the British West Indies, the British could observe what the practices of the others, particularly Spain, had been. The English colonies lacked the large Native American populations of those in Mexico and South American, even after the depopulation caused there by disease. Also, on the mainland, they initially lacked the climate and soil to produce those marketable crops sufficiently in demand in Europe and were not able to pay the high prices required to purchase the limited number of slaves coming from Africa. The labor force and population in the United States would thus consist of fewer Native Americans and slaves than in most other places in the Americas, with a larger role to be played by European immigrants and their descendents. As suggested by Franklin and by Malthus, population growth was influenced by the high ratio of land to labor, leading to early marriage and high fertility by those people able to acquire landholdings at a low price and to a favorable living standard for both the free and enslaved population. The policies introduced to encourage immigration by taking advantage of land availability were highly beneficial to achieving a high rate of population growth, both by attracting new migrants and by permitting early marriage and high rates of childbearing.

An early appraisal of the high rate of population growth in the United States was made in 1751 by Benjamin Franklin, and similar arguments were developed later by Thomas Malthus (Labaree 1961b; Malthus 1960–1961; Zirkle 1957; Aldridge 1949).[3] The key point to Franklin was the availability and cheapness of land, permitting settlers to own and farm their own land and leading to high fertility relative to mortality. There were few direct subsidies granted for this natural increase, but a generous land policy did provide favorable conditions for marriage and fertility (see table 9.2).

The magnitude of free labor migration and the continued increase reflected the outcome of immigration policy. The colonies were long open to migrants, more so than were the colonies of the other settling nations, leading to large inflows and, because there were no broad restrictions on religious or national origins, the colonies were open to migrants from diverse countries and religions (Baseler 1998; Risch 1937; Proper 1900; Brite 1939). It is estimated that the English and Scots accounted for two-thirds of the 1790 population, and the Irish about 10 percent, the Germans 6 percent, and other Northwestern European about 6 percent (McDonald and McDonald 1980). The thirteen colonies each had their own rules regarding immigration and other matters, and it was only after the Revolution that a central

---

3. The basic demographic arguments were made in Labaree (1961a) in the mid-1700s, and this later was used in the arguments of Malthus (1960–1961). See Zirkle (1957). Subsequent debates on the impact of immigration on fertility were rather inconclusive (Easterlin 1971).

Table 9.2   **European-directed transatlantic migration, 1500–1760, by European nation and continent of origin**

Period and country	Africans arriving in the New World, by region (1)		Europeans leaving each nation for New World (net) (2)		Total flow of migrants to New World (1 + 2) (3)		Flow of Africans relative to Europeans (1/2) (4)
	In thousands	%	In thousands	%	In thousands	%	%
1500–1580							
Spain	45	77.6	139	59.9	184	63.4	0.32
Portugal	13	22.4	93	40.1	106	36.6	0.14
Britain	0		0		0		0
Total	58	100.0	232	100.0	290	100.0	0.25
1580–1640							
Spain	289	59.7	188	43.7	477	52.2	1.54
Portugal	181	37.4	110	25.6	291	31.8	1.65
France	2	0.4	4	0.9	6	0.7	0.60
The Netherlands	8	1.7	3	0.6	10	1.1	4.00
Britain	4	0.8	126	29.3	130	14.2	0.03
Total	484	100.0	430	100.0	914	100.0	1.13
1640–1700							
Spain	141	18.4	158	30.7	299	23.3	0.89
Portugal	225	29.3	50	9.7	275	21.5	4.50
France	75	9.8	45	8.8	130	10.1	1.67
The Netherlands	49	6.4	13	2.5	62	4.8	3.77
Britain	277	36.1	248	48.2	525	41.6	1.12
Total	767	100.0	514	100.0	1,281	100.0	1.49
1700–1760							
Spain	271	10.5	193	21.7	464	13.3	1.40
Portugal	768	29.7	270	30.3	1,038	29.8	2.84
France	414	16.0	51	5.7	465	13.4	8.12
The Netherlands	123	4.8	5	0.6	128	3.7	24.60
Britain	1,013	39.1	372	41.8	1,385	39.8	2.72
Total	2,589	100.0	891	100.0	3,480	100.0	2.91
1500–1760							
Spain	746	19.1	678	32.8	1,424	23.9	1.10
Portugal	1,187	30.5	523	25.3	1,710	28.7	2.27
France	491	12.6	100	4.8	591	9.9	4.91
The Netherlands	180	4.6	20	1.0	200	3.4	9.00
Britain	1,294	33.2	746	36.3	2,040	34.2	1.73
Total	3,898	100.0	2,067	100.0	5,965	100.0	1.89

Source: Eltis (1999).

control over migration occurred. Various types of legislation did have some influence on the size of the inflow, including safety restrictions and space limits on transatlantic vessels imposed by states (and later national policy) and then, after independence, the setting of the period of years it would take for immigrants to achieve citizenship and voting rights.[4] Migration patterns included individuals, families, and various groups, religious and otherwise,

4. For a discussion of shipping regulations, see Abbott (1924). On the discussion of citizenship requirements, see Baseler (1998), Kettner (1973), and Hutchinson (1981). For the debates at the Constitutional Convention, see Madison (1984, 406, 419).

some of whom paid their way in full, although in other cases subsidies in full or in part had been provided.

The Native Americans who were present in quite small numbers relative to those in Latin Americas (less than one-tenth) were sometimes used as slaves, generally purchased from Indian tribes, but the numbers used near home locations as nominally free workers were very limited, and unlike in Latin America, these Native Americans were not quantitatively important in the labor force.

As noted, there were two other forms of migrant labor that played a role in settling the mainland. Indentured labor, mainly from the United Kingdom, involved a period of four to seven years of labor time (depending on personal characteristics) in exchange for the cost of transportation to the colonies. At the end of the contract period, the individual was regarded as a free person. In some states, the importer of the individual labor was given a cash subsidy or a subsidy in land for contributing to the region's population increase. Redemptioners, mainly from Germany, arrived after the 1720s, came without signed contracts but contracted themselves after arrival to pay their transport costs. The colonies were also the recipients of convicts from England, who served their time as purchased laborers before being freed. This was not always a popular source of labor increase, at least to Benjamin Franklin, who compared convicts to rattlesnakes, to their detriment (Labaree 1961a, 130–33). When the independent United States refused to take in British convicts, the British then used them to settle Australia. There were also a small number of domestic convicts who could be used for various types of labor by governments or else hired to private individuals by governments.

The most debated of the sources of labor were the slaves imported from Africa and their rapidly growing descendents. The slave trade from Africa to the new world had begun with the period of initial Spanish and Portuguese settlement, and the British colonies had basically followed the previous set of legal arrangements developed elsewhere (Klein 1986). Slavery was legal throughout the colonies, and each colony had some slaves although the numbers varied considerably, based on conditions related to crop possibilities and the required scale of production. The first colonies to end slavery were in the New England, which had relatively few slaves, starting with Vermont in 1777, and then by 1804, most northern states had legislation ending slavery (Zilversmit 1967). The United States ended the transatlantic slave trade in 1808, the same year as did the British. Due to their differences in crop and climate conditions from Latin America and the Caribbean, North American slave labor generally worked on small units producing crops such as tobacco but also rice for export. Unlike tobacco, in the production of rice, there was no direct competition between free white labor and slaves. The regulations imposed by the state and colonial governments did distinguish between the slave trade and slavery itself, and, in North

America, as elsewhere, the slave trade was ended about one half-century before slavery.

Table 9.3 presents data on slave and free migration and population for the four major regions of the British colonies (including the West Indies), presenting the racial breakdown of the preindependence migrations and populations. The late settlement of the British mainland by whites, and the relatively limited number of slaves there, are the most striking characteristics of the North America population pattern, as was the relatively high rate of population growth of both whites and blacks and the small number (compared to Latin America) of Native Americans, who did not provide much of the North American population or labor force. And while most immigrants came from the British Isles, a higher proportion came from the other European nations than was the case for the Spanish and other areas of settlement. The British colonies did have fewer restrictions on migrants than did the colonies of other European nations, helping to account for differences in magnitude and in diversity of origins.

9.3   Education, Health, Migration

The concept of human capital relates to factors that increase the productivity of labor. The four most important categories of human capital formation are education, health, migration, and on-the-job training. Education in the British North American colonies was widely available, from both secular and religious forces, compared to the other colonial regions where education lagged, sometimes for several centuries. Relative to most European nations, the colonies provided more schooling for both males and females. There were variations in regard to who organized schools, religious and secular, and who paid for education, but colonial levels of literacy were, by world standards, quite high, particularly for women (Lockridge 1974). The sense of obligation for education developing out of the colonial period was indicated by the fact that seven of sixteen state constitutions in 1800 mentioned the provision of education, and the number rose to thirteen out of twenty-three by 1820. States such as Massachusetts had required domestic education laws by 1642 and required schooling by 1647. By 1671, all New England states but Rhode Island had compulsory education legislation (Cubberley 1947). Most other states had education systems in place before the Revolution, and these were most often formed by Protestant churches. It is estimated that Massachusetts had a literacy rate for males of about 60 percent in 1650 and 90 percent by 1789, compared to female rates of 30 percent and 50 percent, respectively, rates above those for other states (Lockridge 1974; Axtell 1974; Kaestle and Vinovskis 1980). These literacy rates in New England colonies exceeded those in Europe and Latin America. The Spanish colonies devoted most of their educational expenditures to the university level, while the North American colonies spent considerably more

Table 9.3   **Patterns of net migration to categories of British colonies**

	Destination of migrants							
	New England		Middle Atlantic		South		West Indies	
Ethnic group and period	In thousands	Row percent	In thousands	Row percent	In thousands	Row percent	In thousands	Row percent
Whites								
1630–1680	28	11.0	4	1.6	81	31.9	141	55.5
1680–1730	–4	–1.8	45	19.9	111	49.1	74	32.7
1730–1780	–27	–10.7	101	40.1	136	54.0	42	16.7
Total, 1630–1780	–3	–0.4	150	20.5	328	44.8	257	35.1
Blacks								
1650–1680	0	—	0	—	5	3.7	130	96.3
1680–1730	2	0.5	5	0.9	64	12.0	461	86.7
1730–1780	–6	–0.9	–1	–0.2	150	23.4	497	77.7
Total, 1650–1780	–4	–0.3	4	0.3	219	16.8	1088	83.2
Total								
1630–1680	28	7.2	4	1.0	86	22.1	271	69.7
1680–1730	–2	–0.3	50	6.6	175	23.1	535	70.6
1730–1780	–33	–3.7	100	11.2	286	32.1	539	60.4
Total, 1630–1780	–7	–0.3	154	7.6	547	26.8	1345	66.0

Source: Galenson (1996).

at the primary level, in addition to funding some colleges. Between 1636 and 1769, in the thirteen colonies, there were nine colleges formed, each with some religious affiliation, all of which still remain in existence. The number of colleges increased to twenty-nine by 1829 (Cubberley 1947).

While direct government expenditures by the colonies on health care were few, Massachusetts in 1641 and 1647 and Connecticut after 1663 did introduce provisions for quarantine and vaccination, most frequently as part of the fight against smallpox (Duffy 1953, 1979; Shryock 1960; Tobey 1926, 1939). The first hospital that handled private and poor patients opened in Philadelphia in 1751, and the first medical school opened in Philadelphia in 1765. Municipal boards of health were formed by the 1790s in several states to aid the flow of information on public health related issues. The concern of some colonies with the health on immigrant vessels meant benefits not only for immigrants but also for those already resident, including former immigrants. The positive advantages of health in the colonies were indicated by the high life expectation and the greater heights of the population in the period of settlement (Steckel 2009).

In the pre-Revolutionary period, migration controls, both internal and external, were colonial decisions (Baseler 1998). Important in the eighteenth and nineteenth centuries were restrictions on outmigration from several European nations, limits based either on the migration of entire populations, or, as in the case of Britain, only of skilled mechanics. There were relatively few specific restrictions on intercolonial or interstate migration. There were, in some locations, restrictions regarding pauper residence and parish inflows, as in the English Poor Laws, and rules about times of residence needed for voting (see, for example, Jones 1975). In the nineteenth century, there were state laws concerning the movement of free blacks and of slaves, based on state laws, but, in general, there were no restrictions for whites (Farnam 1938, 211–24).

The period prior to the Constitutional Convention saw some changes in the nature of the colonial labor force. The outcome of the Revolution meant that the United States no longer received convicts from Britain. There were steep declines in the number of the free white and indentured population, as well as of the slaves. These declines, except for convicts, were expected to be reversed when peace was restored, as indeed they were. During the interval of migration decline, however, there was a prolonged recession in domestic economic activity, which, with the wartime activities, served to reduce the inflow of population and labor.

The ending of the war brought about limited legal changes in labor force adjustments. There were no forced declines in contract labor supplies, but there was a significant decline in numbers due to other factors related to war and to disturbances between England and the United States. Immigration of free populations was frequently discussed, but no major interventions were introduced. Following the British discussion after the 1770s, the ending of slave trade was discussed in the colonies, but with no dramatic change until the Constitution's limits of 1787 were introduced. Thus, in the long run, there was only a limited decrease in immigration at this time.

9.4   Constitutional Debates

The debates surrounding the Constitution contained several discussions of policies that had an influence on the magnitude of labor supplies and on the nature of human capital. Some of the measures described were part of the Constitution, other measures were due to legislation by Congress at the national level, and some reflected legislation at the state level; some but not all of the new states followed the same policies.

The discussions at the Constitutional Convention included the setting of rules on various matters to be imposed by the national government (Madison 1984). Except for slaves, there were basically no provisions regarding population inflows and their sources. A major discussion that influenced immigration concerned the period of time to achievement of citizenship, an issue that did lead to several changes in subsequent decades. Later, in 1798, some limit was imposed permitting the deportation of enemy aliens at time of war, as well as preventing aliens from entering (Hutchinson 1981). There were discussions to limit immigrants from monarchies as well as to limit land ownership and voting by recent migrants, but these attempts were not successful. It was believed that subsidies to immigrants were not necessary, because, as Hamilton argued, the favorable economic conditions, including the prospect of higher incomes, lower taxes, "greater personal independence," and the "equality of religious privileges," as well as the availability of land in the United States, would serve to attract labor from abroad (Hamilton 1964).

In his 1791 *Report on the Subject of Manufactures,* Alexander Hamilton pointed to the probability of immigration from Europe as a means to keep agricultural employment high, while at the same time permitting a movement of labor into manufactures. This development was also to be aided by attracting women and children into the labor force, as in Great Britain (Hamilton 1964; Coxe 1965, 40–68; Cooke 1978, 182–200). This policy of open immigration was maintained for those not diseased whose entry was limited after 1838, while after 1891, constraints relating to literacy, insanity, and paupers were introduced. The first limitations on immigration by nationality came with restrictions of Chinese immigrants in 1882. There were also limits on a form of contract labor that was introduced in 1864 and reversed in 1885. The major changes in immigration policy, by numbers and by sources, came in the twentieth century (Hutchinson 1981). Throughout the nineteenth century, the United States received the largest share of immigration from Europe, and this immigration accounted for up to one-third of overall U.S. population growth. In the early antebellum period, the largest population of immigrants came from Ireland, with large numbers also from Great Britain and Germany. The years 1847 to 1854 had the highest ratio of immigrants to population of any period in U.S. history (Cohn 2009; Carter et al. 2006).

There was no mention of indentured servitude in either the Constitution or in Hamilton's report. Perhaps this was because it seemed to have lost its importance with the Revolution. Nevertheless, some indentured labor did persist into the 1810s and 1820s (Grubb 1994; Steinfeld 1991). Then due to some combination of legal changes in the United States and higher European incomes, indentured labor became limited as a source of labor. With the U.S. decline, indentured servitude faded from the world scene, only to be revived with movements to the West Indies and elsewhere from India and China after the 1850s, following the ending of slavery in many parts of the world (Northrup 1996). In the United States, there were, after the Civil War, attempts to bring in contract labor from Europe, mainly as strikebreakers, but these were limited in number, and the recruitment of this form of contract labor ended with the passage of the Foran Act prohibiting contract labor in 1885 (Erickson 1957).

Convict labor was also not mentioned in the Constitution. The British did want to resume sending convicts to the new nation, but this was not acceptable to the United States, and after a brief period of storage on barges in the Thames, they became the settlers of Australia. There was a particular role for convicts described in the Northwest Ordinance because those convicted of crimes could be considered involuntary servants, a provision carried forward in the Thirteenth Amendment, and the same clause required the return of fugitive slaves (*Land Ordinance of 1785; Northwest Ordinance of 1787*). Convict labor by residents did surface as an issue in later years, generally involving the performance of harsh work (particularly in the South) as a form of punishment, whether working for governments or through rental arrangements with private firms or individuals.

Similarly, little was said at this time about Native American labor, and this remained a limited source of the overall labor supply in North America. The issues related to Native Americans debated at the time of the Constitution concerned Indian reservations, and then later, the impact of the westward movement on Indian location and land policy.

It was regarding slavery that major constitutional debates took place, particularly that concerning the international slave trade. The key provision in the Constitution was that the slave trade could not be ended for at least twenty years, and a limit was placed on the tariff that could be imposed on slave imports (Robinson 1971). As was expected, the slave trade was ended in 1808, the same year as for Great Britain, a few years after the ending of the Danish slave trade. To some, closing the slave trade would mean, eventually, the ending of slavery, though the specific time span was not spelled out. In regard to slavery, there was not a constitutional debate, and this was a matter left to state governments. There were, even before the end of the Revolution, several states that ended slavery and also the slave trade, albeit with some differences in specific provisions. Vermont, in 1777, was the first state to end slavery, although with some period of apprenticeship. This freed, at most, nineteen slaves. Within the next decade, New Hampshire and Massachusetts had, in theory, immediate emancipation, but legal issues meant some delay in the time of its accomplishment. Pennsylvania (1780), Rhode Island (1784), Connecticut (1784), New York (1799), and New Jersey (1804) passed legislation that freed those born after a specified date, subject to a period of apprenticeship, but did not free those already enslaved. This meant, in effect, that most of the costs of emancipation were born by slaves and not by taxpayers or slave owners. By 1804, state legislation in all of the Northern states to end slavery had passed although, because of the gradu-ation provisions, slavery still existed in some northern states into the 1840s (Zilversmit 1967). The Northwest Ordinance had limited (but technically not ended) the legality of slavery in the North, but not in the South, and it was not until the Thirteenth Amendment that the national government provided for the national ending of slavery.[5]

Education was not discussed in the Constitution although the North-west Ordinance did provide some set asides from land sales to go toward educational expenditures, with 1/16 from land sales to be used for common schools and two townships in each new state for colleges (*Land Ordinance of 1785; Northwest Ordinance of 1787*). Discussions of education were mainly at the state and local levels, which had the responsibility for determining who would organize the schools (secular or religious), the mix of fees and taxes, and what taxes could be collected for this purpose. As seen by literacy and enrollment rates, educational expenditures and literacy in the United States were quite high by world standards. Compulsory education was not wide-spread until the end of the nineteenth century, but it did not seem necessary for the achievement of high rates of enrollment in most states (see Goldin and Katz 2008; Cubberley 1947).

Medical and health care was primarily a state and local, not federal, func-tion before the twentieth century. One exception was the creation in 1798 of hospitals for merchant seamen, basically a continuation of earlier British practices regarding the navy (Farnam 1938, 231–52).

Until the 1880s, there were no general restrictions on foreign migration although there was some use of the timing of citizenship and voting rights to influence the process of migration. The Constitution provided no limit on internal migration, but several states had laws to prevent the admission of slaves and of free blacks and also prohibited the entry of some undesired

5. Although the Northwest Ordinance banned slavery in the North under most conditions, it did not end slavery if it already existed in those territories and permitted slaves to be brought into two of the territories. Thus, Indiana and Illinois had several slaves recorded in the census through 1840.

groups. There were no federal limits on the interstate slave trade between states where slavery was legal, and none on white internal migration.

Lincoln's policy to limit and then end slavery in the United States was based on the prohibition of slavery in territories. Presumably by increasing the ratio of labor to land in the existing areas, slave prices would ultimately fall and slavery become unprofitable although Lincoln thought that this might take up to about 100 years (Lincoln 1989, 508–27).

Internal migration was encouraged by a land policy that made land more easily accessible to settlers of smaller farms (Gates 1968; Hibbard 1965). Over time, the price per acre fell as also did the minimum size of land to be purchased, and legislation regarding squatters' rights and graduated prices for lands unsold for long periods made for easier acquisition. This meant that the pace of growth of eastern manufacturers was slowed, but the steady inflow of immigrants and the use of women and children meant that any declines in labor in the east were not marked. Debates on land policy also had political implications because population affected the amount of representation by states.

The introduction of labor standards regarding ages, hours, and conditions of work at the state level did not occur until the mid-nineteenth century, and then mainly for women and children. Federally based controls, such as worker's compensation, came even later, at the start of the twentieth century (Farnam 1938).

9.5   Slavery and Migration: A Model

Institutions that shape labor supply can have a profound effect on economic growth, yet, as we argued, the United States Constitution had relatively little to say about labor per se. The important exceptions, as we have noted, concern the date at which the slave trade would be ended (1808) and, indirectly, the influence that Congress possessed by its ability to set naturalization policy and its power to regulate the disposal of public lands, thereby affecting the pace and pattern of western settlement.

How can one assess the impact of a specific constitutional provision or its absence? In general, economists (and economic historians) assess the impact of institutions either using econometric analysis or by applying economic reasoning. For example, one might measure the impact of a constitutional provision by looking for structural breaks in aggregate time series or by comparing outcomes across countries. Practically speaking econometric analysis is impossible in the American case because there are no reliable annual time series on relevant economic aggregates until much later in American history, nor are there reliable cross country data for the period.

Economic reasoning offers the possibility of some insight into the effects of the Constitution. By economic reasoning, we mean an economic model in which some feature can be varied so that a counterfactual prediction can be generated. The specifics of the argument will vary with the question at hand. In this section, we consider several examples of such reasoning.

Our first example is slavery. The Constitution, as we noted, imposed a ban on imported slaves beginning in 1808. By evaluating the effect of the ban on the market for slaves, we could then make predictions as to what the effects of delaying or accelerating the ban might have been.

To evaluate the effects of the import ban, it is useful to begin by specifying the short-run supply curve of slaves prior to the ban. This supply curve has two components—slaves who are already in the United States and slaves who are imported in a given time period. For simplicity, we assume that the marginal cost of importing slaves is constant.

The key feature of this supply curve is that it is perfectly inelastic with respect to the own price of slaves at the quantity of slaves already in the United States but a horizontal (perfectly elastic) function at the marginal cost of importing slaves. If demand for slaves is sufficiently large, slave imports will be positive, and the equilibrium price will equal the marginal cost of importing. A ban on slave imports, therefore, will render the supply curve perfectly inelastic at all prices. Holding the demand curve fixed, the quantity of slaves will equal the number already in the country, and price will increase to some value greater than the marginal cost of importing slaves.[6]

In the long run, the supply of slaves in the United States can be augmented by slave births. As just noted, an effective ban raises the price of slaves above the marginal cost of importing and thus the value of slaves born in the United States. As such, the ban should increase the portion of the value of female slaves that represented their childbearing capacity (see Fogel and Engerman 1974).

In thinking about this prediction, it is important to keep in mind that the date of the actual ban was known in advance, implying that slave traders (and owners) could alter their behavior in advance in ways that would moderate the price increases. The first way would be to import more slaves prior to the ban on imports, especially at young ages. The second way, rationally anticipating that fertility would be the source of slave labor supply in the future, is to import more female slaves. To the extent that both types of reactions occurred, any price effects might be moderated.

Evaluating the predictions is very difficult because the necessary data on slave imports are not available. However, there are good data on slave prices covering the pre- and postban period for Louisiana, allowing at least a partial test of the effects of the ban. Coleman and Hutchinson (2006) estimate

---

6. To see this algebraically, let $p = a - bq$ be the demand curve for slaves, where p = price, q = quantity and the parameters a, b are constants. Let c be the marginal cost of importing slaves and q be the stock of slaves already in the United States. As long as $(a - c)/b > q$, slave imports will be positive and $p = c$. Under an effective ban on imports, the price of slaves will be $p = a - bq$. The condition under which $p > c$ is $(a - c)/b > q$.

regression models of slave prices, controlling for a lengthy list of personal, and other, characteristics. Although the results are not always statistically significant for every type of slave, consistent with our predictions, they do find a broad-based increase in prices after the import ban is imposed, with the price effect being relatively larger for females of childbearing age.

Although the Constitution imposed an eventual ban on slave imports, it obviously did not go further and ban slave labor entirely. We can, however, imagine an extension of the import ban, one that, say, required federal emancipation after a certain point in the nineteenth century, perhaps similar in design to laws passed by state legislatures in the North in the late eighteenth and early nineteenth centuries.

The possible economic effects of a general ban on slavery can be illuminated with the aid of a simple economic model. Imagine that there are three goods (or sectors): "Wheat," "Cotton," and "Manufacturing" (or all other goods). Unlike wheat and manufacturing, cotton is not a final good— rather, it is an intermediate input into manufacturing. Capital is the factor specific to manufacturing, while land is specific to agriculture although it can be shifted between wheat and cotton. Slave labor can be used in any of the sectors, but only in cotton is there the possibility of a positive effect on total factor productivity through the use of the gang system (Fogel and Engerman 1974). Further, the gang system and slavery go hand in hand; if slavery is not possible, the gang system is not profitable (because free labor is unwilling to work in a gang unless paid a wage too high to make use of the system profitable). We assume that output prices are fixed or, equivalently, perfectly elastic demands for outputs. We also assume fixed total amounts of slave and free labor, capital, and land.

Initially, all slave labor is used in cotton because of the productivity effect of the gang system. If, when all slave labor is exhausted, the value of the marginal product of labor in cotton production still exceeds its value elsewhere, free labor will also used. Now imagine that all labor is declared "free." Relative to output levels under slavery in the no-slave equilibrium, cotton and manufacturing outputs are lower and wheat production is higher, but total agricultural output falls. Therefore, relative to output prices, the rental prices of land and capital are lower, as are wages. Because there is no longer a total factor productivity effect in cotton, former slave labor is dispersed across the different sectors; although cotton production declines, the proportion of (formerly) free labor in cotton production increases. These predictions are born out in the aftermath of the American Civil War—wages and land prices fell in the South relative to the non-South, and small-scale "yeoman" production of cotton increased (Margo 2004).

Migration policy can also be illuminated using such a framework. As we noted, the Constitution reserved naturalization policy to the federal government. Although state governments could (and did) pass laws attempting to restrict certain immigrants groups from entering, the efficacy of these laws is questionable. As far as the nineteenth century is concerned, it is probably best to assume that, slave labor aside, the Constitution essentially permitted labor to flow inside the United States where it was most valued and that immigrants could move to the United States essentially without restriction, as long as the economic benefits were greater than the costs.

The fact that Congress did not restrict immigration to the United States (and no state could do this instead) arguably made U.S. population growth greater than it would have been otherwise. This, in turn, may have increased the rate of growth of per capita income in two ways. First, immigrants tended to settle, initially at least, in cities. Although hard evidence is lacking, it is plausible that there were "agglomeration" economies present in early U.S. cities. If this were the case, an increase in urban population due to immigration will raise aggregate total factor productivity and, thus, per capita income.

Within the United States, the absence of restrictions on internal migration—again, with the obvious exception of slave labor in the South—arguably raised the rate of per capita income growth. At first glance, this may seem unlikely because, early in the nineteenth century, per capita income was highest in the Northeast and the flow from east to west; this is the so-called Easterlin paradox (Margo 1999). However, the paradox is more apparent than real: wage data show that real wages were higher on the frontier than in settled areas; hence, a shift of labor from east to west was justifiable on grounds of economic efficiency. In turn, as labor flowed into newly settled areas, wages fell, leading to convergence (Margo 2000). Had each state set its own immigration policy, it is not obvious that, say, the state of Ohio would have permitted a free inflow because the gains would have accrued to landowners, not to labor. Labor, in other words, may have had an incentive to restrict immigration into the state.

What about education, social welfare, and health? As we have noted, the Constitution made no provision for a federal role in these areas of human capital investment; consequently, they were relegated to state (and local) governments. Recent work by Goldin and Katz (2008) argues that the "local" nature of American education was a huge plus. The highly decentralized American education system produced a great deal of competition in organizational forms across locations and efficient solutions to local variation in education demand (Fischel 2009). In other words, in a world like the early nineteenth century United States in which the rate of return to a small amount of education—basic literacy—was probably high but the marginal return was decreasing sharply beyond this point, local institutions—the one-room schoolhouse—were perfectly adequate. The general idea is that if a local government failed to provide a service, people could move to the next town (or county), much more difficult to do if the only option was to move across the county's borders. Although we know of no comparable studies to Goldin and Katz's, it seems likely that similar arguments apply to health policy, particularly in light of the limited state of medical knowledge of the era.

Social welfare policy—by which we mean the care of the disabled, orphans, the indigent, and so on—was also left to the states. While a case can be made for decentralizing health and education expenditures, it is more questionable for social welfare policy because each state had an incentive to keep expenditures low, encouraging the poor to move elsewhere. Residency and other restrictions were common, as were work requirements. Evidence suggests that there was a steep trade-off in the willingness of taxpayers to provide poor support per recipient versus the number of recipients; as the number of recipients increased, support per recipient declined sharply (Kiesling and Margo 1997).

9.6   Conclusion

This chapter has reviewed the early settlement of the United States with an aim of evaluating the impact of the Constitution. Settlement followed a similar pattern for the first three centuries, dictated by the great expanse of fertile land and a set of policies that led to land being made relatively available at low prices in small units and a policy of unrestricted migration of Europeans. The attraction of migrants to provide a labor force took several different forms. Free immigrants were influenced by the availability of inexpensive land as well as by their economic conditions in Europe; immigrants who were unable to pay for their transportation came as indentured servants, and, where economically profitable, slaves were purchased from Africa. The mainland was unique in the very rapid rate of growth of the population, free and slave, with the encouragement of early marriage due to the availability of land as well as the generally high standard of living. The U.S. population growth was unusual in having both a high rate of immigration from Europe and an unusually high rate of natural increase.

In the period of the Revolutionary War, there were declines in the inflow of both slave and free labor. These were, however, soon reversed and continued to increase. The debates at this time did not seem to anticipate any continued declines, and no new policies to enhance migration attracted attention. Indentured labor declined early in the nineteenth century, without prompting by specific legislation. As specified in the Constitution, the slave trade was ended in 1808. Northern states ended slavery by legislation prior to 1804, but slavery did not end in the American South until forcibly achieved by the end of the Civil War in 1865.

We noted that, with the exception of the slave trade, the Constitution and early legislative history of the United States are distinguished by the near absence of clauses directly addressing matters of labor policy. For example, there were no quantitative and other restrictions upon free immigration until the twentieth century regulations controlling numbers and nationalities. We argued that the best way to evaluate the impact of the Constitution and associated legislation is through general equilibrium analysis, possibly with a dynamic component. For example, had slavery itself not been a part of the American landscape in the nineteenth century, the distribution of output between various crops and the allocation of the labor force between agriculture and other sectors would have been quite different.

Policies that restricted free immigration earlier in American history, such as the earlier introduction of legislation restricting the flow of free immigra-

Table 9.4   The distribution and composition of population in New World economies (%)

| Colonial region and year | Composition of population | | | Share in New World population |
	White	Black	Indian	
Spanish America				
1570	1.3	2.5	96.3	83.5
1650	6.3	9.3	84.4	84.3
1825	18.0	22.5	59.5	55.2
1935	35.5	13.3	50.4	30.3
Brazil				
1570	2.4	3.5	94.1	7.6
1650	7.4	13.7	78.9	7.7
1825	23.4	55.6	21.0	11.6
1935	41.0	35.5	23.0	17.1
United States and Canada				
1570	0.2	0.2	99.6	8.9
1650	12.0	2.2	85.8	8.1
1825	79.6	16.7	3.7	33.2
1935	89.4	8.9	1.4	52.6

Source: Engerman and Sokoloff (1997).

Table 9.5   Immigration volume and rates

| Period | Average yearly total (all countries) | Immigration rates (per 1,000 population) | Percent of average yearly total | | | |
			Great Britain	Ireland	Scandinavia and other Northwest Europe	Germany
1630–1700	2,200					
1700–1780	4,325					
1780–1819	9,900					
1820–1831	14,538	1.3	22	45	12	8
1832–1846	71,916	4.3	16	41	9	27
1847–1854	334,506	14.0	13	45	6	32
1855–1864	160,427	5.2	25	28	5	33

Source: Cohn (2009).

tion, would have lowered the pace of land settlement and population growth, thereby likely altering relative factor prices and output levels. Given the abundance of land, it is likely that the absence of restrictions put the United States in a rather favorable position for economic growth in the eighteenth and nineteenth centuries although measuring the quantitative effects await further research (see table 9.4 and 9.5).

References

Abbott, Edith. 1924. *Immigration: Select documents and case records.* Chicago: University of Chicago Press.
Aldridge, Alfred Owen. 1949. Franklin as demographer. *Journal of Economic History* 9:25–44.
Axtell, James. 1974. *The school upon the hill: Education and society in colonial New England.* New York: Norton.
Baseler, Marilyn C. 1998. *Asylum for mankind: America 1607–1800.* Ithaca, NC: Cornell University Press.
Brite, John Duncan. 1939. *The attitudes of European states toward emigration to the American colonies and the United States, 1607–1820.* Chicago: University of Chicago Press.
Carter, Susan, Scott S. Gartner, Michael R. Haines, Alan L. Olmstead, Richard Sutch, and Gavin Wight. 2006. *The historical statistics of the United States: Millennial edition.* Cambridge: Cambridge University Press.
Chapin, Joyce E. 2005. Enslavement of indians in early America: Captivity without the narrative. In *The creation of the British Atlantic world,* ed. E. Mancke and C. Shammas, 45–70. Baltimore, MD: Johns Hopkins University Press.
Coelho, Philip R. P., and Robert A. McGuire. 1997. African and European bound labor in the British new world: The biological consequences of economic choices. *Journal of Economic History* 57:83–115.
Cohn, Raymond L. 2009. *Mass migration under sail: European immigration to the Antebellum United States.* Cambridge: Cambridge University Press.
Coleman, Ashley N., and William K. Hutchinson. 2006. Determinants of slave prices: Louisiana, 1720–1825. Department of Economics Working Paper no. 06-W24. Nashville, TN: Vanderbilt University, December.
Cooke, Jacob E. 1978. *Tench Coxe and the early republic.* Chapel Hill, NC: University of North Carolina Press.
Coxe, Tench. 1965. *A view of the United States of America.* New York: Augustus Kelley. (Orig. pub. 1794).
Craven, Wesley Frank. 1965. The early settlements: A European investment of capital and labor. In *The growth of the American economy.* 2nd ed. Ed. H. F. Williamson, 19–43. Englewood Cliffs, NJ: Prentice-Hall.
Cubberley, Ellwood P. 1947. *Public education in the United States: A study and interpretation of American educational history.* Revised and enlarged ed. Boston: Houghton Mifflin.
Curtin, Philip D. 1969. *The Atlantic slave trade: A census.* Madison, WI: University of Wisconsin Press.
Denevan, William M., ed. 1976. *Native population of the Americas in 1492.* Madison, WI: University of Wisconsin Press.

Duffy, John. 1953. *Epidemics in colonial America.* Baton Rouge, LA: Louisiana State University Press.

———. 1979. *The healers: A history of American medicine.* Urbana, IL: University of Illinois Press.

Easterlin, Richard A. 1971. Does human fertility adjust to the environment? *American Economic Review* 61:399–407.

Ekirch, A. Roger. 1987. *Bound for America: The transportation of British convicts to the colonies, 1718–1775.* New York: Oxford University Press.

Elliott, J. H. 2006. *Empires of the Atlantic world: Britain and Spain in America, 1492–1830.* New Haven, CT: Yale University Press.

Eltis, David, ed. 1987. *Coerced and free migration: Global perspectives.* Stanford, CA: Stanford University Press.

Eltis, David. 1999. Slavery and freedom in the early modern world. In *Terms of labor: Slavery, serfdom, and free labor,* ed. S. L. Engerman, 25–49. Stanford: Stanford University Press.

———. 2001. The volume and structure of the transatlantic slave trade: A reassessment. *William and Mary Quarterly* 57:17–46.

Engerman, Stanley L., and Kenneth L. Sokoloff. 1997. Factor endowments, institutions, and differential paths of growth among new world economies: A view from economic historians of the United States. In *How Latin America fell behind: Essays on the economic histories of Brazil and Mexico, 1800–1914,* ed. S. H. Habar, 260–304. Stanford, CA: Stanford University Press.

———. 2002. Factor endowments, inequality, and paths of development among new world economies. *Economia* 3:41–109.

———. 2005. Five hundred years of European colonization: Inequality and paths of development. University of California at Los Angeles, Department of Economics, Working Paper.

Erickson, Charlotte. 1957. *American industry and the European immigrant, 1860–1885.* Cambridge, MA: Harvard University Press.

Farnam, Henry W. 1938. *Chapters in the history of social legislation in the United States to 1860.* Washington, DC: Carnegie Institution.

Fischel, William A. 2009. *Making the grade: The economic evolution of American school districts.* Chicago: University of Chicago Press.

Fogel, Robert W., and Stanley L. Engerman. 1974. *Time on the cross: The economics of American negro slavery.* Boston: Little, Brown.

Galenson, David W. 1981. *White servitude in colonial America: An economic analysis.* Cambridge: Cambridge University Press.

———. 1996. The settlement and growth of the colonies: Population, labor, and economic development. In *The Cambridge economic history of the United States.* Vol. 1, *The colonial era,* ed. S. L. Engerman and R. E. Gallman, 135–207. Cambridge: Cambridge University Press.

Gallay, Alan. 2002. *The indian slave trade: The rise of the English empire in the American South, 1670–1717.* New Haven, CT: Yale University Press.

Gates, Paul Wallace. 1968. *History of public land law development.* Washington, DC: U.S. Government Printing Office.

Goldin, Claudia, and Lawrence F. Katz. 2008. *The race between education and technology.* Cambridge, MA: Harvard University Press.

Grubb, Farley. 1985a. The incidence of servitude in trans-Atlantic migration, 1771–1804. *Explorations in Economic History* 22:316–39.

———. 1985b. The market for indentured immigrants: Evidence on the efficiency of forward-labor contracting in Philadelphia, 1745–1773. *Journal of Economic History* 45:855–68.

———. 1992. The long-run trend in the value of European immigrant servants, 1654–1831: New measurements and interpretations. *Research in Economic History* 14:167–240.

———. 1994. The end of European immigrant servitude in the United States: An economic analysis of market collapse, 1772–1835. *Journal of Economic History* 54:794–824.

Hamilton, Alexander. 1964. Report on the subject of manufactures. In *The reports of Alexander Hamilton*, ed. Jacob Cooke, 115–205. New York: Harper & Row. (Orig. pub. 1791).

Hibbard, Benjamin Horace. 1965. *A history of the public land policies.* Madison, WI: University of Wisconsin Press. (Orig. pub. 1924).

Hutchinson, E. P. 1981. *Legislative history of American immigration policy, 1798–1965.* Philadelphia: University of Pennsylvania Press.

Inikori, Joseph E. 2002. *Africans and the industrial revolution in England: A study in international trade and economic development.* Cambridge: Cambridge University Press.

Jones, Douglas Lamar. 1975. The strolling poor: Transiency in eighteenth-century Massachusetts. *Journal of Social History* 8:28–54.

Kaestle, Carl F., and Maris A. Vinovskis. 1980. *Education and social change in nineteenth-century Massachusetts.* Cambridge: Cambridge University Press.

Kettner, James H. 1973. *The development of American citizenship, 1608–1870.* Chapel Hill, NC: University of North Carolina Press.

Kiesling, Lynne, and Robert A. Margo 1997. Explaining the rise in antebellum pauperism, 1850–1860: New evidence. *Quarterly Review of Economics and Finance* 37:405–17.

Klein, Herbert S. 1986. *African slavery in Latin America and the Caribbean.* New York: Oxford University Press.

———. 2004. *A population history of the United States.* Cambridge: Cambridge University Press.

Labaree, Leonard W., ed. 1961a. Felons and rattlesnakes. In *The papers of Benjamin Franklin.* Vol. 4, 130–33. New Haven, CT: Yale University Press.

———. 1961b. Observations concerning the increase of mankind. In *The papers of Benjamin Franklin.* Vol. 4, 225–34. New Haven, CT: Yale University Press.

Land Ordinance of 1785. In *Documents of American history, vol. 1* (to 1898), ed. H. S. Commager, 123–4. New York: Appleton-Century-Crofts.

Lauber, Almon Wheeler. 1913. *Indian slavery in colonial times within the present limits of the United States.* New York: Columbia University Press.

Lincoln, Abraham. 1989. *Lincoln: Speeches and writings, 1832–1858.* New York: Library of America.

Lockridge, Kenneth A. 1974. *Literacy in colonial New England: An enquiry into the social context of literacy in the pre-modern West.* New York: Norton.

Madison, James. 1984. *Notes of debates in the Federal Convention of 1787.* Athens, OH: Ohio University Press. (Orig. pub. 1840).

Malthus, T. R. 1960–1961. *An essay on population.* London: J. M. Dent (Orig. pub. 1803).

Margo, Robert A. 1999. Regional wage gaps and the settlement of the Midwest. *Explorations in Economic History* 36:128–43.

———. 2000. *Wages and labor markets in the United States, 1820–1860.* Chicago: University of Chicago Press.

———. 2004. The North-South wage gap, before and after the Civil War. In *Slavery in the development of the Americas*, ed. D. Eltis, F. Lewis, and K. Sokoloff, 324–51. New York: Cambridge University Press.

McCusker, John J., and Russell R. Menard. 1991. *The economy of British America, 1607–1789, with supplemental bibliography.* 2nd ed. Chapel Hill, NC: University of North Carolina Press.

McDonald, Forrest, and Ellen Shapiro McDonald. 1980. The ethnic origins of the American people, 1790. *William and Mary Quarterly* 37:179–99.

McEvedy, Colin, and Richard Jones. 1978. *Atlas of world population history.* Harmondsworth, UK: Penguin.

Menard, Russell R. 2001. *Migrants, servants, and slaves: Unfree labor in colonial British America.* Aldershot, UK: Ashgate.

Northrup, David. 1996. *Indentured labor in the age of imperialism, 1834–1922.* Cambridge: Cambridge University Press.

Northwest Ordinance of 1787. In *Documents of American history, vol. 1* (to 1898), ed. H. S. Commager, 128–32. New York: Appleton-Century-Crofts.

Proper, Emberson Edward. 1900. *Colonial immigration laws: A study of the regulation of immigration by the English colonies in America.* New York: Columbia University Press.

Risch, Erna. 1937. Encouragement of immigration as revealed in colonial legislation. *Virginia Magazine of History and Biography* 45:1–10.

Robinson, Donald L. 1971. *Slavery in the structure of American politics, 1765–1820.* New York: Harcourt Brace Jovanovich.

Shryock, Richard Harrison. 1960. *Medicine and society in America, 1660–1860.* Ithaca, NY: Cornell University Press.

Smith, Abbot Emerson. 1947. *Colonists in bondage: White servitude and convict labor in America, 1607–1776.* Chapel Hill, NC: University of North Carolina Press.

Steckel, Richard H. 2009. Heights and human welfare: Recent developments and new directions. *Explorations in Economic History* 46:1–23.

Steinfeld, Robert J. 1991. *The invention of free labor: The employment relation in English and American law and culture, 1350–1870.* Chapel Hill, NC: University of North Carolina Press.

Tobey, James A. 1926. *The national government and public health.* Baltimore, MD: Johns Hopkins University Press.

———. 1939. *Public health law.* 2nd ed. New York: Commonwealth Fund.

Wokeck, Marianne S. 1999. *Trade in strangers: The beginnings of mass migration to North America.* University Park, PA: Pennsylvania State University Press.

Zilversmit, Arthur. 1967. *The first emancipation: The abolition of slavery in the North.* Chicago: University of Chicago Press.

Zirkle, Conway. 1957. Benjamin Franklin, Thomas Malthus, and the United States Census. *Isis* 48:58–62.

10

Looking Backward
Founding Choices in Innovation and Intellectual Property Protection

B. Zorina Khan

10.1 Introduction

From the distance of more than 200 years, casual consideration of "the Founding" of American institutions tends to convey the impression of a defining discrete moment in time, the outcome of an epiphany experienced by the cadre of extraordinary individuals who established those early rules and standards. The intellectual property clause of the constitution especially might project this aura of inevitability because it was passed unanimously and without debate, with the intent to "promote the Progress of Science and useful Arts, by securing for limited Times to Authors and Inventors the exclusive Right to their respective Writings and Discoveries" (Article 1, Section 8, Clause 8, U.S. Constitution). Instead, a closer examination reveals a less coherent narrative, featuring conflicts among key players, political and personal compromises, and the evolution of views and doctrines over the years. In short, it is worth noting that the Founding was not a moment, but a process, and the Founders' choices were initially expansive and fluid, before crystallizing into a system of patents and copyrights that was unique in its objective and structure relative to any other in the world then and since.

The individuals who met in Philadelphia for the Constitutional Convention of 1787 clearly did not start with a blank slate nor with a well-defined consensus. The Articles of Confederation were a starting point for a number of political and economic issues, but this document failed to address questions of innovation and intellectual property. Instead, the policies that were introduced in the Constitution and the statutes that elaborated on the con-

B. Zorina Khan is professor of economics at Bowdoin College, and research associate at the National Bureau of Economic Research.

stitutional clause were developed from, and in reaction to, an array of other sources. These included the example of other countries (especially France and England), the experience of the American colonies and states, personal views of influential members of the convention, and (more diffusely) the writings of political economists and philosophers.

The framers of the U.S. Constitution and the early statutes were undoubtedly familiar with historical events and with the contemporary European model of intellectual property. Yet they chose to make important changes in the parameters of property rights in invention (broadly defined), including how and to whom they were awarded. Their revealed objectives were to provide more widespread access to such property rights, to facilitate the diffusion of information to the general public, and to develop markets in inventive rights and inventions. If the design of institutions mattered in the direction they predicted, then these "founding choices" in the realm of patents, copyrights, and innovation policies enhanced the rate and direction of economic, technological, and cultural change.

This chapter assesses the options initially available, those exercised, and the consequences of the paths taken in the realm of intellectual property and innovation. Section 10.2 traces the early European use of exclusive privileges to promote the introduction of books, manufacturing, and machine inventions. The next section examines the nature of colonial laws and policies regarding patents, copyrights and innovation, and that is followed by an account of the experiences of the American states between independence and 1787. These precursors ultimately led to the intellectual property clause of the U.S. Constitution, and the two major patent and copyright statutes that were enacted in 1790 to "promote the progress of science and useful arts." The final section summarizes the evolution of the intellectual property system and briefly considers the consequences of these "Founding Choices" for economic and social development in the United States.

10.2   European Precedents

The fundamental element of property rights in invention (broadly defined to include new and improved machines, processes, and cultural products) comprises a right to exclude, and such exclusive rights can be traced back to classical antiquity. Early rights of exclusion were associated with royal and state-created "privileges." The privilege system did not explicitly distinguish between exclusive rights for mechanical inventions and restrictions on rights to copy such items as books and music. Moreover, such proprietary rights were not necessarily associated with novelty and innovation. Instead, privileges tended to establish monopolies in a wide variety of areas, from intellectual endeavors to manufactured products, as well as barriers to entry in guilds and occupations. The notion of rights in intellectual products that could be protected through exclusion or trade secrecy emerged more clearly during the medieval period. Privileges for books and new inventions were frequently granted in fifteenth-century Venice and Florence, but the most notorious and widespread use of such policy devices occurred later in France and England in the sixteenth century.

Books and other written matter were initially regarded as part of the public domain when they were published, but replication rights in cultural products became more significant after the invention of mechanical means of printing. Privileges for both books and inventions were noted in the Republic of Venice in the fifteenth century, a practice that was soon prevalent in a number of other European jurisdictions. For instance, Donatus Bossius, a Milanese author, petitioned the duke in 1492 for an exclusive privilege for his book, successfully argued that he would be unjustly deprived of the benefits from his efforts if others were able to freely copy his work, and obtained a privilege for a term of ten years. However, authorship was not required for the grant of a privilege, and printers and publishers acquired monopolies over existing books as well as new works. Such privileges were granted on a case-by-case basis by a number of different authorities: grantors included religious orders and authorities, universities, political figures, and the representatives of the Crown. The rights they offered varied in geographical scope, duration, and breadth of coverage, as well as in terms of the attendant penalties for their violation.

The extensive French privilege system allowed protection for books or translations, maps, type designs, engravings and artwork, dance, opera and musical performances. Exclusive rights in printed material were introduced in 1498, and such grants were well-established by the end of the sixteenth century (Armstrong 1990). Privileges were under the auspices of the monarch and generally were given for a brief period of two to three years although the term could be as much as ten years or in perpetuity. Petitioners paid formal fees and informal gratuities to the officials concerned. The courts sometimes imposed limits on the rights conferred, such as stipulations about the prices that could be charged and the region in which they applied. Privileges were property that could be assigned or licensed to another party, and their infringement could be punished by fines, imprisonment, or confiscation of the output of "pirates." By the late eighteenth century, an extensive administrative procedure was in place that was designed to restrict the number of presses and facilitate the state's surveillance and censorship of the publishing industry.

A French decree of 1777 established that authors who did not alienate their property were entitled to exclusive rights in perpetuity, but made a distinction in the rights accorded to publishers. Few authors had the will or resources to publish and distribute books, so their privileges were likely to be sold outright to professional publishers, in which case the privilege was only accorded a limited duration, the exact term to be determined in accordance with the value of the work or the influence of the petitioner. Once the publisher's term expired, the work passed into the public domain. Between 1700 and 1789, more than 2,500 petitions for exclusive privileges in books were filed, and about two-thirds were granted. The outcome was a system that resulted in "odious monopolies," higher prices, and greater scarcity, large transfers of revenues to officials of the Crown and their allies, and pervasive censorship.

England similarly experienced a period during which book privileges were granted. A momentous royal charter in 1557 authorized the formation of the Worshipful Company of Stationers, a publishers' guild that would control the book trade for more than 200 years. This company created and controlled the right of their constituent members to make copies, so in effect their "copy right" was a private property right that existed in perpetuity, independently of state or statutory rights. The Stationers' Company maintained a register of books, issued licenses, and sanctioned individuals who violated their regulations. Enforcement and regulation were carried out by the corporation itself through its Court of Assistants. Thus, in both England and France, copyright law began as a monopoly grant to benefit and regulate the printers' guilds and as a means of surveillance and censorship over public opinion on behalf of the Crown.

The English system of book privileges was replaced in 1710 by a copyright statute (the Statute of Anne). The statute intended to restrain the publishing industry and destroy its monopoly power. It was not directed toward authors and had little to do with questions of rewards for creativity. According to this landmark law, copyright was available to anyone, not just to the Stationers. Instead of a perpetual right, the term was limited to fourteen years, with a right of renewal, after which the work would enter the public domain. Subsequent litigation and judicial interpretation added a new and fundamentally different dimension to copyright. In order to protect their perpetual copyright, publishers promoted the idea that copyright was based on the natural rights of authors or creative individuals. If, indeed, copyrights derived from these inherent principles, they represented property that existed independently of statutory provisions and could be protected at common law in perpetuity. As the supposed agent of the author, those rights would devolve to the publisher. The booksellers engaged in a series of strategic litigation that culminated in their defeat in the landmark case, *Donaldson v. Beckett* [98 Eng. Rep. 257 (1774)]. The court ruled that authors did possess a common law right in their unpublished works, but on publication that right was extinguished by the statute, whose provisions determined the nature and scope of any copyright claims.

The transition from publishers' rights to statutory authors' rights was perhaps more based on perception than reality, but it had fundamental implications for the ease with which expansions in such property rights could be defended on the grounds of creativity and personhood. This tension between publishers and authors would recur in the American context, but with less force, because the colonies openly emphasized the pragmatic need to facilitate learning and the diffusion of "useful knowledge," rather than to reward cultural elites who exhibited "genius and creativity."

A similar historical process can be discerned in the development of patents for invention. The modern patent grant also emerged out of Venetian privileges, perhaps as early as the thirteenth century, but certainly by the fifteenth century, the practice of granting exclusive rights for inventions was well established. Novelty was not a requirement, and patents could be granted for foreign innovations that were being introduced by an importer. Many of these early grants comprised petitions that were approved on an individual basis, but a landmark statute in 1474 allowed exclusive rights to authors and inventors for ten years. Despite these precursors at law, Britain stands out for having established a statutory patent system that has been in continuous operation for a longer period than any other in the world. This patent system was an outgrowth of a regime of privileges, whereby the English Crown bestowed vast numbers of monopoly rights in order to raise revenues and to reward favorites. These ultimately caused vociferous popular protests against "odious monopolies" that included specific products and industries, trades and occupations from alehouses to apothecaries, as well as printing and publishing. At the same time, the common law deprecated monopolies but also supported the principle that new inventions and risky ventures deserved protection for a limited time in order to benefit the common good.

The Commons finally succeeded in a petition that outlawed all monopolies, with the exception of new inventions. The Statute of Monopolies in 1624 codified existing common law policies by authorizing patent grants for fourteen years for "the sole making or working of any manner of new manufacture within this realm to the first and true inventor . . . so they be not contrary to the law nor mischievous to the State by raising of the prices of commodities at home, or hurt of trade, or generally inconvenient."[1] The "first and true inventor" was interpreted to include introducers of inventions that had been created abroad, and the roster of successful patentees included employers of the actual inventor, as well as patent agents applying on behalf of their customers. These grants were viewed as monopolies; as such, they were grudgingly granted and narrowly construed and circumscribed.

Another important feature of the British patent system was that it established significant barriers that deliberately limited access to property rights in invention. The application costs were prohibitively high relative to per capita income. Inventors who wished to obtain protection throughout the realm had to contend with the bureaucracy of three patent systems and to pay fees that ranged from £100 for an English patent to more than £300 for property rights that extended to Ireland and Scotland. The complicated

1. 21 Jac. I. C. 3, 1623, Sec. 6.

system also effectively inhibited the diffusion of information and made it difficult, if not impossible, for inventors outside of London to readily conduct patent searches. The cumbersome system (variously described as "mediaeval" and "fantastical") afforded ample material for satire but imposed severe constraints on the ordinary inventor who wished to obtain protection for his or her discovery. Attitudes toward patents were imbued with the distaste felt for speculation, and restrictions on trade in stocks were extended to markets in patent rights.

European states offered a large array of inducements and rewards for innovation, in addition to rights of exclusion in the form of patent and copyright grants. These included a proliferation of institutions directed toward the "the encouragement of arts and manufactures." A board for that purpose was established in Edinburgh in 1727, and in England, the Society for the Encouragement of Arts and Manufactures was founded in 1754, according to a plan published by Benjamin Franklin. In particular, French policies toward inventions and innovations in the eighteenth century are worth a close examination because they comprised a cornucopia of rewards and incentives that illustrate the relative benefits and costs of alternative routes to statutory grants of intellectual property rights. During this period inventors or introducers of inventions could benefit from titles, pensions that sometimes extended to spouses and offspring, loans (some interest-free), lump-sum and land grants, bounties or subsidies for production, exemptions from taxes, and monopoly privileges. Exclusive rights could extend to a specific region or throughout the entire kingdom, and their term varied from five years to perpetuity.

This portfolio of policy instruments provides insights into the efficacy of awards that were administered by the state on a case-by-case basis. On occasion, prior examination by a committee of qualified individuals was required before applicants could receive awards and led to the encouragement and introduction of productive technologies. Nevertheless, such grants and privileges were typically capricious and based on noneconomic criteria. Eighteenth-century correspondence and records provide numerous examples of awards that were made based on court connections. At the other end of the spectrum, large sums were awarded to the "deserving" on the basis of arbitrary factors such as age, deportment, religious piety, or family need. Members of the board of examiners, even if scientifically trained, were not necessarily qualified to assess their potential commercial value. Should the privilege actually prove to be commercially successful, active trade in the rights was inhibited because prior permission had to be secured. Moreover, the administrative and opportunity costs of such a system were nontrivial on the part of both supplicants and the state bureaucracy. Applicants were well aware of the political dimension of innovation (Hilaire-Pérez 2000). They were also aware that promises made as inducements were not necessarily enforceable once the inventor had made fixed investments.

10.3   American Colonies

Any genealogy of eighteenth-century legal codes undoubtedly branches from the seeds of the first colonial governments in America.[2] Colonial legislators did not "dismantle" European legal rules and standards, as popular histories frequently propose. Neither did they slavishly replicate the institutions and practices that prevailed in other countries. Observers have been impressed by the fluidity of the colonial legal institutions and the extent to which they responded to the needs of society.[3] One can detect the influence of the principles and customs of the old world, but at the same time, institutional innovation necessarily occurred to encompass the circumstances that prevailed in the new world. The colonies initially followed a similar model to Europe, allowing monopolies and privileges in the form of patents of introduction, as well as other encouragements for infant enterprises and imported discoveries, and later offered exclusive rights solely for novel contributions.

The original American colonies were subject to the laws of Britain and the terms of their charters, but they also had considerable leeway in their ability to adapt and introduce rules that were more appropriate to domestic circumstances. For instance, the 1691 Charter of the Massachusetts Bay Commonwealth stated that self-government implied the adoption of colonial laws as long as they were "not repugnant or contrary to the Lawes of this our Realme of England." Similarly, the Carolina Charter of 1663 granted full discretion, "Provided nevertheless, that the said laws be consonant to reason, and as near as may be conveniently, agreeable to the laws and customs of this our kingdom of England." The original colonies introduced legal rules and institutions that differed from each other at the time of their establishment, but the laws and their enforcement gradually coalesced and converged. They tended in large part toward the Massachusetts and Virginia models but, in any event, the new American legal order ultimately deviated substantively from their European precedents, especially in the realm of patents and copyrights.

A frequent and significant source of conflict between England and the colonies related to economic policy, including the efforts to promote American innovation at the expense of imports from Europe.[4] Sir Ferdinando

2. "The whole structure of our political institutions is the natural production of the principles laid down by the founders of the several States," according to Towle (1871, 297).

3. This observation is not intended to imply that the law teleogically evolved toward an efficient outcome, nor to underestimate the way in which the interests of certain parties, including slaves and Native Americans, were subsumed in those of the dominant socioeconomic groups.

4. Rhode Island repealed a 1751 act to offer bounties for woolen textiles for fear that "it may draw the displeasure of Great Britain upon us, as it will interfere with their most favorite manufactory." According to Clark, the colonies offered bounties for flax instead in order not to antagonize the British wool manufacturing interests (Clark 1916, 34–35).

Gorges was awarded the monopoly of fishing in New England in the 1620s, but his privilege was never enforced because of protests in the colonies. The colonies were somewhat ambivalent about employing the policy and practice of exclusive rights themselves. On the one hand, the settlers avowed an aversion to monopolies such as the Gorges grant, and the 1629 charter of the Massachusetts Bay Company repeatedly stressed that the colonists "shall have full and free Power and Liberty to continue and use their said Trade of Fishing." In December 1641, the General Court of the colony of Massachusetts adopted "The Body of Liberties," the first code of laws enacted in New England.[5] In particular, the ninth clause is noticeably similar to the Statue of Monopolies: "9. No monopolies shall be granted or allowed amongst us, but of such new Inventions that are profitable to the Country, and that for a short time."[6]

On the other hand, numerous monopoly grants mimicked the privileges that were outlawed by the British Statute of Monopolies in 1624. A few months before the passage of the Body of Liberties, the Massachusetts Bay Colony granted Samuel Winslow a 1641 patent for the monopoly right to produce salt using a new method for ten years, but it is unclear whether he had devised the invention or merely imported it.[7] Salt was important to the colonists and, despite the code, similar awards were made in subsequent years, including a 1656 monopoly to Governor Winthrop's son for yet another method of making salt. Exclusive rights were also permitted for merchants who introduced methods from overseas that were new to the colony. John Clark was even allowed to retain in perpetuity the monopoly right to charge ten shillings per family for use of his stove invention. Some of the patents specified the prices that were to be charged and the quantities. Others included stipulations such as local residency: in April 1641, the town of Plymouth agreed to allow John Jenny and his partners the exclusive rights to make salt for twenty-one years, provided that he sold the salt for two shillings a bushel and did not assign the right to any resident from outside the town. Dirck de Wolff was given a similar privilege to produce salt in New Netherlands in 1661. However, the Dutch colonists exhibited an aversion to monopoly grants "as it is in our opinion a very pernicious management, principally so in a new and budding State, whose population and welfare can not be promoted but through general benefits and privileges, in which every one . . . either as a merchant or a mechanic, may participate" (cited in Clark 1916, 47).

---

5. Nathan Ward, an emigrant from England, compiled this remarkable document. Ward, a minister of the church and a graduate of Emmanuel College of Cambridge University, had also studied and practiced law in England.

6. The document consisted of ninety-eight clauses, a preamble and a conclusion, largely drawn from biblical admonitions and British precedents. These principles comprised the major structure of laws in the colony for much of the rest of the seventeenth century. Clause 9 was preserved in page 62 of the Acts of 1660 and page 119 of the Acts of 1672 (Whitmore 1890).

7. The grant was qualified by a working requirement to establish a factory within one year and also allowed others to make salt using different methods from the one covered by the patent.

This emphasis on open access would be reflected in later conceptions of a uniquely American system.

The colonial legislatures enacted statutes that were designed to protect and encourage domestic manufactures, including an extensive portfolio of such policy instruments as tariffs, loans, bounties, premiums, and subsidies. In 1621, the Virginia Company induced William Norton and his family to immigrate with four Italian artisans to the new world in order to manufacture glass, in part to produce beads to trade with the natives. He was accorded a seven-year privilege for the exclusive manufacturing rights, royalties, and free land; transportation costs, expenses, and tools were provided as well (Brock 1888, 130). Premiums were a popular instrument for encouraging manufactures, such as an award William Penn offered for the highest quality linen made in the colony. Maryland funded its premiums for superior textile products through annual taxes at the county level. However, individual donations and subscriptions also paid for prizes, especially later in the eighteenth century. Virginia tried in 1759 (apparently with limited success) to found a corporation "for encouraging arts and manufactures" to offer prizes for discoveries new to the colony.

Another important innovation for the early colonists, sawmills, were the subject of the first patent in the modern sense of protecting new manufacturing processes and mechanical inventions. The General Court of Massachusetts granted a monopoly in 1646 to Joseph Jenks for fourteen years for his improvements in water mills and the manufacture of scythes: "for a newly invented sawmill that things may be afforded cheaper than formerly, and that for fourteen years without disturbance by any others setting up the like invention so that his study and cost may not be in vain or lost, so as power is still left to restrain the exportation of such manufactures, and to moderate the prices thereof if occasion so require."[8] In 1655, Jenks was issued exclusive rights for another scythe "for the more speedy cutting of grass, for seven years."

Like Massachusetts, Connecticut adopted a code of laws that included a clause regarding monopolies, and in 1672 declared its intention to encourage the importation of foreign methods of manufactures. The legislators established an examination board to assess the apparently large number of applications that inventors and introducers submitted between 1708 and 1789 and made their decisions based on "the comparative importance of the discovery claimed, or the branch of manufactures proposed to be introduced." The term of the patents varied between three and fifteen years. For instance, in 1728, Samuel Higley and Joseph Dewey applied for patent rights for twenty years for improvements in steel making; they were given an exclusive right for ten years, with a two-year probationary period during which they were expected to improve "the art to any good and reasonable

---

8. Jenks's application referred to his "desire to improve this talent for the public good and benefit and service of this country" (Defebaugh 1907, 185).

perfection" (Commissioner of Patents 1850, 550). Many of the petitions stressed the cost to the inventor and the potential benefit to the public. When Benjamin Dearborn approached the New Hampshire legislature in 1786, he declared that "as your petitioner has spent much time and money in a variety of inventions, which may be of public utility, he is desirous of enjoying some exclusive benefit from some of them" (Commissioner of Patents 1850, 577–78). The special act granting him exclusive rights for fourteen years also specified that infringers would have to pay a penalty of double the value of the invention.

The southern colonies were also involved in offering inducements for inventive activity and innovation. Notably, South Carolina passed a 1691 statute "for the better encouragement of the making of engines for propagating the staples of this colony" and early in the eighteenth century granted a number of patents for machine inventions. In 1759 Virginia introduced "an act for encouraging arts and manufactures," which awarded prizes for new discoveries and the establishment of new manufacturing industries (Clark 1916, 38). Similarly, Virginia's "Plan for the encouragement of Arts and Manufactures reported, and unanimously agreed to, Monday, March 27, 1775" urged that "as Salt is a daily and indispensable necessary of life, and the making of it amongst ourselves must be deemed a valuable acquisition, it is therefore recommended that the utmost endeavours be used to establish Salt Works, and that proper encouragement be given to Mr. James Tait, who hath made proposals, and offered a scheme to the publick, for so desirable a purpose." The list of manufactured goods that the colony wished to encourage included saltpeter, sulphur, gunpowder, cloth, and nails. The convention "earnestly recommended that Societies be formed in different parts of this Colony; and it is the opinion of this Convention, that proper Premiums ought to be offered in the several Counties and Corporations, to such persons as shall excel in the several branches of Manufactures."

Privileges comprised part of an economic policy to enhance growth, often a protection analogous to an infant industry subsidy, rather than a fulfillment of any abstract philosophical vision of natural rights. The attitude of these early founders was echoed in a communication of Thomas Jefferson's, dismissing the natural rights argument with the statement that "it would be singular to admit a natural and even an hereditary right to inventors."[9]

9. Thomas Jefferson's letter to Isaac McPherson, August 13, 1813, further stated:

Stable ownership is the gift of social law, and is given late in the progress of society. It would be curious then, if an idea, the fugitive fermentation of an individual brain, could, of natural right, be claimed in exclusive and stable property. If nature has made any one thing less susceptible than all others of exclusive property, it is the action of the thinking power called an idea, which an individual may exclusively possess as long as he keeps it to himself; but the moment it is divulged, it forces itself into the possession of every one, and the receiver cannot dispossess himself of it. Its peculiar character, too, is that no one possesses the less, because every other possesses the whole of it. He who receives an idea from me, receives instruction himself without lessening mine; as he who lights his taper at mine, receives light without darkening me. . . . Considering the exclusive right to invention as given not of

As such, the colonial legislatures frequently appended conditions to the privileges they granted, at the risk of annulment, including working requirements, price controls, assured performance in such dimensions as quantity or quality, and geographical limits on the scope of the monopoly. The patent granted to the Jerom brothers in 1746 to make sea salt in Connecticut would be revoked unless they consistently produced stipulated quantities. Edward Hinman's 1717 patent for making molasses from corn stalks required that the product should be as good and as cheap as the imports from the West Indies.

Both conceptually and in practice, European and colonial histories of privileges and monopolies often bundled exclusive rights without distinguishing between mechanical inventions and cultural inventions. Pennsylvania's Frame of Government in April 1683 presciently declared that it intended to "erect and order all public schools, and encourage and reward the authors of useful sciences and laudable inventions in the said province." Benjamin Dearborn's 1786 grant from New Hampshire bundled a patent for two mechanical inventions with copyright protection for a math textbook. In most other colonies authors applied for special legislative favors, such as John Usher's successful appeal to the Massachusetts General Court for a printing monopoly in *The Book of General Lawes and Liberties.* His 1672 patent ensured for seven years "That no Printer shall print any more Coppies than are agreed and paid for by the owner of the Coppie or Coppies, nor shall he nor any other reprint or make Sale of any of the same without the said Owner's consent upon the forfeiture and penalty of treble the whole charges of Printing and paper of the quantity paid for by the owner of the Coppie, to the said owner or his Assigns." This "patent" may be regarded as the first formal de facto copyright to be granted in the American colonies.

10.4   State Precedents

Intellectual property issues were not addressed in the Articles of Confederation, but the notion of securing protection for authors and inventors was in circulation in the press, in legislatures, and in Congress. In January 1783, a Connecticut representative to Congress, Oliver Wolcott, asserted in a letter

natural right, but for the benefit of society. I know well the difficulty of drawing a line between the things which are worth to the public the embarrassment of an exclusive patent, and those which are not. As a member of the patent board for several years, while the law authorized a board to grant or refuse patents, I saw with what slow progress a system of general rules could be matured.

Jefferson's attitude varied over time, from a rejection of monopoly rights (which he thought should have been included in a bill of rights), to a limited acceptance. In July 1788, he wrote to Madison that "The saying that there shall be no monopolies, lessens the incitements to ingenuity, which is spurred on by the hope of a monopoly for a limited time, as of fourteen years; but the benefit of even limited monopolies is too doubtful to be opposed to that of their general suppression" (Foley 1900, 582). Later in an 1807 letter to Oliver Evans, he opined that the patent term should be longer than the English grant, to take into account the undeveloped state of the American economy.

that "he ever was of Opinion that the Copy Rights of every Author ought to be secured to him under certain Limitations," and later the same year noted that he intended "to secure if I can to Authors their Copy Rights—for Some Time past Congress have been too much Occupied by important Subjects to introduce a Matter of this Nature" (Smith 1976–2000).[10] This might seem to imply that such policies were not regarded as significant but, as Madison (1788) pointed out, "The utility of this power will scarcely be questioned. The copyright of authors has been solemnly adjudged, in Great Britain, to be a right of common law. The right to useful inventions seems with equal reason to belong to the inventors. The public good fully coincides in both cases with the claims of individuals. The States cannot separately make effectual provisions for either of the cases, and most of them have anticipated the decision of this point, by laws passed at the instance of Congress" (Madison 1788).

Indeed, after the Revolution, Congress prompted the individual states to formalize policies toward inventors and authors. Notably, in May 1783, the Colonial Congress recommended that the states "secure to the authors or publishers of any new books not hitherto printed, being citizens of the United States . . . the copy right of such books for a certain time not less than fourteen years from the first publication" (Solberg 1900). That year, Connecticut became the first state to approve an "Act for the encouragement of literature and genius" because "it is perfectly agreeable to the principles of natural equity and justice, that every author should be secured in receiving the profits that may arise from the sale of his works, and such security may encourage men of learning and genius to publish their writings; which may do honor to their country, and service to mankind." Although this preamble might seem to strongly favor authors' rights, the statute also specified that books were to be offered at reasonable prices and in sufficient quantities or else a compulsory license would issue.

Between 1783 and 1786 all of the original states, with the exception of Delaware, likewise complied by enacting copyright laws. These statutes tended to articulate the utilitarian objectives of their legislatures, claiming that copyright was needed in order to encourage learning and education. Pennsylvania's statute was intended "for the encouragement and promotion of learning" and directed toward "useful books." The copyright declaration of the state of New York also included plans to fund an educational academy in Kings County. North Carolina echoed the common theme that "it is proper that men should be encouraged to pursue useful knowledge by

10. See also Paine (1782):

It is more than probable, notwithstanding the declarations it contains, that the copy was obtained for the sake of profiting by the sale of a new and popular work . . . It may with propriety be remarked, that in all countries where literature is protected, and it never can flourish where it is not, the works of an author are his legal property; and to treat letters in any other light than this, is to banish them from the country, or strangle them in the birth.

the hope of reward; and . . . the security of literary property must greatly tend to encourage genius, to promote useful discoveries, and to the general extension of arts and commerce."

In keeping with these social objectives, and to ameliorate any monopolistic consequences, many of the clauses included restrictions on the rights of the copyright holder. South Carolina's "Act For the Encouragement of Arts and Sciences" granted any person who wished to print a copy of a new or existing book "the sole right and liberty of printing such book and books, for the term of fourteen years," on registration with the secretary of the state. However, this exclusive right did not extend to books in foreign languages from overseas. Copyrighted books had to be sold at a reasonable price or else a compulsory license could be issued at the discretion of the courts. Similarly, Georgia's law noted that "it is equally necessary for the encouragement of learning, that the inhabitants of this State be furnished with useful books, &c., at reasonable prices." Massachusetts offered authors exclusive rights for twenty-one years, with a depository requirement.[11] North Carolina's statute allowed for the reprinting of foreign materials and echoed the censorship of British laws by prohibiting copyrights in "books, maps or charts which may be dangerous to civil liberty, or to the peace or morals of society."

Although the majority of states enacted laws toward copyright after 1783, only South Carolina appended a general statement that included patent grants. South Carolina's "Act For the Encouragement of Arts and Sciences" allowed that "the inventors of useful machines shall have a like exclusive privilege of making or vending their machines for the like term of fourteen years," under the same terms as for owners of copyrights. However, this did not imply that patents were automatically available, since inventions were still obtained through ad hoc legislative instruments that responded to petitions filed by specific individuals. As in the case of copyright protection for books, the legislatures conditioned the patent grants on compliance with conditions, such as maximum prices, compulsory licensing, and working requirements.

In 1786, a patent was granted to Peter Belin for "the exclusive right of constructing and vending sundry useful water machines." The patent made reference to the "labor, attention, hazard and expense" of the petitioner, whose discoveries would be "of great utility to the citizens of this State."

11. The Preamble to the Massachusetts Constitution of 1780, Chapter 5, Section 2 proclaimed:

Wisdom and knowledge, as well as virtue, diffused generally among the body of the people, being necessary for the preservation of their rights and liberties; and as these depend on spreading the opportunities and advantages of education in the various parts of the country, and among the different orders of the people, it shall be the duty of legislatures and magistrates, in all future periods of this commonwealth, to cherish the interests of literature and the sciences; . . . to encourage private societies and public institutions, rewards and immunities, for the promotion of agriculture, arts, sciences, commerce, trades, manufactures. . . .

Infringers would have to pay 100 pounds in damages. The patentee had to file models with the authorities and could not refuse requests to build the water works at "a just and reasonable price" or else a compulsory license would issue (Cooper 1838–1839). In 1788, Samuel Knight obtained from the state of South Carolina "the exclusive right of constructing and vending a machine for the pounding of rice" for fourteen years. The patentee was required to deposit a model or "exact plan" with the secretary's office, not to ensure an increase in social knowledge, but for the specific purpose of preventing and proving unknowing infringement. Infringers would be fined fifty pounds sterling, but at the same time, Knight was obligated to issue a license at the set fee of five pounds to anyone who applied. The preamble to another private act that day declared that "authors and inventors should be secured in receiving the profits that may arise from the sale or disposal of their respective writings and discoveries" (Cooper 1838–1839, 69–70).

Several patentees obtained patent rights in more than one state. Henry Guest, a resident of New Brunswick, received the exclusive right to make currier's oil and blubber, from both the Pennsylvania and New York legislatures. He deposited sealed samples and a description of his invention with the clerk of the assembly. The New York law included a provision of treble damages for infringement. The act would not take effect until the inventor filed "a writing containing the names and descriptions of the materials aforesaid, and the method and process of making such blubber and oyl . . . nor until the said Henry Guest shall have a manufactory erected for the purpose . . . within this state" (New York 1886, 780). The steamship inventors, John Fitch, James Rumsey and Robert Fulton, and Robert Livingston (a promoter) lobbied the states strongly to obtain monopoly rights in river transportation. However, the most insistent in trying to gain multistate monopoly rights, before the advent of national laws, was the notorious Oliver Evans. Between 1786 and 1789, Evans obtained patents for a series of inventions in flour mills and steam wagons, from the legislatures of Pennsylvania, Maryland, and New Hampshire.

Throughout the eighteenth century, states continued to offer premiums and subsidies for their favored manufactures. In 1775, the Continental Congress "recommended to the several Provincial Conventions, to grant such premiums, for the refining of Sulphur in their respective Provinces, as may be judged proper." It was also suggested that public patronage should encourage the production of saltpeter. A Committee of the Continental Congress similarly opined in 1783 that domestic manufactures were important to avoid increasing the foreign debt, so it "recommended to the legislatures of the States to countenance and encourage the establishment of useful manufactures either by premiums or by such other means as they may find most effectual which are consistent with the Confederation . . ." (Ford 1905, 516).

The influential Alexander Hamilton advocated an arsenal of commercial policies, including tariffs, restrictions on exports, quotas, subsidies and bonuses, quality controls on manufactures and exports, and improvements in infrastructure necessary for market expansion. He was also a strong supporter of the use of premiums as an integral element in innovation policy.[12] In the critical year of 1787, Tench Coxe (1787, 253) exhorted the Pennsylvania Society for the Encouragement of Manufactures and the Useful Arts to "carefully examine the conduct of other countries in order to possess ourselves of their methods of encouraging manufactories and pursue such of them, as apply to our own situation" and, like his colleague Alexander Hamilton, he recommended the adoption of premiums to achieve these ends. Pennsylvania was already noted for its strong measures to advance manufactures, such as an 1788 Act "to Encourage and Protect the Manufacturers of this State," which imposed fines and jail terms on "ill-designing persons" who exported machines or devices or attempted to lure artisans to leave the country.

10.5   Framing the Intellectual Property Regime

The delegates who gathered in Philadelphia in the summer of 1787 to draw up a blueprint to "promote the general Welfare" had ample suggestions for how to proceed that they could extract from history, recent and more distant. The document they finally produced included a succinct clause (Art. 1, section 8, clause 8) to protect the writings and discoveries of authors and inventors. It was notably the first time in history that an intellectual property provision was included in a national constitution.

The intellectual property clause was not included in the first draft of the Constitution. Instead, the debates record a list of related proposals, which were submitted on August 18, 1787. These included proposals "to secure to

---

12. See, for instance, the *Report on Manufactures* (1791), recommending a fund:

To defray the expences of the emigration of Artists, and Manufacturers in particular branches of extraordinary importance—to induce the prosecution and introduction of useful discoveries, inventions and improvements, by proportionate rewards, judiciously held out and applied—to encourage by premiums both honorable and lucrative the exertions of individuals, And of classes, in relation to the several objects, they are charged with promoting—and to afford such other aids to those objects, as may be generally designated by law . . . The propriety of stimulating by rewards, the invention and introduction of useful improvements, is admitted without difficulty. But the success of attempts in this way must evidently depend much on the manner of conducting them. It is probable, that the placing of the dispensation of those rewards under some proper discretionary direction, where they may be accompanied by collateral expedients, will serve to give them the surest efficacy. It seems impracticable to apportion, by general rules, specific compensations for discoveries of unknown and disproportionate utility . . . The operation and utility of premiums have been adverted to; together with the advantages which have resulted from their dispensation, under the direction of certain public and private societies . . . It may confidently be affirmed that there is scarcely any thing, which has been devised, better calculated to excite a general spirit of improvement than the institutions of this nature. They are truly invaluable. (Syrett et al., eds. 1961, 79)

literary authors, their copyrights for a limited time," "to encourage, by proper premiums and provisions, the advancement of useful knowledge and discoveries," and "to grant patents for useful inventions." It was also proposed "to establish public institutions, rewards and immunities, for the promotion of agriculture, commerce, trades, and manufactures" (Farrand 1937). These provisions were all familiar policy instruments that had prevailed in Europe and in the colonies themselves since the seventeenth century. However, the convention rejected the bundling of incentives for invention and innovation because such powers were "deemed too broad and sweeping" and allowed overly expansive discretion to the government.[13] The unique preamble to the intellectual property clause ("to promote the progress of science and useful arts") implied that private monopolies to benefit privileged individuals or special groups were not to be permitted. Instead, the primary purpose was to encourage social welfare through advances in knowledge and technology, and the means to achieve this objective was through the temporary grant of exclusive rights to authors and inventors alone.

Some might speculate that the silence of the records on the proceedings regarding this clause indicates that the matter was of little interest or import to the delegates. However, that hypothesis is disproved by subsequent events. In the first address to Congress in 1790, George Washington urged: "The advancement of agriculture, commerce, and manufactures, by all proper means, will not, I trust, need recommendation; but I cannot forbear intimating to you the expediency of giving effectual encouragement, as well to the introduction of new and useful inventions from abroad as to the exertion of skill and genius at home . . . Nor am I less persuaded, that you will agree with me in opinion, that there is nothing which can better deserve your patronage, than the promotion of science and literature. Knowledge is, in every country, the surest basis of public happiness."

Congress quickly complied by passing a patent statute 10 April 1790.[14] The United States is noted for creating the first modern patent institution in the world, a system whose features differed in significant respects from those of other major countries. The individuals who shaped early American patent policy were convinced that individuals responded to incentives. Accordingly, they carefully calibrated individual features of the patent system to ensure that the system was effective in promoting inventive activity. This orientation

13. According to Story (1833, Vol. 2, 46):

In regard to the rejection of the proposition in the convention "to establish institutions, rewards, and immunities for the promotion of agriculture, commerce, trades, and manufactures . . . It is notorious, that, in the convention, an attempt was made to introduce into the constitution a power to encourage manufactures; but it was withheld. . . . it involved a direct power to establish institutions, rewards, and immunities for all the great interests of society, and was, on that account, deemed too broad and sweeping. It would establish a general, and not a limited power of government.

14. For accounts of the development of the American patent system see Bugbee (1967), Khan (2005), and Khan and Sokoloff (2001).

was evident at the highest levels (the inclusion of an intellectual property clause in the U.S. Constitution) to the most detailed (provisions to enable patentees in rural areas to mail in their applications without having to pay postage.) The conviction that the design of patent systems mattered was also shared by the inventors themselves and by other participants in the market for technology.

The historical record indicates that the legislature's creation of a uniquely American system was a deliberate and conscious process. In the first place, a combined intellectual property bill, HR 10, was tabled, and instead, separate statutes were enacted for patents and copyrights. Second, the separate patent bill laid before Congress, HR-41, was amended in several places. The most minor of these amendments is suggestive: patents were to be granted in the name of the people of the United States rather than the executive office. The draft of this patent bill echoed a number of other British practices, but the copy that Washington later approved differed significantly from historical precedent, in ways that favored the rights of inventors. The House deleted Section 6, which had imitated the English policy of granting patents for imported inventions. As Justice Joseph Story commented, the Constitution does not permit anyone other than the true inventor to be benefited. The Senate extended the initial definition of novelty: the patent laws still employed the language of the English statutes in allowing patents to the "first and true inventor," but, unlike in England, the phrase was used literally to protect inventions that were new and original to the world, not simply within domestic borders. A section regarding interferences (or conflicting applications) was replaced by a stipulation that information about prior inventions should be readily available to potential patentees. The Senate suggested forcing patentees to work the patent or else license others to do so, but the House rejected this as an unwarranted infringement of the patentee's rights. Moreover, small reductions were made to the fee schedule, which was modest to begin with.

The basic parameters of the U.S. patent system were transparent and predictable, in itself an aid to those who wished to obtain patent rights. The primary feature of the "American system" is that all applications are subject to an examination for conformity with the laws and for novelty. An examination system was set in place in 1790, when a select committee consisting of the Secretary of State (Thomas Jefferson), the Attorney General, and the Secretary of War scrutinized the applications. These duties understandably proved to be too time-consuming for highly ranked officials with other onerous duties, so three years later it was replaced by a registration system. The validity of patents was left up to the district courts, which had the power to set in motion a process that could end in the repeal of the patent. The laws were enforced by a judiciary that was willing to grapple with difficult questions such as the extent to which a democratic and market-oriented political economy was consistent with exclusive rights. Courts explicitly attempted to implement decisions that promoted economic growth and social welfare.[15]

Reforms in 1836 set in place the essential structure of the current patent system. In particular, the 1836 Patent Law established the Patent Office, whose trained and technically qualified employees were authorized to examine applications. In order to constrain the ability of examiners to engage in arbitrary actions, the applicant was given the right to file a bill in equity to contest the decisions of the Patent Office with the further right of appeal to the Supreme Court of the United States. American patent policy likewise stands out in its insistence on affordable fees. Such payments were not intended to exact a price for the patent privilege or to raise revenues for the state—the disclosure of information was the price of the patent property right—rather, they were imposed merely to cover the administrative expenses of the office.[16] The Patent Office itself was a source of centralized information on the state of the arts, and Congress was also concerned with the question of providing for decentralized access to patent materials. Legislation ensured that information about the stock of patented knowledge was readily available and diffused rapidly. As early as 1805, Congress stipulated that the Secretary of State should publish an annual list of patents granted the preceding year, and after 1832 also required the publication in newspapers of notices regarding expired patents.

The American patent system was based on the presumption that patents for new inventions were not monopolies and that social welfare coincided with the individual welfare of inventors. Accordingly, legislators emphatically rejected restrictions on the rights of American inventors. Working requirements or compulsory licenses, standard measures of colonial legislatures to attenuate monopoly power, were regarded as unwarranted infringements of the rights of "meritorious inventors" and incompatible with the philosophy of U.S. patent grants. Patentees were not required to pay annuities to maintain their property, there were no opposition proceedings, and once granted a patent could not be revoked unless there was evidence of fraud. One of the advantages of a system that secures property rights is that it facilitates contracts and trade, and an extensive national network of

15. "The Constitution of the United States, in giving authority to Congress to grant patents for a limited period, declares the object to be to promote the progress of science and the useful arts, an object as truly national and meritorious, and well founded in public policy, as any which can possibly be within the scope of national protection" *Ames v. Howard,* 1 Sumn. 485 (Mass.) 1833.

16. The legislature debated the question of appropriate fees, and the first patent law in 1790 set the rate at the minimal sum of $3.70 plus copy costs. In 1793, the fees were increased to $30, and were maintained at this level until 1861. In that year, they were raised to $35, and the term was changed from fourteen years (with the possibility of an extension) to seventeen years (with no extensions.) The 1869 Report of the Commissioner of Patents compared the $35 fee for a U.S. patent to the significantly higher charges in European countries such as Britain, France, Russia ($450), Belgium ($420) and Austria ($350). The Commissioner speculated that both the private and social cost of patenting were lower in a system of impartial specialized examiners than under a system where similar services were performed on a fee-per-service basis by private solicitors.

licensing and assignments developed early on, aided by legal rulings that overturned contracts for useless or fraudulent patents.

American patent laws provided strong protection for citizens of the United States but varied over time in its treatment of foreign inventors. The statutes of 1793, 1800, and 1832 restricted patent property to citizens or to residents who declared that they intended to become citizens. As such, while an American could not appropriate patent rights to a foreign invention, he or she could freely use the idea without any need to bear licensing or similar costs that would otherwise have been due if the inventor had been able to obtain a patent in this country. In 1836, the stipulations on citizenship or residency were removed but were replaced with discriminatory patent fees: foreigners could obtain a patent in the United States for a fee of three hundred dollars, or five hundred if they were British. The 1832 and 1836 laws stipulated that foreigners had to exploit their patented invention within eighteen months. These clauses seem to have been interpreted by the courts in a fairly liberal fashion because alien patentees "need not prove that they hawked the patented improvement to obtain a market for it, or that they endeavoured to sell it to any person, but that it rested upon those who sought to defeat the patent to prove that the plaintiffs neglected or refused to sell the patented invention for reasonable prices when application was made to them to purchase."[17] Moreover, the records indicate that a significant number of foreign inventors petitioned Congress and readily succeeded in obtaining the right to patent their inventions in the United States.

Such discriminatory provisions proved to be temporary aberrations and were not included in subsequent legislation. After 1861, patent rights were available to all applicants on the same basis without regard to nationality. The patent record itself (figure 10.1) reveals a likely reason for the liberal treatment of foreign inventors: until the middle of the twentieth century, there was relatively little patenting by foreigners in the United States, largely because of the superiority of U.S. technologists and technologies. During the proceedings to celebrate the centenary of the U.S. patent system, this "liberality" was noted as one of its essential features: "Our law gives to all men of all nations the same privileges, and recognizes to the fullest extent the international character of property in inventions. In this respect . . . the United States may claim to have led the world and to be leading it still" (Seeley 1892, 205).

Despite their common source in the intellectual property clause of the U.S. Constitution, copyright policies provided a marked contrast to the patent system in the United States.[18] In the period before the Declaration of Independence, although individual American states recognized and pro-

17. *Tatham et al. v. Lowber et al.,* 23 F. Cas. 721 April 21, 1847.
18. See *Wheaton v. Peters,* 33 U.S. 591, 684 (1834):

It has been argued at the bar, that as the promotion of the progress of science and the useful arts is here united in the same clause in the constitution, the rights of the authors and inventors were considered as standing on the same footing; but this, I think, is a non sequitur for

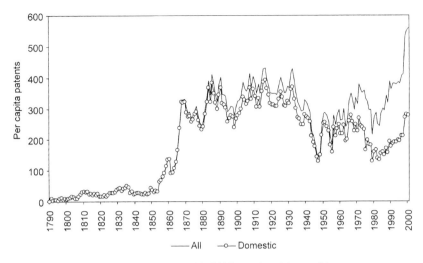

Fig. 10.1   U.S. patents per capita, 1790–2000 (total and domestic)
Sources: U.S. Patent Office and Department of Census, various years.
Note: The data comprise patents per million residents, with figures for domestic patents excluding patents filed by foreign residents.

moted copyright protection, it was not considered to be of equal importance with innovation policies. First, in a democracy, the claims of the public and the wish to foster freedom of expression were paramount. Second, to a new colony, pragmatic concerns were likely of greater importance than the arts, and more substantial literary works were imported from Europe. Demand was sufficiently shallow that an individual could saturate the market with a first run printing, and most local publishers produced ephemera such as newspapers, almanacs, and bills. Third, it was unclear that copyright protection was needed as an incentive for creativity, especially because a significant fraction of output was devoted to works such as medical treatises and religious tracts whose authors wished simply to maximize the number of readers, rather than the amount of income they received.

The earliest federal statute to protect the product of authors was approved on May 31, 1790, "for the encouragement of learning, by securing the copies of maps, charts, and books to the authors and proprietors of such copies, during the times therein mentioned."[19] John Barry obtained the first fed-

---

when congress came to execute this power by legislation, the subjects are kept distinct, and very different provisions are made respecting them.

19. The copyright act required authors and proprietors to deposit a copy of the title of their work in the office of the district court in the area where they lived, for a nominal fee of sixty cents. Registration secured the right to print, publish, and sell maps, charts, and books for a term of fourteen years, with the possibility of an extension for another like term. Amendments to the original act extended protection to other works including musical compositions, plays and performances, engravings, and photographs. Legislators refused to grant perpetual terms, but the length of protection was extended in the general revision of the laws in 1831 and 1909.

eral copyright when he registered his spelling book in the District Court of Pennsylvania, and early grants reflected the same utilitarian character. Policymakers felt that copyright protection would serve to increase the flow of learning and information and by encouraging publication would contribute to democratic principles of free speech. The diffusion of knowledge would also ensure broad-based access to the benefits of social and economic development.

In the case of patents, the rights of inventors, whether domestic or foreign, were widely viewed as coincident with public welfare. In stark contrast, policymakers showed from the very beginning an acute sensitivity to trade-offs between the rights of authors (or publishers) and social welfare. The protections provided to authors under American copyright laws were as a result much more limited than those of most European countries, which increasingly made grants on the basis of moral rights. Of relevance here are stipulations regarding first sale, work for hire, and fair use. Under a moral rights-based system, an artist or his heirs can claim remedies if subsequent owners alter or distort the work in a way that allegedly injures the artist's honor or reputation. According to the first sale doctrine, the copyright holder loses all rights after the work is sold. In the American system, if the copyright holder's welfare were enhanced by nonmonetary concerns, these individualized concerns could be addressed and enforced through contract law, rather than through a generic federal statutory clause that would affect all property holders. Similarly, "work for hire" doctrines repudiated the right of personality in favor of facilitating market transactions.

This difficult quest for balance between private and public good is most evident in the copyright doctrine of "fair use" that (unlike patents) allowed unauthorized access to copyrighted works under certain conditions. The fair use doctrine was initially articulated in England but found its most expansive elaboration in the American system as a way of ensuring that the monopoly costs of an exclusive right in expression would be minimized. One of the striking features of the fair use doctrine is the extent to which property rights were defined in terms of market valuations, or the impact on sales and profits, as opposed to a clear holding of the exclusivity of property. Joseph Story ruled in *Folsom v. Marsh* [9 F. Cas. 342 (1841)]: "we must often, in deciding questions of this sort, look to the nature and objects of the selections made, the quantity and value of the materials used, and the degree in which the use may prejudice the sale, or diminish the profits, or supersede the objects, of the original work." Fair use doctrine thus illustrates the extent to which the early policymakers weighed the costs and benefits of private property rights against the rights of the public and the provisions for a democratic society. If copyrights were as strictly construed as patents, it would serve to reduce scholarship, prohibit public access for noncommercial purposes, increase transactions costs for potential users, and inhibit learning that the statutes were meant to promote.

The basic dimensions of the copyright statute in its domestic provisions were not dissimilar to the English Statute of Anne, but it included a startling innovation in the treatment of international copyright protection. The 1790 Copyright Act specified that "nothing in this act shall be construed to extend to prohibit the importation or vending, reprinting or publishing within the United States, of any map, chart, book or books . . . by any person not a citizen of the United States." The United States was long a net importer of literary and artistic works, especially from England, which implied that recognition of foreign copyrights would have led to a net deficit in international royalty payments. The legislators explicitly acknowledged the imbalance in the cultural ledger and, therefore, authorized Americans to take free advantage of the cultural output of other countries.[20] The tendency to reprint foreign works was encouraged by the existence of tariffs on imported books that ranged as high as 25 percent.

The United States stood out in contrast to countries such as France, which prohibited counterfeiting of both foreign and domestic works. Other countries that were affected by American "piracy" retaliated by refusing to recognize American copyrights. Despite the lobbying of numerous authors and celebrities on both sides of the Atlantic, the American copyright statutes did not allow for copyright protection of foreign works for fully one century. As a result, the nineteenth century offers a colorful episode in the annals of intellectual property as American publishers and producers pirated foreign literature, art, and drama in accordance with its own laws.

It is widely acknowledged that copyrights in books tended to be the concern of publishers rather than of authors (although the two are naturally not independent of each other). As a result of the lack of legal copyrights in foreign works, publishers raced to be first on the market with the "new" pirated books, and the industry experienced several decades of intense, if not quite "ruinous," competition. These were problems that publishers in England had faced before in the market for uncopyrighted books, such as Shakespeare and Fielding (Collins 1927). Their solution had been to collude in the form of strictly regulated cartels or "printing congers," which created divisible alienable property in books. Cooperation resulted in risk sharing and a greater ability to cover expenses. The unstable races in the United States similarly settled down during the 1840s to collusive standards that were termed "trade custom" or "courtesy of the trade."

The industry achieved relative stability because the dominant firms cooperated in establishing synthetic property rights in foreign-authored books.

---

20. Senator John Ruggles was one of the leading authorities in Congress on the patent system and a strong proponent of the 1836 changes in the patent law. He was also a key member of a committee to consider reforming international copyrights and argued that "American ingenuity in the arts and practical sciences would derive at least as much benefit from international patent laws, as that of foreigners. Not so with authorship and book-making. The difference is too obvious to admit of controversy" (Barnes 1974, 71).

American publishers made payments (termed "copyrights") to foreign authors to secure early sheets, and other firms recognized their exclusive property in the "authorized reprint." Advance payments to foreign authors not only served to ensure the coincidence of publishers' and authors' interests—they were also recognized by "reputable" publishers as "copyrights." These exclusive rights were tradable and enforced by threats of predatory pricing and retaliation. Such practices suggest that publishers were able to simulate the legal grant through private means. However, such private rights naturally did not confer property rights that could be enforced by law. The case of *Sheldon v. Houghton* [21 F. Cas 1239 (1865)] illustrates that these rights were considered to be "very valuable, and is often made the subject of contracts, sales, and transfers, among booksellers and publishers." The court pointed out that:

> If anything which can be called, in any legal sense, property, was transferred to this partnership, this was based on the custom of the trade, which is very far from being a legal custom, furnishing a solid foundation upon which an inviolable title to property can rest, which courts can protect from invasion. . . . It may be an advantage to the party enjoying it for the time being, but its protection rests in the voluntary and unconstrained forbearance of the trade. I know of no way in which the publishers of this country can republish the works of a foreign author, and secure to themselves the exclusive right to such publication . . . For this court to recognize any other literary property in the works of a foreign author, would contravene the settled policy of Congress.

Thus, synthetic rights differed from copyrights in the degree of security that was offered by the enforcement power of the courts. Nevertheless, these title-specific rights of exclusion decreased uncertainty, enabled publishers to recoup their fixed costs and avoided the wasteful duplication of resources that would otherwise have occurred.

It was not until 1891 that the Chace Act granted copyright protection to selected foreign residents. Thus, after a century of lobbying by interested parties on both sides of the Atlantic, based on reasons that ranged from the economic to the moral, copyright laws only changed when the United States became more competitive in the international market for cultural goods. However, the act also included significant concessions to domestic printers' unions and printing establishments in the form of "manufacturing clauses." Books had to be published in the United States before or at the same time as the publication date in its country of origin. The work also had to be printed here or printed from type set in the United States or from plates made from type set in the United States. Copyright protection still depended on conformity with stipulations such as formal registration of the work. These clauses resulted in U.S. failure to qualify for admission to the Berne Convention until 1988, more than 100 years after the first Convention for the harmonization of international copyright laws.

10.6   Looking Backward

The framers of the American system of intellectual property intended to promote social progress in a democratic society. This utilitarian objective explains the elements that were drawn from prior examples across time and region, as well as the innovations in the design of the system. The framers wished to avoid the "pernicious monopolies" that plagued the prior grant of privileges in Europe and American colonies, hence the rejection of premiums and broad powers to encourage innovation. In the new Republic, only true inventors were to be benefited, not importers, the well-connected, or monopolists. In order to identify those who deserved these rights, an examination system was instituted, and protection would be allowed to only those inventions that were new to the world. Moreover, all inventors, not just the wealthy or well-connected, would be allowed access to exclusive rights, and the determination of useful knowledge would be left to the market rather than to judges or committees. Once granted to "meritorious patentees," these rights were not to be infringed on, either by other inventors, or by society itself in the form of working requirements or price controls. The diffusion of information was ensured through the deposit of models and information and publication of specifications.

As for copyright, the interests of authors were less aligned to those of a democratic society, which had a critical interest in the diffusion of information, education, and learning. Moreover, the European experience raised concerns about the use of copyright powers to impose censorship and limit free speech. Hence, Congress would be less generous in its provisions for the protection of authorship, allowing shorter terms than in any other developed country, and requiring strict compliance with the statutory provisions, on pain of annulment of the right. The judiciary likewise permitted unauthorized access to copyrighted products through a stronger "fair use doctrine" than any that had previously existed. Moreover, effective public policy required withholding protection to the rights of foreign authors while the balance of trade was unfavorable to American citizens. Thus, for both patents and copyrights, the calibration of systemic design was directed toward allowing rights to individuals in order to offer enough incentives for productivity and creation, while ensuring that overall social welfare was enhanced through wider access to these cultural inventions. This calculus created property rights in patents that were the strongest in the world, and a system of copyrights that were among the weakest in the world.

Comparisons across Europe and the United States suggest that their respective policy choices regarding intellectual property affected the rate and direction of inventive activity. Differences in the design of patent institutions were responsible in part for the contrasts in the American experience relative to other countries. As figure 10.1 shows, per capita rates of patenting in the United States grew rapidly, and contemporary observers credited favorable institutions for its competitiveness. American technologies were soon recognized as the most productive and innovative in the world. Patterns of inventors and inventions were also affected by the intellectual property rules: U.S. inventors were drawn from a wider spectrum of the population than in Europe, and inventiveness was also far more broadly distributed across all industries. Markets in patent rights and patented inventions flourished, and this market orientation was especially beneficial to patentees who did not have the financial resources to exploit their patents. These observations are consistent with the patterns of productivity and economic growth across countries. U.S. productivity gains were evident in all sectors, even labor-intensive industries, and its growth were balanced. In Britain, by contrast, patented inventions tended to be quite capital-intensive and clustered in a few industries such as steel and textiles; it is likely not coincidental that British productivity was lower, limited to these few industries, and they experienced unbalanced economic growth.

The historical evidence regarding intellectual property and technological innovation, therefore, strongly suggests that the design of rules and standards mattered. The U.S. patent system was universally acknowledged to be the model prototype for the protection of inventions and inventors, and in order to benefit globally competitive American patentees, the United States took the lead to encourage other countries to strengthen their patent laws in line with American policies. However, we should not overlook the fact that patent systems are embedded in a set of related institutions, such as the legal system, markets for technology, and organizations that facilitate the acquisition of skills and learning. For, if other institutions are not responsive and enabling, even a well-designed patent system can be ineffective. The Founding Choices regarding intellectual property proved to be eminently favorable for social and economic development, but the flexibility of these institutional mechanisms in accommodating change and new circumstances was equally important. When the British finally restructured their patent system in the direction of the American system, reforms were limited by incapacity in other directions such as unresponsive legal and educational institutions.

American exceptionalism was also evident in the area of copyrights, but in the opposite direction to patents. The United States emphasized the importance of mass literacy and public education, and abridged copyrights when a conflict might exist between learning and copyright. Thus, it lagged behind the rest of the world in terms of both domestic and foreign copyright protection. Americans not only refused to adhere to international copyright treaties long upheld by European countries, but for a century they also continued to engage in copyright piracy of foreign cultural products even in the face of widespread protests and condemnation. It is very likely that such American "copyright piracy" benefited the country initially when the United States was a net debtor. But once the balance of trade moved in its favor, the

United States had an incentive to adopt stronger laws to protect its authors internationally. By way of contrast, European policymakers regarded copyright owners as geniuses who were deserving of strong protection for the products of their personality, and their copyright regimes evolved in the direction of inherent and inalienable author's rights. Consequently, France took the lead in promoting the harmonization of international copyright laws. Today's movement to harmonize patent and copyright laws can thus be traced to these two separate sources that culminated in stipulations for a system of uniformly strong patents and strong copyrights regardless of the level of economic development. Such a system did not exist anywhere in the world during the period when countries enjoyed greater freedom to choose appropriate institutions.

In the United States of the twenty-first century, as in the eighteenth century, there is no shortage of proposals regarding policies that might best promote social and economic development. Ironically, in direct contrast to the Founding Choices, the prevailing policies comprise measures that result in weak patents and strong copyrights. The patent system has departed from the original objectives of the creators of the system, with a faulty examination system, proposals to issue patents to first filers rather than to the first inventor, judicial considerations of utility and creativity in determining validity, and patentable subject matter held to include "anything under the sun" that man can create. A number of economists have been persuaded by the superior theoretical properties of such alternative policy instruments as state-sponsored awards, buyouts and prizes, and some even echo nineteenth-century European advocates for the abolition of intellectual property rights. The departures are even more blatant in the copyright regime. Today, copyright laws are largely determined by industry lobbies bent on securing their own objectives, with few to defend the public interest. Similarly, international copyright harmonization has created a mixed and muddled domestic system that conflicts with the intent of the founders. The Supreme Court has approved a virtually perpetual copyright and, rather than the public domain being the default, copyright is now the default. Extensions to the power of copyright owners are now justified on the basis of the creativity of authors, rather than the benefits to society. New technologies such as encryption and the threat of costly litigation allow owners the ability to expand their rights of exclusion in ways that avoid the limitations and constraints that the early laws incorporated to protect public welfare.

Thomas Jefferson pointed out that he was "not an advocate for frequent and untried changes in laws and constitutions . . . But . . . laws and institutions must go hand in hand with the progress of the human mind."[21] The extent to which institutions must alter to accommodate social and economic

---

21. In a letter to Samuel Kercheval, July 12, 1810. Available online at the Electronic Text Center, University of Virginia Library.

change is a subtle question that admits of a number of equally valid and opposing answers. At the same time, it is always worthwhile to reconsider the fundamental principles on which those laws and constitutions were originally founded. Looking backward to that extraordinary summer in 1787, it is useful to speculate whether today's intellectual property institutions have diverged too far afield from the original founding choices that comprised the constitutional blueprint for promoting the progress of science and useful arts.

References

Armstrong, Elizabeth. 1990. *Before copyright: The French book-privilege system, 1498–1526.* Cambridge, UK: Cambridge University Press.

Barnes, James J. 1974. *Authors, publishers, and politicians: The quest for an Anglo-American copyright agreement, 1815–1854.* Columbus, OH: Ohio State University Press.

Brock, R. A., ed. 1888. *Abstracts of proceedings of the Virginia Company of London.* Vol. 1. Richmond, VA: Virginia Historical Society.

Bugbee, Bruce W. 1967. *Genesis of American patent and copyright law.* Washington, DC: Public Affairs Press.

Clark, Victor. 1916. *History of manufactures in the United States, 1607–1860.* Washington, DC: Carnegie Institution.

Collins, A. S. 1927. *Authorship in the days of Johnson.* London: Robert Holden.

Commissioner of Patents. 1850. *Annual report of the Commissioner of Patents.* Washington, DC: Government Printing Office.

Cooper, Thomas, ed. 1838–1839. *Statutes at large of South Carolina.* Columbia, SC: Johnston.

Coxe, Tench. 1787. An address to an assembly of American manufactures. *American Museum.* Vol. 2. Philadelphia: Matthew Carey.

Defebaugh, James E. 1907. *History of the lumber industry of America.* Vol. 2. Chicago: American Lumberman.

Farrand, Max, ed. 1937. *The records of the Federal Convention of 1787.* Revised ed., 4 vols. New Haven, CT: Yale University Press.

Foley, John P., ed. 1900. *The Jeffersonian cyclopedia.* New York: Funk and Wagnalls.

Ford, Worthington Chauncey, ed. 1905. *Journals of the Continental Congress, 1774–1779.* Washington, DC: Government Printing Office.

Hilaire-Pérez, Liliane. 2000. *L'invention technique au siècle des Lumières.* Paris: Albin Michel.

Khan, B. Zorina. 2005. *The democratization of invention: Patents and copyrights in American economic development.* New York: Cambridge University Press.

Khan, B. Zorina, and Kenneth L. Sokoloff. 2001. The early development of intellectual property institutions in the United States. *Journal of Economic Perspectives* 15 (3): 233–46.

Madison, James. 1788. *The Federalist* no. 43. New York: J. and A. McClean.

New York. 1886. *Laws of the State of New York.* Vol. 1. Albany, NY: Weed & Parsons.

Paine, Thomas. 1782. A letter addressed to the Abbe Raynal, on the affairs of North

America, in which the mistakes in the Abbe's account of the Revolution of America are corrected and cleared up. www.gutenberg.org.

Seeley, F. A. 1892. International protection of industrial property. In *Proceedings and addresses: Celebration of the beginning of the second century of the American patent system.* Washington, DC: Gedney & Roberts.

Smith, Paul H., Gerard W. Gawalt, Rosemary F. Plakas, and Eugene R. Sheridan, eds. 1976–2000. *Letters of delegates to Congress, 1774–1789.* 25 vols. Washington, DC: Library of Congress.

Solberg, Thorvald, ed. 1900. *Copyright enactments: 1783–1900.* Copyright Office Bulletin no. 3. Washington, DC: Library of Congress.

Story, Joseph. 1833. *Commentaries on the Constitution of the United States.* 3 vols. Boston: Little, Brown, and Co.

Syrett, Harold C. et al., eds. 1961. *The papers of Alexander Hamilton.* 26 vols. New York: Columbia University Press.

Towle, Nathaniel C. 1871. *A history and analysis of the Constitution of the United States.* Boston: Little, Brown.

Whitmore, William H. 1890. *Biographical sketch of the laws of the Massachusetts Colony from 1630 to 1686.* Boston: Rockwell and Churchill.

Contributors

Howard Bodenhorn
John E. Walker Department of
    Economics
College of Business and Behavioral
    Science
201-B Sirrine Hall
Clemson University
Clemson, SC 29634

Stanley L. Engerman
Department of Economics
University of Rochester
Rochester, NY 14627-0156

Farley Grubb
Economics Department
University of Delaware
Newark, DE 19716-2720

Douglas A. Irwin
Department of Economics
Dartmouth College
Hanover, NH 03755

B. Zorina Khan
Department of Economics
Bowdoin College
9700 College Station
Brunswick, ME 04011

Robert A. Margo
Department of Economics
Boston University
270 Bay State Road
Boston, MA 02215

Sonia Mittal
Department of Political Science
Encina Hall West, Room 100
Stanford University
616 Serra Street
Stanford, CA 94305-6044

Jack N. Rakove
Department of Political Science
Stanford University
616 Serra Street
Stanford, CA 94305-2024

Peter L. Rousseau
Department of Economics
Vanderbilt University
VU Station B #351819
2301 Vanderbilt Place
Nashville, TN 37235-1819

Richard Sylla
Stern School of Business, Economics
New York University
44 West 4th Street
New York, NY 10012-1126

John Joseph Wallis
Department of Economics
University of Maryland
College Park, MD 20742

Barry R. Weingast
Department of Political Science
Stanford University
616 Serra Street
Stanford, CA 94305-2024

Robert E. Wright
Division of Social Science
Madsen Center 111
Augustana College
2001 South Summit Avenue
Sioux Falls, SD 57197

Author Index

Subject Index

Page numbers followed by f or t refer to figures or tables, respectively.